Critical Communication
Theory

CRITICAL MEDIA STUDIES
INSTITUTIONS, POLITICS, AND CULTURE

Series Editor
Andrew Calabrese, University of Colorado

Advisory Board

Patricia Aufderheide,
American University
Jean-Claude Burgelman,
Free University of Brussels
Simone Chambers,
University of Colorado
Nicholas Garnham
University of Westminster
Hanno Hardt, University of Iowa
Gay Hawkins,
The University of New South Wales
Maria Heller, Eötvös Loránd
University
Robert Horwitz,
University of California at San Diego
Douglas Kellner,
University of California at Los Angeles
Gary Marx,
Massachusetts Institute of Technology
Toby Miller, New York University

Vincent Mosco,
Carleton University
Janice Peck,
University of Colorado
Manjunath Pendakur,
University of Western Ontario
Arvind Rajagopal,
New York University
Kevin Robins, Goldsmiths College
Saskia Sassen,
University of Chicago
Colin Sparks,
University of Westminster
Slavko Splichal,
University of Ljubljana
Thomas Streeter,
University of Vermont
Liesbet van Zoonen,
University of Amsterdam
Janet Wasko, University of Oregon

Recent Titles in the Series
Deliberation, Democracy, and the Media,
    edited by Simone Chambers and Anne Costain
Deregulating Telecommunications: U.S. and Canadian Telecommunications, 1840–1997,
    Kevin G. Wilson
Floating Lives: The Media and Asian Diasporas,
    edited by Stuart Cunningham and John Sinclair
Continental Order? Integrating North America for Cybercapitalism,
    edited by Vincent Mosco and Dan Schiller
Social Theories of the Press: Constituents of Communication Research,
1840s to 1920s, second edition,
    Hanno Hardt
The Global and the National: Media and Communications in Post-Communist Russia,
    Terhi Rantanen
Privacy and the Information Age,
    Serge Gutwrith
Global Media Governance: A Beginner's Guide,
    Seán Ó Siochrú and Bruce Girard

Forthcoming in the Series
From Newspaper Guild to Multimedia Union: A Study in Labor Convergence,
    Catherine McKercher
The Eclipse of Freedom: From the Principle of Publicity to the Freedom of the Press,
    Slavko Splichal
Elusive Autonomy: Brazilian Communications Policy in an Age of
Globalization and Technical Change,
    Sergio Euclides de Souza
Internet Governance in Transition,
    Daniel J. Paré
Herbert Schiller,
    Richard Maxwell
Digital Disability: The Social Construction of Disability in New Media,
    Gerard Goggin and Christopher Newell

Critical Communication Theory

Power, Media, Gender, and Technology

Sue Curry Jansen

ROWMAN & LITTLEFIELD PUBLISHERS, INC.
Lanham • Boulder • New York • Oxford

ROWMAN & LITTLEFIELD PUBLISHERS, INC.

Published in the United States of America
by Rowman & Littlefield Publishers, Inc.
A Member of the Rowman & Littlefield Publishing Group
4720 Boston Way, Lanham, Maryland 20706
www.rowmanlittlefield.com

PO Box 317
Oxford
OX2 9RU, UK

British Library Cataloguing in Publication Information Available

Library of Congress Cataloging-in-Publication Data

Jansen, Sue Curry.
  Critical communication theory : power, media, gender, and
technology/ Sue Curry Jansen.
    p. cm. — (Critical media studies)
Includes bibliographical references and index.
  ISBN 0-7425-2372-1 (cloth : alk. paper) — ISBN 0-7425-2373-X (pbk. :
alk. paper)
    1. Communication—Social aspects. 2. Critical theory. 3. Knowledge,
Sociology of. 4. Ideology. 5. Intellectuals. I. Title. II. Series.
  HM651 .J36 2002
  302.2—dc21

2002009077

Printed in the United States of America

∞™ The paper used in this publication meets the minimum requirements of American
National Standard for Information Sciences—Permanence of Paper for Printed Library
Materials, ANSI/NISO Z39.48-1992.

Contents

Acknowledgments

Academic books are never done. There is always more data that could be collected, more to be read, thought, and clarified. Authors must, however, periodically force tentative closure on their work if they are to be authors at all.

The sense of forced closure is especially keen with this work. I finished this manuscript during the first week of September 2001. The following week, history took one of its unexpected turns. The attacks in New York, Washington, and Pennsylvania brought an end to the "post–Cold War period," the subject, directly or indirectly, of several of my case studies. With the bipartisan support of Congress, President George W. Bush declared a new war, both hot and cold, on terrorism. Still in the formative stages, the domestic and global ramifications of the "War on Terrorism" remain subjects for speculation.

What is already clear, however, is that, like the Cold War, this new war will involve a permanent war mentality and a permanent war economy. That is, there is no end in sight, and none is anticipated. To secure and sustain this new worldview, new political linguistics, metaphors, categories of thought, and agenda-setting strategies are being cultivated by the government and its corporate partners. The White House has set up a Communications War Room; the State Department has hired an advertising executive to direct a global marketing initiative to sell America to the world; and the Pentagon created a new Office of Strategic Influence, which it subsequently dismantled as a result of widespread criticism from the international press. Even the long-standing government-sponsored War on Drugs media campaign has been revamped and recruited to the service of the War on Terrorism.

To force closure on my book at this juncture in history is therefore as logical as it is difficult. So much of what I have written about—political linguistics, generative metaphors, historical rupture, the gendering of war, silences and erasures in international news reporting—is currently being reactualized as the American government and its allies mobilize their long-term response to the threat of terrorism. The temptation is, of course, to try to capture and report as much of this political dramaturgy as possible. But the reality is that this is another book, perhaps my next book. The compromise that I decided upon instead was to undertake a limited revision of the manuscript to take into account September 11, 2001, and its immediate aftermath, but to do so with a clear publishing deadline in sight. Like most compromises, this one is less than fully satisfying. I know my examinations of these developments are superficial because information is thin due to wartime censorship. Yet, to ignore these horrific events and their aftermath seems a greater folly.

One entry in my own political linguistics deserves explanation. The word "terrorism," has always been problematic for students of critical political linguistics. Like the term "deviance," those in power determine its definition, and historically the definition of terrorism has been notoriously fluid. The term is never used by government spokespersons to describe their government's actions or actions of its agents or allies. It is a devil term that is always ascribed to the actions of enemies. Consequently, many analysts prefer the term "political violence." I share this preference. But the events of September 2001 have made the word terrorism an inescapable term in the new and evolving American political vocabulary. The best critical thinkers can do now is to try to keep critical analysis of the term, and its references, alive and razor-sharp.

This book has had a *very* long gestation. Several chapters had prior lives in conference papers, lectures, and in earlier published works. The cobwebs of fading memories make it impossible to adequately acknowledge everyone who contributed to the book's development. I do, however, owe immediate debts to a number of people for their abiding support. First, and foremost, Marsha Siefert, who frequently shares her morning coffee with me across the Atlantic via e-mail: Marsha endured my daily progress reports during the periods of intensive writing of this book, and always returned words of encouragement. Without that support, this work might well have been silenced or erased. Llewellyn Z. Gross, who long ago served as my dissertation advisor, and who continues to serve as role model *extraordinaire*, dear friend, and the embodiment of good rationality: many of the kernels of ideas developed in these case studies first took form in letters to Lew. Letters to Lew have played an eccentric but very important role in my scholarship. They have sometimes provided quick and painless cures to writer's block as I followed advice Lew gave in one of his seminars, "If you can't write, write about what you can't write." Conversely, in those rare but glorious moments scholars live for, when a rush of new insights has them dancing around in delight, a letter to Lew has been the medium for me to safely bring these wild ideas to coherence and to test their logic. Don Sabo, my longtime collaborator and friend of the mind, is responsible for my forays into sports studies. He is coauthor of chapter 8; without his mastery of the literature in sports sociology, that chapter would not exist. Without his friendship, my life would be diminished. Susan Leggett, former student, current colleague, and expert in her own right on sports, gender, and technology, brought contagious enthusiasm to our frequent discussions of many of the topics and perspectives developed in this work. She has multiplied the illumination of whatever small candles I lit for her long ago, and generously returned their amplified light to me many times over. Finally, I am keenly aware in some still inarticulate way of the enormous intellectual debts I owe my former teacher, the late Ed Powell. His death during the summer of 2001 hung heavily over the writing of this book. Although we had not been in direct contact for years, I nevertheless felt his absence. I became a scholar as an undergraduate in his classes; ours was an agonistic relationship. He provoked me to knowledge; in defending my views against his, I was sometimes transported to new and unexpected places. His pedagogy taught me both the strengths and the limitations of dialectical (and dialogic) reasoning. I am, however, aware that my own teaching and scholarship have been indelibly influenced by his, and that, in the end, our agreements far outweighed our differences.

Beyond these immeasurable debts, there are also many tangible and measurable ones. Andrew Schmidt, my former student, was the first reader of the completed manuscript. He lightened my load considerably by untangling endnote formatting problems; doing detective work on mystery notes; and above all, by asking substantive questions that led to clarifying revisions. In addition to Susan Leggett, my other colleagues in the Communication Department at Muhlenberg College comprise an exceptionally stimulating and supportive community of critical scholars: David Tafler, Susan Kahlenberg, Susan Ross, Jim Schneider, John Sullivan, and Lora Taub make work a pleasure. Jayne Spring and Jane Flood have also been sustaining presences and sources of encouragement throughout the development of this project. Others have exerted considerable influence over specific chapters as supporters and critics. George Gerbner's critical challenges to a very early version of chapter 3 helped me clarify and reinforce my arguments. His enthusiastic support for the ideas developed in chapter 9 made that chapter possible. My debts to George and to his work are much larger than these few lines can possibly begin to convey. Brenda Dervin's work, friendship, and formidable dialogic skills have no doubt exerted influence far beyond what is overtly acknowledged within these pages. Thanks to Brenda, I had the opportunity to observe and participate in sessions and workshops she led on sense-making methodology at the meetings of the International Communication Association. The

x

Acknowledgments

democratic dialogic model that serves as the template for those interactions, as well as the generous participatory ethos of the remarkable network of scholars working within the sense-making approach, have reaffirmed my conviction that the dialogue on dialogue still holds considerable promise despite some premature obituaries that have been written for it. Members of the Feminist Scholarship Division of the International Communication Association, especially during its formative "interest group" years, provided sympathetic audiences for some of my early explorations of ideas developed in this book, especially Mary Ellen Brown, Nina Gregg, and Angharad Valdivia. Muhlenberg College provided both summer grant and sabbatical support that allowed for some of the focused writing time that was necessary to bring this project to fruition.

Finally my family, Paul, Timothy, Michael, and Cathlin Jansen, and Linda, Brian, Edward, and Emily Schmitt, are my life support systems; without them, there would be no writing at all.

Chapter 2 of this book, which was originally written as its introduction, was previously published as "'The future is not what it used to be': Gender, History, and Communication," *Communication Theory* 9, no. 3 (May 1993): 136–48. It is reproduced here with only minor revisions and is reprinted by permission of Oxford University Press and the International Communication Association. Some parts of other chapters have been published in much earlier forms and in some instances as constituents of different arguments in the following publications. Part I of chapter 5 is both an abridgment and extension of part of a review essay that was originally published as, "Is Science a Man? New Feminist Epistemologies and Reconstructions of Knowledge," *Theory and Society* 19 (1990): 235–46. Other earlier publications are "Beaches Without Bases," in *Invisible Crises*, ed. George Gerbner, Hamid Mowlana, and Herbert I. Schiller (Boulder: Westview, 1996), 131–44; "The Sport/War Metaphor: Hegemonic Masculinity, the Persian Gulf War, and the New World Order," *Sociology of Sport Journal* 10, no. 2 (March 1994): 1–17; "Market Censorship Revisited," in *Communication Yearbook* 17, ed. Stanley Deetz (Thousand Oaks, Calif.: Sage, 1994), 481–504; "Gender and the Information Society: A Socially-Structured Silence," *Journal of Communication* 39, no. 3 (Summer 1989): 196–215; and "Power and Knowledge: Towards a New Critical Synthesis," *Journal of Communication* 33, no. 3 (Summer 1983): 342–54.

Part I

SILENCES AND WHISPERS

If they can get you asking the wrong questions, they don't have to worry about the answers.

—Thomas Pynchon

Chapter One

Introduction: Scholarly Writing Is an Unnatural Act

In Ireland, that tiny country that has produced such literary giants as Swift, Wilde, Synge, Yeats, Joyce, and Beckett, writers are dismissed with mock disparagement as "failed conversationalists." The charge can, however, be leveled without the courtesy of the Celtic wink against many, perhaps even most, scholars. Failed conversations are, in fact, primary sources of original scholarly ideas. Scholarship begins where current language and explanatory structures falter; it culminates in a form of discourse that would bring most ordinary conversations to an abrupt end.

Scholarship tries to communicate ideas and relationships among ideas that cannot be easily said or even thought. It is usually composed for the eye, not the ear: to be read, not said. It tames the swirling winds of ordinary language into starchy monologues, parses them into major and minor propositions, and defends them with batteries of footnotes and bibliographies. Indeed, scholarly writing reaches its purest form when it tries to move beyond the messy ambiguities of language by reducing thought to numbers, formulas, diagrams, charts, and other esoteric codes.

This is an unnatural act. No one talks that way, not even us. Academic writing inverts many of the norms of conversational etiquette. It interrupts, takes statements out of context, competes, criticizes, contradicts, and insists that virtually every position except the one that its author is currently espousing is flawed or at least in some sense incomplete. Even its affirmations are frequently contentious and defensive. It can press individualism and iconoclasm to the edge of nihilism. But it can also display fierce paradigm-centered group loyalties. Paradoxically, it can sometimes do both of these things at the same time. Scholarship employs modes of reasoning that would be regarded as antisocial, possibly even pathological, if they were displayed in other social settings. Moreover, it does so in the name of higher forms of thought.

In everyday encounters, conversations fail for many reasons. We are not quick enough, knowledgeable enough, facile enough, loud enough, deferential enough, crude enough, and so on, ad infinitum. We must seize the moment or lose it. Scholarly discourse, by contrast, stops time. Recursive U-turns, which allow us to reflect, retract, and repair semantic mishaps, are rare and fortuitous exceptions when they occur in ordinary conversation. In scholarly writing, they are the rule. Not only can we return to the moment of lost opportunity, we can linger there for weeks, months, even years. We can argue with the dead, put words in their mouths, shore up their sagging theories, claim them as our intellectual ancestors, or shoot fresh arrows through their ancient hearts.

The stakes of these exchanges are actually very high, but their significance is often obscured by their familiarity. They are the grist of the academic mill: the sources of lecture notes, term papers, theses, dissertations, theories, equations, models, and the like. Yet, the troubled and troubling silences that force thinkers to seek explanations on paper are also portals to the transcendent intellectual breakthroughs that can change the way we think about, act within, adapt to, or alter the world.

Such breakthroughs are, of course, infrequent and largely unpredictable. They are, however, the goal, the raison d'être, of scholarly communication. Within the circles of failed academic conversations, discovery as well as almost every shade of interest, indifference, ignorance, error, and illumination are incubated. Dreary prose may multiply geometrically and even prosper within these circles; but "cultures of critical discourse" also provide the discursive spaces where anomalies, paradoxes, gaps, and evasions in prevailing explanatory frameworks can be interrogated and exposed, and new ways of seeing can take form.[1]

Spectacular breakthroughs, for example, Einstein's theory of relativity, decoding the structure of DNA, and the big bang theory, reverberate far beyond their scholarly incubators. They make headlines and careers. They leave us all in awe at the power of the human imagination. Even the more overtly ideologically contested triumphs of social scientists and humanists, for example Marx's analysis of capital; Weber's theory of rationality; Peirce, James, and Dewey's pragmatic conceptions of truth; and Keynes or Friedman's concepts of markets can change minds, policies, and social practices.

Most scholars are, however, destined to plant more modest gardens. Yet, even we small potato growers can produce life-transforming changes, although these changes may be less audible and more incremental than those memorialized in headlines and textbooks. And we may go to our graves wholly unaware of them.

Works of acknowledged genius frequently acknowledge their own dependence on the insights of obscure tillers of the fields. Minor clarifications can prepare the ground for major ones. Teachers can teach more than they know. Students sometimes say that reading a particular scholarly article "changed everything" for them: changed their entire worldview. An amazing feat when we allow ourselves to seriously contemplate it: as little as twenty or thirty pages of print, read at the right moment, can change everything! Or seem to.

Martin Luther said print gives words wings. Once they are airborne, authors lose control over their flight paths. What the reader across the world or across the hall makes of my words reveals as much and sometimes more about her mind than it does about mine. Moreover, the consequences of being understood are sometimes as daunting as the consequences of being misunderstood. Yet, the job of the professor is to profess. A professor's publications are an archive of his or her most carefully considered professions.

DEFINING QUESTIONS AND EPISTEMOLOGICAL QUANDARIES

The archive assembled between these covers represents some provisional outcomes of my extended engagement with two questions that lie at the heart of a critical politics of communication: What do you know? and How do you know it? Simply framed but fraught with existential and epistemological implications, these probes are shorthand renderings of the concerns that have driven the "communicative turn" in contemporary scholarship. They are symptomatic of the interrogations of the current postmodern or, as some would say and hope, "post-postmodern" intellectual climate.

Consequently these are also loaded questions. Their intent is to cultivate reflexivity, and, in their best moments, to induce humility rather than to elicit definitive answers. In asking you to take an inventory of *what* you know, the first probe is actually pressing you to reflect on how little you know and how little can be known. It foregrounds limits: the limits of your personal knowledge and, if you are scholar, the limits of knowledge and even the limits of human intelligence itself.

By directing your attention to *how* you know, the second probe is asking you to reflect upon the mediated nature of all forms of knowing. It is highlighting the radical contingency of knowledge: the dependence of knowledge upon communication and society. This probe encourages you to think about the ways mediation limits, filters, blocks, or distorts your access to knowledge. It raises the twin specters of censorship and hidden manipulation. It evokes caricatures of powerful men with fat cigars in hidden chambers conspiring to mislead you (and me). But is also raises more profound and intractable doubts about our reliance on sources, the technologies of communication, the politics and economics of mediation, and even the reliability of the data supplied by our own senses. It raises a battery of related questions. Who is supplying our information? What institutional arrangements and distribution networks shape the platforms for this supply? Can we trust our sources? What makes sources trustworthy? What should we do if reliable sources conflict? What role does language play in mediating knowledge? Do the limits of our languages (and social locations) circumscribe the limits of our worlds? What is firsthand knowledge? Can we trust our perceptions? Is perception already constituted as conception? If knowledge is contingent, what is truth? Reason? How is society possible? Politics? Ethics?

My questions are the questions—the worries—that define, energize, and deeply trouble scholarship today. Every generation likes to think its problems are unique, and that its sensibility and its angst are unlike any that have come before it. Yet, all of these questions have been asked before. Indeed, in many ways, these are distinctly modern questions. What is *post*modern is our period's response to them: our hyperawareness of the epistemological implications of these questions and our agnosticism about the possibilities of providing definitive answers to them. In *The Birth and Death of Meaning*, Ernest Becker eloquently evokes the new awareness when he writes:

> The world of human aspiration is largely fictitious, and if we do not understand this we understand nothing about man. . . . Man's freedom is a fabricated freedom, and he pays a price for it. He must at all times *defend the utter fragility of his delicately constituted fiction, deny its artificiality.* . . . The most astonishing thing of all, about man's fictions, is not that they have from prehistoric times hung like a flimsy canopy over his social world, but that we should have come to discover them at all. It is one of the most remarkable achievements of thought, of self-scrutiny, that the most anxiety-prone animal of all could come to *see through himself* and discover the fictional nature of his action world. Future historians will probably record it as one of the great liberating breakthroughs of all time, and it happened in ours.[2]

Scholarly responses to this breakthrough have filled several thousand volumes. They range from giddy embraces of aesthetic hedonism to soulful laments for the fate of a god-forsaken world. Some declare the impossibility of theory. Some embrace radical constructivism, declare the world a text, and construct their own, highly individualized life rafts on a sea of floating signifiers. Some retreat to the new tribalism of identity politics. Some see equations of power and knowledge as opportunities to stake personal, positional, or professional claims to power. Some see the past, especially the egalitarian claims of the Enlightenment, as fraudulent, a pack of ideological lies, and issue manifestos calling for reconstruction of knowledge, *ex nihilo*, even though the same insight that inspires this impulse also legislates against its feasibility. And some of us settle for less dramatic alternatives that are faithful to the past in their break with the past.

That is, we honor the labors and achievements of our intellectual ancestors by learning from the conundrums and paradoxes they harvested. Our approach views the breakthrough that Becker describes as a rationale for more humble forms of theory, research, politics, and community-building: forms that are contextual, contingent, process-oriented, symbol-based but embedded ever so tenuously in critical realism, self-correcting, always struggling with and against the pull of relativism, modest in their claims, and reconciled to the presence of paradox and uncertainty in the human condition and in our capacities to make knowledge claims. This path is full of hazards, yet, in my judgment, it is the one that will take us as close as humans can get to rationality, justice, and truth. To be sure, this is not as close as we would like or as we once thought we were; but it may be as close as an anxiety-prone animal can get in an imperfect world.

In mapping the topography of my location, I am not making any claims to originality as the ample weight of my footnotes testifies. Rather I am only trying to position the modest critical claims that these case studies can make in relation to what has been called the great "schizoid split" in Western consciousness.[3] Until recently, this split, and the dualism it has supported, has allowed scholars to deny their own, always imperfect, agency as mediators and makers of knowledge. That is, it has allowed them/us to act as if we were ventriloquists for God, Nature, and Truth. It supported Promethean delusions of disembodied and disinterested knowledge, which can no longer be sustained.

Long before postmodernism enveloped and destabilized the foundations of contemporary scholarship, Michael Polanyi described the new, post-Promethean terms of human engagement with knowledge:

> We have plucked from the Tree a second apple which has forever imperilled our knowledge of Good and Evil, and we must learn to know these qualities henceforth in the blinding light of our new analytical powers. Humanity has been deprived a second time of its innocence, and driven out of another garden which was, at any rate, a Fool's Paradise.[4]

The intellectual distance from Polanyi's garden to mine is enormous and humbling. He rethinks the nature of thought. In contrast, I till much more pedestrian grounds: the weedy plots of contemporary forms of mediation. Yet, even these grounds must now be viewed differently in light of our new analytical powers. Not only must we approach them with the same weighty epistemological baggage that we would take to the high courts of philosophy. We must also recognize that these weedy plots, which are so often filled with trivial contents, nevertheless exercise significant, even profound, influence over what and how we know.

My explorations raise more questions than they answer about the fragile fictions that make community and communication possible. These critical probes seek to expose some of the cruel fictions that fracture communities and thwart dreams of democracy. With the burden of epistemological perplexity that is now everyone's lot, my work recognizes that some of the same fictions do both. That is, they simultaneously create and fracture community, absorbing and refracting change.

Cautionary Signal: Both/And

In an attempt to foreground and flag my attempt to keep the schizoid character of the *dis-ease* of contemporary thought in the foreground, I frequently invoke the awkward terminological amalgamation "both/and." Both/and has been used by feminists to mark their—our—break with Cartesian dualism.[5] When I use the term in my work, it signals a commitment to pursue modes of thinking that avoid the reductive binary categories of dualism, even though I know frequent relapses are inevitable because dualism is built into the very categories and structures of Indo-European languages, and possibly into our perceptual apparatus.[6] In that sense, the both/and qualifier marks intention more often than achievement. It signals an ongoing desire to recognize the complexity, ambiguity, and paradoxical qualities of human perceptions, conceptions, and communications.

The challenge that both/and modes of thinking pose can be illustrated by considering an old truism of practical reason that many children have put to the empirical test: "You can't chew gum and skip at the same time." "Both/and" raises the bar for reason. It requires us to skip and chew simultaneously, knowing full well that we will frequently stumble and bite our tongues. That is, it urges us to go forward and do our work of repairing, remaking, or replacing the failed conversations of our disciplines while at the same time remaining alert to the disruptive tension that underscores the fragility of our own claims. It is a mandate for epistemological humility.[7]

For me both/and is, or should be, much more than a conciliatory gesture. I use it to signal a friendly initiative—a handshake, if you will—in an academic language game that usually takes no prisoners. I intend it as an acknowledgment and appreciation of the fact that all arguments, including my own, are always incomplete and flawed.

Throughout this book, I probe the limits of language and the slipperiness of metaphors, yet I relish the taste of language and the magic of metaphors. I am critical, sometimes hypercritical, of mass-mediated forms, but I remain in awe of their powers and continue to dream hopeful dreams of what they could do. In short, both/and is also "Yes, but. . . ."

The primary focus of most of these essays is on language and representational practices; it is therefore, by definition, a limited plane of analysis. This focus supplements and complements more broadly based researches on cultural production and the political economy of communication, but it does not, in any sense, supersede or supplant them. To the contrary, they provide the impetus for these studies.

YES, BUT . . . WHAT? WHERE I
ENTER THE CONVERSATIONS IN THIS BOOK

In this volume, I explore the following interrelated themes: (a) how words and ideas shape and are shaped by material conditions and human agency; (b) how Promethean myths of transcendence condition and gender contemporary thought and social practices; (c) how the gendering of thought and practices intersects with, inflects, and is inflected by other forms of social inequality, for example, race, class, nation, and the ever-fluid "et cetera," which must always accompany inventories of injustices; (d) how metaphors incubate mythic thinking, act as agents of ideological transfer, and sanction the political linguistics that, at particular moments in history, provide more or less convincing explanations of the world; (e) how generative metaphors like the Enlightenment, the Cold War, the New World Order, globalization, and the War on Terrorism construct their flimsy canopies over our social worlds, and how the resulting structures coordinate and mobilize social resources and actions; (f) how the liberation that accompanies discovery of the transparency of our human fictions heightens our ethical and epistemological responsibilities without relieving our species of its dependence upon fictions—our need for narratives to constitute and make sense of the social world and to provide grounds for human communication and action; and (g) how the airy abstractions enumerated in this very long sentence actually manifest themselves in tangible social practices such as science, technology, information, sport, war, news, and critical scholarship.[8]

A number of both/ands—ambivalences, conceptual inversions, and conundrums—place inconvenient demands on this agenda. Some of the repeat offenders are readily identifiable: (a) the tensions inherent in my dual commitments to critical social theory and critical feminisms; (b) the messiness that accompanies commuting among competing theoretic claims and disciplinary loyalties, which court the wrath of both disciplinary purists and the logic police; (c) the paradox or near-paradox implicit in arguing against Promethean conceptions of knowledge while at the same time arguing for recovery of the utopian impulse in human affairs; and (d) the familiar dilemma that every scholar and every intellectual generation must come to terms with, which is how to define and perform the role of critical scholar under social conditions that almost always impose heavy tolls on those who would speak inconvenient truths to or about the powerful.

CRITICAL SOCIAL THEORY AND CRITICAL FEMINISMS

Critical social theory, as I use that compound term here, refers to a fairly broad and fluid configuration that drew its original inspiration from what has been called "the classic tradition" in nineteenth-century social thought.[9] The intellectual heirs of this tradition include a motley array of thinkers who would never list themselves in the same playbook. Within communication and media sociology, critical social theory has exerted significant influence in four overlapping areas: (a) political economy; (b) institutional analyses; (c) what I call "media critical" theory; and (d) (with significant qualifiers) the prolific newcomer, cultural studies. While the classic tradition has produced prominent feminists, it has not generally been friendly to feminism.[10] Feminists have found their voice in critiquing the critique. They have been the willful daughters or errant sons of a tradition that is secured in what Bakhtin refers to as "the word of the fathers."[11]

The cultural studies approach is an exception to this generalization. The nature of this exception requires brief amplification here because I constantly bundle my subsequent references to cultural studies in qualifiers. Gaining influence across the disciplines in the wake of feminism and women's studies and in tandem with queer studies, the cultural studies approach has provided a welcome refuge for work that places gender and/or sexuality at its center.[12] Initial articulations of the approach, for example the Birmingham School, derived directly from and served as a "cultural" corrective to critical social theory. As cultural studies gained the momentum and experienced the heady success of a movement, however, it lost much of its critical edge. Many of its U.S. converts have been unwilling or unable to skip the skip of cultural analysis while at the same time chewing the gum of sociological analysis. The "social," as that term has been historically understood and deployed by sociologists, was the first casualty of the theory and disciplinary wars that ensued as cultural studies began to vie for paradigmatic status in the United States. Much of the scholarship that now operates under the eclectic flag of cultural studies on this side of the Atlantic is actually literary studies reborn and expanded to encompass literary analyses of the "texts" of popular culture, for example, film, television, advertising, and fashion. Except for some faint derivative Marxian echoes, poststructuralist versions of cultural studies acknowledge few debts to classic social theory and are largely hostile to its premises.[13]

Critical feminisms, as I use that designation here, denote feminist theories and practices that are critical of the limits of their own horizons of class, race, empire, heterosexisms, generation, et cetera—feminisms that remain open to further conversations and to coalition building. More influential today in Europe, Canada, Australia, and New Zealand than in the United States, critical feminisms extend critique of "the woman question" to comprehensive and systemic analyses of the historical and sociological roots of "structures" of dominance and subordination.[14] Some critical feminists express deep skepticism about what they refer to as the "cultural feminism" of recent, primarily U.S., feminist epistemological critiques of science and philosophy, for example, the work of Merchant, Keller, Harding, Haraway, and Bordo.[15] I do not fully share this skepticism. I believe the feminist epistemological critique has opened up some crucial discursive spaces that have, at least in the U.S., long silenced or disabled systemic critical analyses of formidable structures of power and knowledge. I do, however, acknowledge that cultural feminism shares some of the vulnerabilities of cultural studies. That is why I emphasize my allegiances to "critical" feminisms.

Critical social theory and critical feminisms share many common commitments. Both recognize that the Cartesian dream of pure thought is an impossible dream. That is, they conceive of scholarship as a social practice, which is inextricably embedded in the historical contexts, social values, material interests, and social struggles that produce and constitute it. As a result, both approaches embrace the unity of theory and practice. Critical social theory and critical feminisms are products of the incomplete egalitarian struggles of the Enlightenment. Both fault the often unspoken exclusionary clauses in the liberal democratic visions of the Enlightenment, yet they remain committed to the project of translating the theory of participatory democracy into practice. They therefore affirm a shared sense of solidarity with the oppressed. While they recognize the "systemic" character of oppression, they also recognize that categories of oppression are fluid and require constant monitoring so that solidarity with yesterday's underdog does not empower tomorrow's tyrants. In that sense, then, both perspectives place criticism before solidarity in interventions in public life; although, to be sure, being the work of flawed humans, few of their/our interventions ever achieve full fidelity with this principle.

In this book, I press the discourses of critical social theory and critical feminisms into conversation with each other. That is far from an original move. Indeed, by now, if for no other reason than a generational shift, most thoughtful people on both sides of the divide acknowledge its logic.[16] If my attempt possesses any identifiable distinction, it may be its longevity and persistence: a wage of age.

ELUDING THE LOGIC POLICE: STRUCTURAL METAPHORS

To acknowledge the resonance of Becker's claim that humans construct canopies of meaning over their social worlds and then take up residence under them is to embrace a form of social constructivism. It is to salute the power of words, ideas, and reason in human affairs. Yet, to insist, as I do, that social structures and material conditions also exert very real constraints on the conduct of human affairs is to cast a vote for realism. This is a both/and move that purists find untenable.

My response to this objection is both complex and (alas, poor reader) somewhat convoluted. The fundamental question, "How is society possible?", posed long ago by Georg Simmel, remains the core question of social theory.[17] I view metaphors as the long lamented missing link in sociological analysis: the dynamic force that connects individual consciousness and society and ignites lifelong struggles between them. For me, coming to terms with the powers of metaphor enables a vision of social reality, which both embraces the communicative turn in scholarship and reconstitutes a platform for structural analysis. Here is how it works.

Hard-nosed realists and idealists agree on one thing: Social structure is a metaphor. As a result, purists in both camps maintain that little will be lost if they discard the concept; however, this common conclusion is supported by conflicting rationales. To realists, metaphors lack substance; for example, you can't see, touch, taste, or smell social structures. That is not a problem for idealists. However, idealists prefer more elegant, fluid, process-oriented metaphors that capture and amplify the fleeting qualities of human interactions and that emphasize the fragility of meaning-making and the wonder of communication—for example, conversational and textual metaphors and their antecedents, weaving and web imagery; even metaphysical and religious metaphors, such as surrender and catch, communion, and telos. A both/and compromise acknowledges the complaints of both camps: social structure is a metaphor, an abstraction that is often reified in social analyses; moreover, it is a clumsy metaphor that suggests more solidity and permanence than the fragile fictions of the human species can support. Yet, my both/and compromise stubbornly hangs onto this flawed idea and affirms its continuing utility. That is, this compromise treats social structure as a heuristic or generative metaphor for social theory.

Heuristic metaphors focus perception and attention. They make some "things" easier to see, think, and say than others. Social structure is a metaphor that focuses attention on issues of power, hierarchy, social inequality, social relationships and processes of dominance and subordination, social stratification, the systemic effects of allocation of social and economic resources, et cetera.[18] As a crutch or tool of critical analysis, it helps us apprehend conceptual as well as material processes of power relations. Structure is, however, an abstraction that glosses over the subtleties and nuances of the multiplicity of ways people actually make sense of their life worlds. Borrowed from the language of the material world of mortar, bricks, and steel, the metaphor implies more solidity and permanence than exists in the social world; hence Anthony Giddens's useful corrective, "structuration," which emphasizes process and accommodates change.[19] Analysis of social structure tells us little about art, music, poetry, or literature. It is not a very useful heuristic for analyzing the production of texts or for interpreting their cultural meanings. It tells us little about human dreams, aspirations, nature, bodies, or individuality. It is a bare-bones abstraction: necessary but never sufficient. It only acquires analytic power when the malleable forms of the blood and flesh of historical testaments give it temporal locations and palpable meanings. It is, in short, a crude and clumsy metaphor, but one that can nevertheless help critical theorists keep faith with the oppressed.

Surrendering the concept of structure to the logic police silences critical analysis of the big picture. It proscribes the use of master narratives. Moreover, it does it at precisely the historical moment when the master narratives and generative metaphors of globalization and the War on Terrorism are being deployed throughout the world to bring it into alignment with Western interests.

In this work, then, I use the term "structure" to refer to a dynamic set of institutional rules, practices, processes, and institutionally mediated meanings that are used to constitute, organize, and coordinate behavior in the world. By world, I mean that place outside of our heads where even radical poststructuralists must go to sharpen their pencils, brew coffee, cash checks, and bury their dead.

Large scale (macro) structural analysis will continue to be imperative, methodologically and politically, for as long as powerful entities such as nation-states, corporations, and the international organizations they create to represent their interests (like the World Bank, the International Monetary Fund, and the World Trade Organization) continue to cultivate master narratives, policies, and practices that have profound social and environmental consequences. In short, responsible forms of critical theory will not be able to discard it for the foreseeable future.

PROMETHEUS'S CORPSE

I endorse an epistemological stance that conceives of knowledge as the unique and extraordinary achievement of embodied humans, not the work of gods. This stance rejects correspondence theories of truth that cast the scientist, poet, or scholar in the role of a privileged intermediary who speaks for God or Nature. That is, it calls mind back to the body and struggles against Western dualism. In short, it attempts to clip the wings of Prometheus. Yet, at the same time, I also support Pierre Bourdieu and Günter Grass's recent call for a recovery of the utopian impulse in politics and human affairs.[20] This is an audacious both/and move, which should raise the critical antenna of any serious reader.

An explanation is required. In our time, utopianism has been equated with totalitarianism: with Promethean flights of imagination that impose the ideas of one thinker, party, or vanguard on all. The twin terrors of the twentieth century, Nazism and Soviet Communism, are offered as definitive evidence. Victims of these horrors argue with persuasive passion and clarity against the "lunatics of one idea" and remind us that in the twentieth century, "the executioners' best friends have often turned out to be writers and intellectuals."[21]

Yet, the great achievements of human emancipation, the decline of feudalism, the birth of democracy, the formal (though not always actual) abolition of slavery in most parts of the world, the relative decline of torture as a routine tool of state-craft, the emancipation of women, and the emergence of laws and covenants recognizing human rights are all products of long and still incomplete struggles of principled people who dared to imagine something better and to commit themselves to achieving it.

To accept "what is" as all that can be is to surrender the dream of democracy and to betray the oppressed. Dreams of democracy are, however, by definition, multiple dreams that can only be achieved by means that are consistent with their ends. There are, of course, no sure guarantees that demagogues—the lunatics of one idea—will not hijack these dreams. But, in my judgment and in the judgment of many thinkers who are far wiser than me, democratic dreams and the political practices they support still offer the best defense that our anxiety-prone species has against the seductions and tyrannies of totalizing systems.

And here is where both/and adds its tonic. By surrendering Promethean delusions of certainty, we create mandates for more grounded, decentralized, community-based forms of political legitimization as well as for the more humble epistemological claims I have been affirming up to this point. In a passage that I cite repeatedly in the chapters that follow because, in my judgment, it cannot be repeated too often, Donna Haraway describes the epistemological and political challenges that we now face:

"[O]ur" problem is, how to have simultaneously an account of radical historical contingency for all knowledge claims and knowing subjects, a critical practice for recognizing our own "semiotic technologies" for making meanings and a no nonsense commitment to faithful accounts of a "real" world; one that can be partially shared and that is friendly to earthwide projects of finite freedom, adequate material abundance, modest meaning in suffering, and limited happiness.[22]

In our time, the major semiotic technologies for representing the "real" worlds of politics—what are now almost universally referred to in everyday usage in the singular term "the media"—are now owned and controlled by a handful of global corporations. As a result, in the twenty-first century, *how* we know is more imperiled than ever before by the threat of the singular, commodified vision of powerful corporations that not only control the contents but also the conduits of our semiotic technologies: our newspapers, books, radio, television, telephony, satellites, Internet access, et cetera.[23] In short, the multiplicity of political viewpoints that are both the means and ends of democracy are now disappearing from major media: the media that most people rely upon for most of their news and political information.

This is why Robert McChesney argues that communication scholars must now play a central role in raising public awareness of the relationship between media and democracy. "Only communication scholars," he asserts, "have the resources and institutional basis to move forward with honest independent scholarship and instruction, with a commitment first and foremost to democratic values." If the field of communication does not take up this charge, McChesney warns, the lesson of the last fifty years makes it clear that "nobody else will."[24] Unless we, communication scholars, systematically document what is missing under neoliberal (that is, privatized, conglomerate, and globalized) control of media and find the courage to imagine something better, to entertain utopian possibilities, then the unfulfilled dreams of democracy may be deferred indefinitely. Utopian visions that are produced by careful analysis of actual social conditions are not visions of "no place" or an impossible place but of a better place, a good place, which can be reached from the current place. They are "reasoned utopias."[25] This kind of utopianism is not only consistent with the assumptions of the classic tradition of social theory; it is its mandate.

SPEAKING TRUTH TO POWER

The duty, the moral obligation, of critical scholars is to think "otherwise," to question established orthodoxies and to speak truth about and, when possible, to power.[26] Whether they take to the streets, to the study, or to the lectern, scholars working within this tradition share the conviction that scholarship is not just another career choice like accounting or public relations. They tap into an ancient tradition, which conceives of scholarship as a calling or vocation that entails sacrifice and obligation as well as intellectual pleasures. To think otherwise is to choose a life on the margins: a location, which is antithetical to the usual requirements for career advancement. This marginality usually places the scholar in tension with, and sometimes in overt conflict with, a sense of personal well-being and comfort. For most of its practitioners, this tradition makes heavy personal demands but returns relatively modest material rewards.

Compensation comes from living one's convictions and from the intrinsic value of the work itself: from the romance and, dare I say it, the erotics of "adventures of ideas."[27] Here, however, I must add a qualifying note, which is expanded in the concluding chapter. Given the present and perhaps only partially mutable order of the world, this calling almost always extracts a higher toll from women than men. Because "woman" is constructed within larger discourses of imperial, racial, and class domination, this toll is also assessed in more complex and usually harsher ways for women *and* men who experience multiple layers of oppression.[28] Moreover, this qualifier also needs to be qualified in another both/and move. Academics see themselves as materially disadvantaged in the contemporary corporate dominated world; however, occupying an academic position *always* carries class privileges regardless of one's gender, race, ethnicity, sexual orientation, or even income, and regardless of whether one is an apologist of power or its self-anointed critic. And all academics are always and justly vulnerable to suspicion when they presume to speak for those who do not speak the idioms of scholarship or other forms of print-based literacies. Yet, speak they must! And try to find ways of making themselves heard, too.

MEDIA-CRITICAL THEORY: RECOVERING EMANCIPATORY TENSIONS

In locating this book under the umbrella of media-critical theory, I revisit an old academic debate. Not a failed conversation, but an incomplete one: It began in a generative chapter of Alvin W. Gouldner's *The Dialectic of Ideology and Technology*, entitled "Towards a Media-Critical Politics." Reading that chapter, almost a quarter of a century ago, actually did change everything for me: the direction of my scholarly work and even my disciplinary identity and location.

Emphasizing that the future of emancipatory politics is contingent upon developing a theory of media freedom, Gouldner asserts,

Critical theory must reopen the question of media freedom. It must recenter that problem, exposing the manner in which all kinds of freedom today hinges on issues of media censorship—of news, news interpretation, and of entertainment. . . . It is through the mass media and through them alone that there is today any possibility at all of a truly mass public enlightenment that might go beyond what universities might elicit, i.e. beyond small elites and educated elitism. It is through the media that the system may be made to "dance to its own melody," or to expose itself. From *l'affaire Dreyfus* to the Watergate scandal, the powerful role of media in monitoring the management of public affairs has been notable, even if sporadic. For those who can see, it is profoundly at variance with any simple-minded stereotype of media simply as an agency reproducing the existent system of domination.[29]

Gouldner did not articulate a media-critical theory. That was not his project, but he does articulate a warrant for such a perspective.

I believe Gouldner's insight remains fundamentally important today, even as the Internet and digital convergence compound what we mean by mass media and transform how media function. More obvious than innovative now, the implications of Gouldner's view are even more sobering. Yet, in 1978 when the flames of Cold War rhetoric were still burning brightly, his claim that "[t]he news-producing system is thus a news *withholding* and *censoring* system" was not fully appreciated. The technological and organizational infrastructures required for corporations and some states to mobilize and coordinate their power for sustained withholding and censoring across the world were still largely hypothetical. Today these infrastructures are in place. Their coordinated use to overtly censor or withhold news about specific political issues is still infrequent. But instances of this kind of state and market censorship can be identified. For example, in the wake of the attack on the World Trade Center, the U.S. government directly and (to its merit, if censorship can have merit) *openly* intervened in news processes, with full cooperation from U.S.-based news organizations, to prevent rebroadcast on U.S. television of videotaped messages produced by Osama bin Laden's forces, which were broadcast on Arab television. Most state and market censorships do not operate openly although they do frequently operate in tandem. For example, market censorship in the U.S. muffled debate and provided a virtual news blackout that underreported, silenced, or preempted public debates on the Telecommunications Act of 1996, as well as the NAFTA and GATT treaties. This censorship gave Congress and industry lobbyists free hands in crafting legislation that has profound global consequences. What has, however, been more common in the post–Cold War era has been saturation of news with sex scandals, trivial stories about celebrities, and high profile crime stories, combined with thin coverage of international news and highly skewed coverage of political protests that target globalization. In the immediate wake of the attacks on New York and Washington, mainstream media organizations placed renewed emphasis on hard news and international coverage; however, they soon returned to the ratings-centered entertainment model of news.

The central insight of media-critical theory is still not fully grasped by many sociologists who acknowledge the power of media in the social reproduction of inequalities in capitalist societies. To wit, media and mediation are practices that must be understood on their own terms and in their full (and fully nuanced) complexity. That is, as Gouldner affirms, representational practices cannot be understood simply by understanding ownership patterns, although those patterns are an important component of political economy and institutional analysis of media structures. Contradictions within the profit structures of media systems of neoliberal societies must also be understood, and, where possible, supported through alliances with cultural workers; for, as Graham Murdock and Peter Golding emphasize, media workers operate within traditions, codes, and occupational ideologies, and with personal and social aspirations that retain some autonomy despite media ownership patterns.[30]

Ben Bagdikian provides useful metaphors for thinking about these contradictions in contemporary media systems when he describes journalism as a house divided.[31] On the one side, there are those who think of journalism as a "cathedral," including reporters and editors who retain the hoary values of the Jeffersonian concept of the press as a watchdog of democracy, independent, crusading, championing the rights of the underdog. On the other side of the house is the "bank": the business offices where the bottom line rules and pressures to pander to advertisers prevail. The two sides of the house have never been as hermetically sealed as the apologists of the cathedral like to imagine; but the theoretical separation has historically served as a useful fiction that has preserved some degrees of freedom within the cathedral. It has often kept the bankers on the defensive against charges of censorship; and the struggles between the two sides of the house have allowed the commercial press in liberal societies to be both profitable and relatively free. Given the current conglomerate control and vertical integration of global media, I share Bagdikian's worry that the bank is winning the struggle, and I share his conclusion that the watchdogs bear watching now more than ever.

The tensions between the bank and the cathedral are openings to emancipatory possibilities. The mandates of media-critical theory are to reconnect analyses of cultural forms to analyses of the institutions and the political economy of communication, to form alliance with cultural workers, and to link critical scholarship to struggles for meaningful forms of social and political freedom, not just cultural freedom. That is, to recover and amplify definitions of human freedom that position meaningful citizen participation at their center. Freedom then becomes more than just the freedom to consume controversial cultural products, even though these consumer rights may assume importance when the powerful attempt to quash them. Nevertheless struggles to preserve access to pornographic websites or to controversial art exhibits in publicly funded museums, which always command extensive media coverage in the United States, deflect attention away from the larger democratic struggles of our time. Moreover, they trivialize what is actually at stake in these larger struggles: the political freedom of all citizens, not just the cultural freedom of elite artists or crass pornographers.

NOTES

1. Alvin Gouldner, *The Dialectic of Ideology and Technology* (New York: The Seabury Press, 1976); and *The Future of Intellectuals and the Rise of the New Class* (New York: The Seabury Press, 1979). While I freely indulge the "conversation" metaphor in this introduction, I do not yield to the postmodernist or neopragmatic temptation to conceive of scholarship as only conversation, only a rhetorical exercise. To the contrary, I recognize that scholarship bears the weight of the world. That is, it is constrained by and embedded within the limits imposed by the "real," external, material world.

2. Ernest Becker, "The Fragile Fiction," in *The Truth About Truth: De-Confusing and Re-Constructing the Postmodern World*, ed. Walter Truett Anderson (New York: G. F. Putnam's Sons, 1995), 34–35. Becker's widely cited book, *The Birth and Death of Meaning* (Glencoe, Ill.: The Free Press, 1962), from which this passage is excerpted, has exerted considerable influence because of its timely appearance and its stunning eloquence.

3. Houston Smith, *Beyond the Post-Modern Mind* (New York: Crossroads, 1982).

4. Michael Polanyi, *Personal Knowledge* (Chicago: University of Chicago Press, 1958), 268.

5. The both/and terminological pairing has had wide circulation in feminist critiques of binary thinking. Eve Tavor Bannet provides a useful analysis in "The Feminist Logic of Both/And," *Genders* 15 (Winter 1992): 1–19. For me, the "logic" resonates *both* within *and* beyond feminisms. Susan Bordo's valuable essay, "The Cartesian Masculinization of Thought," *Signs* 11, no. 3 (1986): 439–56, which was subsequently amplified in *The Flight to Objectivity: Essays on Cartesianism and Culture* (Albany: State University of New York Press, 1987), has exercised significant influence over my thinking about Western dualism. I am, however, far less optimistic than Bordo is about prospects for reconciliation and a new synthesis. I think we will face the intellectual burden and awkwardness of both/and conceptual gymnastics for the foreseeable future.

6. Perception is not only conception, but it is, as Jerome Bruner has pointed out, conceived within narrative frames and categories. Moreover, cognitive science has demonstrated that the brain pads that are habitually used develop more fully than those that are dormant. See Bruner, *Actual Minds, Possible Worlds* (Cambridge, Mass.: Harvard University Press, 1986).

7. Polanyi saw *Personal Knowledge* as an argument for a "new humility" in the theory of knowledge. Anderson tries to mediate the implications of the epistemological crises posed by new approaches to the theory of knowledge in *The Truth about Truth*.

8. This summarizing sentence is packed with synthetic statements drawn from many sources that are cited and examined in depth later in the book. This footnote cannot possibly catalog nor do justice to them all. There are, however, some direct borrowings that do require acknowledgment here. Obviously I draw upon and play heavily with Becker's description of the fictive character of human meaning cited earlier; see Becker, "The Fragile Fiction." Many influences have shaped my approach to metaphor from Nietzsche, Richards, Burke, and Blackman to more recent work by Bloor, Lakoff and Johnson, Steiner, and Rorty. Feminist probes of language by Daly, Merchant, Haraway, Keller, Bordo, and legions of others have also been extremely important to me. Bloor's discussions of how metaphors transfer ideology into mathematics have been especially useful to my own thinking. See David Bloor, *Knowledge and Social Imagery* (London: Routledge and Kegan Paul, 1977). Herbert Marcuse introduced the concept of "political linguistics" in *Eros: A Philosophical Inquiry into Freud* (Boston: Beacon Press, 1955).

9. C. Wright Mills, *Images of Man: The Classic Tradition in Sociological Thinking* (New York: G. Brazeller, 1960). I cite Mills's work a matter of convenience here. Courses in classic social (or sociological) theory are standard offerings in sociology departments throughout the United States. They typically cover such thinkers as Comte, Marx, Weber, Durkheim, Tarde, Tonnies, and Simmel.

10. This mapping of the field is, at best, a tentative effort to locate a disparate set of critical inquiries in order to locate my own point of departure. There have been a number of excellent recent attempts to rethink and remap the territory of communication inquiry from critical perspectives that are far more thorough and nuanced than the shorthand I use here. See, for example, Vincent Mosco, *The Political Economy of Communication* (London: Sage, 1996); Armand Mattelart and Michele Mattelart, *Rethinking Media Theory: Signposts and New Directions* (Minneapolis: University of Minnesota Press, 1992); John Durham Peters, *Speaking into the Air: A History of the Idea of Communication* (Chicago: University of Chicago Press, 1999); and Dan Schiller, *Theorizing Communication* (New York: Oxford University Press, 1996). Mosco also provides some interesting reflections on the mapping process itself.

11. There are historical exceptions or partial exceptions, of course, for example, John Stuart Mill, Georg Simmel, and Max Weber were supportive of the feminist arguments of their times, although they were nevertheless also beneficiaries of its prevailing gender order. Socialist-feminism, of course, applies the insights of the thinking of Marx and Engels to its articulations of critical analyses of patriarchy; Engels's *The Origin of the Family, Private Property and the State* (New York: International Publishers, 1972) contributed significantly to the development of feminist thought. The quote is from Mikhail Bakhtin, *The Dialectical Imagination* (Austin: University of Texas Press, 1981), 342.

12. This claim requires some qualification. To be sure, early work in British cultural studies shared the gendered blindspot of other forms of communication inquiry.

Feminist struggles exposed that blindspot, and, to some significant degree, opened up the range of inquiry encompassed by cultural studies. However, the tendency to slip back into old patriarchal patterns continues, as do the struggles against it. What passes as cultural studies in the U.S. lacks both the theoretical coherence and the political mission of the original: its eclecticism has made it a convenient location and identifier for interdisciplinary work that does not fit within established subfields of the social sciences or humanities. Its openness to feminist and queer studies is, at least in part, an artifact of this eclecticism.

13. For a discussion of the problems in the humanities, and especially English, that led to the ascent of cultural studies in the humanities, as well as a tracking of its theoretical roots, see Anthony Easthope, *Literary into Cultural Studies* (New York: Routledge, 1991). For a scathing critique of the transformation of cultural studies as it has been appropriated by the humanities in the U.S., see Rita Felski, "Those Who Disdain Cultural Studies Don't Know What They're Talking About," *The Chronicle of Higher Education* (23 July 1999): 6(B). For a critique of cultural studies that draws upon the same traditions as British cultural studies, see Nicholas Garnham, *Capitalism and Communication: Global Communication and the Economics of Information* (London: Sage, 1990); and Nicholas Garnham, *The Media and Modernity* (London: Oxford University Press, 2000). For a careful explication of the debates within the British left involving E. P. Thompson, Raymond Williams, and Stuart Hall, which resulted in the privileging of culture in the work of the Birmingham School, see Schiller, *Theorizing Communication*.

14. Naming the names of all of the scholars who have directly influenced my thinking about feminist theory over many years of reading, conferencing, and agitating would be impossible. Since my purpose here is simply to flag an affinity with modes of feminist thought that more or less consistently keep their eyes on the systemic effects of oppression as well as on its cultural expressions (including those that oppress men as well as women), I arbitrarily list only a few influences here, for example, Dorothy Smith, Eva Figas, Ann Oakley, the early Germaine Greer, Dale Spender, Bob Connell, Cynthia Cockburn, Maureen McNeil, and Mary O'Brien. American feminism has, of course, also had an enormous, indeed shaping, influence on my thinking, and much of that influence has come from thinkers outside of the academy. Some of these influences are catalogued in the endnotes.

15. See, for example, the prefatory comments to Judy Wajcman, *Feminism Confronts Technology* (University Park: The Pennsylvania State University Press, 1991), 2. I do, however, more generally agree with the emphasis that Wajcman places on the "social" constituents of technology development.

16. For three recent, book-length rethinkings of critical theory that are responsive to the feminist critique, see Mosco, *The Political Economy of Communication*; Peters, *Speaking into the Air*; and Schiller, *Theorizing Communication*. While focused on political economy, rather than on the communication field as a whole, Mosco's work presses toward a synthesis of feminism and critical theory in his rethinking of the political economy of communication.

17. Georg Simmel, *The Sociology of Georg Simmel* (Glencoe, Ill.: The Free Press, 1964). The question "How is society possible?" is the fundamental question underlying all of Simmel's (1858–1918) work. Others critical sociologists have expressed

their truces with constructivism more efficiently by describing the relationship between communication and society as mutually constitutive, a position that is consonant with my position. My added verbiage and qualifications are, however, necessary because much of the work in this book examines the roles metaphors play in those constitutive processes. As a result, my own metaphors require more interrogation.

18. In *The Political Economy of Communication*, Mosco, following Connell, describes his critical realist's truce with constructivism much more efficiently by describing the social as mutually constituting.

19. Clifford Geertz played a crucial bridging role, at least in the United States, in the movement from literary study to cultural studies. Long an eloquent in-house critic of positivistic approaches to anthropology, Geertz's work reads very differently as literary apology than it does as anthropological critique. Anthropologists know that the temptation to reify the concept of social structure by structural-functionalists has long been critiqued within social science even by functionalists, for example Alfred R. Radcliffe-Brown. See Alfred R. Radcliffe-Brown, *Structure and Function in Primitive Society: Essays and Addresses* (Glencoe, Ill.: The Free Press, 1965). They know that these reflexive moves have been moves away from naïve realism. They also know that critical, conflict, or neo-Marxian traditions have long used the term by linking it dynamically to struggles of domination and resistance. In short, they know that the term, the metaphor or heuristic model, has a much richer and more nuanced history and set of critical associations than is presence in the mechanistic determinism of Marx's analytic categories of sub- and superstructure (that even Marx qualified and later criticized). Moreover, they also know that while reductive dreams have certainly prospered in all of the social sciences, the "structure" of Suassurian linguistics is but one rather specialized meaning of the term. Its failure to satisfy the reductive dreams of students of literature does not, however, mean that all other uses of the term are illegitimate or that social science itself has little of value to say about culture and communication. Geertz has often been misused, albeit without protest, especially by English professors to dismiss, without investigation, the entire corpus of pre-Geertzian anthropology and virtually all structural sociology.

20. Anthony Giddens, *The Constitution of Society: Outline of the Theory of Structuralism* (Berkeley: University of California Press, 1974).

21. Günter Grass and Pierre Bourdieu, "A Literature from Below," *The Nation* (July 3, 2000): 25–28; and Pierre Bourdieu, "A Reasoned Utopia and Economic Fatalism," *New Left Review* 227 (1988): 125–30.

22. The phrase "lunatics of one idea" is from Wallace Stevens. It is cited by Charles Simic in his powerful testament against utopian thought, "Refuges," in *Letters of Transit: Reflections on Exile, Identity, Language, and Loss*, ed. Andre Aciman (New York: The New Press, 1999), 134. Simic claims, "Barbarism, intolerance, and fanaticism have been the by-products of all utopian projects in this century. Infallible theories of history and human progress brought about the most repellent forms of repression. The noble-sounding attempt to make the whole of society accept a particular worldview always leads, sooner or later, to slaughter of the innocents" (133). In my view Simic rightly equates fanaticism with claims to infallible theories of history and progress. However, his equation of all utopian thought with claims to infallibility

and the reductive lunacy of one idea is hyperbolic and ahistorical. Although he celebrates the individual rights valorized by Western democracies (in this case the United States), Simic ignores the history of democratic movements: of movements to expand human rights franchises, the civil rights movement, the women's movement, Mandela's triumph over apartheid, et cetera. Even such modest social reform initiatives like providing shelters for the homeless, crises hotlines to comfort and counsel the traumatized, or school lunch programs require some vision of a better, more just society.

23. Donna Haraway, "Situated Knowledge: The Science Question in Feminism and the Privilege of Partial Perspective," *Feminist Studies* 14, no. 3 (1988): 579. I not only endorse macroanalysis of national and transnational neoliberal structures and initiatives, but also activism that exposes the human costs they extract, for example sweatshops and environmental toxicity. However, given the ways major mass media have represented this activism to date, emphasizing violence and anarchy and framing it as the work of radical fringe groups and naïve tagalong youths, I am not optimistic that this activism can spark a groundswell of public support any time soon. I am, however, more hopeful about some other initiatives to counter globalization that are emerging from within the life worlds of ordinary people as the effects of globalization impinge upon their immediate environments and their respective pursuits of "adequate material abundance, modest meaning in suffering, and limited happiness." Most people, for example, do not want to drink water that contains arsenic or eat produce that is laced with pesticides, meat that contains growth hormone residues, or food that has been chemically altered or radiated. These bread-and-butter issues bring globalism home to the family dinner tables of ordinary people in tangible ways that distant protests at summits of corporate and government leaders do not. For most people, WTO, WMF, GATT, and NAFTA are vague abstractions, and big media prosper from keeping them that way. Conversely, bread-and-butter issues are mobilizing people in many parts of the world into community-based acts of social responsibility that are also, at least in part, acts of "resistance" to reducing all values to market values. Moreover, this resistance cuts across ideological spectrums. To cite a few examples: European skepticism and activism against radiation of food before its long-term effects can be assessed (which, yes, is also a form of anti-Americanism); initiatives that support recycling, which in the U.S. have popular support even when they are not cost effective; the Slow Food Movement in Italy, which seeks to protect artisan food production and practices and the ways of life that support them against imposition of production standards favored by U.S. agribusiness; and even the growing popularity of home gardening using organic methods, reintroducing heirloom plants, and home canning and other food preservation techniques. *Organic Gardening* is, for instance, the world's largest gardening magazine with a circulation of 600,000. While the visibility of such efforts has had an upscale, yuppie, or "bobo" (bourgeois-bohemian) lifestyle edge, the "back to nature" methods they draw upon have deep roots in peasant experiences of scarcity. The challenge for critical scholarship is to connect the dots among these macro- and micro-movements. See Alexander Stille, "Slow Food: An Italian Answer to Globalization," *The Nation* (August 20/27, 2001):11–16; and Irene Kraft, "Rodale Goes Organic with Style," *Allentown (Pa.) Morning Call*, 20 August 2001, 1(D), 4(D).

24. Nicholas Johnson, "Freedom, Fun, and Fundamentals: Defining Digital Progress in a Democratic Society" in *Invisible Crises: What Conglomerate Control of Media Means for America and the World*, ed. George Gerbner, Hamid Mowlana, and Herbert I. Schiller (Boulder: Westview Press, 1996), 82–90. Johnson, a former federal communication commissioner, points out that in the U.S., until recently, combined control over media contents and the conduits for distribution of contents was barred by FCC regulations.

25. Robert W. McChesney, "The Political Economy of Communication and the Future of the Field," *Media, Culture, and Society* 22 (January 2000): 115. McChesney offers an excellent analysis of the recent malaise in communication scholarship and provides a compelling plea for revitalization of communication research. Unfortunately I discovered this article late in the writing of this book; however, my arguments resonate closely with McChesney's. McChesney also provides an excellent brief for utopian thinking in media reform movements, which is also grounded, in part, in Bourdieu's concept of "reasoned utopias." See Bourdieu, "A Reasoned Utopia and Economic Fatalism."

26. In his vast history of Western culture, Jacques Barzun also presents a strong argument for recovering "eutopian" thought, pointing out that it has contributed much to social thought and struggles for democracy. Barzun, *From Dawn to Decadence: 500 Years of Western Cultural Life, 1500 to the Present* (New York: HarperCollins, 2000). In their recent book, Liberation Sociology (Boulder: Westview Press, 2001), Joe R. Feagin and Hernan Vera also remind us that until the mid-twentieth century when sociology was "Parsonized" (shaped by the objectivist interpretations and social positioning of Talcott Parsons of Harvard University), commitments to social reform and to activism on behalf of the oppressed were hallmarks of the field. Like feminism, multiculturalism, and "political correctness" before it, the conception of the intellectual as gadfly who is obliged to "speak truth to power" has recently come under heavy fire from the conservative right in the U.S. This is a curiously inconsistent move since the right has stridently claimed that privilege since the 1960s in challenging what it has insistently characterized as the "liberal" dominance of U.S. politics, academics, media, and popular culture. See Richard Posner, *Public Intellectuals: A Study of Decline* (Cambridge, Mass.: Harvard University Press, 2001).

27. Max Weber, "Science as a Vocation," in *From Max Weber*, ed. H. H. Gerth and C. Wright Mills (New York: Oxford University Press, 1958), 147. See also Edward Said, *Representations of the Intellectual* (New York: Random House, 1996). Said acknowledges large debts to C. Wright Mills's discussions of the role of the intellectual in *Power, Politics, and People* (New York: Ballantine, 1963). Mills's thinking, in turn, was, of course, strongly influenced by Weber's.

28. Alfred North Whitehead, *Adventures of Ideas* (New York: The Free Press, 1967, original 1933).

29. See Edward Said, *Orientalism* (New York: Pantheon, 1978); Edward Said, *Culture and Imperialism* (New York: Random House, 1977); bell hooks, *Yearning: Race, Gender, and Cultural Politics* (Boston: South End Press, 1990); and John Gabriel, *Whitewash: Racialized Politics and the Media* (London and New York: Routledge, 1998).

30. See Gouldner, *The Dialectic of Ideology and Technology*, 164; and Graham Murdock and Peter Golding, "Culture, Communications, and Political Economy," in *Mass Media and Society*, ed. James Curran and Michael Gurevitch (London: Edward Arnold, 1991), 26.

31. Ben Bagdikian, interview, *Fear and Favor in the Newsroom*, videocassette (Seattle, Wash.: Northwest Passages Productions, 1997).

Chapter Two

The Future Is Not What It Used to Be

Napoleon described history as the fable agreed upon. During the closing decades of the twentieth century, explorations of the grounds for such agreements became the sites of highly charged epistemological and cultural conflicts. Theories about communication have provided the cognitive maps for many of the explorations. These theories have not, however, originated within the academic discipline that we know as communications.

Except for studies in rhetoric, communication research has been largely ahistorical. The usual excuse for this lapse, the newness of this branch of inquiry, does actually have some merit in this instance. The field, like the political, economic, and cultural practices that it studies, is now an international enterprise. Nevertheless, communication research initially articulated its identity as an independent area of academic inquiry in the United States; the structures of knowledge it supports continue to carry the signature of this historical genesis.

Established in the wake of the communications revolutions that took place during World War II, communication research claimed modern, technology-based forms of communication as its primary foci. In short, it created a space for itself by identifying a subject matter that was of immense importance to the economic, cultural, and social alignments of the United States in the post-war era but of marginal interest to traditional academic disciplines.

This strategic move situated communication research within the categories and the historically dependent structures of thought that the publisher, Henry Luce, had heralded in 1942 as "the American century." It defined a set of contemporary Western artifacts, social resources, and cultural practices as the subject of communication research and invested the emerging discipline's methodological commitments in the then-current understandings of the nature of empirical inquiry. This positioning did not merely predispose the field to historical and cultural myopia; it came close to mandating it.

Yet, communication—even contemporary forms of communication—cannot be understood without understanding history. Mary Mander strongly underscores this point when she asserts:

> At the heart of communication, however defined, is the fact that it is mediated. Because all communication is mediated, the nature of communication is necessarily connected to historically dependent dispositions.[1]

RECOVERING HISTORY: COMMUNICATION AS SITUATED KNOWLEDGE

Ironically, communication research achieved academic legitimacy by securing its claims in empiricism at precisely the historical juncture when scholars in more established disciplines were beginning to discover that empirical claims are themselves "speech acts"; and that these speech acts are socially and culturally "situated" forms of communication.[2] The so-called communicative turn within epistemology has yet to be fully acknowledged, appreciated, absorbed, or accommodated by the prevailing domain assumptions of communication research.[3]

Where the field of communications has been responsive to these developments, it has usually been in ways that continue to support impoverished conceptions of history. Thus, for example, Michel Foucault's concept of "discourse," which recognizes that knowledge and knowers are always constructed within, and indelibly marked by, a field of power relations, has gained significant currency in communications.[4] There have, however, been few reflexive explorations of the ways this idea radically challenges conventional, textbook understandings of disciplinary histories and research practices, including the history and practice of communication research.

Pressing the Foucault example further, how many of us have seriously considered the methodological problems that the concept of historical discontinuity or "rupture" poses? Foucault not only contends that the categories with which we know, think, and make sense—both as scholars and ordinary citizens—are historically and culturally dependent dispositions; he also points out that these dispositions can be radically disjunctive. He uses a by now familiar but possibly fictive quotation from a Chinese encyclopedia, which he borrowed from Jorge Luis Borges to illustrate this phenomenon:

> [It] is written that "animals are divided into: (a) belonging to the Emperor, (b) embalmed, (c) tame, (d) suckling pigs, (e) sirens, (f) fabulous, (g) stray dogs,

(h) included in the present classification, (i) frenzied, (j) innumerable, (k) drawn from a very fine camelhair brush, (l) et cetera, (m) having just broken the water pitcher, (n) that from a long way off look like flies."[5]

Foucault cites this example to demonstrate not only the "exotic charm of another system of thought" but also "the limitation of our own" and "the stark impossibility [for Europeans] of thinking that."[6]

Awareness of "that" has become a tenet of cultural and postcolonial studies. This is an advance. Yet, too often, this new cultural awareness has generated pat validations of "difference" that offer easy excuses for relativism. These validations have, in turn, created a ready arsenal of stock charges of implicitly or explicitly racialized "essentialism" and "reductionism" that are levied against anyone who presses researchers to do the very hard, systematic, and disciplined historical and sociological work necessary to make some, albeit always incomplete, sense of "that." Without this work, each of us will remain incarcerated in "her own zoo," to use Trinh T. Minh-ha's metaphor.[7] When this happens, all possibilities of developing rational models of intergroup communication and coalition politics are foreclosed.

The apartheid approach to scholarship that results from the nonreflexive valorization of historical discontinuity and cultural difference ensures that communications will remain "a field of isolated islands of thought."[8] It also excuses its practitioners from participation in the very difficult, conflict-laden dialogues that are a necessary prologue to articulating ways of knowing that are no longer intractably embedded in logics and categories of domination and submission. The remainder of this essay focuses on some of the ways the new feminist epistemologies can be seen as marking radical breaks with conventional, empirical conceptions of science and communication. I use this exposition to try to show why most attempts (including friendly attempts) to integrate feminist perspectives within mainstream research programs and publications fail, and suggest some possible avenues for re-marking this impasse as a site of discovery rather than conceding it as a point of terminus for dialogues within the field of communications.

LOSING HISTORY IN THE TRANSLATION

Like the Chinese encyclopedia, new feminist epistemologies and theories of communication weave together categories, concepts, and cultural practices that are impossible to think within the Baconian and Cartesian methodologies that have provided the warrant for empirical studies in social science. To be sure these empirical methodologies have always functioned more as professional ideology than as practical recipes for conducting scientific research.[9]

Feminist claims are "unthinkable" within the domain assumptions of established social science not only because they forthrightly assert that the discourses of science are manmade, but also because they subscribe to the far more radical claims that the epistemologies and the theories of knowledge that produced these discourses are systematically skewed by both Eurocentric and masculinist interpretative and textual practices. Or, to put it in the terms of Mander's proposition: the rules governing the communications that comprise scientific talk and texts have been secured by "the historically dependent dispositions" of a select group of well-educated Western men.[10] According to the feminist view, then, the substantive claims of science are neither "neutral" nor "neutered."[11] To the contrary, feminist epistemologies treat the forms of "objectivity," which science has valorized, as contingent cultural artifacts: artifacts that were crafted by formalizing and codifying the subjective views of the men who participated in the founding conversations of modern science.

Feminists have identified some of the gendered practices that shaped these artifacts. First, women were excluded from science at its inception. This was, in part, a strategic move that was designed to distance the powders and potions of scientists from those of the womanly arts of herbal medicine and witchcraft, and thereby protect scientists from the bloody Inquisition that swept Europe during the formative years of the scientific revolution.[12] Second, modern science marked this distance by securing its vision in highly sexualized and sexist metaphors: instrumental metaphors that characterized nature as a woman and recommended her domination—even, in Bacon's much cited graphic hyperbole, her "rape."[13] Third, the categories of Western science emphasize discrete boundaries, hierarchies, binary logics, and abstractions that, paradoxically, support both disembodied and homoerotic patterns of thinking and writing about natural phenomena.[14]

Feminist accounts of the history and cultural practices of science partially overlap and converge with accounts of the scientific enterprise that have been independently arrived at by sociologists and historians of science.[15] The feminist project is not, however, merely an analytical or critical endeavor. To the contrary, it is committed to social change: to radical revision and re-creation of the terms and fields of power relations that provide the auspices for the discourses of science, history, and capitalism.

Feminist revisionism does not claim that the discoveries or the laws of the Sciences of Man are invalid or obsolete. It does, however, claim that these sciences are not only socially and historically contingent but also incomplete. For this reason, feminist epistemologies patently reject all strategies for redressing this partiality that do anything less than undertake a comprehensive revision of existing categories and structures of knowledge.[16] Yet, established structures of knowledge in science and history contain no terms and few spaces for thinking "that." This is why these structures cannot support integration of feminist ideas within existing paradigms and definitions of the problematics of communication studies.

In contrast to the "view from nowhere" that the epistemics of Baconian and Cartesian objectivity support, feminist epistemologies recognize that all forms of knowledge, including the disciplined knowledges of the academy, are, in Donna Haraway's terms, "situated knowledges": knowledges that are historically, materially, culturally, and linguistically mediated, finite, and secured within, although not necessary homologous with, a field of power relations.[17] This recognition does not necessitate an embrace of relativism. To the contrary, it is the first move in what Haraway describes as a "no-nonsense commitment" to the hard work necessary to provide "rational," "objective," and "faithful accounts of a 'real' world" that can be partially shared and that are "friendly to earthwide projects of finite freedom, adequate material abundance, modest meaning of suffering, and limited happiness."[18]

Contra Foucault's theory of mediation, however, feminist epistemologies do not assume that all roads to resistance and emancipation are blocked by hegemonic discursive practices. They recognize that Foucault's concept of "discourse," like Bacon's and Descartes's concepts of "objectivity," failed to adequately account for its own vantage point: the situation of its own production.

Foucault's "data," the texts and expert claims that he used to expose the panoptic disciplining of modern forms of authority and sexuality, were situated within the epistemic of what Nancy Hartsock calls "abstracted masculinity."[19] Consequently, a sociologically informed feminist epistemological position supports Jurgen Habermas's indictment of Foucault as a "young conservative," although not only or fully on the charges specified by Habermas, whose own theory of emancipatory communication is also punctuated by gendered "blindspots."[20]

Dorothy Smith implicitly recognizes Foucault's (and philosophy's) masculinist positioning when she reinterprets his concept of "discourse" from a sociological perspective:

because we are talking sociology, not philosophy, we want to address discourse as a conversation mediated by texts, that is, not a matter of statements alone but of actual ongoing practices and sites of practices, the material forms of texts (journals, reviews, books, conferences, classrooms, laboratories, etc.), the methods of producing texts, the reputational and status structures, the organization of powers intersecting with other relations of ruling in state agencies, universities, professional organizations, and the like. Attention to discourse as socially organized does not discard or invalidate the statements, conventions, and knowledges that its texts bear. Rather texts are understood as embedded in and organizing relations among subjects active in the discourse. *We are talking then about actual people entering into actual relations with one another* [emphasis added].[21]

Smith reminds us that "the actual people entering into actual relations with one another" in the laboratories, seminars, government offices, and publishing houses that produced Foucauldian "discourses" were (and are) primarily, although not exclusively, male and that these men operate within a gendered field of power relations that is based upon a complex dialectic of "dominance" and "submission." And, these men do so largely oblivious to the gendered constituents of these power relations and the entitlements that accompany them. In the case of academics, these entitlements also, of course, typically include the privileges of class, race, and imperial locations.

Since Foucault attended to the sexual rather than the gendered constituents of the anatomy of power relations, he was unable to gain access to a persistent site of tension, conflict, and sometimes resistance to hegemonic discourse: women's cultures, and their "ways of knowing" and of performing gendered identities.[22] The specific contents and artifacts of these subcultures or "residual" cultures have generally been of marginal interest to male institutions and disciplinary practices.[23] Consequently, these residual cultures have retained significant diversity across ethnic, religious, color, and class lines, even within Western industrial societies. Unlike the disciplined, homogenized, and in their own ways repressive and commodified values, practices, and artifacts of the dominant male culture, "woman" is still, as Luce Irigaray put it, the "sex which is not *one*" (emphasis added).[24]

As women, the actual people of Smith's formulation, become increasingly integrated into the structures of global capitalism, they are, however, experiencing increasing pressures to surrender this diversity and to assimilate the values of the dominant and still misogynist corporate culture. That is, they are resocialized, even, in a sense, "remanufactured" to fit the specifications of the commodified corporate gender regime. The image of the ideal corporate woman cultivated in U.S. popular media today is that of "a babe," in quasi-pornographic terms, as well as a "killer woman," a ruthless instrumentalist who takes no prisoners and has no patience with traditional feminine, qua humanistic, values.[25] Hypersexed according to the specifications of adolescent male fantasies, this new hybrid type comes equipped with a female body, frequently amplified by breast implants and, depending upon the fashion dictates of the season, sculpted by rigorous body-building regimes and/or near anorexic nutritional deprivation. Her mind is, however, fully colonized by masculine cultural values. She is an operative of the commercial world who coexists (possibly even doubly exists) with a softer more private and presumably traditionally docile type: wife, mother, daughter, girl next door.

When women are represented within the discourses of abstracted masculinity (and they often are), it is as "the sex"—the marked category—in the field of power relations.[26] These representations usually define women in essentialized and heterosexist terms based upon the roles they play in men's lives as sexual partners, wombs, and nurturers. Even the "killer" corporate woman, who challenges this conception by fiercely competing with men, nevertheless compensates for her challenge, at least in the mythos of popular culture, by submitting to framing within traditional pornographic representations of the "bad girl," qua insatiable dominatrix.

These representations leave much of women's experience "hidden from history."[27] What is hidden from the disciplined discourses of abstracted masculinity, including Foucault's corpus, is:

> the experience of spinsters, lesbians, unionists, prostitutes, madwomen, rebels and maiden aunts, manual workers, midwives and witches. And what is involved in radical sexual politics, in one of its dimensions, is precisely a reassertion and recovery of marginalized forms of femininity in the experience of groups like these.[28]

Since Foucault ascribes special epistemological status to the outlaw—"the condemned man"—who, he claims, represents "the symmetrical, inverted figure of the king" in the "darkest region of the field of political power-relations," his disinterest in marginalized forms of femininity is especially telling. It is masculinist if not overtly misogynist.[29]

Adequate accounts of the contributions that women have made to the development of the disciplines, either by attending to the material needs of male scientists and scholars or by acting as silent partners in the research process, still remain largely absent from the historical record.[30] Speculation about the role Einstein's first wife may have played in developing the special theory of relativity is just one, albeit dramatic, example of this kind of gap in the official archives of science. A more prosaic but pervasive example of women scholars hidden from history, including the history of communications, is the two-person academic career in which wives, cast as silent partners, function as researchers, typists, editors, and sometimes ghostwriters. Such careers were very common, almost normative, in the United States after World War II, when academic women, like their working-class sister, Rosie the Riveter, were dismissed from their positions en masse to make room for men returning from the military and war-related government work.

Moreover, the historical eraser rubs both ways. When, for example, the history and cultural practices of science are apprehended through the lens of "abstracted masculinity," the absence of women from the laboratory or research team is routinely taken to mean gendered behavior is also absent. That is, abstracted masculinity cultivates the peculiar conclusion that male institutions are not gendered institutions. It allows scholars like Steve Shapin, coauthor of *Leviathan and the Air-Pump: Hobbes, Boyle, and the Experimental Life* (1991), and others to maintain, for instance, that gender is not relevant to explaining Boyle's science because it was a "gentlemen's" activity. Because women were excluded, Shapin contends that gender is not a significant variable for studying the formative texts of modern science. David Noble's *A World Without Women* (1992) provides an excellent corrective to this kind of myopia.[31]

In contrast, feminist epistemologies conceive of the absence of women from the laboratories, research teams, public fora, and archives of science as decisive markers of gendered terrain. Thus, for example, science, technology, war, and sport are usually conceived of as predominantly homosocial and sometimes homoerotic institutions within feminist research protocols.[32] Recent feminist research in communications indicates that news, information science, and certain other research venues are also illuminated by viewing them as sites of gendered knowledges.[33]

In sum, feminist epistemologies assume that gender is a crucial constituent for the analysis of all fields of power relations and all disciplined subjects and structures of knowledge.[34] This assumption mandates radically new ways of conceiving, legitimating, and building structures of power and knowledge.

THE "BRAVE NEW WORLD" OF COMMUNICATION

Communication research is peculiarly positioned in relationship to gender studies. Empirical research in the field has confirmed gender-based differences in taste cultures, audience responses, conversational behavior, decision-making processes, leadership styles, voting and consumer behaviors, and much more. Gender is therefore well established as an important variable for most forms of research in the field.

Empirical social science research methodologies produced these findings. In the 1970s and early 1980s, feminists interpreted such findings as evidence of patriarchal domination and incorporated them in briefs for reform in both science and society. In the past two decades, however, as Sandra Harding points out, feminist empiricism has discovered that gender is not merely an important variable in explaining social behavior, but it is also the difference that makes a difference within social hierarchies.[35] This discovery not only radically alters the future of feminist research; it transforms the ways feminist sociologists and historians conceive of the past.

Moreover, this discovery is producing a body of research that is increasingly exercising influence beyond feminism.[36] This research is demonstrating that gender is a primary constituent of the anatomy of all forms of knowledge and power-relations. So that, for example, if we want to study the structures, processes, and achievements of Plato's academy, the Crusades, the medieval monastery, the Royal Academy, or the National Football League, we must consider and examine the exclusion of women as a constitutive, gendered behavior rather than as an incidental practice of these organizations.

This move opens up what Stuart Hall describes as a "brave new world" for researchers: one that radically alters the topographies of knowledge and social relations. According to Hall, a "revolution in thinking" follows

> in the wake of the recognition that *all* social practices and forms of domination—including the politics of the Left—are always inscribed in and to some extent secured by sexual identity and positioning. If we don't attend to how gendered identities are formed and transformed and how they are deployed politically, we simply do not have a language of sufficient explanatory power at our command with which to understand the institutionalisation of power in our society and the secret sources of our resistances to change.[37]

Even the brave enter this new world knowing that they must rewrite their personal intellectual histories as well as the histories of their disciplines, and that these revisions will significantly transform their investments in the future.

Yet, such reflexive exercises can also secure the grounds for forms of rationality and politics that are no longer situated in the unexamined assumptions of Western structures of gendered knowledge. Thus, for example, they make it possible to uncover and partially repair the gender-based blindspots in Foucault's archaeology of knowledge and Habermas's concept of emancipatory communication, and thereby to recraft and amplify the power and resonances of these ideas. Such exercises will, of course, also have less salutary effects. A reflexive history of communication research would surely show that situating the field within the prevailing assumptions of the power-knowledge of "the American century" contributed to cultural imperialism, Cold War ideologies, and replications of gender orders based upon what Bob Connell calls "hegemonic masculinity."[38] In my judgment, however, the risks and embarrassments we face are far outweighed by the opportunities.

A blindspot that requires immediate redress, in light of the lessons of the new feminist epistemologies as well as the work of Foucault, Lacan, Derrida, and many others, is the fundamental, even constitutive, error in most current protocols for empirical communication research, which treats gender as a "variable."[39] This error is produced by the nonreflexive practice of importing and replicating the compulsory heterosexuality of the larger culture that forces data into the logics and structures of discrete, implicitly hierarchical, binary categories, which reflect hegemonic definitions of masculinity and femininity.

One methodological strategy, already in use in communication, that may have the capacity to accommodate this correction is the sense-making approach pioneered by Brenda Dervin. Based in part on Paulo Freire's process of "conscientization," it requires researchers to constantly interrogate their own epistemological positions. This insistent reflexivity is the point of departure for conducting open-ended sense-making interviews in which subjects explain how they make sense of their own life worlds in specific contexts: how they solve problems, bridge gaps in their knowledge, and so on. Both researchers and subjects (who might better be described as dialogic partners) are engaged in a dynamic process of "verbing," in which all accounts are always incomplete; are open to revision, correction, refinement; and are amenable to change as conditions change. The goal of sense-making, like the goal of feminist critiques of science, is to tell "less false stories about nature and social life."[40]

LOST INNOCENCE, NEW POSSIBILITIES

The communication revolution in epistemology has robbed contemporary scholarship of its philosophical innocence and naïveté. Developments in politics and the global marketplace have changed the terms, technologies, agendas, social relations, and material conditions for the production of knowledge. New structures for securing, testing, and validating knowledge claims recognize location and positioning as pivotal because, as Hall notes, "This insistence on 'positioning' provides people with coordinates, which are specially important in the face of the enormous globalisation and transnational character of many of the processes which now shape their lives."[41] In short, this insistence makes all scholarship more accountable than it was during "the American century."

The communication turn in epistemology creates extraordinary opportunities for the field of communications. Some of the architects of this revolution have turned to communication scholars for guidance in mapping the terrain of the brave new world they have created. For example, in 1991 Donna Haraway—who, at the time, was perceived as perhaps the most prescient of all of the technovisionaries by virtue of her authorship of "The Cyborg Manifesto"—saw the discipline of communication as posed on the cutting edge of further developments in the new scholarship.[42] Yet, more than a decade later, communication has contributed little to this discourse; increasingly, the discipline risks irrelevance as its subject matter becomes the common feast and fodder of the social sciences, humanities, and the commercial world. To meet this challenge, communication needs to create methodologies with sufficient analytic power to systematically investigate the multiple and multifaceted ways that gendered patterns of communication and gendered distributions of power are variously constructed and replicated in different social institutions and structures of knowledge. Moreover, gender is, of course, but one of what Judith Butler (1990) calls "the exasperated 'etc.'" (of race, class, gender, etc.), albeit it is one that asserts its claims in most of the actual relations we have with one another in constructing and performing social reality.

My account has underscored some of the ways that empirical approaches within science and history have secured their vision—their way of seeing by not seeing gender. It has also identified some of the blindspots in prominent theories of mediation and emancipatory communication. Finally, it has located some of the sources of Eurocentric and masculinist blinders in the power-knowledge of the American century, and in the socially situated knowledge that secured the legitimacy of the field of communications.

Poised on the threshold of a brave new world, some of us now regard the shadow histories that these approaches to discovery supported (but denied) as very promising sites for new discoveries. To effectively develop these sites, however, we need fully equipped conceptual toolboxes. Consequently, we cannot afford to throw the proverbial infant out with the soiled suds. Empirical social science, and the forms of rationality it supports, remain powerful tools for knowing and being in a world wired together by global communication and market structures. We need to acknowledge the continued relevance and utility of this form of inquiry as well as its gaps and blindspots.

Positioning communications within the context of the American century gave researchers privileged access to the cultural artifacts and forms of power-knowledge that are currently being reproduced and transformed by globalization. That globalization is now making the cultural and gendered constituents of that power-knowledge increasingly transparent should not be read as a failure of the empirical project but rather as a delayed affirmation of its critical and self-correcting powers. Documenting the denials that cultivated cultural amnesia and secured the delayed deployment of disciplinary reflexivity is a crucial emancipatory move. Nevertheless, it should not eclipse the fact that the project for empirical study of communication, conceived a half-century ago, has been productive. Indeed, it has been so successful that it has undermined its own grounding, and thereby opened up new vistas for reflection and discovery.

The challenges and opportunities we now face involve rethinking and resituating our conceptions of that past in light of what we now know. Awareness of the gaps in the power-knowledge that secured the academic study of communication enriches the quest for, and multiplies the paths to, more adequate grounds for "rational" inquiry. It also provides more open and responsible templates for situating and adjudicating claims to reliable knowledge. In sum, this awareness moves us closer to knowing how to craft "faithful accounts of a 'real' world" that can be partially shared, and that are "friendly to earth-wide projects of finite freedom, adequate material abundance, modest meaning in suffering, and limited happiness."[43]

NOTES

1. Mary S. Mander, "Communications Theory and History" in *Communications in Transition: Issues and Debates in Current Research*, ed. Mary Mander (New York: Praeger, 1983), 12. This historical deficit is now beginning to be addressed. See, for example, Hanno Hardt, *Critical Communication Studies: Communication, History and Theory in America* (London: Routledge, 1992); Vincent Mosco, *The Political Economy of Communication* (London: Sage, 1996); John Durham Peters, *Speaking into the Air: A History of the Idea of Communication* (Chicago: University of Chicago Press, 1999); and Dan Schiller, *Theorizing Communication: A History* (New York: Oxford University Press, 1996).

2. John R. Searle, *Speech Acts: An Essay on the Philosophy of Language* (Cambridge: Cambridge University Press, 1970); and Donna Haraway, "Situated Knowledges: The Science Question in Feminism and the Privilege of Partial Perspective," *Feminist Studies* 14 (1988): 575–99.

3. Jurgen Habermas, *Knowledge and Human Interests* (Boston: Beacon Press, 1971).

4. Michel Foucault, *The Order of Things: An Archaeology of the Human Sciences* (New York: Vintage Books, 1970); Michel Foucault, *Discipline and Punish: The Birth of the Prison* (New York: Pantheon, 1977); and Michel Foucault, *The History of Sexuality: Volume I: An Introduction* (New York: Pantheon, 1978).

5. Jorge Luis Borges, quoted by Foucault, *The Order of Things*, xv.

6. Foucault, *The Order of Things*, xv.

7. Donna Haraway, presentation at the National Endowment in the Humanities Summer Institute on Science as a Cultural Practice, Wesleyan University, Middletown, Conn., 1991. See also Trinh T. Minh-ha, *Woman, Native, Other: Writing Postcoloniality and Feminism* (Bloomington: Indiana University Press, 1989), 80–86.

8. Trinh T. Minh-ha, *Woman, Native, Other*; and Everett N. Rogers, "Communication: A Field of Isolated Islands of Thought," in *Rethinking Communication, Vol. 1: Paradigm Issues*, ed. Brenda Dervin, Larry Grossberg, Beverly J. O'Keefe, and Ellen Wartella, (Newbury Park, Calif.: Sage, 1989), 209–10.

9. Bruno Latour, *Science in Action: How to Follow Scientists and Engineers Through Society* (Cambridge, Mass.: Harvard University Press, 1987); and Steve Woolgar, *Science: The Very Idea* (London: Tavistock, 1988).

10. Mander, "Communications Theory and History," 12.

11. Catherine A. MacKinnon, "Feminism, Marxism, Method and the State: An Agenda for Theory," *Signs 7* (1982): 515–44.

12. Brian Easlea, *Fathering the Unthinkable: Masculinity, Scientists, and the Nuclear Arms Race* (London: Pluto Press, 1983); Carolyn Merchant, *The Death of Nature: Women, Ecology and the Scientific Revolution* (New York: Harper & Row, 1980); and Hugh R. Trevor-Roper, *The European Witch-craze of the Sixteenth and Seventeenth Centuries* (New York: Harper & Row, 1969).

13. Evelyn Fox Keller, *Reflections on Gender and Science* (New Haven, Conn.: Yale University Press, 1985); and Merchant, *The Death of Nature*.

14. Susan Bordo, "The Cartesian Masculinization of Thought," *Signs* 11 (1986): 439–56; Keller, *Reflections on Gender and Science*; David F. Noble, *A World Without Women: The Christian Culture of Western Science* (New York: Knopf, 1992); and Hillary Rose, "Hand, Brain and Heart: A Feminist Epistemology for the Natural Sciences," *Signs* 9 (1985): 73–90.

15. Easlea, *Fathering the Unthinkable*; James Hillman, *The Myth of Analysis: Three Essays in Archetypal Psychology* (Evanston, Ill.: Northwestern University Press, 1972); and Latour, *Science in Action*.

16. In this respect, it embraces Audre Lorde's assertion that "the master's tools will never dismantle the master's house." See Audre Lorde, "The Master's Tools will Never Dismantle the Master's House," in *Sister Outsider: Essays and Speeches* (Trumansburg, N.Y.: Crossing Press, 1984), 110–13. Because existing structures of knowledge are based upon a dialectical relationship involving domination and subordination, the new feminist epistemologies assume that any strategy that simply adds women's contributions to existing equations will not produce the necessary corrective. Both terms in that equation (masculinity and femininity) are damaged by the exploitive nature of the architecture of the field of power relations in which they are situated. For discussions of this point, see Kathy Ferguson, *The Feminist Case against Bureaucracy* (Philadelphia: Temple University Press, 1984); and R. W. Connell, *Gender and Power: Society, the Person, and Sexual Politics* (Palo Alto, Calif.: Stanford University Press, 1987). For a fast and easily accessible examination of what happens when mainstream models of scholarship attempt to "add women and stir," see Carol Berkin's "'Dangerous Courtesies' Assault Women's History," *The Chronicle of Higher Education* (11 December 1991): 44(A). For a recent take on the implications of this stance in technology studies, see Ruth Woodfield, *Women, Work and Computing* (Cambridge: Cambridge University Press, 2000).

17. Donna Haraway, "Situated Knowledges."

18. Donna Haraway, "Situated Knowledges," 579.

19. Nancy Hartsock, *Building Feminist Theory: Essays from the Quest* (New York: Longman Press, 1981), 117–18.

20. Jurgen Habermas, "Modernity versus Postmodernity," *New German Critique* 22 (1981): 3–14. For discussion of some of these blindspots, see Nancy Fraser, *Unruly Practices: Power, Discourse and Gender in Contemporary Social Theory* (Minneapolis: University of Minnesota Press, 1989) and chapter 4 of this book.

21. Dorothy Smith, *The Everyday World as Problematic: A Feminist Sociology* (Boston: Northeastern University Press, 1987), 210.

22. Mary Field Belenky, Blythe McVicker Clinchy, Nancy Rule Goldberger, and Jill Mattuck Tarule, *Women's Ways of Knowing: The Development of Self, Voice, and Mind* (New York: Basic Books, 1986); Combahee River Collective, "A Black Feminist Statement 1977," in *All the Women Are White, All the Blacks Are Men, but Some of Us Are Brave: Black Women's Studies: A Black Feminist Statement*, ed. Gloria T. Hull, Patricia B. Scott, and Barbara Smith (New York: Feminist Press, 1982), 13–22; Carol Gilligan, *In a Different Voice: Psychological Theory and Women's Development* (Cambridge, Mass.: Harvard University Press, 1982); Carol Smith-Rosenberg, *Disorderly Conduct: Visions of Gender in Victorian America* (New York: Knopf, 1985); and Judith Butler, *Gender Trouble: Feminism and the Subversion of Identity* (New York: Routledge, 1990).

23. Raymond Williams, *Problems in Materialism and Culture* (London: Verso, 1980).

24. See Lucy Irigaray, "The Sex which is Not One," in *New French Feminisms: An Anthology*, ed. Elaine Marks and Isabelle de Courtivron (Amherst: University of Massachusetts Press, 1980), 99–106.

25. Benjamin DeMott, *Killer Woman Blues: Why Americans Can't Think Straight about Gender and Power* (Boston: Houghton Mifflin, 2000). For a brief discussion of the marketing of the tough girl image to girls, see Martha Irvine, The Associated Press, "New Breed of Female Icon are Hardly Wilting Flowers," *Allentown (Pa.) Morning Call*, 9 May 2001, 13(A).

26. Women are, of course, very amply represented in male discourses. Indeed, the surplus of such representation was, in part, the provocation that led Virginia Woolf to write *A Room of One's Own* (London: Hogarth, 1929).

27. Connell, *Gender and Power*; and Sheila Rowbotham, *Hidden From History: Rediscovering Women in History from the Seventeenth Century to the Present* (New York: Pantheon, 1974).

28. Connell, *Gender and Power*, 188.

29. Foucault, *Discipline and Punish*, 29.

30. Rose, "Hand, Brain and Heart"; and Anne Sayre, *Rosalind Franklin and DNA* (New York: W. W. Norton, 1975). For recent autobiographical account of what graduate education at Columbia was like during the postwar era, see Carolyn G. Heilbrun, *When Men Were the Only Models* (Philadelphia: University of Pennsylvania Press, 2002).

31. To be sure, Shapin and Schaffer demonstrate that class is the salient variable of the narrative they construct to explain the working relationship between Boyle and Hooke. See Steven Shapin and Simon Schaffer, *Leviathan and the Air-Pump: Hobbes, Boyle, and the Experimental Life* (Princeton, N.J.: Princeton University Press, 1985); and Noble, *A World Without Women*.

32. Carol Cohn, "Sex and Death in the Rational World of Defense Intellectuals," *Signs* 12 (1987): 687–718; Sally Hacker, *Pleasure, Power, and Technology: Some Tales of Gender, Engineering, and the Cooperative Workplace* (Boston: Unwin and Hyman, 1989); Keller, *Reflections on Gender and Science*; B. A. Reardon, *Sexism and the War System* (New York: Teachers College Press, 1985); Donald F. Sabo and J. Panepinto, "Football Ritual and the Social Reproduction of Masculinity," in *Sport,*

Men, and the Gender Order: Critical Feminist Perspectives, ed. Michael Messner and Donald F. Sabo (Champaign, Ill.: Human Kinetics Books, 1990), 115–26; and chapter 8 of this book. Conceiving these institutions as primarily homosocial amplifies our analytic powers, but it also inadvertently contributes to the homosocial practices that erase women's achievements within or at the margins of these practices. For a recent example of how this framing has worked within the history of sport, see Susan Leggett, *Atlanta's Sisters: Sport, Gender and Technology in Popular Press, 1921–1996,* Ph.D. diss., University of Massachusetts at Amherst, 2001.

33. See for example Lana F. Rakow and K. Kranich, "Woman as Sign in Television News," *Journal of Communication* 41, no. 1 (1991): 8–23; Stuart Allan, "The Gendered Realities of Journalism," in *News Culture,* ed. Stuart Allan (Buckingham, England: Open University Press, 1999), 130–56; and chapter 4 of this book.

34. It should be noted that recognition of the ubiquity of gendered knowledges and structures of power does not preclude or marginalize consideration of class, race, ethnicity, and other important social categories. To the contrary, as Connell points out, his theorization of "hegemonic masculinity" facilitates analyses of social structures in general rather than forcing the researcher to place a priority on class or gender relations. This point requires emphasis because sociologists are, in my judgment, legitimately suspicious of theoretical programs that obscure or deflate the importance of class analysis, particularly at a point in history when large scale redistributions of wealth are taking place in countries like the United States and the United Kingdom— redistributions that are designed to reverse the social benefits of the welfare state.

35. Sandra Harding, *The Science Question in Feminism* (Ithaca, N.Y.: Cornell University Press, 1986).

36. Studies of the processes and products of the scientific enterprise by feminists such as Bleier, Hacker, Haraway, Hubbard, Henefin, Fried, Keller, Martin, Rapp, and Traweek have demonstrated just how powerful the lens of gender is in examining the social construction of knowledge. So much so that many male sociologists, historians, and philosophers of science without feminist commitments wanted a piece of the action by the early 1990s. Witness developments in the science and technology studies (STS) journal, *Social Epistemology,* as well as inclusion of Keller and Haraway in the programming of the 1991 National Endowment in the Humanities Summer Institute on Science as Cultural Practice at Wesleyan University, Middletown, Connecticut. The STS research group appears to be largely unaware that male scholars such as Connell, Easlea, and Paul Edwards have for some time used the concept of gender and feminist theories very effectively in their respective explorations of the sciences and technologies of militarism. See Ruth Bleier, *Science and Gender: A Critique of Biology and its Theories on Women* (New York: Pergamon, 1984); Hacker, *Pleasure, Power, and Technology*; Donna Haraway, *Primate Visions: Gender, Race, and Nature in the World of Modern Science* (New York: Routledge, 1989); Ruth Hubbard, M. S. Henefin, and B. Fried, eds., *Biological Woman, the Convenient Myth: A Collection of Feminist Essays and a Comprehensive Bibliography* (Cambridge, Mass.: Schenkman, 1982); Keller, *Reflections on Gender and Science*; Emily Martin, *The Woman in the Body: A Cultural Analysis of Reproduction* (Boston: Beacon Press, 1987); Rayna Rapp, "Chromosomes and Communication: The Discourse of Genetic Counseling,"

Medical Anthropology Quarterly 2 (1988): 121–42; Sharon Traweek, *Beamtimes and Life-times: The World of High Energy Physicists* (Cambridge, Mass.: Harvard University Press, 1988). For studies of gender and militarism, see Connell, *Gender and Power*, and Connell, "The State, Gender, and Sexual Politics"; Easlea, *Fathering the Unthinkable*; Paul Edwards, "Border Wars: The Science and Politics of Artificial Intelligence," *Radical America* 19, no. 6 (1985): 39–50; and Paul Edwards, "The Army and the Microworld: Computers and the Politics of Gender Identity," *Signs* 16 (1990): 102–27.

37. Stuart Hall, "Brave New World," *Marxism Today* (October 1988): 24–29.

38. Connell, *Gender and Power*.

39. Jacques Derrida, "White Mythology: Metaphor in the Text of Philosophy," *New Literary History* 6 (1974): 5–74; Jacques Derrida, *Of Grammatology* (Baltimore: Johns Hopkins University Press, 1976); and Michel Foucault, *The History of Sexuality: Volume 1: An Introduction*.

40. Brenda Dervin et al., "Freedom is Another Word for Nothing Left to Lose," paper presented at the annual meeting of the International Communication Association, Washington, D.C., May 28, 2001. Sandra Harding describes the objectives of the feminist critique of science in essentially the same terms. See chapter 5. For further discussion of the sense-making approach and its convergences with feminism, see Brenda Dervin, "Users as Research Inventions: How Research Categories Perpetuate Inequities," *Journal of Communication* 39, no. 3 (Summer 1989): 216–32; and Vickie Shields and Brenda Dervin, "Making Sense of Methodology: On Feminist Scholarship and Sense-making Research," paper presented at the annual meeting of the International Communication Association, Chicago, May 27, 1991. For a comprehensive introduction to sense making, visit the sense-making website at <http://communication.sbs.ohio-state.edu/sense-making/default.html> (accessed July 15, 2002).

41. Hall "Brave New World," 29.

42. Haraway, "Science as Cultural Practice." See also Donna Haraway, "A Manifesto for Cyborgs: Science, Technology, and Socialist Feminism in the 1980s," *Socialist Review* 80 (1985): 65–107.

43. Haraway, "Situated Knowledges," 579.

Chapter Three

Paris Is Always More than Paris

Pascal's assertion that "there is a time to call Paris Paris and a time to call it the capitol of the Kingdom" implicitly recognizes the knot that binds power and knowledge. But the legacy of Western rationalism encourages us to deny or ignore its epistemological implications. Thus, for example, formalism directs us to regard synonymous expressions as equivalencies: interchangeable "markers" that can be represented by a common symbol in the manipulations of machine languages. Only rhetoric has consistently applied the Pascalian insight. Following the precedent set by Aristotle, however, philosophers have generally dismissed rhetoric as a secondary art, at best a form of salesmanship, so that even the work of a great rhetorician like Kenneth Burke has remained at the margins of contemporary thought about thought.

During the past two decades, however, the ranks of those who recognize that Paris is not just Paris have swollen. Crisis within the philosophy of science as well as growing political cynicism among the general population have led to widespread questioning of established modes of legitimating both knowledge and power. During the 1970s and 1980s, this questioning generated a renewal of interest in the Frankfurt School of critical social theory. Initially articulated by Max Horkheimer, Friedrich Pollock, Theodor Adorno, and their associates at the *Institut fur Sozialforschung* in the 1930s, the approach was subsequently enriched by Herbert Marcuse and Jurgen Habermas in their respective attempts to secure a basis for emancipatory communication (and politics) in industrial (or postindustrial) societies.

The two waves of critical theory explicitly recognized the bond that unites power and knowledge. They affirmed the familiar dictum that "power is knowledge and knowledge, power." They did so, however, through the lens of a radical critique of Enlightenment-based epistemology. Frankfurt School critical theory does not merely acknowledge that power uses and corrupts knowledge, but also recognizes that it sets the conditions for knowledge: that power-relations provide the auspices for knowledge and cultural production, and establish the rules of permission and proscription that endow them with coherence. The resulting theory of knowledge is realistic but also deeply pessimistic. With Nietzsche, apologists of the first wave of critical theory recognize the impossibility of "immaculate perception." They acknowledge that "we all harbor hidden gardens and plantings." But, with Marx, they also realize that capital usually determines how those gardens are planted.

The German Ideology of 1846 was, of course, the immediate textual precedent for critical theory's perspective on repressed or distorted communication. In the relevant passages, Marx and Engels contend that the abstract (formal) language of philosophers that creates the impression that thought is free of practical interests is only "the distorted language of the actual world": a language that reflects and secures the prevailing form of the division of labor.[1] They point out that, under capitalism, even the categories that lie behind our semantic conventions are skewed by property relations, so that "in language [as in life] the relations of buying and selling have been the basis of all others."[2]

Taking up their charge nearly a century after these fathers of world revolution had completed their mischief, critical theorists chose their prefix and defined their theoretical enterprise deliberately, reflexively. Critical theorists sought to distance their perspective from vulgar (mechanical) Marxism and to establish kinship with the Hegelian and philological roots of Marx's conceptions of alienation, consciousness, and ideology. They were students of Dilthey, von Humboldt, Schiller, Heine, Grimm, Nietzsche, Weber, and Freud, as well as Marx. But they were also contemporaries of Hitler, Mussolini, and Stalin.

Contra positivism, including the positivistic strains in Marxism, they regarded the Enlightenment as a betrayal of reason rather than an extension of it, a betrayal that established the hegemony of instrumental reason and thereby prepared the way for the emergence of monopoly capitalism.[3] Moreover, they rejected the prevailing liberal view, which regarded fascism as a singular historical aberration. Rather, they saw it as a logical extension of the structures of crisis-ridden advanced capitalism. Consequently, the Frankfurt School tried to outline a perspective on capitalist social institutions that was both "scientific" (amenable to documentary validation) and at the same time "critical" (committed to the creation of a more robustly rational and just social order).[4]

Their theory of personality and culture was also radically revisionist. Consistent with the German philological tradition and the then-emergent Freudian perspective, they maintained that we are captives of culture trapped in "the hermeneutic circle" of language. They were far less optimistic than Marx regarding prospects for breaking out of that captivity, believing instead that, in the twentieth century, mass media and mass entertainments (what Adorno would later call "the culture industry") had so thoroughly colonized the consciousness of the industrialized masses that they were no longer able to even conceive of resistance, let alone articulate a platform for emancipatory social change. Indeed, Horkheimer and Adorno contended that the culture industry had actually invaded the collective unconscious, so that even the hopes, dreams, desires, and utopian fantasies of the masses had come to bear the imprimatur of Hollywood, the world headquarters of the culture industry.[5] As students of Freud and residents of Nazi Germany (until their self-imposed exile after 1933), Horkheimer and Adorno were keenly aware of the roles mythic thought and storytelling play in human motivation, even in a scientific age. They believed that apologists of capital not only control the institutions of popular culture through ownership, but also exercise dominion over the popular imagination.

Horkheimer and Adorno could see no way out. The first wave of critical theory offered no practical plans for resistance, no program for translating criticism into collective action; at best, it invested some limited hope in the generative powers of critical knowledge. Consequently it is generally regarded, even by sympathetic interpreters, as deeply pessimistic despite its emancipatory commitments.

Reread today, in the wake of a virtual flood of postmodern critiques of the Enlightenment, the sweep and originality of Horkheimer and Adorno's work remains striking. Their heavy-handed wielding of the dialectical hammer is, however, also striking. It forces evidence into the either/or of the binary logics of the dualistic (cum dialectic) patterns of Western thought that they sought to implode. The net effect of this conceptual overkill is to underestimate the historical vitality of the lost or betrayed democratic potential of French and American Enlightenment thought. That is, the dialectical structure of the argument itself combined with the brutal realities of the dire historical moment in which Horkheimer and Adorno wrote to prevent them from fully grasping the resilience of democratic impulses: a resilience that is nicely, if perhaps a bit too optimistically, evoked by Charles Douglas Loomis, who writes,

> The word democracy has been . . . used and betrayed by state, party, sect, and interest. Yet it still has honest lovers, who detect in it something that has mysteriously remained immaculate and true.[6]

Despite its egalitarian goals, the first wave of Frankfurt critical theory is nevertheless pockmarked with elitism.[7] Horkheimer's and Adorno's arguments imply that only critical theorists and other trained dialecticians possess the conceptual resources necessary to see through the trickery of the culture industry. Whether this apparently elitist assumption is evidence of an endemic arrogance (and implicit vanguardism) within the perspective or a testament to the power and cogency of critical theory in illuminating the hidden mechanics of the culture industry—or both—is for the reader to decide.

Failure to effectively resolve these issues combined with the hostile political climate of the Cold War to lead many postwar Anglo-American social scientists to dismiss much of the work of those associated with the first wave of critical theory as irrationalist and nihilist. Some associates of the original Frankfurt School (e.g., Erich Fromm, Franz Neumann, Karl Mannheim, and Paul Lazarsfeld) established reputations in philosophy, political theory, sociology, and communication scholarship independent of their earlier affiliations with the Frankfurt Institute. Others, like Horkheimer, Adorno, Leo Lowenthal, and Herbert Marcuse, worked throughout their lives to resolve the impasse of the first wave of critical theory.

A second generation of critical theorists, led by Jurgen Habermas, subsequently took up the challenge. Marcuse's analysis of linguistic domination and its dialectical counterpart, his proposal for "linguistic therapy," as well as Habermas's theory of "communicative competence" and his attempt to specify the conditions of an "ideal speech situation," are of special interest to students of political linguistics. Both of these thinkers try to chart escape routes out of a language and culture dominated by instrumental reason.

In this chapter I describe the topography of the proposed escape routes, note their limitations, and review some related explorations in critical theory that suggest new possibilities for countering the antidemocratic effects of linguistic domination. What the thinkers examined in this chapter have in common is the conviction that "just communication is an index of the good society."[8]

A ROAD NOT TAKEN

A few prefatory remarks are, however, in order. The revival of interest in the Frankfurt School in communication and sociology was relatively short-lived. By the late 1980s, it became fashionable in many circles to dismiss the entire project because its progenitors were not able to bring it to full fruition. The readily identifiable flaws in some of the work were treated as synecdoche for the entire corpus. Adorno and Horkheimer were tagged as elitist, cultural mandarins: the passages in their work that displayed shallow or erroneous understandings of specific contents of American popular culture were repeatedly cited. Marcuse was framed, in Cold War terms, as a quasi-totalitarian;

and the argument of his most popular and, from the perspective of 2002, prescient book, *One-Dimensional Man* (1964), was widely faulted as overdetermined. Similarly Habermas's early explorations of the communicative constituents of participatory democracy were variously labeled as "naïve," "idealistic," "utopian," and packed away among the relics of a more buoyant moment in history. To be sure, the cultural terrain identified by the Frankfurt School has continued to productively engage serious thinkers who do not ride the tides of intellectual trends.[9] Such work is, however, a continuance of a resistant tradition of research, which John Lent aptly characterizes as "a different road taken" and a road I would describe as still sparsely traveled, especially in the United States.[10]

This book aligns itself with that resistance. It distances itself from the easy glamour of the intellectual fashion shows that too often privilege the new over the profound or the difficult. That is, I argue that the bold and trenchant questions posed by the Frankfurt School, not its incomplete answers, are what continue to make this work relevant and instructive. The agenda these thinkers set is an agenda that those who still believe in the ideal of participatory democracy cannot ignore. Their questions retain their relevance precisely because they resist definitive answers. The point of participatory democracy is to continuously struggle with such questions, not to settle them. As Goethe pointed out long ago, freedom can only be earned by daily conquering it anew.[11]

The conundrums in Habermas's work were already apparent by the late 1970s: its idealism, which fails to contend with the formidable powers of mass media; the problematic role psychoanalytic concepts play in his work; the liberal bias of his approach to democracy and the state; and his gendered blindspots. Yet, few living thinkers have struggled as long or as hard as Habermas has to find ways to regenerate the public sphere and to energize the democratic discourse that can sustain it. To paper over that struggle with cynicism is to play into the hands of the enemy. As James Carey points out, the public sphere exists as "desire" in our life world, not simply as nostalgia for what never was or might be in the future.[12] We feel its presence as desire. We know something is missing from our collective life. Habermas may not have found the way, but he points the way to a democratic quest for something better. Habermas's "ideal speech situation" is indeed, as his critics repeatedly charge, a utopian construct; but I would argue that this utopianism is a strength as well as a limitation of Habermas's work. It proposes a normative standard or democratic ideal, which helps us identify and assess what is missing in actual power talk and in the tightly scripted spin that passes as political communication today. Marcuse's concept of "linguistic therapy" is also utopian, as is much of his later work, which overcorrects the determinism of some of his earlier work.

Within the current cultural climate of postmodern cool, to call a piece of work utopian is to call in the gravediggers. Yet, democracy itself is a utopian formation: an ideal that always falls short, even in its best moments, of its promises. Utopian thought—the desire for something better—is a necessary precondition to improvements in the human condition: the theory that gives birth to practice. Practice, alas, like all human endeavors, is always imperfect. Rejecting postmodern paralysis, Jacques Barzun uses the term "eutopian" to suggest that writers like More, Campanella, Bacon, and Rabelais were not writing about "no place" but about a "good place," and that they contributed much to social thought in doing so.[13] The same could be said of Erasmus, Diderot, Voltaire, Jefferson, Madison, Sojourner Truth, Susan B. Anthony, Gandhi, Martin Luther King Jr., Lech Walesa, Nelson Mandela, and many others. Without the capacity to identify what is missing and to articulate the desire for something better, we resign ourselves to current antidemocratic trends and thereby invite something worse.

EMANCIPATORY COMMUNICATION

The concept of emancipatory communication is an eutopian idea: its users sensed that something was missing in the age of administered public discourse. They tried to imagine something better: a good place where the link between community and communication could be affirmed—I am even tempted to say "consecrated." I use the past tense here because emancipatory communication, like its sister term "liberation," has fallen out of fashion: a casualty of the end of the Cold War and the triumph of globalization.

Critical resources have been redirected toward resisting cultural homogenization and preserving local cultures. These worthy pursuits have underwritten some of the best recent work in cultural studies; nevertheless, a just world cannot be constructed within a museum of cultural diversity. Politics is still necessary. The goal of critical theory is to expand participatory democracy at the local as well as national and international levels. Therefore local cultures are not protected from critical scrutiny.

To interrogate local cultures is, however, to court charges of Western imperialism; such charges need to be given a full and fair hearing in fora that are sensitive to local traditions. Western cultural imperialism has never been more pervasive than it is today. Moreover, it must be acknowledged that the human rights charters that provide the legally recognized transnational platforms for interrogating local practices do reflect Western values.

This is not, however, an excuse for romanticizing local traditions. Some local traditions, such as torture and slavery, are now considered inhumane and illegal by most of the world's governments.[14] Recent human rights discourses on female infanticide, female circumcision, child prostitution, and child labor are instructive. Locals who benefit from these practices defend them against human rights monitoring groups by framing them as practices that are integral to local cultural traditions and economies. In short, emancipatory politics in non-Western nations, as in Western nations, are often sites of conflict between traditional, patrimonial forms of authority and more broadly based, inclusive, and participatory forms.

Democracy is an emancipatory project. To retreat from the word is to retreat from the quest. To tread cautiously in unfamiliar terrain is sensible; to listen before one speaks is prudent; to interrogate one's own positions before others is the beginning of wisdom; but to remain silent in the presence of brutality is to become complicit in it.

For these reasons, I continue to swim against the cynical, anti-utopian current. I argue that terms like liberation and emancipation do what Virginia Woolf once said good words should do: they soak up a lot of truth. These particular good words also galvanize action. The neoliberal globalizers, who denounce them as polemical, are right. They are polemical! This is an argument for their recuperation by friends of democracy, not an argument for their censure.

Fixing damaged words is, of course, not enough. Systematic research in the political economy of communication, media institutions, and propaganda analysis is imperative. Moreover, this work needs to be combined with political activism dedicated to reforming social practices. Without these efforts, wordsmithing is an idle pursuit.

POLITICAL LINGUISTICS

Building upon the foundations crafted by Adorno and Horkheimer, Herbert Marcuse forged his classic statement on political linguistics in 1955.[15] Because he framed his argument within the context of his longstanding debate with "revisionary neo-Freudians," especially Jungians, these ideas remain relatively unfamiliar to most communication theorists. One need not share Marcuse's Freudian sympathies to find his perspective on language and communication compelling. In essence, Marcuse tried to preserve the liberating message in Freud's theory of repression. He saw it as the essential subtext of the Freudian breakthrough. Thus, he maintained that, at its inception, "psychoanalysis was a radically critical theory" because it provided a method for demystifying repression and nurturing desires for real autonomy.[16] Marcuse contended, however, that the neo-Freudians had transformed psychoanalysis into an ideology that justifies repression as the price that must be paid for civilization.

Contra this "ideological" reading of Freud that reifies repression, Marcuse offered a "sociological" reading. That is, he insisted on viewing every collective form of repression in relative and historical terms. Thus, he maintained that, in our time, domination is based upon (a) "surplus repression," which supports a complex hierarchical division of labor, and (b) "the performance principle," which subordinates all life-affirming energies to the demands of work. He contended that this system of domination has made a sham of participatory democracy, and that even science—once the cutting edge for human freedom—is now implicated in legitimating and maintaining the sham. Marcuse's *One-Dimensional Man*, published in 1964, was intended as an extension of this sociological analysis.[17] He conceived it as an empirical case study of the increasingly invisible structures of social control in advanced capitalist societies: control effected by subordinating all human needs to the imperatives of the instrumental reason of the market. Marcuse's description of the dehumanization of American language and culture in *One-Dimensional Man* rivals the most desolate passages in the writings of Horkheimer, Adorno, and Walter Benjamin.

But the work of the dialectician does not end with critique. Unlike many of his followers in the New Left of the 1960s and 1970s who were too often content to sloganize and vulgarize Marcuse—cry "cooptation" and retreat to a comfortable narcissism—Marcuse himself combined critical rigor with an unwavering commitment to a "new sensibility" that could transcend instrumental domination. He continued to pursue all paths that might lead those who had been socialized into silence and subservience to discover new vocabularies that could prepare the way for "a return of the repressed." Marcuse's somber testaments, like Freud's, contain promises of transcendence, promises that could be realized through "linguistic therapy."

To describe the way those in power are able systematically to skew semantic conventions, linguistic rules, and epistemological criteria, to deny dissent and preserve their own interests in the maintenance of the status quo, Marcuse used the term "political linguistics." He characterizes political linguistics as the "armor of the Establishment" and points out that "one of the most effective rights of the Sovereign is the right to establish enforceable definitions of words."[18] So, for example, "in the established vocabulary, "violence" is a term which one does not apply to the action of the police, the National Guard, the Marshals, the Marines, the bombers."[19] Conversely, "terrorism" is never used to describe the actions of friendly governments, no matter how abhorrent. In contemporary pseudo-liberal societies, "censorship" has become a pejorative code word reserved for those who posit constructions of reality different from the established one. For example, in current debates in the United States about the separation of church and state, those who seek to remove displays of the Ten Commandments from courthouses or the words "under God" from the Pledge of Allegiance are frequently dismissed as censors. However, many of these activists see themselves as defenders of the First Amendment and advocates of religious diversity and intellectual freedom.

Politically engaged rhetoricians like Kenneth Burke and Murray Edelman have provided invaluable tools for decoding political linguistics.[20] However, Marcuse's approach to linguistic therapy is far more radical. He contends that development of a new sensibility and a new consciousness requires a new language to create and communicate new values: "the rupture with the continuum of domination must also be a rupture with the vocabulary of domination."[21] Linguistic therapy, then, is an attempt to liberate words (and thereby concepts) from distortion of their meanings by established systems of domination. Marcuse acknowledged that this may be a utopian quest. He admitted that the process of linguistic domination has been with us throughout history and that no revolution has transcended it: no revolution has severed the hierarchical scaffolding of language and power. Yet, he expressed the hope that, when humankind is released from the most demeaning forms of labor by advanced technology, a new, humanistic reality principle will displace the imperatives of "surplus repression" and "the performance principle."

Marcuse regarded linguistic therapy as prologue to, and building block of, an enlarged concept of rationality in which "the aesthetic dimension" of human sensibility is no longer repressed.[22] He maintained that, so far, black Americans have been the most effective agents of linguistic therapy. He cites their refusal and aesthetic reversal of the language of oppression as expressed in words and phrases like "soul," "black power," and "black is beautiful." Similar claims have, of course, been made in recent years for rap and hiphop.[23] The mandate of linguistic therapy, then, is to restore the dialogic powers of the people by rescuing language from the control of the dominators. Marcuse did not assume that words were free of history in the precapitalist era. But he did contend that it is possible to strip away the veneer of surplus distortion acquired by language under the rule of instrumental reason. So, for example, it would be possible to recover and restore the critical edge that words like "freedom," "equality," and "justice" had during the seventeenth and eighteenth centuries, when they were essential terms in the language of the repressed rather than in the vocabulary of ideological control.

There are, of course, problems with Marcuse's formulation. Despite his acute awareness of capitalism's power to absorb and domesticate criticism, Marcuse failed to come to terms effectively with the pervasive role mass media, especially television, play in colonizing consciousness and extending linguistic domination. Today, more than ever, technovisions and techno-toys cultivate the values, priorities, and interests of cultural hegemony. Moreover, the apostles of postmodernism have convincingly demonstrated that the aesthetic dimension itself has now been captured and rather thoroughly colonized by the marketplace.[24] Marcuse's belief—hope, really—that technology could liberate humankind from surplus repression appears, from the perspective of 2002, as a both/and prospect at best. Some lives have been dramatically enhanced by technological prosthetics: these technologies have given speech to the mute, hearing to the profoundly deaf, sight to the blind, mobility to the paralyzed, and more. Ordinary people in technologically advanced societies now enjoy some of the lifestyle comforts that were once the exclusive preserves of princes and robber barons. Yet, these advances carry significant material and social costs: adding to the ecological strain on an increasingly fragile planet, exacerbating inequalities in the international division of labor and resources, and constraining as well enabling their beneficiaries. So that, for example, globalization has undermined unionization and worker's rights in developed countries by exporting jobs and repression to developing nations where slave wages are the norm. Labor-saving technologies have not produced more leisure; to the contrary, workers in the United States are working longer hours than they did before the computer revolution. According to the Bureau of Labor Statistics, for example, an average married couple now works 26 percent longer than comparable working married couples did thirty years ago.[25]

As Dallas Smythe demonstrated in *Dependency Road*, more time away from the factory or office does not necessarily mean greater freedom from instrumental relations; for, under advanced capitalism, productive labor includes consumption.[26] Mass media and, more recently, the Internet keep people "working" by marketing consumer products to themselves, even during their so-called leisure time. So most Americans spend their hours away from paid work with the National Football League, General Mills, Burger King, home shopping networks, and commercial websites rather than in liberative play, creative craftsmanship, or emancipatory dialogue. Until critical theory devises adequate strategies for countering the effects of hierarchically dominated media systems and the passive consumerist approaches to citizenship they cultivate, the return of the repressed will be delayed, and linguistic therapy will remain an interesting but esoteric idea.

MONOLOGIC INSTITUTIONS

At once more encompassing and less radical than Marcuse's view, Habermas's version of critical theory focuses directly on the problem of linguistic domination and the question of communicative competence. Thus, he maintains, "Today the problem of language has replaced the traditional problem of consciousness."[27] Like Marcuse, Habermas is concerned with the way science has been used to extend the hold of linguistic domination. Specifically, he is interested in the way expert technical and managerial knowledge is used by those in power to disenfranchise citizen participation in political debates by fostering the impression that many issues are inherently too complex for a layperson to comprehend or debate competently. According to Habermas, this disenfranchisement has led to the collapse of "the public sphere" and passive acceptance of technocratic elitism. Thus, he claims, all modern governments, whether capitalist or socialist, violate the terms of classic social contract theories of state power. None are legitimated by dialogic consensus.

Rejecting Chomsky's pursuit of linguistic universals as ill-conceived, Habermas's early work on emancipatory communication arrives at a theory of knowledge that bears striking resemblance to Burke's rhetoric.[28] Both thinkers, for example, propose pragmatic definitions of truth founded in dialogue.[29] Habermas maintains that truth can only be secured pragmatically: it is founded upon consensus that is realized in discourse. For Habermas, truth means "warranted assertability." He contends that a "model of pure communicative action (interaction)" presupposes that all parties involved in an interaction are accountable: that their behaviors are intentional and that they are capable of justifying their beliefs and norms. But he points out that the monologic actions of contemporary institutions do not fit this model. Therefore, Habermas maintains, these institutional acts are embedded in systematically distorted communication:

> The barriers to communication which make a fiction of the reciprocal imputation of accountability support at the same time the belief in legitimacy which sustains the fiction and prevents it being found out. That is the paradoxical achievement of ideologies, whose individual prototype is the neurotic disturbance.[30]

Ideological legitimations of ideas and states are secured in monologic fictions. They are based upon false or forced consensus: hence the Orwellian deformations of the vocabulary of modern politics. Habermas argues that a genuine, rationally motivated consensus can be reached only if the conditions of an "ideal speech situation" can be anticipated during legitimating discourses. He regards the semantic analysis of the classic (Freudian) psychoanalytic dialogues of patient and therapist as prototypes of the ideal, reflexive speech situation. In an ideal speech situation, Habermas contends, all potential participants must have equal chances to initiate and perpetuate discourses; all participants must have equal opportunities to criticize, ground, or refute all statements, explanations, interpretations, and justifications; and discourse must be free from the external constraints of domination, for example, violence, threats, and sanctions. If these conditions prevail, the preconditions for a rational order will be met. If these conditions are also realized *within* the actual course of the dialogue, the resulting consensus will be free of internal and external constraints. It will be based upon *the power of the best argument.*

Habermas does not bar instrumental arguments from the arena of debate; he merely tries to ensure that other arguments can be heard. The ideal speech situation is both the means and the end—double objectives—of Habermas's emancipatory project. In Marcuse's critical theory, linguistic therapy and exploration of the aesthetic dimensions of dialogue were merely prologue: means whereby more humane visions of social organization might be articulated. Habermas's work is an apology for more rationality and more democracy in interactions between dominators and the dominated. It does not promise an end to domination. It offers no strategies for countering the massive agenda-setting machinery of today's culture industry. Moreover, his conception of rationality is quite narrowly, one might even say parochially, framed when viewed from the perspectives of postcolonial, feminist, or postmodern positions. Habermas successfully demonstrates the importance of language and communication in legitimating knowledge and power. He does not successfully transcend positivism and instrumentalism. Therefore, he has been correctly labeled a "right-wing Marxist" or a "radical Liberal."[31] Habermas has, however, clarified the issues and demonstrated that the impasse in the emancipatory project of his critical theory is not an impasse in critical theory per se. Moreover, his extended engagement with the problems of deliberative democracy has set an agenda for a robust transdisciplinary conversation that continues to resonate with partisans of participatory democracy.

DEMOCRATIC POWER-TALK

Ben Agger has offered a provocative synthesis of the ideas of Habermas, Marcuse, and the liberal American legal theorist Bruce Ackerman.[32] In Agger's critical theory, dialogue is regarded as both a means to discrediting and overcoming repressive institutional arrangements and as "an imaginative model—a telos—of free human activity."[33] Like Habermas, Agger contends that technocratic capitalism is supported by a scientization of ideology that not only discourages dialogues between laypeople and experts, but also encourages a "socially structured silence" among citizens. He contends that "the monopoly of capital goes hand in hand with the monopoly both of information and of dialogue-chances."[34]

Agger's synthesis has three essential components: (a) a conversational basis for delegitimating a repressive social order, through which the powerless can engage the powerful in justificatory dialogues, (b) a critique of the ideology of technocratically induced silence that *uses* the public experience of delegitimation as a means of generating more sophisticated political dialogues, and (c) an outline of concrete social and political action in which the human capacity for competent involvement in person-nature, person-symbol, and person-person dialogues is affirmed. Ackerman's "neutral dialogue" provides the first component, Habermas's critical theory the second, and Agger's conception of dialogue as an exemplar of free human activity the third.

Ackerman's neutral dialogue provides an independent criterion for identifying illegitimate, nonrational, "constrained power talk." Constrained power talk entails failure to engage in dialogue or, once engaged, failure to offer rational justifications for one's advantaged position. According to Ackerman:

> A power structure is illegitimate if it can be justified only through a conversation in which some person (or group) must assert that he is (or they are) the privileged moral authority: Neutrality. No reason is a good reason if it requires the power holder to assert:
>   (a) that his conception of the good is better than that asserted by any of his fellow citizens, or
>   (b) that regardless of his conception of the good, he is intrinsically superior to one or more of his fellow citizens.[35]

Pulling rank, citing credentials instead of reasons, using technical data to obfuscate, and invoking procedural rules to mute or deflect justificatory dialogues are, by definition, illegitimate, repressive communications, violations of democratically grounded free speech. As Ackerman puts it, "A sustained silence or a stream of self-contradictory noises are decisive signs that something very wrong is going on."[36]

Ackerman is not a critical theorist. He posits his conception of neutral dialogue in an attempt to breathe new life into liberalism. However, he demonstrates that, by virtue of their monologic stances, most existing liberal institutions are illegitimate. He provides a perspective for principled recognition of corruption, but no program for purging corruption. He is interested in the ground rules of free speech, not in the sociology of communicative competence. Thus, he has nothing to say about socially stratified inequalities in educational and linguistic opportunities which, according to sociologists like Basil Bernstein, cause the disadvantaged to abstain from participation in public forums.[37] Habermas's perspective, however, criticizes technocratically induced silence and encourages the powerless to respond to failed justificatory dialogues by developing communicative competence and thereby renewing political dialogues and actions.

Agger, like Marcuse, sees the first step—identifying illegitimate power relations—and the second step—developing communicative competence—as prologue to the third step—articulating a new sensibility that replaces instrumental control with humanistic productive and organizational relations grounded in dialogue liberated from repression. Thus, Agger contends: "Communicative competence in this sense is nothing less than a competence to manage all the facets of our lives, in transcendence of an ideology that robs us both of our political voices and our substantive social and economic freedom of self creation."[38] It is not just the power to generate fluent reports or warranted assertions; it is the power to transform ourselves and the world. This power does not necessarily preclude hierarchy. But it does require such hierarchical moves to be secured in egalitarian dialogues. Thus, in contrast to historical (Marxist-Leninist) socialism, for example, it insists that the processes and the product of socialism cannot be divorced. If the ends are social democracy or communitarianism, these ends can only be justified if they can be secured by democratic means: egalitarian dialogic processes. To Dag Hammarskjöld's wise prescript, "Only he [or she] deserves power who everyday justifies it," might be added the caveat that he or she must justify it in both theory and practice.[39] In short, Agger's robust concept of communication competence is unapologetically eutopian.

POLICY IMPLICATIONS

What Paulo Freire tried to do to create conditions that would develop critical consciousness and articulation among those repressed by neocolonial structures of oppression, Agger's work attempts to do for those disenfranchised by technocratic structures.[40] He provides them/us with a dialogic warrant for recovering their voices and discovering their competencies. Agger's synthesis transcends the praxeological impasse of the first wave of critical theory. The standard of neutral dialogue, as radicalized by Agger, advances critical theory beyond ideological critique. It provides a practical interactional test of the symmetry (and democracy) of dialogic relationships: not just political relationships, but also the organization of work and of social and domestic relationships. Moreover, it provides a prophylaxis against vanguardism: the perennial problem of the left whereby the emancipatory vision is distorted and betrayed by leaders who predicate their claims to speak for the people on a refusal to listen to the people. Agger's approach is interested in encouraging the repressed to speak for themselves, to make policy. Therefore, he does not examine in a concrete way the policy implications of institutionalizing neutrality, although he does suggest that it would revolutionize the division of labor in society.

As I interpret these policy implications, they would seem to suggest, at a minimum, that in a truly democratic state, all institutional spokespersons would be instructed in the rules of neutral dialogue rather than in the principles of technocratic management, advertising, public relations, and spin control. The institutions of such a state would be structured to maximize opportunities for generating justificatory dialogues. Racism, sexism, classism, and ageism would be outlawed as violations of the terms of neutral dialogue. A primary responsibility of the press would be to report breaches of the rules of neutral dialogue by those in positions of power as violations of their trust. The press itself would have to rethink its covenant because, by definition, the hierarchical concentration of control of mass media that prevails in technocratic societies is an abrogation of neutrality.

Similarly, claims by the press to the superior moral authority of "journalistic objectivity" would have to be abandoned. Copyrights, royalties, patents, and other reified concepts of information ownership would also have to be thoroughly rethought. Present trends toward privatization of information resources would be reversed. A new international information order would be established that would bear little resemblance to that presently envisioned by either its proponents or opponents. The culture industry as we know it, with its monologic programming, would talk itself out of existence, and the knowledge industry would manufacture a new warrant through which scientists would invent less manipulative relationships with nature, objects, and people, and thereby articulate more nurturing vocabularies of motive and expression. Clearly, this simple and eminently reasonable paradigm for free speech is a very radical idea—perhaps as radical as ideas like "freedom," "equality," "justice," and "liberalism" were in the seventeenth and eighteenth centuries.

FLIES IN THE OINTMENT

Neutral dialogue, as it is conceived by Ackerman and Agger, is not just a good place. It is also a distant place. It will remain an unreachable place (or value) unless critical theory recovers its political will, its commitments to participatory democracy, and its investment in the future. The odds against its realization are great, even monumental.

Media Industries

The most obvious, pernicious, and intractable obstacles are, of course, the established powers of mass media and the culture industry more generally.

Given the present organization of media and the corporate economic stranglehold on national politics, at least in the United States, it is pie in the sky to contemplate reforming national politics from the top-down through neutral dialogue. New media mergers are constantly shifting the alignments and increasing the conglomeration, integration, and synergy within the handful of global communication companies that now control most of the world's media.

Moreover new, user-friendly media technologies, post-Fordian modes of production (flexible, stratified, and targeted), and personalized marketing techniques threaten to dismantle remaining vestiges of the public sphere by erasing the shared universe of discourse upon which an informed citizenry depends. Technovisionaries tell us that Internet-mediated infobots, which allow users to design personalized newspapers and other information resources by filtering out entire categories or genres of messages in advance, are the wave of the future. So, for example, Consumer A can bypass political news entirely and immerse himself in sports media, while Consumer B tunes into political news but filters out all viewpoints that challenges her ideological presuppositions, and so on. Personalized media—so inviting from an efficiency standpoint in an age of information overload—may in fact create "technological echo chambers," which preclude encounters with people and perspectives that are unfamiliar or challenging to their users.[41] Yet, as Cass Sunstein points out, free expression and deliberative democracy depend upon: (a) unplanned and unanticipated exchanges of diverse viewpoints that people do not seek, frequently find disturbing, and must struggle to integrate into their understandings of the world; and (b) a citizenry that has a range of shared experiences. He maintains that these requirements hold in any large nation, but that

> [t]hey are especially important in a heterogeneous nation, which is bound to face an occasional risk of fragmentation. They have all the more importance as each nation becomes increasingly global, and each citizen becomes to a greater or lesser degree, a "citizen of the world."[42]

Computer-enabled target marketing and consumer tracking further erode these democratic requirements. Intended to use advertising dollars more efficiently, these practices not only respond to self-selecting taste cultures and lifestyle differences, they cultivate them. Segmenting markets and media audiences, these profit-maximizing strategies also divide consumer/citizens based upon age, gender, race, class, and other variables. That is, they create echo chambers as well as reinforce and amplify the filtering mechanisms that insulate these chambers.[43]

Failures of Critical Theories and Politics

The logical counter to both new and old forms of media hegemony is, of course, broadly based democratic media activism. The recent attempts to create coalitions of media scholars, media activists, and media workers have, however, been notorious for their own forms of fragmentation and factionalism, infighting, and identity politics. As neutral dialogue, most of these efforts fail.

Would-be media reformers need to get their own houses in order. Some of the fault lines in failed efforts at critical media coalition politics are readily transparent. None is perhaps more crucial than the absence of coherent vision (or amalgamation of visions).

From its inception, critical social theory has been committed to recovering the unity of theory and practice: to discovering what is missing and imagining something better. That is, it has been eutopian. Since the collapse of the Soviet dystopia, neoliberalism, the anti-ideological ideology of globalization, has succeeded in censoring all utopian visions except the technovisions upon which its own future depends.[44] Framing itself as the "end of history"—as both the telos and terminus of historical evolution—neoliberalism thereby positions itself to reject all challenges to its hegemony as regressive, ahistorical, irrational, reductive, and potentially totalitarian.[45] This alchemy has worked relatively well, at least within neoliberal states where the left, with some exceptions, has largely surrendered (if only by default) to the "end of ideology" thesis that it once roundly rejected.[46] Yet, without some shared vision, some bridging of ideals, coalition politics are impossible.

The current intellectual fashion of blaming the Enlightenment for all of the errors of modernism misses the point. As the conservative economist Friedrich Hayek pointed out long ago, it was the marriage of scientism and Marxist-Leninism that led to totalitarianism: a universalistic, reductive, unitary, and ultimately closed vision.[47] A similar and similarly dangerous but unacknowledged scientism, rooted in social evolutionary assumptions, lies at the core of current neoliberal apologetics for globalization.

Eutopian ideals, unfettered by scientism and articulated on more modest, even local, scales, are still needed to build just communities and viable coalitions. The Golden Rule is such an ideal, one that can be found in some form as a normative standard in all enduring societies: never fully realized, but as a perennial dream. Those who find something missing in the current subordination of all values to market values need to dare to dream again; to recover the eutopian impulse and to exercise it wisely, reflexively, with a clear-eyed realism. They need to once again find the courage to speak truth to those in power: to take risks, including risking the possibility of once again making humiliating errors.[48]

Feminist Questions

Then, there is "the feminist question." Gestures that are friendly to feminism can be found or read into all of the theories of emancipatory communication explored in these pages; however, none of their authors engages directly with the feminist critique of patriarchal language, structures of thought, or discursive practices. None considers what recent feminist epistemological critiques of rationalism and empiricism would mean for a theory of dialogue; how the feminist project would reconstruct models of rationality and discursive rules or how it has deconstructed social contract theory; how the gendering of public and private spheres and conceptions of good arguments can be reconciled in comprehensive theories of dialogue; or how Cartesian mind-body dualism conditions contemporary concepts of communication, information, and mediation. Indeed, all of these theories of emancipatory communication appear to import unstated and nonreflexive images of imaginary dialogic partners who already share some fundamental agreements about how public issues, rationality, and warranted assertability should be defined. Yet, these elements are the problem of the feminist epistemological critique. In sum, feminism poses some profound, though not necessarily insurmountable, problems for critical theory and for dialogic theories of democracy. Some of these challenges are more fully explored in part II of this book.

Elitism and Moral Tyranny of Dialogic Models

The most daunting challenges to dialogic models of emancipatory communication cut to their logical core. In his thoughtful and imaginative book, *Speaking into the Air* (1999), John Durham Peters radically questions both the desirability and tenability of using dialogue as a "normative model for the extended, even distended, kinds of talk and discourse necessary to large-scale democracy."[49] He points to the simple and obvious, but frequently glossed over, fact that dialogic relations are dyadic, person-to-person, reciprocal interactions involving "the marriage of true minds." Dialogic couplings are both exclusionary and very rare; moreover, they sometimes involve tyranny and exploitation.

Socrates, the Socratic method of questioning, and the dyadic relationship of mentor and student are the prototypes for romanticizing dialogue as an idealized model for communication in Western culture. Socratic dialogues are elitist, in Peters's view, because the reciprocity they offer requires (a) orientation through education; and (b) the junior partner to successfully negotiate intellectual contests to achieve relative equality. They are not open to all; in historical fact, they were open only to an elite few within the limited franchises of Athenian democracy.

In place of the Socratic ideal of dialogue, Peters proposes "dissemination" as a more accurate, and in his view, more democratic model for mass communication. Here, he offers Jesus and the Gospels as prototypes of dissemination. Peters locates democracy in reception rather than in transmission; that is, receivers are free to accept, reject, ignore, or reconfigure messages.

More specifically, for our purposes, Peters criticizes the "moral tyranny" that he believes is implicit in Ackerman's apparently congenial invitation to dialog because it does not leave potential dialogic partners free to refuse the invitation.[50] Peters's moral objection is justified if neutral dialogue is taken as a model for all forms of dialogue. However, Ackerman is a political theorist, not a social psychologist. He intends neutral dialogue as a means whereby citizens can take back (or create) democracy by making corrupt monologic institutions accountable for their actions by, in effect, making them more dialogic. That is, Ackerman intends neutral dialogue as a model for legitimating dialogues in which the governed ask governors to justify their exercises of power. In this context, institutional structures and procedures are already heavily stacked in favor of the powerful, giving them many ways of preemptively opting out of dialogues. Within Ackerman's liberal schema, then, the refusal of representatives of monologic institutions to justify their actions to the people is a violation of the democratic social contract of liberalism. This refusal is tyranny. Conversely, the threat of the people to engage in violence if the representatives of monologic institutions refuse their invitation to dialogue, which Peters objects to, is not tyranny—at least not to a Jeffersonian or Ackermanian liberal. It is entirely consistent with the democratic premises of the liberal social contract, which originated in both United States and France in violent revolutions against the monologic regimes of monarchies. In short, the threat of violent resistance by the people is part of the bargain of liberalism.

Nonetheless Peters's larger point about the inappropriateness of dialogue as a model for public communication does identify serious conundrums in communication theory and liberalism. Dissemination is a far more accurate description of how mass media and public communication work today; however, I am not persuaded by his advocacy for the democracy of reception. To be sure, receivers are not the passive puppets that many theories, especially Marxist theories, of communications have assumed, but without a diverse media and a viable public sphere, even actively resistant receivers are poorly positioned to do the work of democracy.

Peters's conception of communication is, however, far richer and, and in my judgment, truer than the theories of communication he critiques. Peters recognizes that there is a kind of "permanent kink" in the human condition, which makes perfect communicative reciprocity impossible; our efforts to "reconcile self and other" always involve some "strangeness."[51] There are always gaps that are filled with contradictions, ironies, wit, word play, logical inversions, and awkwardness; yet, he claims, these gaps are the sources of love and justice. In negotiating them, we become fully human.

Peters is surely right in claiming that the liberal dialogic models of Habermas and Ackerman are much too sober to take into account the strangeness and wonder of human communication. These models only tap our highest cerebral functions: the upper attic of our minds where formal logic eliminates all of the noise of life and engages in the simplistic reductions of rationalism. These models ignore the fact that we all live in bodies, bring different gendered, racialized, class experiences, life histories, educational backgrounds, semantic resources, and creative cunning to legitimating conversations.

If we accept Peters's enriched conception of communicative processes, must we surrender our dialogic dreams? Must we settle instead into the congregations of nay-sayers or yeah-sayers that his "dissemination" model appears to offer?

Not necessarily! Within Peters's work, there is a loophole that saves dialogue from extinction in communicative ethics and in developing rules for engaging in power talk. In a move that is less slick than it initially seems, he turns the demands of reflective dialogue inside out, or more precisely "outside in." That is, Peters imposes the rules of dialogue on the self rather than on the other:

> The motto of communication theory ought to be: Dialogue with the self, dissemination the other. This is another way of stating the ethical maxim: Treat yourself like an other and the other like a self.[52]

He makes explicit what has always been implicit, but not always honored in practice, in theories of emancipatory communication: theorists need to practice what they preach.

RETURNING TO PARIS: LINGUISTIC
THERAPY FOR DAMAGED THEORIES OF DIALOG

Was the communication turn in critical theory a wrong turn? Should we abandon dialogues about dialogue, repress our "desire" for more satisfying forms of collective life, and return to just calling Paris Paris?

I think not. To be sure, we need to do much more than talk about talk. Studies in political economy and institutional analysis, which examine the material and social conditions in which public communications take place in contemporary societies, need to be reinvigorated and recentered within communication research.[53] But talk about talk remains an essential part of critical theory's emancipatory mission. The thinkers profiled in this chapter have contributed much to the advancement of that talk even when (and sometimes especially when) they have talked themselves into corners. The dream of full reciprocity in communication may be a romantic fiction. But the desire for reciprocity is not only what makes us human, it is what makes society possible. Conversational rules or etiquettes, which are designed to bring a wider range of voices into democratic debates, may not work. Or, if they do, the conversations they produce may end in stalemates. But to give up on the possibility of such conversations is to give up on democracy.

A first step toward opening up richer dialogues about dialogic theory might be to abandon the abstractions of the armchair and engage in real conversations that test and amend the rules of neutral dialogue in practice. This is because ultimately the rules for such dialogues, if they really are to be open and just, must be articulated contextually by committed participants. A vast research literature is now available on the ways gender, race, class, heterosexism, and other positionings intersect and condition actual and perceived communication competence in a wide range of intercultural contexts. There is, in short, an ample knowledge base to put theory into practice if participants are committed to coalition building. Moreover, liberal models for coalition building, which often impose rather than achieve consensus, have been extensively critiqued; and alternative, equity based models, which can accommodate irreducible differences, have been developed and successfully deployed by activists, for example, by some antiglobalization groups.

Testing communication models in micropractice—in the palpable, participatory presence of real talking, gesturing, and touching people—should also short-circuit some of the abstract logorrhea that has led so much high theory astray in the last two decades. Or, as Peters bluntly notes, in an otherwise mixed assessment of Jacques Derrida's work, "[T]o think of the longing for the presence of other people as a kind of metaphysical mistake is nuts."[54]

Putting the house of critical theory in order also requires fidelity to what Ackerman calls consistency in practice as well as in dialogic claims. That is, it requires consistency within the micropolitics of critical theory whether those politics function in theory groups, academic gatekeeping, or in political organizing. If critical theorists are genuinely committed to participatory democracy, then they must submit their own practices to its frequently inefficient, usually time-consuming, sometimes irresolute, often frustrating and disorderly, but self-reflexive, litmus test.

Consistency is always a heavy burden for humans: our flawed souls are battlefields of conflicting desires. Yet, perhaps in no scholarly endeavor is the mandate clearer: in theorizing emancipatory communication, we are obligated, both logically and morally, to strive for consistency. Ultimately the most valuable outcome of this striving may be the ethic it imposes on the theorist/activist (as in Peters's redeployment of dialogue). Taken seriously, the norm of consistency can serve as a self-reflexive ethic for modeling and monitoring our own contributions to justificatory dialogues. That is, those who claim to be seriously committed to communicative and community justice could begin their reformation by interrogating their own dialogic motives and practices. In *Doing Documentary Work* (1998), Robert Coles provides an insightful, if inescapably tension-laden, model for conducting such self-interrogations in research settings that involve communications across class, race, and status. The reflexive, personal, and social ethic that Coles advocates in the research process can also serve as a useful, self-imposed normative standard for guiding participation by intellectuals in justificatory dialogues and community activism.[55]

Today, much, perhaps even most, of our discursive space is technologically mediated. Practicing what I preach in a milieu in which most of my potential conversational partners are engaged in mediated experiences most of their waking hours may be morally uplifting, however, except in very rare instances, it is likely to be politically irrelevant. Yet, counter-hegemonic, Internet-based mediating technologies could be designed to facilitate political dialogues that embody the values of and conform to the rules of reflexive power-talk.[56] A long shot? Yes indeed! But a long shot is better than cashing in one's chips and resigning oneself to the "end of history."

The clock is ticking. While media reformers have been factionalizing, the media monoliths have been conglomerating, consolidating, and integrating. They have been using their increased financial clout to "reform" communication law, to dismantle the mandates of regulatory agencies like the Federal Communication Commission, and to foreclose public debate about international trade agreements that further advance their global hegemony. As Herbert Schiller pointed out more than two decades ago, globalization, the convergence of "new electronic industries, the changing sites of industrial production, and instantaneous international communication are imposing a new form of hierarchical organization on much of the world."[57]

The Agger-Ackerman critique of "monopolies of both information and of dialogue chances" is incomplete; and neutral dialogue is a preliminary and flawed formulation, perhaps at best a provocative hypothesis. It may not prove viable in practice even in the micropolitics of organizations dedicated to democratic social change. Nevertheless, the questions it addresses— questions posed so long ago by the Frankfurt School when the specters of earlier totalitarian ambitions were at their heels—are still salient questions.

There is now considerable research that shows that participatory democracy is still possible in small groups.[58] Powerful arguments have also been made for the indispensability of coalition politics of resistance under present political arrangements.[59] Critical scholars have a role to play in coalition building, not as vanguards or authoritative experts, but as collaborators in genuinely democratic processes. Within these collaborations, consistency, with democratic principles, may often require scholars to consume salutary servings of humble pie by assuming secondary roles as research associates.

Realization of neutral dialogue and self-reflexive dialogic ethics will not sever the knot that binds power and knowledge. Struggles to identify and reduce surplus repression cannot undo the "kink" in human communication processes. But revised, historicized, and contextualized, struggles for norms of emancipatory communication are still worth pursuing.

Many critical theorists are, in my judgment, too eager to declare this pursuit a dead end and move on to the next game. Yet, this declaration comes at exactly the moment in history when feminism and other subaltern perspectives are actively interrogating the power talk of critical theory, seeking to reverse its exclusionary clauses, hold it to norms of reflexivity and consistency, and effect transformative syntheses. Changing the subject before everyone has her say is, of course, also a breach of the rules of reflexive power-talk, as well as a familiar move in the politics of gendered conversation.

NOTES

1. Karl Marx and Friedrich Engels, *The German Ideology* (New York: International Publishers, 1970, original 1846), 119.

2. Marx and Engels, *The German Ideology*, 102.

3. Max Horkheimer, *Eclipse of Reason* (New York: Seabury Press, 1974); and Max Horkheimer and Theodore W. Adorno, *Dialectics of Enlightenment* (New York: Herder and Herder, 1972).

4. Max Horkheimer, *Critical Theory: Selected Essays* (New York: Seabury Press, 1972); Martin Jay, The *Dialectical Imagination: A History of the Frankfurt School and the Institute of Social Research 1923–1950* (Boston: Little, Brown, 1973); Trent Schroyer, *The Critique of Domination* (New York: Braziller, 1973); and Jules Sensat, *Habermas and Marxism: An Appraisal* (Beverly Hills, Calif.: Sage, 1979).

5. Horkheimer and Adorno, *Dialects of Enlightenment*.

6. Charles Loomis quoted by John Gastil, *Democracy in Small Groups: Participation, Decision Making and Communication* (Philadelphia: New Society Publishers, 1993), vii.

7. Ben Agger, "Work and Authority in Marcuse and Habermas," *Human Studies* 2 (1979): 191–208; and Paulo Freire, *Pedagogy of the Oppressed* (New York: Seabury Press, 1970).

Chapter Three

8. John Durham Peters, *Speaking Into the Air: A History of the Idea of Communication* (Chicago: University of Chicago Press, 1999), 269.

9. Douglas Kellner, *Television and the Crisis of Democracy* (Boulder: Westview Press, 1990); Vincent Mosco, *The Political Economy of Communication* (London: Sage, 1996); and Dan Schiller, *Theorizing Communication: A History* (New York: Oxford University Press, 1996).

10. John A. Lent, ed., *A Different Road Taken: Profiles in Critical Communication* (Boulder: Westview Press, 1995).

11. Paul Carus, *Goethe* (Chicago: Open Court, 1915).

12. James W. Carey, "Public Sphere," plenary address presented at the annual meeting of the International Communication Association, Chicago, May 23, 1996.

13. Jacques Barzun, *From Dawn to Decadence: 500 Years of Western Cultural Life, 1500 to the Present* (New York: HarperCollins, 2000); and Roger Shattuck, "Decline and Fall?" *The New York Times Review of Books*, 29 June 2000, 55–58.

14. This is at least formally true for all members of the United Nations although, of course, subscription to human rights charters produces, at best, imperfect results.

15. Herbert Marcuse, *Eros: A Philosophical Inquiry into Freud* (Boston: Beacon Press, 1955).

16. Marcuse, *Eros*, 217.

17. Herbert Marcuse, *One-Dimensional Man* (Boston: Beacon Press, 1964), 217.

18. Herbert Marcuse, *An Essay on Liberation* (Boston: Beacon Press, 1969), 73.

19. Marcuse, *An Essay on Liberation*, 72.

20. Kenneth Burke, *A Grammar of Motives and Rhetoric of Motives* (Cleveland, Ohio: Meridian, 1962); and Murray Edelman, *Political Language: Words that Succeed and Politics that Fail* (New York: Academic Press, 1977).

21. Marcuse, *An Essay on Liberation*, 33.

22. Herbert Marcuse, *The Aesthetic Dimension: Toward a Critique of Marxist Aesthetics* (Boston: Beacon Press, 1978).

23. Michael Eric Dyson, *Between God and Gangsta Rap: Bearing Witness to Black Culture* (New York: Oxford University Press, 1997).

24. Andreas Huyssen, "The Hidden Dialectic: The Avant Garde-Technology-Mass Culture," in *The Myths of Information: Technology and Postindustrial Culture*, ed. Kathleen Woodward (Sun Prairie, Wisc.: Baumgartner Publications and the University of Wisconsin, 1980), 151–64; and Thomas Frank, *The Conquest of Cool: Business Culture, Counterculture and the Rise of Hip Consumerism* (Chicago: University of Chicago Press, 1998).

25. From *Parks and Recreation* (October 2000), cited in "Time Out," UTNE Reader (April 2001): 62.

26. Dallas Smythe, *Dependency Road: Communications, Capitalism, Consciousness and Canada* (Norwood, N.J.: Ablex, 1981).

27. Jurgen Habermas, *Knowledge and Human Interests* (Boston: Beacon Press, 1971), 220.

28. Burke, *A Grammar of Motives*.

29. In this regard, they share common, if not always acknowledged, roots in the American pragmatism of Dewey and James who, like their current apologist Richard Rorty, also valorize the conversational grounding of truth-making.

30. Quoted in Thomas A. McCarthy, "A Theory of Communicative Competence," *Philosophy of Social Science* 3 (1973): 135–56.

31. Ben Agger, "A Critical Theory of Dialogue," *Humanities in Society* 4, no. 1 (Winter 1981): 201.

32. Agger, "Work and Authority."

33. Agger, "Work and Authority," 7.

34. Agger, "Work and Authority," 9.

35. Bruce A. Ackerman, *Social Justice in the Liberal State* (New Haven, Conn., and London: Yale University Press, 1980), 10–11.

36. Ackerman, *Social Justice*, 8.

37. Basil Bernstein, *Class Codes and Control* (London: Routledge & Kegan Paul, 1971).

38. Agger, "Work and Authority," 28.

39. Dag Hammarskjöld, *Markings* (New York: Knopf, 1964), 138.

40. Paulo Freire, *Pedagogy of the Oppressed* (New York: Seabury Press, 1970); Agger, "Work and Authority"; and Agger, "A Critical Theory of Dialogue."

41. Cass Sunstein, "Exposure to Other Viewpoints Is Vital to Democracy," *The Chronicle of Higher Education* (March 16, 2001): 10(B)–11(B). See also Sunstein, *Republic.com* (Princeton: Princeton University Press, 2001).

42. Sunstein, "Exposure to Other Viewpoints," 10(B)–11(B); and Sunstein, *Republic.com*.

43. Joseph Turow, *Breaking up America: Advertisers and the New Media World* (Chicago: University of Chicago Press, 1997).

44. Günter Grass and Pierre Bourdieu, "A Literature from Below," *The Nation* (July 3, 2000): 25–28.

45. Grass and Bourdieu, "A Literature from Below." The end of history thesis was articulated (or rearticulated within the post–Cold War context) by Francis Fukuyama, "The End of History?" *National Interest* (Summer 1989): 3–18, and expanded in a book, *The End of History and The Last Man* (New York: The Free Press, 1992).

46. Russell Jaccoby, *The End of Utopia: Politics and Culture in an Age of Apathy* (New York: Basic Books, 1999).

47. Friedrich Hayek, *The Road to Serfdom* (Chicago: University of Chicago Press, 1996, original 1942).

48. Edward Said, *Representations of the Intellectual* (New York: Random House, 1996).

49. Peters, *Speaking into the Air*, 34

50. Peters, *Speaking into the Air*, 159.

51. Peters, *Speaking into the Air*, 9 and 29.

52. Peters, *Speaking into the Air*, 57.

53. On this point, I strongly agree with Vincent Mosco and Dan Schiller who stress the important of reemphasizing the study of the material and social relations of cultural production in the wake of the ascendancy of cultural studies and postmodernism. See Vincent Mosco, *The Political Economy of Communication* (London: Sage, 1996); and Dan Schiller, *Theorizing Communication: A History* (New York: Oxford University Press, 1996).

54. Peters, *Speaking into the Air*, 270.

68 Chapter Three

55. Robert Coles, *Doing Documentary Work* (New York: Oxford University Press, 1998).

56. Benjamin Barber is exploring development of such software. Benjamin Barber, presentation to Faculty Humanities Seminar, Muhlenberg College, February 13, 2001. See also Brenda Dervin's ongoing experimentations with computer mediated dialogic designs. For a recent installment, see Brenda Dervin et al., "Freedom is Another Word for Nothing Left to Lose: The Inextricable Necessity of Theorizing/ Philosophizing in Disciplined Communication Policy/Practice," paper presented at annual meetings of the International Communication Association, May 26, 2001.

57. Herbert Schiller, *Who Knows: Information in the Age of the Fortune 500* (Norwood, N.J.: Ablex, 1981), 2.

58. Gastil, *Democracy in Small Groups*.

59. William Julius Wilson, *The Bridge over the Racial Divide: Rising Inequality and Coalition Politics* (Berkeley: University of California Press, 1999).

Part II

IMPERTINENT QUESTIONS

We are what we pretend to be, so we must be careful about what we pretend to be.

—Kurt Vonnegut

Chapter Four

Is Information Gendered?

There really is a man behind the curtain, Dorothy. Pay no attention to the convergence pyrotechnics. There's a lot at stake, and it just might be your digital future.

—Mark Stallman, *Wired*, March 1994

Technological designs are also social designs. Cultural values, economic interests, and political decisions are as integral to their composition as mathematical calculations, motors, cams, circuits, and silicon chips. During the closing decades of the twentieth century, debates provoked by commercial and military designs for a global "information age" or "information society" became prime sites for international political, economic, and cultural struggles.

These struggles, in turn, provided the auspices and impetus for ambitious agendas of politically engaged critical communications research. Data-driven, yet theoretically rich, this research offered systematic assessments of the institutional architecture, economic constituents, technological possibilities, and occupational and class arrangements of emerging national and global structures of information-capitalism. The international character of this research in the political economy of communication was especially salutary in exposing the Eurocentric values, priorities, and biases that condition the development of designs for global information systems: values such as technical progress, economic growth, productivity, efficiency, and control. Nevertheless, this body of theory and the empirical assessments it produced remained largely silent about a crucial dimension of the power-knowledge of the information age: its gender politics.

The sources of this exclusion, this socially structured silence, are paradoxically both transparent and puzzling. They are transparent because, in a sense,

71

social and linguistic constructions of the term "technology" in Western languages and discourse practices mandate this silence. Even a cursory review of the scholarly literature on technology reveals that constitution of the terms "woman" and "technology" are not separate practices; they are related terms in a vocabulary of power-relations that defines the objects men make and manipulate and the work they do as "technical." Conversely, this vocabulary treats the objects women make and manipulate and the work they do as "nontechnical," "natural," sometimes even "nurturing," "humane," or "humanistic."[1] This practice is also, of course, congruent with theoretical conventions in economics, sociology, and history, which have considered men's paid labor as productive and part of a nation's economy and women's unpaid labor as reproductive and outside calculations of gross national products.

As a result of these constitutive practices, histories of Western technology have been histories of male activities.[2] They examine the tools and techniques that have built industry and advanced warfare. They do not examine birthing, cooking, or childcare skills or devices.[3] Often these histories are secured by evolutionary assumptions that carry unexamined masculinist (and Eurocentric) cargoes. When histories of technology mention women (and they do so rarely), women are usually conceived as "consumers" of technology, as users of bicycles, telephones, typewriters, word processors, and fax machines.[4]

In short, it is easy to understand why mainstream debates on technology were able to ignore the question of gender for so long. The established categories and conventions of Western languages and thought direct attention away from this question. The silence that results is so pervasive and deeply entrenched that Jane Caputo describes the advanced technologies it produces as "phallotechnologies."[5]

TROUBLING SILENCES IN
CRITICAL COMMUNICATION THEORY

Nevertheless, the unreflective replication of these practices in critical theories and assessments of information technologies is puzzling and counterproductive for a number of reasons. First, when communications scholars invade territories already occupied by other disciplines, they incur special obligations to survey the communicative features of those territories. When they study technology, they are therefore presumably required to display greater linguistic reflexivity than scientists, engineers, technologists, or even historians.

Second, critical communication theorists, especially neo- or post-Marxists and postmodernists, directly and aggressively challenge the Enlightenment-based vocabulary of power-knowledge that supports these linguistic practices.[6]

Third, many critical communication scholars publicly profess support for the egalitarian goals of feminism. Yet, these practices obstruct realization of those goals.

Fourth, critical researchers are interested in what Harry Braverman characterized as "de-skilling" processes in communications industries.[7] The gendering of skills is particularly pronounced in technology-intensive industries, especially computer and other electronics industries, so much so that government and industry task forces are now busily addressing ways of closing the so-called digital divide, which separates technological "haves" from "have-nots" both domestically and globally including males and females, rich and poor, and whites and nonwhites.[8]

Fifth, studies of the history and social effects of the computer revolution suggest that the knowledge "lost" in the digitalization of information may be the humanistic knowledge that has preserved many cherished values of Western civilization.[9] These are the same values that were marginalized and feminized by gendered discourses on technology (phallotexts?) during the Industrial Revolution.[10]

Sixth, putting the new wine of critical and cultural theory in the old bottles of patriarchal linguistic categories inhibits, perhaps even precludes, the kinds of radical reconceptualizations of structures of everyday life—of authority, difference, community, and relations with the nonhuman environment—valorized by current critical and postmodernist perspectives within communications studies.[11] In sum, the absence of a critical consciousness regarding the gendering of technological discourse concedes contestable territory to technological designs that reproduce old patterns of power and privilege.

The socially structured silences supported by gendered vocabularies of power and knowledge are such consistent and persistent furnishings of discussions of technology that feminism has issued "a challenge and invitation to malestream researchers to question, for example, the assumption that men in the West have a location which is separate and adequate for theorizing about communications and technology without consideration of the origin of the imposed hierarchical social divisions of such polar terms as female/male, East/West, and black/white."[12] Or, to put it bluntly, feminists ask, Is technology gendered?

BREAKING THE SILENCE

This chapter takes up the challenge of interrogating the gendered constituents of information designs and technologies. It breaks the silences that have buried these constituents beneath a veneer of phantom objectivity. Countering these silences requires the articulation of new languages, paradigms, and politics for creating and studying technologies. This is work that cuts across disciplines, work that requires an epochal change in consciousness and generations of effort. This chapter offers some preliminary reflections on the nature of that work and suggests some resources that may provide productive points of departure. Like the mainstream texts it criticizes, this text is also skewed by its own positioning within a Western, indeed American, vantage point. It too contains many silences that require critique, correction, and amendment by other "others."[13]

Although I am convinced that further development of critical and cultural perspectives in communications is contingent upon adequate theorizations of the gender question, I do not think that viable feminist rethinkings of technology can be achieved without effecting a *partial* truce with malestream research. Mainstream discourse on technology has ignored the world of the everyday, the private sphere, the traditional sites of female-gendered skills; however, within feminist perspectives, the public sphere still remains undertheorized.[14] This theoretical tension needs to be radically reinterrogated. Not necessarily to close the gap—as liberals would have it—but to probe the sources of this tension and its resistance to closure, to inspire alternative conceptualizations of the public-private nexus, to encourage rethinking of processes of community-building, and to examine the role technology plays in shaping and mediating contemporary concepts and practices of community.

At the present juncture in the struggle to articulate new vocabularies for constituting dialogues on technology, feminist choices are limited. To engage in creditable discussions of technology, feminists must engage with and use the language of the authoritative discourses—what Mikhail Bakhtin called "the word of the fathers."[15] There are four major ways of coming to terms with this language: (a) surrendering; (b) escaping to the interior, where separate feminist colonies and critical codes can be established; (c) infiltrating the ranks in order to engage in what Umberto Eco calls "semiological guerrilla warfare"; or (d) "commuting" between points (b) and (c).[16] In my judgment, the last option is the most responsible as well as the most politically effective posture. The first two, by leaving the boys alone with some very dangerous toys, may increase the risks of chemical, biological, and nuclear disaster.[17] The third approach can stand alone, but it stands in the middle of the dialectical process; it can deconstruct the old ways, but it lacks the creative resources necessary to empower a new vision. The trick, then, is to take from mainstream discourses without being (entirely) taken in by them. This is not an easy task, but it is one that is consistent with the professed dicta of critical and postmodernist cultural theories, which include theoretical, methodological, and ideological reflexivity.[18]

In the remainder of this chapter, I try to put some additional teeth into the feminist challenge to the "word of the fathers" by very briefly reviewing some feminist deconstructions of the epistemological "location" of white Western males. These deconstructions suggest that, like black females from the East, members of the malestream also see from a particular vantage point or perspective that influences what and how they see, conceive, construct, and use technologies. Then, I consider some of the distinctive properties of the language and models of communications, which make them especially resistant to displays of the perspectivity of knowledge. Finally, I identify some ways in which such displays may be used to secure new models of systematic (even "objective" and scientific) knowledge that are responsive to postcolonialist and feminist perspectives.

FEMINIST EPISTEMOLOGICAL CRITIQUE

A virtual revolution in feminist thought about thought has taken place since the publication of Carolyn Merchant's *Death of Nature* in 1980. Feminist analyses of the founding texts of modern science have established their historicity and intertextuality as well as their strategic positioning within debates involving church, state, commerce, witchcraft, and alchemy.[19] Feminist recoveries of the submerged texts that informed the gender politics of early science demonstrate that scientific reasoning is grounded in metaphors and mythos drawn from the Inquisition, which were designed to purge male fears of the diabolical powers of witches, place the promises and potions of scientists beyond inquisitors' suspicions, and remove the mystique of "mother" earth so that her resources could be exploited by commerce. Although the project is driven by other agendas, it contains within it some provocative insights into the political economy of early science.

These studies have demonstrated that "nature" is a social category. Its representation in the definitive texts of Western science was constructed from the specific reference point of a particular group of males who were interested in escaping the inquisitor's sword and developing mining resources. By exposing this reference point (and subsequent ones) from which the discourses of Western science have been articulated, feminist critics believe they have established that there is no "organic or natural standpoint" from which any of us can apprehend nature or the social world.[20]

This insight has, in turn, led feminist epistemologists to radically problematize established/malestream concepts of observation, empiricism, and objectivity.[21] According to the new feminist epistemologies, the models, theories, and methodologies of modern science and technology bear the scars of their troubled history. Both Baconian empiricism and Cartesian rationalism carry their inscriptions.[22] These inscriptions, in turn, skew the kinds of problems that have interested scientists and the kinds of methods they use to study these problems.[23] The feminist epistemological critique traces these inscriptions to what Sandra Harding calls the primitive "totemic" of gender; they maintain that gender is the *difference* that has made the difference in the generative categories, rules, and structures of Indo-European languages.[24] Feminists point out that within these languages, woman is constructed as the "other." Male subjectivity is established hierarchically by marking its difference from the "objects" of his gaze, desire, affection, and contempt. Woman is conceived as the negative pole in a series of hierarchical oppositions that result from this semiotic occlusion: activity/passivity, culture/nature, head/heart, and logos/pathos. Within this code, only those who control the power to name remain unmarked, unmediated, and disembodied.[25]

Conceived in this way, gender does not simply classify body types or prescribe norms for their representation; it "inflects an entire universe of objects and behaviors with masculine or feminine attributes, most of which remain unstated."[26] Feminist deconstructions of this symbolic economy explode the myth of male "aperspectivity"; the claim that the dominant view is the unbiased view. They reject the premise that the "neutral observer" is neutral and neuter.[27] In short, they identify the all-seeing eye that informs the objectivist logics of mainstream science as the eye of the patriarch.

Feminist re-visions of the logic of science are not merely theoretical or metatheoretical undertakings. Many of the authors of these revisions are practicing scientists. Citing the achievements of Rachel Carson, Barbara McClintock, and Jane Goodall, feminist scientists assume that some forms of inquiry can be better served by attempts to understand and preserve rather than master and control nature. They seek to expand the methods, metaphors, and models of science.

Thus, for example, biologist Ruth Hubbard reconceives narratives of reproduction from a feminist perspective and tells a new story of embodiment in which the female egg is an active partner in the process of fertilization rather than a passive princess waiting patiently for the sperm prince to awaken her from her slumbers.[28] Hubbard looks at what happens to scientific questions when the gender totemic is treated as a null hypothesis: what happens when we look at similarities instead of differences in males and females of the same species. Sarah Blaffer Hrdy examines the mating behaviors of monkeys and discovers that females are not nearly as discreet, selective, or unappreciative of the pleasures of the flesh as male scientists since Darwin and the Victorian era have claimed.[29] Evelyn Fox Keller and Catherine E. Grontowski speculate on what physics would sound or feel like if it had been constructed on aural or tactile instead of the spatial metaphors favored by men.[30] Ann Oakley displays the masculinist assumptions of standard interview protocols in social science and proposes a dialogic approach for research on women that is contiguous with female-gendered communicative patterns.[31]

With the significant exceptions of primatology and, more recently, medical research, the feminist epistemological challenge has had little direct impact on mainstream science and technology—although it has incited some vociferous backlash.[32] Nonetheless, despite its paradigm-shattering rhetoric, the transformative powers of feminism in science and technology may turn out to be more gradual and cumulative. For example, changing pedagogies, inspired, at least in part, by feminist epistemologies creates more women-friendly instruction in science and mathematics, which, in turn, recruits more women practitioners to these fields. Changing sensibilities and practices may slowly erode the patriarchal foundations of science, although not necessarily in ways that feminist epistemologists might anticipate or desire.

Social science has also largely resisted the incursions of feminist epistemologies, except for gender studies, which continue to be marginalized.[33] The humanities, however, have proven more hospitable to the new feminist constructions of knowledge. In fields like history, literature, and to some extent, philosophy—fields that have always preserved some space for the "subjective" (in the terms of positivist discourse, the "feminine")—the feminist challenge has brought about a renewal of creative energies, which, in turn, have opened new areas of inquiry. Within communication research per se, the humanistic and interdisciplinary specialties, such as film and cultural studies, have been most receptive to integrating feminist perspectives into their domain assumptions.

Within feminist scholarship, the authority of the old masculinist and Eurocentric models has been permanently displaced. The feminist epistemological critique has demonstrated that, in the words of John Hillman, "the specific consciousness we call scientific, Western and modern is the long sharpened tool of the masculine mind that has discarded parts of its own substance, calling it 'Eve,' 'female' and 'inferior.'"[34]

ORIGIN MYTHS: THE SNAKE IN
THE GARDEN OF COMMUNICATION

Mainstream communications research has been somewhat receptive to reformist efforts that stress the salience of gender-related variables in studies of language patterning, interpersonal, visual, and some facets of organizational communications; however, it has been virtually untouched by attempts to change conventional research designs to accommodate feminist epistemologies.[35]

Like other disciplines secured by social science orientations, communications is heavily invested in objectivist theories of knowledge: these theories provide the auspices for its disciplinary boundaries, textual authority, institutional positioning, and funding resources. There may, however, be an additional reason for this insularity. The language and models of mainstream communications studies may be especially resistant to displays of the perspectivity of knowledge because of their special relationship to Cartesian concepts of "information."

David Bloor has pointed out that every field has its "origin myth," which it makes major investments in protecting.[36] These myths launder the past. They cleanse the record of the confusions, conflicts, and defeats that accompany the births of all disciplines. They tell more palatable and palpable stories of disciplinary origins, provide props for paradigmatic thinking, endow heirs to the tradition with a collective identity and sense of purpose, and foster temptations to hubris.

"In the beginning," many mainstream communications textbooks tell us, there was Claude Shannon's mathematical theory of communications.[37] Everett Rogers explains, "Shannon's information theory in the 1950's offered the potential of unifying not only the field of communications but also the social sciences and other sciences." Alas, a snake appeared in the garden. "When this theoretical approach to communication was institutionalized in U.S. universities," Rogers reports, "it was mainly absorbed into existing departments of speech and journalism, transforming them but also being bifurcated by this placement in an existing university organizational structure."[38] According to Rogers, the result is a "Balkanization of communication research and theory," which produces "a low degree of coherence to communication research."[39] But the dream of a unified science of information lives on in the hearts of the faithful.[40]

Subscription to this origin myth is not universal even within the mainstream, and the mainstream itself is becoming increasingly difficult to locate. And, it should be noted, Shannon himself never shared the grand ambitions that social scientists like Rogers attached to information theory. He knew he was only describing the mathematics of inanimate circuits, not cracking a master code of human communication.[41] Nevertheless, the origin myth has had significant currency within the field of communication. Like origin myths in other disciplines, it has provided scholars seeking to distance themselves from the mainstream with a benchmark (and straw man) with which to chart their critical departures. In short, whether as ticket or target, communications scholars have strong attachments to information theory.

INFORMATION THEORY:
CARTESIAN DREAMS OF CLEAN MACHINES

Information theory may represent the purest articulation—the exemplary model—of what Susan Bordo characterizes as "the Cartesian masculinization of thought."[42] The father of Cartesian rationalism, René Descartes (1596–1650), entered Western philosophy at a crucial juncture. The growing influence of mechanistic models and metaphors was undermining the authority of the organic worldview that had secured Francis Bacon's (1561–1626) justification of scientific inquiry. The achievements of mechanistic science occurred at the same time that the great "witch craze" swept across Europe, claiming (according to conservative estimates) between 50,000 and 300,000 lives; and, as H. R. Trevor-Roper points out, the fury of the craze was not entirely "separable from the intellectual and spiritual life of those years."[43]

The Inquisitioners required assurance that scientists were doing God's work. Cartesian dualism provided this assurance by valorizing an approach to inquiry that emphasizes separation and difference, and establishes firm boundaries between man and nature (the "other" that in the gendered inflections of seventeenth-century France also included "woman"). The Cartesian method separates reason and emotion, and extols detached, dispassionate, calculating, and abstract modes of cognition; within the ethos of this quasi-secular form of Puritanism, embodiment became an obstacle to reason. The Cartesian recipe maps the coordinates upon which Shannon defined his mathematical theory of information and Alan Turing devised his theory of computational numbers and conceived of his "logic machine"; their work, in turn, provided partial blueprints for development of the modern digital computer.[44]

Realization of the Cartesian dream of a clean machine of reason had profound philosophical, mathematical, theological, political, economic, and social implications. These implications have been extensively explored in the literature on the computer revolution.[45] However, the implications for the gendering of information have been neglected. By relocating the sites of numbers and arithmetic operations from mind to electronic circuits, Shannon and Turing's clean machines reduce the concept of information to the kinds of messages these circuits can accommodate. Magoroh Maruyama describes the truncated form of information valorized by information theory as "classificatory information"; he points out that this mode of reasoning is only one of the forms of information routinely used by humans (in the West) to organize and analyze data.[46] Maruyama reports that, unlike their electronic surrogates, human "information processors" also regularly rely upon "relational," "relevance," and "contextual informations" in making sense and reaching decisions.

THE GHOSTS IN THE MACHINE: MIND AS PROGRAM

The information of information theory (Maruyama's "classificatory information") is a distinctly modern, Western, market-oriented construct that is [mis]represented in discourses of power as the issue of an immutable, universal, evolutionary logic.[47] Nevertheless, the information technologies it produces bear the marks of their social genesis. Thus, for example, David Bolter points out that computer operating systems such as MS-DOS, UNIX, and CPM are based upon the rules of the "command" and "control" functions of military hierarchies and business accounting systems.

The epistemological and methodological assumptions of information theory invite recruitment to representation within discourses of power.[48] The quest for a unified science embraces methodological imperialism in its search for the "one true story"—the master narrative—of human reason. It also engages in a reductionism that would purge all information except "classificatory information" from inclusion within the master narrative. Thus, for example, artificial intelligence modelers claim that all "interesting" forms of human intelligence can be captured within computer programs.[49] The social counterpart of this methodological imperative is an appropriationist logic (the Western gaze) that seeks to master all it surveys—even the extraterrestrial (for example, the Star Wars weapon system).

"Classificatory information," which information theory conceives of as a neutral construct, drained of all cultural meaning, is, however, anything but an empty receptor. It is not only an artifact of Western dualism; it is also a gendered construct.[50] The assumptions and rule structures reified by computer logics—the underpinnings of "classificatory information"—are, to reiterate and paraphrase Hillman, literal extensions of the minds of the men who made and programmed these machines. And, paradoxically, some of the most convincing testimony in support of this claim has, in fact, come from these men themselves, specifically the scientists associated with the Artificial Intelligence Movement.

Studies of science and technology have been faulted for conflating science and technology; Judy Wajcman points out that scientists and technologists possess different cultural resources, for example, the know-how of the technologist is visual and tactile, not just verbal and mathematical.[51] Relationships between the two spheres have varied historically, culturally, and within different branches of science and technology. Throughout the Cold War period, however, when virtually all research and development in computer science in the United States was funded by the Defense Department, the two spheres were tightly integrated. For this reason, the culture of computer scientists during that period provides an especially rich site for studying both the relationship of science and technology and the ways applied scientists and technologists think about and relate to the material objects they make. Some of the more reflective thinkers associated with the Artificial Intelligence Movement were self-consciously aware, from the very inception of the enterprise, that their goal was quite literally to model the logical structures of their own minds.[52] That is, these thinkers viewed the mind as a hierarchically organized structure, and they conceived of the logical operations of mind as its highest form of functioning. Their job, as they saw it, was to peel that logic off the top of the mind and replicate it in programs. Of course, these scientists were de facto Kantians who assumed, at least initially, that the logical structures of mind are natural structures largely uncontaminated by culture.

The story of the failure of the original research program of the Artificial Intelligence Movement, as told in the self-reflexive critiques of its former apologists, is the story of (a) the discovery that separating the logical patterns of mind from its biological constituents yields limited results; (b) that memory, emotion, interest, and tacit knowledge, not just formal structures of logic, are integral parts of purposive action; and (c) that the ghost in the machine is the scientist himself, a reflection of his culture and ego, not a mirror of nature. That is, what can be peeled off the top of mind is not "pure reason," but "classificatory information": the abstract, reified, and ultimately narcissistic extension of the form of thought most highly prized by the cultural values of Western dualism.

CLASSIFICATORY INFORMATION AND MASCULINE MORALITY OF RULES

Classificatory information, the kind of information that can be accommodated by information theory, is largely homologous with the form of reasoning that developmental psychologist Carol Gilligan codes as masculine in her widely influential, but always controversial, study of gendered forms of reasoning. Since its publication in 1982, Gilligan's *A Different Voice* has been the site of an ideological divide for feminism: essentialism versus anti-essentialism.[53] For a significant number of academic feminists, anti-essentialism is a litmus test of feminism. Gilligan leaves the question of essentialism open in *A Different Voice*. Consequently, readers often read or misread Gilligan through heavily politicized lenses. Let me therefore make it very clear that throughout this chapter, indeed throughout this book, I am doing sociology, not biology. I am describing social and cultural patterns; in this instance, cultural performances of gender.

Moreover, I am not, in any sense, endorsing Gilligan's methods or privileging her findings. To the contrary, I treat her work, like the work of information theorists and artificial intelligence scientists (and, for that matter, all work including my own) as fully amenable to analysis through the lens of the sociology of knowledge. In Gilligan's case, it is precisely because the social fingerprints on her models of developmental psychology are (and perhaps should be) so transparent that her work strongly supports my claims. That is, the Western, indeed American, middle-class, twentieth-century, binary/heterosexual, and possibly essentialist elements of Gilligan's early models of gendered reasoning are evidence for my argument, not against it.

With these qualifiers in place, consider the intersections of Maruyama's models of information and Gilligan's models of moral decision-making. These intersections affirm that classificatory information is the kind of information well-educated Western men draw upon most frequently in analyzing data and making decisions. Unlike Maruyama, Gilligan reduces reasoning patterns to two major types: what she calls a "morality of rules" and an "ethic of responsibility." She found that the men she studied generally relied upon the morality of rules, while the women usually referred to an ethic of responsibility in reaching moral decisions. The rules that guide Gilligan's masculine-gendered mode of reasoning are the same rules that construct classificatory information. Conversely, the principles that guide the ethic of responsibility, Gilligan's feminine-gendered mode of reasoning, are based upon forms of information that cannot be readily accommodated by information theory: what Maruyama called "relational," "relevance," and "contextual information."

Gilligan's male subjects, Harvard students, shared many of the same background characteristics, including patterns of gender, racial, and social class socialization, as information theorists and artificial intelligence scientists at the elite institutions like MIT and Carnegie-Mellon University, where the Artificial Intelligence Movement thrived. That is, they are highly intelligent, highly educated people, who are, for the most part, from white, middle- or upper-class, American backgrounds: a socially and culturally homogeneous group. In sum, the overfed but undernourished modern concept of classificatory information is, at least to a significant degree, a reification of the cultural values and instrumental logic valued by elite masculine cultures.

THE DIGITAL DIVIDE AS GENDER DIVIDE

Current research efforts to identify the gendered constituents of the so-called digital divide and to reform gender-biased educational practices in mathematics, engineering, and computer science; gender inequities in access to information technologies; gender-based segmentation of technical skills; and

Table 4.1 Comparison of Constituent Assumptions

Maruyama's Concept of "Classificatory Information"
Constituent Assumptions:

- Discrete: domain consists of substances or objects that obey the law of identity and mutual exclusiveness.
- Hierarchical: substances and objects within the domain can be classified into a hierarchy of categories, subcategories, and supercategories.
- Information value of a "message" increases with the categorical specification of the message, or a message's information value is greater if it describes an event that has a lower probability (for example, "It snowed in Florida in summer" as opposed to "It snowed in Quebec during the winter").
- Information is not context-bound: a piece of information has an objective meaning which is universally understandable, without reference to other pieces of information.
- Consistency and transparency: discrepancies within messages or differences between messages must have been caused by error.
- Intolerance of ambiguity: discrepant positions should be discarded as inaccurate.

Gilligan's Concept of "Morality of Rules"
Constituent Assumptions:

- Thinking is goal-oriented.
- A hierarchical order of (universal) rules guides decision-making.

- Decisions are made by identifying available means and applying the rules to identify the appropriate (moral/utilitarian) choice.
- Transparency: available means can be articulated.
- Consistency: articulation of means involves resolution of ambiguities.
- Hierarchy: the hierarchy of rules is used to infer relations among alternatives, and the rules are used as templates for understanding new, unusual, or ambiguous situations.
- Principles of justice, equality, and fairness are formalized in the rules, and decision-making is conceived as an attempt to realize these values.
- Systematic, internally consistent, and rational.

Gilligan's Concept of "Ethic of Responsibility"
Constituent Assumptions:

- Nonhierarchical: embedded in "web-like relations" rather than hierarchies or formal rules.
- Contextual: emphasizes contextual reasoning and equivocation.
- Permeable categories: stresses care, attachment, affiliation, and interdependence.
- Conceives of power as nurturance.
- Embraces principles of equity and nonviolence; defines self in relationships with others.
- Systematic, internally consistent, and rational.

Sources: Magoroh Maruyama, "Information and Communication in Poly-Epistemological Systems," in *The Myths of Information,* ed. Kathleen Woodward (Milwaukee: University of Wisconsin Press, 1980), 28–40; and Carol Gilligan, *In a Different Voice* (Cambridge, Mass.: Harvard University Press, 1982).

gendered mentoring systems in science and engineering deal with symptoms, albeit very important symptoms. Reformist framings of these research initiatives seldom adequately grasp or treat the causes of these inequities.[54] Explorations of the experiential—tacit and tactile—dimensions of technological cultures probe more deeply. This includes research that examines the role that

adolescent "tinkering" plays in developing mechanical interests and aptitudes; male and female patterns of participation in Internet-based communications; the prevalence of masculinist "search and destroy" narratives in
video and computer games; the masculine subcultures of computing, including the close links between technophilia and technoporn; and the cultivation
of gendered differences in consumer desire in technomarketing.[55]

Nevertheless, there appears to be significant resistance to pressing the findings of such research into deeper syntheses, which would raise larger and
more radical questions about the relationship of technology and society. This
synthetic move would not only interrogate the significant role technology
plays in reproducing gendered, class, and racially based social hierarchies; it
would raise more general questions about decision-making in democratic societies, including decisions about technological design, assessment, and deployment.

The very conceptualization of the digital divide presupposes that the ambivalence that many women and girls experience in relation to technology is a defect
or deficit in them. The mission of these initiatives is to extinguish the ambivalence and fill the void with cyber-values and skills. The possibility that women's
ambivalence about the values built into the social designs of the digital revolution might have some merit is either not considered or only peripherally acknowledged. Framed within the either/or logic of domination, the message, cum
directive, to women and girls is clear: adapt to the imperatives of informatics or
you will be left behind in poverty and dependency. Gear up or shut up.

How the gap will be closed—what means will most efficiently bring females up to speed and into conformity with the digital culture—is open to
question within the discourse of the digital divide, but the end, digitalization,
is not. Yet, even research sponsored by groups dedicated to closing the divide
shows that many girls are actively resisting their initiatives; consider the following passage from a report on AAUW Educational Foundation's Commission on Technology, Gender, and Teacher Education:

> Girls say, in effect, "We can, but we don't want to." These findings, the com-
> mission says, can't be dismissed as girls' anxiety or incompetence. Girls are
> pointing to critical deficits in the computer culture that require attention.[56]

Digital divide initiatives are, however, dedicated to *re-forming* girls, not
technologies.

To some extent, the tone-deafness of liberal digital dividers is an artifact of
their methods: that is, they rely heavily on the protocols of empirical social
science that, of course, privileges classificatory information and research
questions and data-gathering techniques that can be numerically coded and
crunched with a minimal N = 500.

In this regard, European and Canadian researchers have been more imaginative and open to methodological experimentation than Americans in conceptualizing and researching technological divides. Using social constructivist approaches to document gendered constituents in design, deployment, and use of information technologies, they have produced more richly nuanced and frankly paradoxical data than their U.S. counterparts. Yet, paradoxical findings are what one would expect, given many, though not all, women's professed ambivalences and resistances to informatics. European and Canadian data does, however, indicate to a very significant extent that information technologies are technologies of gender. That is, it supports the conclusion that the primary currents within the social designs and uses of these technologies produce, not simply reproduce, gendered hierarchies.[57] Women who resist their uncritical acceptance are therefore not simply reactionary or recalcitrant; they are frequently acting, whether consciously or intuitively, in their own self-interest. When women have been brought into the production process, it has been mainly in systems development rather than in product design.[58] And they have often found that once they have helped design women-friendly computer systems, fewer women are needed to run them.[59] Women have also, of course, been used as tools for displacing higher paid and/or unionized male workers in automation processes, for example female secretaries replacing male typists in the early part of the twentieth century and female word processors displacing male lithographers in the later part of the century.[60]

Ambivalence does, however, make messy arguments. It therefore needs to be acknowledged that there are also women technophiles, including both self-styled cyber-girls eager to be incorporated within the regimes of informatics and critical feminist cyber-activists who use digital technologies to critique informatics. Moreover, many, possibly even most, women, including myself, as well as many men are, to varying degrees, genuinely ambivalent about digital technologies, welcoming some aspects of their incorporation in contemporary life and apprehensive about others. Moreover, not every top-down institutional initiative to bring women workers into info design produces cyber-systems that are counterproductive to their interests. When the domestic U.S. market for male computer users was saturated, the computer industry, acting purely from profit motives, did nonetheless produce more user-friendly computers to increase sales to women, who typically have less leisure time than men to use computers for entertainment purposes. Similarly, the Florence project has even demonstrated that digital technologies can be used to advance traditional feminine caring agendas. This project created conditions where nurses could articulate the caring and communicative facets of their work, and press for a new computerized work system, which valorized these qualities and affirmed an understanding of their work that amplified their professionalism.[61] These are, however, countercurrents within a complex set of layered meanings and practices that usually reproduce gendered hierarchies.

THE FEMINIST DIVIDE

Feminists themselves are divided over the digital divide. Dale Spender, for example, maintains that we are in a period of profound cultural transformation comparable to the advent of print.[62] According to Spender, early print culture secured hierarchical values and structures of masculine culture, which systematically disadvantaged women in the ensuing five hundred years; she believes that digitalization is currently repeating this process. Therefore, Spender argues, women must change the signs and appropriate the new technologies to feminist ends. In her view, women do indeed need to gear up and they must do it fast because the information revolution is already a *fait accompli*.

In contrast, Ellen Balka argues that when cyber-feminism is divorced from rigorous and ongoing interrogations and assessments of technological impacts on social life including distributions of global power and resources, labor processes, human relationships, and structures of knowledge, it surrenders, de facto, to capitalism's antidemocratic imperatives.[63] Balka concedes Spender's point that wired women can communicate more widely and rapidly than ever before, and without malestream gatekeepers censoring their messages. They can, in effect, use online communications for feminist organizing. Yet, Balka points out that women "sitting alone in front of web-ready computers" are having a far different experience and social impact than women who are organizing in social movements and intervening in the world: in technology design, assessment, policy processes, and in socially responsible forms of technological implementation.[64]

Where Spender advocates a strategic, remedial, feminist approach that appropriates the means—the tools and skills of the digital revolution—Balka calls for more radical feminist and democratic interrogations of the end: the digital revolution. These two positions are not, in my judgment, as mutually exclusive as Balka's framing appears to suggest. To be sure, in a genuinely democratic society, technology assessment debates would be ongoing and debate would *always* precede social implementation. There have been no such democratic debates about digitalization in the United States; the Clinton-Gore Administration's National Information Initiative, which in 1993 made digitalization a national priority, was a top-down policy and one that was intended to have global, not merely national, reach. Yet, the need for the kinds of debates Balka calls for remains as urgent as ever. The irony is that it is almost impossible to conceive of any way of mounting those debates today without relying heavily on digital technologies and skills. Thus, feminist engagement with and resistance to informatics is now a both/and proposition that draws upon the commuting metaphor developed earlier in this chapter. Feminists need to commute between a position that allows them to ask the crucial, radical, feminist, and democratic questions Balka poses; at the same time, they need to appropriate digital skills to feminist ends, as Spender suggests, but appropriate them without being appropriated by them.

We are now far enough into the social implementation of the technovisions of the digerati to see that digitalization is a fairly transparent synonym for globalization, cum expanding capitalist (and American) hegemony. And that technological convergence is also homologous with economic convergence or vertical integration of information industries.[65] It is now apparent that women and children, wired or not, are among the primary losers in the newly wired world.[66] Beyond the digital divide of skills per se, the economic exploitation of women and girls within the specialized, export-based labor markets of developing countries is a common, even defining, feature of the global economy; the Internet has rationalized and globalized the marketing of the sex trades and sexual tourism; and websites featuring pornographic representations of women and children are among the most popular (most hit) sites on the Internet. Therefore, feminist and critical theorists must radically interrogate the roles that digitized information and digital screens, mediated by commercial sources, are increasingly playing in our lives, simulating and displacing "live" interaction and community building. In addition, we must render the men behind the screens visible, legible, and accountable to the procedures of democratic legitimization.[67]

SEMIOTIC OPPORTUNITIES

Remedial education and feminist boycotts of digital technologies may have some roles to play in these struggles, but they are not solutions. What is needed instead (or in addition) is a bold rethinking of the relationship of technology and society for, as Robert Romanyshyn points out:

> Technology is not just a series of events, which occurs over there on the side of the [material] world. It is, on the contrary, the enactment of the human imagination in the world. In building a technological world we enact and live out our experiences of awe and wonder, our fantasies of service and control, our images of exploration and destruction, our dreams of hope and nightmares of despair.[68]

Technology is "the creation, the making, the working out of a shared cultural dream."[69] The digital dividers are right in seeking to broaden the base of those who share in working out the cultural dream. But they are wrong, anti-democratic, in attempting to impose the dreams of a small, technocratic elite on the rest of the planet. Today we require nothing less than a renaissance in the ways we conceive, design, create, code, theorize, and use technologies, gender, information, epistemology, and communications.

The challenges new feminist epistemologies pose to mainstream and critical communications research on technology and society are, of course, only part of a much larger international and interdisciplinary response to the perceived depletion or corruption of the legacy of the Western Enlightenment. Poststructuralism, postmodernism, and some forms of social constructivism share feminism's skepticism of universal and universalizing claims about existence, language, reason, science, and progress; these perspectives also conceive of their critical projects as forms of resistance to the reified fictions of the naturalized, essentialized *human* of humanism that has historically denied the subjectivity of women, blacks, sexual minorities, and members of non-Western cultures.

In short, a broad and varied intellectual constituency is struggling to articulate epistemological stances that recognize and conserve the irreducible differences and radical multiplicity of local cultures. This project is viewed as urgent in light of the homogenizing thrust of globalization. Donna Haraway describes the stakes of this struggle:

> "[O]ur" problem is, how to have simultaneously an account of radical historical contingency for all knowledge claims and knowing subjects, a critical practice for recognizing our own "semiotic technologies" for making meanings and a no nonsense commitment to faithful accounts of a "real" world; one that can be partially shared and that is friendly to earthwide projects of finite freedom, adequate material abundance, modest meaning in suffering, and limited happiness.[70]

The critique of gendered technologies and information theory developed in this chapter indicates that Western/modernist/masculinist "semiotic technologies" have historically excluded female-gendered beings, modes of reasoning, and skills from their discourses. Further, this critique indicates that remedial efforts toward inclusion continue to be based on conquest models that "ask women to exchange major aspects of their gender identity for a masculine version without prescribing a similar 'degendering' process for men."[71]

Poststructuralists such as Jacques Lacan and Jacques Derrida would argue that such exclusions and exchanges are inescapable; they claim that the feminine is characterized by the impossibility of representation.[72] The French feminist version of this argument conceives of language as a "binary trap"; the most radical form of the argument mandates creation of a new language (*l'ecriture feminine*) secured in the prelinguistic imagery of female bodily pleasures and drives.[73] Anglo-American feminists have been less metaphysical and more pragmatic in confronting the problem of (mis)representation. They have conceived women's languages as submerged or residual practices residing largely outside of the discourses of power (and theory), but nevertheless integral to the creation and sustenance of the "everyday world."[74] Rather than an empty term in what Helene Cixous and Catherine Clement call a "phallogocentric" language, Anglo-American feminists maintain that malestream languages and philosophies contain well-established conventions for representing women.[75] These conventions inscribe woman as "embodied" (albeit from the limited perspective of the male gaze).

Feminist materialism treats this sexist precedent as a semiotic opportunity— a dialectical opening or staging ground—for making a necessary epistemological correction. As the ones "who are not allowed *not* to have a body," a finite position, and situationally embedded knowledges, female thinkers are well placed within the struggle to articulate responsible post-Cartesian and perhaps postmodern theories of knowledge.[76] Haraway describes the paradox: "We need the power of modern critical theories of how meanings and bodies get made, not in order to deny meanings and bodies, but in order to build meanings and bodies that have a chance for life."[77] In short, feminist critics need to use these critical theories to document the embodiment of male knowledge, including what Nancy Hartsock describes as abstract masculinity.[78]

The immediate feminist linguistic, artistic, and technological project requires women to claim the power to reinscribe and re-present women's experience of embodiment and skill.[79] The larger feminist, poststructuralist, and postmodernist epistemological projects require recognition of the embodiment of all knowledge: recognition that white men do not have the eyes of gods or cyclops. Like the vision of women, walleyed pike, and turkey vultures, the vision of human males is embodied, finite, and situationally embedded. No one sees from nowhere. Men, even accomplished scholars like Bacon, Descartes, Turing, and Shannon, view the world from specific human vantage points. Therefore, we require epistemologies that can account for positioning: what Haraway calls "situated" or "embodied" knowledges. We need to be able to locate the sources of all knowledge claims in order to rationally assess their truth value. Recognition of the situational embeddedness of knowledge does not require acceptance of relativism or rejection of the quest for "objective" knowledge. Haraway points out that

the alternative to relativism is not totalization and single vision, which is always finally the unmarked category whose power depends on systematic narrowing and obscuring. The alternative to relativism is partial, locatable, critical knowledges sustaining the possibility of webs of connections called solidarity in politics and shared conversations in epistemology. Relativism is a way of being

nowhere while claiming to be everywhere equally. The "equality" of positioning is a denial of responsibility and critical inquiry. Relativism is the perfect mirror twin of totalization in the ideologies of objectivity; both deny the stakes in
location, embodiment, and partial perspective; both make it impossible to see
well. Relativism and totalization are both "god tricks" promising vision from
everywhere and nowhere equally and fully, common myths in rhetorics surrounding Science. But it is precisely in the politics and epistemology of partial
perspectives that the possibility of sustained, rational, objective inquiry rests.[80]

Accepting epistemologies that recognize the embodiment and situational and
linguistic embeddedness of knowledge does not require rejecting science. To
the contrary, it demands finally that we display fidelity to a long-professed
but too seldom-honored covenant of modern science: the idea that science is
an ongoing, open-ended, and fundamentally democratic process that is never
subject to final closure, a process that is fueled by criticism and delighted by
surprise. Within the objectivity of situated knowledge, there are no unprob-
lematic "objects."[81] All objects and observations are mediated by language,
culture, and vantage points. The purpose of conducting semiological guerrilla
warfare within the territories of mainstream science is not to bring down the
house of science but to remodel and expand it: to create what Harding calls a
"successor science."[82]

ALTERNATIVE DESIGN AESTHETICS

What would this successor science do for social science? It would open up an
enormous array of new research questions, and it would radically alter the
ways we approach and frame those questions. It would make epistemological
and linguistic reflexivity routine features of all our inquiries. It would restore
methodology to the privileged position it held in nineteenth-century articulations of warrants for the "human sciences."[83] It would not require wholesale
rejection of the achievements of mainstream theory and research. The
Promethean vision that secures the achievements of Bacon, Descartes, Darwin, Turing, and Shannon is skewed, partial, and incomplete, but it is also extraordinarily acute, insightful, and productive. A successor science would not
discard the man with his myopia; however, it would require regrounding and
resituating the claims of mainstream science within a responsible theory of
knowledge. That is, it would provide a warrant for fully embracing what
Bloor calls "the strong program" in the sociology of knowledge.[84]

This successor science would reopen the questions and perhaps reclaim the
values marginalized by the twin triumphs of industrialism and instrumental
rationality. Instead of settling for the fast foods of the easily processed and en-

coded message systems of classificatory information, it would provide entry to the lavish banquet of research possibilities provided by more holistic reintegrations of "classificatory," "contextual," "relational," "relevance," and other information and communicative modes and practices. It would empower ongoing interrogations of the design codes and communicative models contained within plans for global information systems. In sum, it would do what male critics of instrumentalism such as Max Weber, Karl Jaspers, Karl Mannheim, Max Horkheimer, Theodor Adomo, Lewis Mumford, and Jurgen Habermas have long recommended: subordinate instrumental or "functional" forms of rationality to the claims of "substantive" rationality.[85] That is, it would require us to reflect upon and justify the ends as well as the means of technological decisions.

What kinds of information sciences and technologies would a successor science support? Beyond debates that relate to the future of reproductive technologies, feminist theory has not, to my knowledge, directly addressed this question in any comprehensive way; although feminist science fiction, like science fiction generally, is proving to be a fertile ground for reimagining technologies. At this point, however, history may still be a better guide than fiction.

Technologies are extensions of structures of power and capital as well as derivatives of scientific and engineering discourses. Women and men in Western cultures have, of course, been differentially situated in relation to structures of wealth and power. As a result of their subordinate position in these relations, women have developed alternative information networks and conceived of alternative social designs, for example, witchcraft, keening rites, old wives' tales, midwifery, motherwit, communal laundering activities, sewing circles, moral uplift movements, and consciousness-raising groups. They have created and circulated handcrafted information systems: recipes, home remedies, gossip, samplers, quilts, letters, publications, performances, and works of art. Women have also "misused," or reconfigured, malestream information technologies to serve alternative purposes. Thus, for example, Lana Rakow points out that the telephone was initially conceived as a tool of business; American women transformed it into a household necessity.[86] Judy Smith, Ellen Balka, and Dale Spender report that similar processes are at work today as women use computer networking to accommodate feminist chatting and organizing.[87] That is, women's uses or "misuses" of technology affirm Liesbet van Zoonen's claim that "the meaning and social significance of technology is not pregiven but established in ongoing historically and culturally specific discursive practices."[88] Within the residual, sometimes resistant feminine subcultures, the masculine social designs built into technologies have been variously accepted, rejected, perfected, or ignored.

Similarly feminist-informed technologies would presumably incorporate elements drawn from these alternative networks, designs, artifacts, and uses. Women's residual cultural articulations of principles of social order have historically relied on decentralized, egalitarian decision-making processes; they emphasize context, personal responsibility, and interactional processes in mediating formal rules; they treat skills and knowledge as resources to be pooled to enhance group efforts; they avoid hierarchical arrangements and formal divisions of labor; when divisions of labor are introduced, horizontal rather than vertical structures are often adopted so that creative and routine aspects of task forces can be distributed among all members.[89]

These principles reflect gendered differences in orientations to power and authority: where men in groups assume that a general, captain, coach, or dean will lead the charge, women have, at least historically, conceived of power as a process rather than a privilege of office or person. Thus, for example, conceiving of power from a feminist perspective, Hartsock defines it in terms of empowerment: "To lead is to be at the center of a group rather than in front of others."[90]

A feminist design aesthetic would presumably favor development of decentralized, egalitarian, accessible, process-oriented information technologies that advance expressive as well as instrumental values.[91] Such an aesthetic would subvert, invert, or divert the design logic that has fostered development of the capital-intensive information systems, which currently facilitate global control systems. It would challenge the single-minded, malestream commitment to what Mumford calls "authoritarian technics": system-centered, immensely powerful, but inherently unstable technologies.[92] Instead, a feminist design aesthetic would presumably seek to realize the telos of "democratic technics": it would articulate social designs that incorporate human-centered, diverse, resourceful, and durable technologies.[93]

To be sure, the virtues of suppressed groups can be, and often are, overestimated and romanticized by standpoint epistemologies. Prisoners see the world through bars, and their visions of freedom are shaped by that perspective, which is both the merit and limitations of their epistemological locations. Truly democratic technics do not replace one skewed vision with another. Rather, all positions need to be open to question; what is missing in current technologies of power needs to be articulated within fora for power-talk that monitor, negate, and counter, insofar as humanly possible, all gender, racial, class, and other forms of discursive privilege. And technological designs secured within democratic values need to be envisioned and developed. Pie in the sky? Perhaps, but then so are most innovations and virtually all eutopian visions before they become realities.

There are signs that a new, post-Promethean sensibility is now taking form at the frontiers of science. Although this sensibility does not identify itself as feminist, it is nevertheless motivated by attempts to transcend the limits of dualism and to create models for construction of scientific knowledge that are contextual and connective rather than binary and reductive. The new "sciences of complexity" conceive of scientific modeling in ways that are more consonant with feminist approaches than were Baconian or Cartesian science.[94] Within computer science, complexity emphasizes parallel over serial processes, neural networks that facilitate learning and are self-correcting, fuzzy logics rather than Cartesian reductions, and holistic modeling that can accommodate relevance, contextual, and relational informations as well as classificatory information. To be sure, these new models also have darker sides; the ghosts of scientific conquistadors still lurk within them.[95] Nonetheless they do represent a movement towards more conceptually rich ways of conceiving of nature and our position within it.[96]

A design aesthetic that is "friendly to earthwide projects of finite freedom, adequate material abundance, modest meaning in suffering, and limited happiness" *cannot simply substitute one partial perspective* for another. We face problems that require global action: environmental contamination, global warming, famine, and nuclear threats that have multiplied rather than dissipated since the end of the Cold War. Instrumental thinking created these problems, and instrumental thinking will be required to redress them; but, unless instrumentalism is resituated within grammars of human motives, contexts, relationships, values, concepts of community, democratic dialogue, and social responsibility, we are all imperiled by the emergent global structures of information-capitalism.

NOTES

1. Zillah Eisenstein, ed., *Capitalist Patriarchy and the Case for Socialist Feminism* (New York: Monthly Review Press, 1979); Annette Kuhn and Ann Marie Wolpe, eds., *Feminism and Materialism: Women and Modes of Production* (London: Routledge & Kegan Paul, 1978); Pam Linn, "Gender Stereotypes, Technology Stereotypes" in *Gender and Expertise*, ed. Maureen McNeil (London: Free Association Books, 1987); Mary O'Brien, *Reproducing the World: Essays in Feminist Theory* (Boulder: Westview: 1989); and Dorothy E. Smith, *The Everyday World as Problematic: A Feminist Sociology* (London: Open University/Milton Keynes, 1988).

2. Feminist informed rewritings of the history of technology are beginning to fill in the blank spaces in this historical record. See, for example, Ruth S. Cowan's groundbreaking *More Work for Mother: The Ironies of Household Technology from the Open Hearth to the Microwave* (New York: Basic Books, 1983); Anne Balsamo, *Technologies of the Gendered Body: Reading Cyborg Women* (Durham, N.C.: Duke University Press, 1996); Cynthia Cockburn, *Machinery of Dominance: Women, Men and Technical Know-How* (London: Pluto Press, 1985); Cynthia Cockburn and Susan

Ormrod, *Gender and Technology in the Making* (Thousand Oaks, Calif.: Sage, 1993); Ann Gray, *Video Playtime: The Gendering of a Leisure Technology* (London: Routledge, 1992); Sally Hacker, *Pleasure, Power and Technology: Some Tales of Gender, Engineering and the Cooperative Workplace* (New York: Routledge, 1989); Jean Rothschild, *Machina Ex Dea: Feminist Perspectives on Technology* (New York: Pergamon Press, 1983); and Judy Wajcman, *Feminism Confronts Technology* (New York: Routledge, 1989).

3. See Cheris Kramarae, "Gotta Go Myrtle, Technology's at the Door," in *Technology and Women's Voices: Keeping in Touch*, ed. Cheris Kramarae (New York: Routledge & Kegan Paul, 1988); Linn, "Gender Stereotypes, Technology Stereotypes"; McNeil, "*Gender and Expertise*, introduction; Rothschild, *Machina Ex Dea*, introduction; and Jan Zimmerman, *The Technological Woman: Interfacing with Tomorrow* (New York: Praeger, 1983).

4. For a provocative interpretation of the multiple connotations of the coding of women as "consumers" of technologies, see Campbell and Wheeler, "Filofaxions," *Marxism Today* (December 1988): 32–33. Even some revisionary histories of technology unreflexively adopt mainstream framing conventions that render women invisible. Thus, for example, a widely influential 1987 volume entitled *The Social Construction of Technological Systems,* ed. Wiebe E. Bijker, Thomas P. Hughes, and Trevor Pinch (Cambridge, Mass.: MIT Press, 1987) ignores the question of gender except for brief references to women as a "social group" that may require special consideration in explaining some parts of the development of the bicycle.

5. Jane Caputo, "Seeing Elephants: The Myths of Phallotechnology," *Feminist Studies* 14, no. 4 (Fall 1988): 487–524.

6. Murray Edelman, *Political Language: Words That Succeed and Politics That Fail* (New York: Academic Press, 1977); Marike Finlay, *Powermatics: A Discursive Critique of New Communications Technology* (London: Routledge & Kegan Paul, 1987); Cary Nelson and Lawrence Grossberg, *Marxism and the Interpretation of Culture* (Urbana: University of Illinois Press, 1988); Herbert I. Schiller, *Who Knows: Information in the Age of the Fortune 500* (Norwood, N.J.: Ablex, 1981); Dallas Smythe, *Dependency Road: Communications, Capitalism, Consciousness, and Canada* (Norwood, N.J.: Ablex, 1981); and Dallas Smythe, "Needs Before Tools? The Illusions of Electronic Democracy," paper presented at the annual meeting of the International Communication Association, Honolulu, May 28, 1985.

7. Harry Braverman, *Labor and Monopoly Capital: The Degradation of Work in the Twentieth Century* (New York: Monthly Review Press, 1974); J. W. Freiberg, *The French Press: Class, State and Ideology* (New York: Praeger, 1981); and Frank Webster and Kevin Robins, *Information Technology: A Luddite Analysis* (Norwood, N.J.: Ablex, 1986).

8. Cockbum, *Machinery of Dominance*; Sonia Liff, "Gender Relations in the Construction of Jobs," in *Gender and Expertise*, ed. Maureen McNeil (London: Free Association Books, 1987); and Jane Nash and Maria Patricia Fernandez-Kelly, *Women, Men, and the International Division of Labor* (Albany: State University of New York Press, 1983).

9. Hubert L. Dreyfus, *What Computers Can't Do: The Limits of Artificial Intelligence* (New York: Harper & Row, 1979); Jean-François Lyotard, *The Postmodern*

Condition: A Report on Knowledge (Minneapolis: University of Minnesota Press, 1984); John Durham Peters, "Information: Notes Toward a Critical History," *Journal of Communication Inquiry* 12, no. 2 (1988): 9–23; and Joseph Weizenbaum, *Computer Power and Human Reason* (San Francisco: W. H. Freeman, 1976).

10. Annette Kuhn and Ann Marie Wolpe, eds., *Feminism and Materialism: Women and Modes of Production* (London: Routledge & Kegan Paul, 1978); Jean Baker Miller, *Toward a New Psychology of Women* (London: Penguin, 1978); Sheila Rowbotham, *Hidden from History: Rediscovering Women in History from the Seventeenth Century to the Present* (New York: Random House, 1974); Carroll Smith-Rosenberg, "The Feminist Reconstruction of History," *Academe* (September/October 1983): 26–37; and Eli Zaretsky, *Capitalism, the Family, and Personal Life* (London: Pluto Press, 1976).

11. Nelson and Grossberg, *Marxism and the Interpretation of Culture.*

12. Kramarae, *Technology and Women's Voices,* preface.

13. Chandra Mohanty, "Under Western Eyes," *Boundary* 2, no. 3 (1984): 333–58; and Gayatri Chakravorty Spivak, *In Other Worlds: Essays in Cultural Politics* (New York, Routledge, 1988). Constitution of the category of non-Western peoples as other "others" is, of course, highly problematic, as postcolonial studies repeatedly demonstrate. Within the writings of white feminists, this discursive practice replicates the appropriationist frames of the Western (masculinist) logics.

14. Kathy Ferguson, *The Feminist Case against Bureaucracy* (Philadelphia: Temple University Press, 1984); and Dorothy E. Smith, *The Everyday World as Problematic.*

15. Mikhail Bakhtin, *The Dialogic Imagination* (Austin: University of Texas Press, 1981).

16. Umberto Eco, *Travels in Hyper-Reality* (New York: Harcourt Brace Jovanovich, 1986); and Bette J. Kauffman, *Women Artist: Communicating Social Identity,* Ph.D. diss., University of Pennsylvania, 1990. The "commuter" image is developed by Kauffman in describing the psychic and practical strategies women artists use in pursuing careers within male-dominated art worlds.

17. Carol Cohn, "Sex and Death in the Rational World of Defense Intellectuals," *Signs* 12, no. 4 (1987): 687–718; Brian Easlea, *Fathering the Unthinkable: Masculinity, Scientists and the Nuclear Arms Race* (London: Pluto Press, 1983); Hilary Rose, "Hand, Brain and Heart: A Feminist Epistemology for the Natural Sciences," *Signs* 9, no. 1 (1983): 73–90; and Bill Joy, "Why the Future Doesn't Need Us," *Wired* (April 2000): 1–15.

18. An excellent demonstration of the advantages of this kind of "commuting" is provided by Cohn in "Sex and Death in the Rational World of Defense Intellectuals," in which she undertakes a provocative deconstruction and critique of the role played by metaphors of sex and death in articulations of the "rational World" of defense intellectuals. Cohn uses the trope of a spy to describe her work in order to retain a critical perspective while traveling between the two worlds of feminism and militarism.

19. Susan Bordo, "The Cartesian Masculinization of Thought," *Signs* 11, no. 3 (1986): 439–56; Sandra Harding, *The Science Question in Feminism* (Ithaca, N.Y.: Cornell University Press, 1986); Evelyn Fox Keller, *Reflections on Gender and Science* (New Haven, Conn.: Yale University Press, 1985); Carolyn Merchant, *The Death of Nature: Women, Ecology and the Scientific Revolution* (New York: Harper

& Row, 1980); and David F. Noble, *A World Without Women: The Christian Clerical Culture of Western Science* (New York.: Alfred A. Knopf, 1992). My brief assessment of the growing literature on gender, science, and epistemology cannot begin to do justice to the diversity or complexity of the arguments developed by feminists, historians of science, and philosophers. For an extended analysis of some of the generative texts, see chapter 5. For a current assessment of the prospects for and controversies within feminist approaches to science, see *Signs* 26, no. 2 (2001), including Sylvia Walby, "Against Epistemological Chasms: The Science Question in Feminism Revisited," 485–509; Sandra Harding, "Comment: Can Democratic Values and Interests Ever Play a Rationally Justified Role in the Evaluation of Scientific Work?" 511–25; Joey Sprague, "Comment: Structured Knowledge and Strategic Methodology," 527–36; and Sylvia Walby, "Reply to Harding and Sprague," 537–40.

20. Donna Haraway, "A Manifesto for Cyborgs: Science, Technology, and Socialist Feminism in the 1980s," *Socialist Review* 80 (1985): 65–107; and Carol P. MacCormack, "Nature, Culture and Gender: A Critique," in *Nature, Culture and Gender*, ed. Carol P. MacCormack and Marilyn Strathern (Cambridge: Cambridge University Press, 1980).

21. Bordo, "The Cartesian Masculinization of Thought"; Marike Finlay, *Powermatics: A Discursive Critique of New Communications Technology* (London: Routledge & Kegan Paul, 1987); Grant Fjermedal, *The Tomorrow Makers: A Brave New World of Living-Brain Machines* (New York: Macmillan, 1986); Barbara Garson, *The Electronic Sweatshop* (New York: Simon & Schuster, 1988); Jurgen Habermas, *Knowledge and Human Interests* (Boston: Beacon Press, 1971); Max Horkheimer, *Eclipse of Reason* (New York: Seabury Press, 1974); Max Horkheimer and Theodor W. Adorno, *Dialectic of Enlightenment* (New York: Herder and Herder, 1972); Carolyn Merchant, *The Death of Nature: Women, Ecology and the Scientific Revolution* (New York: Harper & Row, 1980); and Jean Baker Miller, *Toward a New Psychology of Women* (London: Penguin, 1978).

22. Bordo, "The Cartesian Masculinization of Thought"; Keller, *Reflections on Gender and Science*; and Merchant, *The Death of Nature*.

23. Ruth Bleier, ed., *Feminist Approaches to Science* (New York: Pergamon Press, 1986); Donna Haraway, "A Manifesto for Cyborgs: Science, Technology, and Socialist Feminism in the 1980s," *Socialist Review* 80 (1985): 65–107; and Donna Haraway, "'Situated Knowledge': The Science Question in Feminism and the Privilege of Partial Perspective," *Feminist Studies* 14, no. 3 (1988): 575–99; Sandra Harding, *The Science Question in Feminism*; Sandra Harding and Merrill B. Hintikka, eds., *Discovering Reality* (Dordrecht, Netherlands: D. Reidel, 1983); Keller, *Reflections on Gender and Science*; and Evelyn Fox Keller and Catherine E. Grontowski, "The Mind's Eye," in *Discovering Reality*, ed. Sandra Harding and Merrill B. Hintikka.

24. Harding, *The Science Question in Feminism*. This claim is secured in the linguistic postulate, which asserts that phonemes and signs achieve intelligibility only through difference; in Saussure's words, "whatever distinguishes one sign from the others constitutes it." Saussure quoted by Terrence Hawkes, *Structuralism and Semiotics* (Berkeley: University of California Press, 1977), 28.

25. Donna Haraway, "Situated Knowledge."

26. Nancy Armstrong, "The Gender Bind: Women and the Disciplines," *Genders* 3 (Fall 1988): 1–23.

27. Catherine A. MacKinnon, "Feminism, Marxism, Method and the State: An Agenda for Theory," *Signs* 7, no. 3 (Spring 1982): 515–44.

28. Ruth Hubbard, Mary Sue Henifin, and Barbara Fried, eds., *Biological Woman—The Convenient Myth* (Cambridge, Mass.: Schenkman, 1982).

29. Sarah Blaffer Hrdy, "Empathy, Polandry, and the Myth of the Coy Female" in *Feminist Approaches to Science*, ed. Ruth Bleier (New York: Pergamon Press, 1986), 119–46.

30. Keller and Grontowski, "The Mind's Eye."

31. Ann Oakley, "Interviewing Women: A Contradiction in Terms," in *Doing Feminist Research*, ed. Helen Roberts (London: Routledge & Kegan Paul, 1981).

32. Bleier, *Feminist Approaches to Science*. For a sampling of the backlash, see Richard Dawkins, *Unweaving the Rainbow: Science, Delusion and Appetite for Wonder* (Boston: Houghton Mifflin, 1998); and especially Paul R. Gross and Norman Levitt, *Higher Superstition: The Academic Left and Its Quarrels with Science* (Baltimore: Johns Hopkins, 1994).

33. Marcia Millman and Rosabeth Moss Kanter, *Another Voice: Feminist Perspectives on Social Life and Social Science* (Garden City, N.Y.: Anchor Doubleday, 1975).

34. James Hillman, *The Myth of Analysis* (New York: Harper & Row, 1972).

35. Lana Rakow, "From the Feminization of Public Relations to the Promise of Feminism," paper presented at the annual meeting of the International Communication Association, San Francisco, May 26, 1989.

36. David Bloor, *Knowledge and Social Imagery* (London: Routledge & Kegan Paul, 1977).

37. Claude Shannon, "The Mathematical Theory of Communication," in *The Mathematical Theory of Communication*, ed. Claude Shannon and Warren Weaver (Urbana: University of Illinois Press, 1964, original 1948).

38. Everett M. Rogers, "Communication: A Field of Isolated Islands of Thought," in *Rethinking Communication, Volume I Paradigm Issues*, ed. Brenda Dervin, Lawrence Grossberg, Barbara J. O'Keefe, and Ellen Wartella (Newbury Park, Calif.: Sage, 1989).

39. Rogers, "Communication."

40. James R. Beniger, *The Control Revolution* (Cambridge, Mass.: Harvard University Press, 1986); and John Durham Peters, "Information: Notes Toward a Critical History," *Journal of Communication Inquiry* 12, no. 2 (1988): 9–23.

41. George Johnson, "Claude Shannon," obituary, *New York Times*, 27 February 2001, <www.newyorktimes.com> (accessed March 14, 2001).

42. Bordo, "The Cartesian Masculinization of Thought."

43. H. R. Trevor-Roper, *The European Witch-Craze of the Sixteenth and Seventeenth Centuries* (New York: Harper & Row, 1969).

44. David Bolter, *Turing's Man: Western Culture in the Computer Age* (Chapel Hill: University of North Carolina Press, 1984); and Hans Moravec, *Mind Children: The Future of Robot and Human Intelligence* (Cambridge, Mass.: Harvard University Press, 1988).

45. Bolter, Turing's Man; Dreyfus, *What Computers Can't Do*; Fjermedal, *The Tomorrow Makers*; Marvin Minsky, *Society of Mind* (New York: Simon & Schuster, 1987); Moravec, *Mind Children*; Sherry Turkle, *The Second Self: Computers and the Human Spirit* (New York: Simon & Schuster, 1984); Joseph Weizenbaum, *Computer Power and Human Reason* (San Francisco: W. H. Freeman, 1976); and Norbert Wiener, *God and Golem, Inc. A Comment on Certain Points Where Cybernetics Impinges on Religion* (Cambridge, Mass.: MIT Press, 1964).

46. Magoroh Maruyama, "Information and Communication in Poly-Epistemological Systems," in *The Myths of Information*, ed. Kathleen Woodward (Milwaukee: University of Wisconsin Press, 1980), 28–40.

47. Wilhelm Dilthey, *Pattern and Meaning in History*, ed. H. P. Rickman (New York: Harper & Row, 1962); and John Durham Peters, "Information."

48. Sue Curry Jansen, "Mind Machines, Myth, Metaphor, and Scientific Imagination," paper presented at the annual meeting of the International Communication Association, San Francisco, May 26, 1989; Paul N. Edwards, "Border Wars: The Science and Politics of Artificial Intelligence," *Radical America* 19, no. 6 (1985): 39–50; and Peters, "Information."

49. Minsky, *Society of Mind*.

50. Sue Curry Jansen, "Science, Gender, and a Feminist Sociology of Science: The Case of Artificial Intelligence," paper presented at the annual meeting of the American Sociological Association, Chicago, August 26, 1987; Jansen, "The Ghost in the Machine: Artificial Intelligence and Gendered Thought Patterns," *Resources for Feminist Research/Documentation sur la Recherche Feminist* 17, no. 4 (December 1988): 4–7; and Jansen, "Mind Machines."

51. Judy Wacjman, *Feminism Confronts Technology* (University Park: The Pennsylvania State University Press, 1991).

52. Norbert Wiener, *Human Use of Human Beings: Cybernetics and Society* (New York: Morrow, 1986); and Douglas R. Hofstadter, *Godel, Escher, Bach: An Eternal Golden Braid* (New York: Random House, 1980).

53. To some significant degree, Gilligan is used as a synecdoche and straw woman by American feminist sociologists who are dismayed by postfeminist celebrations of difference, which are actually largely derived from European social theory, especially French feminisms. Gilligan herself, it needs to be emphasized, has contributed a large corpus of feminist work, which focuses primarily on the ways in which masculinist American cultural values and institutions impact negatively on girls' social development. Monique Wittig forcefully asserts the sociological argument: "The *ideology of sexual difference* functions as censorship in our culture by masking, on the ground of nature, the *social opposition between men and women*. Masculine/feminine, male/female are the categories which serve to conceal the fact that the difference is social" (emphases in original). Whether the origins are in biology, culture, or both, feminist interventions have demonstrated that masculinist texts and practices are subject to revision. See Monique Wittig, "On the Social Contract," *Feminist Issues* 9, no. 1 (Spring 1989): 10.

54. Thus, for example, Sherry Turkle's studies of computational reticence suggest that for some women technophobia may be partly based in their discomfort with the

martial language and macho metaphors of hackers. For example, women may be repelled by concepts like "sport death"; they may prefer to "communicate" rather than "command." Turkle sees this female computational reticence as a transitional phenomenon that will disappear as female socialization offers greater opportunities to interact with formal systems. Because Turkle believes that users impute their own personal meanings to what she calls "intimate machines," she is optimistic about this outcome. See Turkle, "Computational Reticence: Why Women Fear the Intimate Machine," in *Technology and Women's Voices*, ed. Cheris Kramarae (New York: Routledge & Kegan Paul, 1988). While there is surely much truth in Turkle's analysis of girls' responses to the culture of violence and their relative lack of experience with formal systems, I am nevertheless far less sanguine about long-term prospects for women in cyberspace. Users do indeed bring their own meanings to machines, but the designs of information machines and programs also set limits. That is, they seem to exercise a kind of ersatz Sapir-Whorf effect, whereby some meanings and uses can be much more readily accommodated than others. Some users may create their own codes, but most do not. The kind of accommodation to formal systems Turkle anticipates may be an accommodation to the appropriationist logic valorized by Minsky, *Society of Mind*; Moravec, *Mind Children*; and others.

55. Hacker, *Pleasure, Power and Technology*; Cockburn and Ormrod, *Gender and Technology in the Making*; Wacjman, *Feminism Confronts Technology*; and Lucy Suchman, *Plans and Situated Actions: The Problem of Human-Machine Communication* (Cambridge: Cambridge University Press, 1987).

56. Leslie Oliver, "Techno-Tips for Educating Tech-Savvy Girls," *AAUW in Action* news release (Spring 2000): 1.

57. Valerie Frisson, ed., *Gender, ITC's and Everyday Life: Mutual Shaping Processes* (Amsterdam: European Commission, 1997).

58. Frisson, *Gender, ITC's and Everyday Life*.

59. Janine Morgall, *Technology Assessment: A Feminist Perspective* (Philadelphia: Temple University Press, 1993). See also Juliet Webster, "Gendering Information Technologies: Lessons from Feminist Research" in *Gender, ITCs and Everyday Life*, ed. Valerie Frisson (Amsterdam: European Commission, 1997), 81–111; Eileen Green, Jenny Owen, and Den Pain, "City Libraries: Human-Centered Opportunities for Women?" in *Gendered by Design: Information Technologies and Office Systems* (London: Taylor and Francis, 1993), cited by Webster, "Gendering Information Technologies: Lessons from Feminist Research"; J. Grunfeldt and S. Kanrup, "Women, Work and Computerization," in *Women, Work and Computerization: Opportunities and Disadvantages*, ed. A. Olerup, L. Schneider, and E. Monod (Amsterdam: Elsevier, 1985), cited by Webster, "Gendering Information Technologies"; and Ruth Woodfield, *Women, Work and Computing* (Cambridge: Cambridge University Press, 2000), especially the introduction, "The Myth of the Neutral Computer," 1–29.

60. Cynthia Cockburn, *Brothers: Male Dominance and Technological Change* (London: Pluto, 1983).

61. G. Bjerkens and T. Brattenteig, "Computers—Utensils or Epaulets? The Application Perspective Revisited," *AI and Society* 2, no. 3 (1989): 258–66, cited by Webster, "Gendering Information Technologies."

62. Dale Spender, *Nattering on the Net: Women, Power and Cyberspace* (New South Wales, Australia: SpinFex Press, 1996).

63. Ellen Balka, "Where Have All of the Feminist Tech Critics Gone?" *Loka Alert* <www.loka.org> (accessed November 12, 1999).

64. Balka, "Where Have All. . . ."

65. Robert W. McChesney, *Rich Media, Poor Democracy: Communication Politics in Dubious Times* (Champaign: University of Illinois Press, 1999); and Benjamin R. Barber, "Commonwealth: Globalizing Democracy," *The American Prospect* (September 11, 2000): 16–19.

66. Benjamin Barber, "On Civil Society," lecture, Muhlenberg College, February 13, 2001.

67. Richard Sennett, *The Fall of Public Man* (New York: W. W. Norton, 1992); and Sue Curry Jansen, *Censorship: The Knot That Binds Power and Knowledge* (New York: Oxford University Press, 1988).

68. Robert Romanyshyn, *Technology as Symptom and Dream* (New York: Routledge, 1989).

69. Romanyshyn, *Technology as Symptom and Dream*.

70. Haraway, "Situated Knowledge," 579.

71. Wacjman, *Feminism Confronts Technology*. In this regard, Benjamin DeMott's portrait of Ester Dyson, the most powerful women within the higher circles of the digerati, is devastating. See DeMott, *Killer Woman Blues* (Boston: Houghton Mifflin, 2000).

72. Clara Juncker, "Writing (With) Cixous," *College English* 50, no. 4 (April 1988): 424–36; and Patricia McDermott, "Post-Lacanian French Feminist Theory: Lucy Irigaray," *Women and Politics* 7, no. 3 (Fall 1987): 47–64.

73. Feminists give postmodernism a mixed review. Some readily embrace what Teresa de Lauretis describes as "a possible love affair between feminism and postmodernism." See Teresa de Lauretis, *Technologies of Gender: Essays on Theory, Film, and Fiction* (Bloomington: Indiana University Press, 1987), x. Others (for example, Jane Flax, Haraway, and Harding) embrace it with qualifications. Still others (for example, Frigga Haug and Mary Hawkesworth) rigorously reject it. Hawkesworth succinctly states the feminist case against postmodernism: "At a moment when the preponderance of rational and moral argument sustains prescriptions for women's equality, it is a bit too cruel a conclusion and too reactionary a political agenda to accept that reason is impotent, that equality is impossible. Should postmodernism's seductive text gain ascendancy, it will not be an accident that power remains in the hands of the white males who currently possess it. . . . In confrontations with power, knowledge and rational argumentation alone will not secure victory, but feminists can use them strategically to subvert male dominance and to transform oppressive institutions and practices." See Mary Hawkesworth, "Knowers, Knowing, Known: Feminist Theory and Claims of Truth," *Signs* 14, no. 3 (Spring 1989): 557; and Juncker, "Writing (With) Cixous," 424–36.

74. Ann Oakley, The Sociology of Housework (New York: Pantheon, 1975); Mary O'Brien, *Reproducing the World: Essays in Feminist Theory* (Boulder, Colo.: Westview, 1989); Hilary Rose, "Hand, Brain and Heart"; Rose, "Beyond Masculinist Re-

alities: A Feminist Epistemology for the Sciences," in *Feminist Approaches to Science*, ed. Ruth Bleier; and Smith, *The Everyday World as Problematic*.

75. Helene Cixous and Catherine Clement, *The Newly Born Woman*. (Minneapolis: University of Minnesota Press, 1986).

76. Haraway, "Situated Knowledge." George Lakoff's studies of language and metaphor also make a strong case for developing a theory of language based upon embodiment; his argument is developed without reference to the feminist literature. See, for example, George Lakoff, *Women, Fire, and Dangerous Things: What Categories Reveal About the World* (Chicago: University of Chicago Press, 1987); and George Lakoff and Mark Johnson, *Philosophy in the Flesh: The Embodied Mind and Its Challenges to Western Thought* (New York: Basic Books, 1999).

77. Haraway, "Situated Knowledge."

78. Nancy Hartsock, *Money, Sex, And Power: Toward a Feminist Historical Materialism* (New York: Longman, 1983). In the 1990s studies of the body, including studies of its relationship to and the limits it sets upon knowledge, became a minor cottage industry. At the same time, popular culture accelerated its obsession with bodies at many levels, including emphasis upon sport and fitness as well as global expansion of the pornographic industry and importation of pornographic representational conventions into mainstream culture.

79. This project is, of course, well underway in literature and the arts. It is making significant inroads in discourses on reproduction and reproductive technologies. See Emily Martin, *The Woman in the Body: A Cultural Analysis of Reproduction* (Boston: Beacon Press, 1989). Feminist film theory and filmmaking has also been influenced by this project. Thus, for example, Teresa de Lauretis's deconstruction of the male voyeuristic gaze of film technologies and conventions has inspired some experimental feminist filmmakers to articulate feminist alternatives. See de Lauretis, *Technologies of Gender*.

80. Haraway, "Situated Knowledge."

81. Haraway, "Situated Knowledge."

82. Harding, *The Science Question in Feminism*.

83. Dilthey, *Pattem and Meaning in History*; and Michael Polanyi, *The Study of Man* (Chicago: University of Chicago Press, 1963).

84. David Bloor, *Knowledge and Social Imagery* (London: Routledge & Kegan Paul, 1977).

85. Horkheimer, *Eclipse of Reason*; Horkheimer and Adorno, *Dialectic of Enlightenment*; Karl Jaspers, *Man in the Modem Age* (Garden City, N.Y.: Anchor Books, 1957); Karl Mannheim, *Ideology and Utopia* (New York: Harcourt, Brace, 1936); Lewis Mumford, "Authoritarian and Democratic Technics," *Technology and Culture* 5, no. 1 (Winter 1964): 1–8; and Max Weber, *The Theory of Social and Economic Organizations* (Glencoe, Ill.: Free Press, 1964).

86. Lana Rakow, "Women and the Telephone: The Gendering of a Communications Technology," in *Technology and Women's Voices*, ed. Cheris Kramarae (New York: Routledge & Kegan Paul, 1988), 207–28.

87. Judy Smith and Ellen Balka, "Chatting on a Feminist Computer Network," in *Technology and Women's Voices*, ed. Cheris Kramarae (New York: Routledge & Kegan Paul, 1988), 82–97; and Spender, *Nattering on the Net*.

88. Liesbet van Zoonen, "Feminist Theory and Information Technology," *Media, Culture and Society* 14 (1992): 9–29.

89. Ann Bookman and Sandra Morgen, eds., *Women and the Politics of Empowerment* (Philadelphia: Temple University Press, 1988); and Kathy Ferguson, *The Feminist Case against Bureaucracy* (Philadelphia: Temple University Press, 1984).

90. Nancy Hartsock, "Staying Alive," in Nancy Hartsock, *Building Feminist Theory: Essays from Quest* (New York: Longman, 1981), 117–18.

91. Alison M. Jagger, "Love and Knowledge: Emotion in Feminist Epistemology," *Inquiry* 32, no. 2 (June 1989): 161–76; Rose, "Hand, Brain and Heart"; and Rose, "Beyond Masculinist Realities."

92. Mumford, "Authoritarian and Democratic Technics," in *Technology and Culture*.

93. Mumford's recognition of the gendered constituents of technological designs predates the second wave of feminism. He associates masculinist cultures and technologies with authoritarian politics and conversely relates the ascendancy of "the feminine principle" to the development of democratic technics. Moreover, he does so within a conceptual framework that survives the test of feminist critique. See his "Authoritarian and Democratic Technics" as well as his *Technics and Civilization* (New York: Harcourt, Brace, 1964, original 1934). To be sure, Mumford's work is only suggestive. What he calls feminine might as easily be called humanistic, spiritual, or more directly, the dimension that partially resists, moderates, and balances the hegemonic pressures of capital.

94. Hans Pagels, *Dreams of Reason: The Computer and the Rise of the Sciences of Complexity* (New York: Simon & Schuster, 1988); and Evelyn Fox Keller, *The Century of the Gene* (Cambridge, Mass.: Harvard University Press, 2000).

95. Pagels, *Dreams of Reason*; Joy, "Why the Future Doesn't Need Us"; and William Bechtel and Robert C. Richardson, *Discovering Complexity: Decomposition and Localization as Strategies in Scientific Research* (Princeton, N.J.: Princeton University Press, 1993).

96. Keller, *The Century of the Gene*.

Chapter Five

Is Science a Man?

The structure of this chapter differs from that of its companions. The departure is designed to simultaneously offer prospective and retrospective takes on feminist standpoint approaches to science. The format for doing this is simple. Part I: Prospects, is a revision of a review essay, "Is Science a Man? New Feminist Epistemologies and Reconstructions of Knowledge." Part II: Retrospects, entitled "Yes, Dorothy, There is a Man Behind the Microscope Too," offers a more informal set of reflections on subsequent developments within, and in response to, feminist approaches to science.

The original review essay was written when the feminist perspective on science was initially breaking through the barriers to print, with the provocative energy and revolutionary sense of possibility that usually accompanies long suppressed ideas. I wrote the essay with two major goals in mind. First, I closely followed publication of all of the early, generative contributions to the feminist critique of science, and I did so from multiple positions: (a) as a longtime student of the sociology of knowledge, interested in the ways "objectivity" is construed in science, law, journalism, and the gender politics of everyday life; (b) as a feminist committed to expanding the discursive space for women's voices and experiential knowledge; and (c) as a student of censorship committed to investigating and witnessing silencings of unpopular voices and epistemological stances. The radical implications of this work for the sociology of knowledge and for knowledge itself were immediately apparent to me. I wanted to call it to the attention of a broader academic audience of critical thinkers, including nonfeminists and feminists outside of science studies. In that sense, I sought to explicate and share what was, at the time, perceived as a difficult body of work. I also conceived of the essay as a feminist intervention, albeit a very modest one.

Second, the essay was intended to offer a timely synthesis and assessment of the lively, but largely discrete, parallel debates that were taking place at the time in feminist epistemology and science studies and in social constructivist approaches to the history, sociology, and philosophy of science. Most of the feminist work was fresh and as yet either unknown or unacknowledged by constructivists. My goal was to bring these two discourses together and to thereby amplify their authority and resonances. I wrote the essay quickly and with a sense of urgency that, I think, still marches through its pages.

The conservative world of academic editors and referees did not, however, share my breathless enthusiasm for these provocative new ways of thinking. The manuscript collected several rejections before *Theory and Society* published it in 1990.[1] Rejecting editors and referees seemed united in their determination to preserve their paradigms. Some referees implied I was dangerous. Some wanted proof of my scientific credentials. One advised a remedial writing program; another found my arguments unintelligible. Some gave me reading assignments. Karl Popper was frequently invoked. Since I was only synthesizing—acting as, at most, a proactive scribe—I was surprised by the intensity of the personal attacks and dismissals. The experience enhanced my appreciation of the courage of the originals: the feminist scientists and philosophers of science who had dared to take Virginia Woolf's question seriously. And Woolf herself!

Despite its delayed debut, this essay seemed to fill a need by serving as a translation for scholars who understood the stakes of these debates but whose own scholarly interests did not require them to go inside of them. Over the years, I have received more requests for reprints of this essay than for anything I have ever published. Most of these requests have been from abroad. Judging from the comments that accompanied these requests, it appears that "Is Science a Man?" has also been useful to its international readers in positioning American feminist critiques of science within the context of broader social critiques of positivism, empiricism, and realism.

Rethinking the essay today, I am encouraged by how much these disturbing books have disturbed.

PART I: PROSPECTS 1988: IS SCIENCE A MAN? NEW FEMINIST EPISTEMOLOGIES AND RECONSTRUCTIONS OF KNOWLEDGE

In *Three Guineas*, Virginia Woolf asserted, "Science it would seem is not sexless; she is a man, a father and infected too."[2] Although scientific discourse has been deeply implicated in processes of rationalizing and legitimizing women's oppression, until well into the 1980s feminist scholars routinely treated displays of male bias in science as errors produced by bad scientific practices: errors that could be corrected by greater objectivity and methodological rigor. With few exceptions, they resisted Woolf's claim that masculine bias is a constituent principle of the modern, Western, scientific outlook.

There were very good reasons for this resistance. The established theories of knowledge (empiricism, realism, instrumentalism, and neo-positivism) treated scientific reasoning as the exemplar of rational thought. To be taken seriously, feminist scholars had to take the canons of scientific reasoning seriously. To accept Woolf's claim was to risk being labeled and dismissed, as Woolf was during her lifetime, as "irrational" or "hysterical."

By the mid-1980s, however, developments within philosophy, feminist theory, and the culture at large had significantly reduced this risk. The growing influence of social constructivist conceptions of science made it possible to raise epistemological questions that were beyond the limits of permission for scholarly discourse only a decade earlier. New feminist epistemologies were able at last to examine the social etiology of the masculinist scientific infection; advances in communication technologies had radically shifted human experiences of space and time in ways that made multiculturalism and cultural relativism routine aspects of everyday life. These developments, in turn, undermined the fundamentalist and universalistic claims of the Western Enlightenment.

Sexing the Paradigms

In part I of this chapter, I examine some early contributions to the debate; situate these contributions within the larger context of the radical new turn in feminist epistemology; and briefly identify some of the challenges, paradoxes, and resistances facing those who seek either to reconstruct science or to find emancipatory alternatives to it. These contributions defined the salient questions, legitimized new modes of inquiry in science studies, and set the agenda for the virtual flood of feminist research on gender, science, and knowledge that has followed. They are definitive works: the creative touchstones and benchmarks for amplification, emendation, critique, and backlash.

Unlike earlier feminist attempts to *correct* or *reform* science, the new feminist epistemologies raise fundamental questions about the nature of truth, objectivity, observation, empiricism, verification, and rationality. They represent a radical break with conventional thinking in the sociology and philosophy of science. They push the implications of Wittgenstein's claim—that the limits of language establish the limits of knowledge—in new directions by locating the source of Baconian and Cartesian dualisms in the binary categorical structures of Indo-European languages, which they see as extensions, elaborations, and reifications of primitive totemics of sexual difference. These thinkers cut through the disciplinary boundaries of the natural, physical, and social sciences. Their perspectives are heterodox but potentially revolutionary because they seek to dismantle or reconstruct the structures of power-knowledge that have informed and administered Western culture since the Enlightenment.

In *The Science Question in Feminism* (1986), Sandra Harding articulates the essential question of the new feminist epistemological studies: "Is it possible to use for emancipatory ends sciences that are apparently so intimately involved in Western, bourgeois, and masculinist projects?" The radical feminist response is a resounding "No!" According to Harding, who embraces the radical stance, this position rejects conventional science on three interrelated grounds: "that the epistemologies, metaphysics, ethics, and politics of the dominant forms of science are androcentric and mutually supportive; that despite the deeply ingrained Western cultural belief in science's intrinsic progressiveness, science today serves primarily regressive social tendencies; and that the social structure of science, many of its applications and technologies, its modes of defining research problems and designing experiments, its ways of constructing and conferring meanings are not only sexist but also racist, classist, and culturally coercive."[3] The claims of the new feminist epistemologies are not just premises for position papers; they are propositions to be tested by an ambitious research program undertaken by feminist scientists, philosophers, historians, and sociologists of science.

The philosophic and methodological warrants for these research programs are reinforced by recent changes in thought about thought that have taken place outside of feminist research: (a) post-Kuhnian studies in the sociology and history of science; (b) the social constructivism of Mary Hesse, Bruno LaTour, Steve Woolgar, David Bloor, and Barry Barnes, and the pragmatism of Richard Rorty and many others; (c) studies in the archaeology and sociology of knowledge that seek to recover the "submerged" or "residual texts" of Western culture, as in the work of Foucault, Williams, the "new history," and others; and (d) poststructuralist and postmodernist approaches to textual analysis and epistemology, as in Derrida, Lacan, Kristeva, Cixous, Irigaray, and many others.

Traditional philosophies of science maintain that studies of the origins of science can add nothing of significance to the body of scientific knowledge. They claim that such studies commit the genetic fallacy, that is, they contend that the origins of ideas do not affect their truth-value and are therefore irrelevant to discussions of science. Thomas Kuhn's research, however, established the relevance of the history of science to discussions of processes of formulating and legitimizing scientific paradigms, defining what counts as fact, and articulating methods of verification.[4] David Bloor's work carried critique of conventional approaches to the philosophy of science a step further by demonstrating that "the strong program" in the sociology of knowledge (a research program that applies the assumptions of scientific naturalism to the study of science itself) can introduce a new dimension to discussions of the "genetic fallacy" of modern science. Specifically, Bloor claims that the founders of modern science violated the terms of their own covenant by: (a) ascribing a "sacred" character (in the Durkheimian sense) to science, and (b) proscribing all inquiries into the validity or reliability of its founding premises. Bloor recommends violation of these interdictions; he endorses "methodological relativism" on the grounds that,

> [l]ike many features of a landscape, knowledge looks different from different angles. Approach it from an unexpected route, glimpse it from an unusual vantage point, and at first it may not be recognizable.[5]

Feminists have followed this recommendation. Recent feminist analysis of the founding texts of modern science reveal their historicity and intertextuality as well as their strategic positioning within debates involving church, state, commerce, witchcraft, and alchemy. Feminist recoveries of the submerged texts that informed the gender politics of early science demonstrate that scientific reasoning is secured by metaphors and myths drawn from the Inquisition. In short, they indicate that the landscape of modern science, like other landscapes, can only be approached from a specific angle or reference point. They identify the reference point of the collective voice of Western scientific discourse as the "I" of educated white males.

The groundbreaking work is Carolyn Merchant's *The Death of Nature* (1980). A historian of science, Merchant presents a meticulously detailed recovery and analysis of seventeenth- and eighteenth-century scientific and humanistic texts. The focal point of her investigation is a reconstruction of the contexts that produced the founding texts of Western science. She shows (a) why Francis Bacon and other members of The Royal Society claimed "knowledge is power," and (b) how Baconian empiricism ultimately became a form of power-knowledge that was instrumental in securing the mechanistic worldviews that facilitated the development of capitalism.[6] The achievement of Merchant's book is its radical problematization of nature. Through exhaustive (and exhausting) documentation she affirms Mary Hesse's contention that nature is altered by cultural conceptions of it.[7] That is, Merchant demonstrates that how we name nature affects the way we treat it: how we organize our adaptive efforts, how we use resources, how we intervene in and transform natural processes, and how we relate to other species, races, and genders. She marshals an impressive array of historical evidence that indicates that people do not treat a "mother" (the traditional image of nature) the same way they treat a "bride," "mistress," or "common harlot," the descriptive terms Bacon uses to name nature. Entering a mother's womb and robbing it of its hidden treasures of gold, silver, iron, and coal is, within the discourse and ethos of Western males, a very different act than seducing or even ravaging a sexual consort or "object." The two acts carry different cultural connotations and value orientations, and are accompanied by different social rituals and interdictions. Similarly, Merchant shows that when nature "dies"—is rendered lifeless or becomes "a great pregnant automaton" (Boyle) or a "world machine" (Newton)—the change in signs has revolutionary consequences for science, commerce, and ecology.

Evelyn Fox Keller continues the work begun by Merchant. Trained as a physicist, Keller does not just record the history of science, she retheorizes critical moments in scientific history by asking, "What might have happened if. . . ?" In one of her most interesting efforts, a collaboration with Christine Grontowski (1983), Keller and her coauthor ask what physics might sound or feel like if it had been constructed on aural or tactile models instead of the spatial metaphors favored by the discourse of males in Western cultures.[8] The nine essays collected in Keller's *Reflections on Gender and Science* range from detailed deconstructions of Bacon's sexual and reproductive metaphors to a biographical study of the career of Nobel Laureate Barbara McClintock. Thomas Kuhn receives generous bouquets in Keller's acknowledgments for his "careful readings and incisive criticism of drafts of all of the material in this book."[9]

The weakest link in Keller's argument is the unnecessary and unwarranted psychological reductionism that results from wholesale adaptations of Nancy Chodorow's "reproduction of mothering" thesis and D. W. Winnicott's object-relations theory. Too often, these developmental theories are simplistically invoked as universal explanations of gender differences in cognitive and affectual patterns; as a result, both the cultural variability of gender performances and the powerful role societal reward structures play in reproducing gender differences are occluded. Keller, it should be noted, has subsequently abandoned this line of argument in response to the criticisms of social scientists.[10]

The formidable achievement of Keller's book is that it radically problematizes epistemology. Like Margaret Mead's *Sex and Temperament in Three Primitive Societies* (1947), which provided its readers with three provocatively instructive fairy tales about alternative social constructions of gender, Keller's work offers her readers a challenging framework for conceiving of alternative constructions of knowledge. Her analysis builds upon Merchant's insights by demonstrating the centrality of sexual metaphors in articulating conceptions of knowledge. It also shows how these conceptions condition the questions that can be asked about nature, self, and society. Keller deconstructs the gender politics underlying three epistemological stances that have had some currency in Western cultures: first, Plato's homoerotic view of knowledge, which conceives of knowledge as a product of a spiritual union between a male mentor and male disciple, a view that proscribes violence and aggression in pursuit of knowledge; second, Bacon's concept of knowledge as power, which equates women and nature, and seeks domination over both; and third, the Paracelsian alchemists' construction of knowledge, which uses the metaphor of heterosexual intercourse to suggest that the unity of two different, but in a sense equal, partners is required to produce knowledge. For decades students of anthropology have come away from Mead's text wondering what Western culture would have been like if it had adapted the gender patterning of the gentle Arapesh. Keller leaves many of us wondering what would have happened to Western science and culture if the Paracelsians had triumphed over the Baconians during the early modern period? What would have happened if Eros rather than aggression had animated the Western quest for knowledge?

The collection edited by Ruth Bleier, *Feminist Approaches to Science* (1986), carried the dialogue a step further by raising the following questions: If modern science is a man, what would an alternative feminist science look like? And what would such a voice sound like? How would science be different? How would our perceptions of the natural world, of women and men, be transformed?[11]

Bleier, a physician and neurophysiologist, brought together ten provocative essays on feminist science, most of them written by women trained in the physical and natural sciences. For these women, science is, to paraphrase Donna Haraway, a way of practicing politics by other means.[12] Thus, for example, Haraway, anticipating the argument of her subsequent work *Primate Visions* (1989), examines the narrative practices of primatologists and concludes that primatology is a promising site for articulations of feminist perspectives on human origins, evolution, and behavioral biology. Sarah Blaffer Hrdy looks at mating behaviors of monkeys and discovers through carefully controlled observation of female primates that they are not nearly as discrete, selective, or unappreciative of the pleasures of the flesh as male scientists since Darwin have claimed. Bleier's essay shows how the ideological propaganda smuggled into the language of science by the metaphors that secure scientific models influences interpretations of findings in brain lateralization research. Elizabeth Fee's "Critiques of Modern Science: The Relationship of

Feminism to Other Radical Critiques" encourages feminists to practice what
they preach by building critical self-reflexivity into feminist perspectives. Fee
perceptively anticipated the divisive identity politics that have subsequently
fractured many attempts at coalition building among feminists and other critical theorists. Her essay identifies problematic assumptions and tensions
within the new feminist epistemologies; she explores possible points of convergence with other critical projects and movements resisting human domination. In "Beyond Masculinist Realities: A Feminist Epistemology for the
Sciences," Hilary Rose extends the arguments initially formulated in her
widely cited 1983 article, "Hand, Brain and Heart."[13] Rose offers a reconstruction of epistemology that seeks to mend the mind fractured by Baconian
and Cartesian dualisms; she locates a model for this epistemology in feminist
materialism, in the invisible caring labor of women that has kept females
from fully embracing the separations of mental and menial labor reified by
philosophic dualism and industrial capitalism.

The papers collected by Bleier are reports from the front. They were
"not simply conceived *within* a particular social and political context, they
are themselves *part* of the larger international social struggle about the po-
litical-symbolic structure, history, and future of Woman and women."[14]
They are attempts by activists to recover the submerged texts of modern
science; as such, they exhibit the energy and enthusiasm of revolutionary
ferment and possibility. For this reason, these essays provide an excellent
and accessible entry point for newcomers to the literature on science and
gender. There is no official line here, no common ideological grammar beyond the shared conviction that there is something suspect, dangerous,
even potentially lethal about the way science is currently practiced. That
is, these essays represent a moment of creative ferment and vision when a
sense of what was missing could, at last, be freely articulated: a moment in
which long-suppressed questions could be asked and at least partially legitimized.

Although primarily a work in the history and feminist reinterpretation of
epistemology rather than a contribution to feminist approaches to science
per se, Susan Bordo's *The Flight to Objectivity: Essays on Cartesianism and
Culture* (1987) has profound implications for feminist rethinkings of science
and knowledge.[15] What Merchant and Keller do in their respective histori-
cizing of Baconian empiricism, Bordo does to Descartes's rationalism. That
is, she demonstrates that conceptions of sexual difference, conditioned by
the cultural values of seventeenth-century France, provide the template for
Cartesian dualism. Specifically they provide the basis for the separation, hierarchies, and reifications of the binary categories of Descartes's theory of
knowledge: mind-body, subject-object, nature-culture, and so on. According

to Bordo, Descartes's "flight to objectivity" is also a flight from the feminine, and the destination of that flight is the masculinization of reason.

Sandra Harding's *The Science Question in Feminism* (1986) is much more than a dispatch from the field; it is an attempt to summarize, classify, synthesize, and clarify the issues, challenges, and tensions that have generated the ferment.[16] In short, Harding sets an impossible task for herself and comes very close to achieving it. This important book should be required reading for all graduate students in the natural and social sciences. It will make some very angry, but it may change forever the way a few readers conceive of science, scholarship, and the human predicament. Harding's value commitments are feminist, egalitarian, and socialist; her scholarship is impressive; her prose is lucid and sometimes even eloquent; however, for reasons I discuss below, the fruit of her synthesis, "feminist postmodernism," remains problematic.

Feminist methodologies depart from standard academic practice by probing across and "insistently against" the disciplines. Harding identifies and carefully explains five discernible interdisciplinary research trends in feminist studies of science: first, equity studies motivated by liberal reformist politics, which examine resistance to and discrimination against women in science, scientific education, and in socialization processes that cultivate aptitudes for and interests in science; second, studies investigating the uses and abuses of the biological and social sciences and their technologies, which reveal sexist, racist, homophobic, and classist social projects; third, social constructivist studies that challenge the possibility of the existence of pure science, even if the biases generated by current "isms" could be eliminated; fourth, studies informed by rhetoric, deconstructionism, and other forms of discourse analysis that analyze science as "text" in order to determine how scientific reports are conditioned by the limits of language and rhetorical structures of writing, including how metaphors smuggle ideology and mythology into science; and fifth, epistemological studies that explore the groundings of knowledge in social relations, embodiment, and structures of power.

Harding locates three different (and differing) positions in which these feminist critical claims are grounded. The first position is feminist empiricism, which maintains that sexism and male-centered conceptions of reality are social biases that deform the quest for objective knowledge. Feminist empiricism initially conceived of these biases as errors resulting from faulty implementations of empirical methods. Increasingly, however, scrutiny of scientific empiricism has led this group to question the adequacy of empiricism per se. As a result, a growing number are abandoning reformist stances and seeking to transform and, in some cases, transcend science.

The second position is feminist standpoint epistemologies, which claim men have been corrupted by power; this position regards patriarchy as a partial and perverse perspective because it is blind to its own blindness. In contrast, feminist standpoint epistemologies maintain that women's subjugated position requires them to see more and to see more clearly (the power of the powerless). Because we must all see from some perspective, immaculate perception, objectivity, and pure science are impossible. Therefore advocates of this position maintain that feminism is a morally and scientifically more tenable position for grounding interpretations and explanations of nature and society.

The third position is feminist postmodernism, which assumes that modern life fractures identities. Like many other contemporary strains of critical thought, this view adopts a radical skepticism regarding all universal and universalizing claims about existence, the nature and powers of language, reason, and science. It marks a conscious break with the legacy of the Enlightenment, including such ideas as progress and contractual theories of politics. This perspective presents itself as a form of resistance to the reified fictions of the naturalized, essentialized, *human* of humanism, which have historically oppressed women, as well as men of laboring classes, colonized nations, and racial, ethnic, and sexual minorities by denying them subjectivity. In short, it explodes the myth of male "aperspectivity": the claim that the dominant male view is the unbiased view, the claim that the "neutral observer" is really neutral and neuter.[17] Feminist postmodernism assumes its own claims are more plausible because they are grounded in awareness of fractured identities and in the tensions created by solidarity with and between these identities. Harding explores each of these perspectives in rich detail and presents an exhaustive review of the substantive contributions of scholars working within each perspective. She also takes readers on some interesting excursions of her own, with her discussion of Taylorism in science offering an especially stimulating side trip.

Harding concludes that each of these positions (as well as feminism generally) suffers from inadequate conceptualizations of gender. This is not an original idea, but it is an important corrective to the tendency of some early second-wave feminist thinking (circa 1970s), which embraced an easy optimism that suggests that the fractured mind can be repaired by an androgynous reunion of masculinity and femininity. Harding reminds the optimists that masculinity and femininity are not simply complementary poles of thought, not two symmetrical halves of the fruit of the tree of knowledge. Both are partial, distorted, and damaged renderings of the range of male and female potential. As a result, she points out that putting master and slave in the same bed will not liberate either of them.

In *The Science Question in Feminism*, Harding very tentatively casts her own lot with feminist postmodernism because it abandons the defensive masculine impulse to imagine a "transcendental ego" (the Promethean leap) with a singular voice that determines whether knowledge claims tell the "one true story" of how the world works. This perspective seeks reciprocity and solidarity among heterodox groups rather than essentialized and naturalized identities; as a result it supports pluralistic, decentered forms of knowledge. In short, it bears very little resemblance to what we now know as science.

On the surface, postmodern perspectives are appealing. They appear to represent an alternative to domination and coercion; and they open up important questions and areas of inquiry that the constituent assumptions of Enlightenment-based epistemologies foreclosed. Postmodernism is, of course, a protean term that resists precise definition; it encompasses a broad and eclectic set of ideas, aesthetics, cultural diagnostics, and intellectual trends that often have little in common with one another except that they are all responses to the ruptures within or the breakdown of the authority of Enlightenment thought. Generalizing about postmodernism, which itself eschews generalizing, is therefore always a very precarious move.

Within the context of feminist science studies, however, postmodern perspectives are problematic on several grounds. First, they do not represent a victory of domestic or humane science over big science. At best, they can support a handicraft alternative to established science; one that will presumably operate at the level of what Lewis Mumford called "democratic technics."[18] Postmodern perspectives do not create a culture of critical discourse that can effectively counter or contain the destructive thrusts of what Rose has called exterminatory science.[19] Second, they embrace relativism without articulating a theory or developing a politics that can institutionalize constraints on totalitarian exercises of state or corporate power. Third, postmodernism abandons the unfinished project of the democratic Enlightenment at the very juncture when women, minorities, and colonized people throughout the world are demanding that it finally realize its inclusionary telos. Fourth, trading a flawed consensually based democracy for an aesthetically based anarchic individualism is a dangerous move at a time when private (corporate) power is gaining ascendancy over public (national) power structures, systems of accountability, and powerful and potently destructive forms of scientific and technological knowledge. The fractures postmodernism supports provide de facto warrants for dismantling the last remnants of the public sphere and clearing the path for the triumph of what Marilouise and Arthur Kroker characterize as "ultracapitalism."[20] Fifth, in spite of its embrace of pluralism, postmodernism is, in Hans-Georg Gadamer words, "too self-regarding."[21] Postmodernism easily slips into an avant-gardism that permits those who possess comfortable levels of cultural and real capital to flirt with nihilism. It provides no recipes for sharing the wealth or relieving human misery. Indeed, avant-garde and postmodernist aesthetics have proven to be potent vehicles of advertising and marketing in the post-Fordian economy.[22] For these reasons, it is difficult to see how postmodernism can provide epistemological anchors for democracy, socialism, or feminism. Sixth, postmodernism abandons the quest for human covenants informed by a shared moral vision and ethical commitments. In summary, postmodernism may serve as a creative platform for poetic and aesthetic experimentation; however, as now constituted, it does not provide a viable platform for constructing communities or crafting portals to wisdom.

Harding herself almost immediately reengaged the postmodern question in two important anthologized essays, "Epistemological Questions" (1987) and "Feminism, Science, and the Anti-Enlightenment Critiques" (1990); abandoning postmodernism, she maintains that feminist empiricism and feminist standpoint epistemologies, which want "less false stories about nature and social life," contribute in "important ways to the continuation of the modernist and Enlightenment projects."[23] In her two subsequent books, *Whose Science? Whose Knowledge?* (1991) and *The Racial Economy of Science: Toward a Democratic Future* (1993), she clearly commits herself to preserving and advancing what she sees as the "progressive" political elements in the feminist critique of science, and insistently rejects the radical relativism and consequent political paralysis of many postmodern perspectives.

Extending her critique of the social constituents of Western science to include "the racial economy of science" and its historical positioning within class and colonial hierarchies, Harding attempts to reclaim and recuperate the critical spirit of early modern science.[24] That is, she recognizes that Western science and Western democracy share a common genesis; and she believes that if science can turn its critical lens on its own practices, and become self-reflexive and truly self-correcting, it can contribute much to the world. Not, to be sure, the transcendent, omniscient, Promethean view that traditional philosophies of science valorized, but it can provide a valuable "indigenous," or socially situated, Western way of seeing, "a strong objectivity" that remains very useful in solving certain kinds of problems.[25] Decentered but still representing a substantial constituency in a newly democratized and pluralized global republic of knowledge, Western truth claims can coexist along with other socially situated cultural formations, which also represent coherent worldviews.

EARLY RECEPTION AND CRITICAL REFLECTION

It is too early to tell whether the power of the new feminist theories of knowledge, like the power of the genie, comes from being in the bottle: whether

they will function only as critique of male science or whether they can articulate new ways of knowing. By 1990, feminist critiques of science had: (a)
posed profound challenges to conventional understandings of Baconian and
Cartesian dualisms; (b) exposed the destructive thrusts of the Baconian
legacy, and documented the embeddedness of big science in a "culture of
death"; and (c) posited strong claims in support of the hypothesis that the survival of the human species requires new approaches to knowing and being in
the world.[26] However, two gaps in the new feminist epistemologies still
needed to be addressed before they could move from critique to construction.

First, most early feminist critiques of science did not fully embrace the dialectic of history. The scientific revolutions of the seventeenth and eighteenth
centuries were complex and sometimes contradictory social movements that
changed the world. They cannot be fairly assessed by reducing interpretations
of their effects to linear (and male-dominated) binary codes. Baconian science
was a project of both domination and emancipation. It was an egalitarian project that helped break the hereditary rule of feudal societies; its epistemology
not only rationalized domination of nature (which included women), fueled industry, and eventually split the atom; it also improved crops, battled disease,
extended lifespans, and ultimately freed Western woman from the annual oc-
cupations of her womb that had kept her bound to home and hearth and frequently sentenced her to an early death. Modern science has not achieved the
progress that positivism promised, but it has made some of the daily labors of
ordinary women and men less oppressive. The new epistemologies need to
identify and systematically acknowledge the emancipatory elements within
the modern scientific outlook. If these elements cannot be freed from infection
and incorporated in the feminist project, then the new epistemologies should
devise a litmus test to determine what scientific assumptions, practices, and
procedures are directly implicated in the culture of death and what science
may warrant cautious accommodation. Donna Haraway (1988), an advocate of
the standpoint approach, has made some promising moves in this direction by
suggesting criteria for assessing "situated knowledges."[27]

Second, while these now classic works in feminist epistemology provided
effective platforms for critiquing the masculinist groundings of Western dualism; it is not yet clear how images, metaphors, and cognitive models drawn
from the traditional spheres of women's experience and culture can reinvent
science. Images of domesticity and necessity keep our feet on the ground, but
the achievements as well as the perversions of modern science have taken
flight on the wings of Promethean metaphors. The question remains, can
"heart," Eros, and the caring labors of women generate semantically rich and
methodologically fruitful alternatives to the disembodied abstractions valorized by Baconian and Cartesian dualisms?

Except primatology, mainstream sciences have largely ignored feminist attempts to rename nature and reconstruct science. Beyond suggesting models and taxonomies that are less hierarchical, more permeable, and more reflexive than the male prototypes—which is, to be sure, an extraordinarily valuable corrective—it is not yet clear what feminist revisions and reconstructions of science will entail. Feminist practices may generate new ways of being in the world—of caring for it and each other—and thereby give birth to new ways of knowing and describing the world. Or, perhaps the ultimate achievement of the new epistemologies will be to map the limits of language and knowledge: to chart the embeddedness of knowledge in structures of (gendered) power-relations. In either case, it is clear that Woolf's voice can no longer be dismissed as an irrational voice in the wilderness. For Baconian science, it would seem, is a man, a father too, and still infected by his capitalist, colonial, and misogynist past.

PART II: RETROSPECTS: 2002: YES, DOROTHY, THERE IS A MAN BEHIND THE MICROSCOPE TOO

What a difference a decade has made! Today it would be impossible for any single scholar to review the current literature on feminism and science. The sheer volume of the work that has been produced in the relatively short time since these original works were published, as well as the multiplicity of ways in which feminist and gender-sensitive lenses have been applied by both male and female scientists within specialized subareas of science make such a project impossible. In this regard, the feminist revolution in science has been successful and far-reaching.

The number of women entering science has increased significantly during the ensuing period; although, it should be emphasized, like other members of their generation, relatively few young women scientists self-identify as feminists even though most strongly support fundamental tenets of liberal feminism such as equal political rights for women and equal pay for equal work.

Pedagogical approaches to the teaching of science, especially in American higher education, are undergoing radical rethinking in response both to declining enrollments in science majors and the changing demographics of the general college population (e.g., women now constitute the majority of students in American higher education although they remain a minority in science).

Protocols within scientific research, which once either assumed women and men were the same and/or eliminated women from sampling procedures because they exhibited too much variability as compared to males who were treated as the human norm, are now generally recognized as outdated and invalid. In that sense, we have moved closer—progressed—to what Sandra Harding originally envisioned: a science that tells "less false stories about nature and social life."

Moreover, the once-heretical insight of Mary Hesse that metaphors enable scientific vision, which was creatively amplified through feminist lenses by Merchant, Keller, and many others, has now gained fairly broad acceptance, even among nonfeminists or antifeminists, within mainstream science.[28] It has made practices that were once covert a little more overt, consciously creative, and reflexively accountable. Some of the metaphors of contemporary science could be conceived as, if not directly responsive to, more compatible with the agendas of feminist approaches to science than their mechanistic predecessors were. Examples include the use of metaphors based on complexity rather than reductionism, the embrace of conservancy or caring metaphors in environmental science, and even the displacement of mechanical metaphors with biological metaphors in computer and cognitive science modeling.

Feminist critiques of science have also reenergized studies in the history of science, which, if the feminist critique is correct, requires complete reconceptualization; David Noble's *World Without Women* (1992) is one of the most ambitious works to undertake this kind of reconceptualization of the history of science. In addition, the feminist critique of science itself has subsequently contextualized and positioned its own arguments within broader historical analyses as well as provided numerous specialized histories and biographies of women in science.

MEDIEVAL LANGUAGE IN MODERN RESEARCH CENTERS

Is science still a man? Yes, but he is a little less blind to his own blindness, slightly more aware of the social constituents of his practice, and increasingly sensitive to the presence of difference within his midst. Some scientists welcome the change: the opening up of paradigms to new creative possibilities and the enrichment of scientific vision that new voices and perspectives offer. Others, probably the majority, like Thomas Kuhn's "old" paradigmers continue to put in their time, with minor accommodations, still largely relying on the scientific orthodoxies that prevailed during their own education and early professional socialization within their fields.

Some scientists—perhaps, I say hopefully, only a minority but a minority whose voices have been amplified by the media because they provide the most colorful quotes—are firmly entrenched in rearguard antifeminist and

sometimes misogynist positions. The most notable contribution to the latter
genre is Paul R. Gross and Norman Levitt's *The Higher Superstition: The
Academic Left and Its Quarrels with Science*, which conflates all analyses of
the social constituents of science, including nonfeminist sociological and
philosophical approaches, with left political agendas, and denies metaphors
play an important role in scientific conceptions.[29] These authors dismiss feminist critiques of science as irrational and superstitious: a form of magical
thinking that would deny the realities of female disadvantage in the order of
nature.

All of the authors of the pioneering works in the feminist critique of science have arsenals of war stories to tell about the early, and in many quarters
continuing, hostile receptions of their work by self-styled "hard scientists": a
metaphor that has been so widely deconstructed that it now evokes a smile of
critical solidarity among feminists when it is used by their adversaries. I personally witnessed angry responses to public appearances by Harding, Haraway, and Keller during the early 1990s. I recount briefly here one of those
incidents because it illustrates how old images continue to find expression in
current forms of resistance, albeit usually amply coated in irony. Yet, it is
telling when the language of reason fails self-styled defenders of reason.

The occasion was a guest lecture by Sandra Harding, "What is Feminist
Science?", at a top-twenty research university. Sponsored by the university's women's studies program, a sizable and vocal contingent of the male
science faculty had protested against the invitation and threatened to dis-
rupt the lecture. Unfamiliar with the campus (and, at the time, the protest
of the scientists), I arrived early to find the building and lecture room. I
was fully a half-hour early, and was surprised to find the lecture hall already more than half-full with an audience that was all male and far too
gray and bearded to be composed of students. I had to be in the wrong
place, I thought. But it soon became clear I was in the right place, although
I was not expected so early. I had crashed the warm-up meeting of the hostile reception committee of the "hard scientists." But if I was not invisible,
I was inconsequential. There was much bravado: some of it was angry,
some of it was ironic, and all of it seemed somehow lurid, as if I had stum-
bled into a stag party during a pornographic film. The salient words were
"spectacle," "inquisition," "witch," and its canine rhyming partner. There
was a bill of particulars in the form of questions circulating, apparently
formulated by one of the ringleaders who had actually looked at a copy of
Harding's book, *The Science Question in Feminism*. The questions, which
did not seem to have much to do with the book that I had read, were assigned to various lieutenants positioned in different parts of the room.
Clearly the specter of "a feminist science" had caused a stir!

When Harding stepped up to the podium, the crowd was silent. None of the anticipatory theatrics were visible. She gave a finely choreographed talk. When the question and answer period began, the men came through. All the hands that were immediately raised belonged to men; all of the questions they asked were adversarial. Harding responded with personal warmth but cool and insistent rationality. She anticipated and systematically disarmed virtually all of the questions. Silent or silenced until they were released into the hallway, where corridor courage resuscitated and pyrrhic victories were proclaimed, the would-be witch-burners had their moment but apparently not nearly as much fun as they had anticipated. Later at a women studies–sponsored dinner, I apologized to Harding for the audience's behavior. Since I was a part of that audience, my own silence made me an accomplice. Harding (actually, at that point, she became Sandra) said it was standard fare and that her entire presentation is crafted in defensive mode to counter charges of irrationality. Still, I should note that this by-then internationally prominent figure gave a copy of my review of her talk, which was published intramurally in my own college's women's newsletter, to her dean—to, she said, prove to him she that she is doing scholarly work when she does these presentations.[30]

READINGS AND MISREADINGS:
FEMINIST APPROACHES TO SCIENCE
AND SOCIAL STUDIES OF SCIENCE TODAY

Even the hardest of the hard scientists, who actively engage in debates about the social constituents of science today, acknowledge that there is a communicative constitutive to science. That is, scientific findings must inevitably be conveyed using language, symbols, and images, and these linguistic and visual technologies must be framed within arguments using recognizable narrative structures and rhetorical devices. Positivism and naïve realism are easier to practice than to preach (and are still widely practiced); consequently, they have few vocal defenders in scholarly fora (Gross and Levitt being notable exceptions). Similarly, radical constructivist approaches to science have fewer defenders today than they did a decade ago. Nature, however we name it, seems to have a way of grounding views of science that stray too far from materialism; hence the current resurgence of popularity of pragmatism within the philosophy of science.

One of my original reasons for writing the review essay was to bring together in dialogue the parallel, but then largely discrete discourses of feminist critiques of science and social constructivist approaches to the history, sociology, and philosophy of science. That conversation has now taken place and continues on a sporadic basis, but without producing the happy synthesis that I had envisioned. Many issues divide the two sets of discourses, among them the fact that a multiplicity of internally distinct and sometimes disparate viewpoints exist under each broad umbrella. Moreover, the two broad currents of thought have different relationships to and agendas for science: to paraphrase Marx, the philosophers (as well as the historians and sociologists) seek to describe it, while the feminists want to change it. To be sure, there are dissenters among the philosophers et al. who also want to transform and humanize science but they are dissenters who are at odds with the domain assumptions of their respective fields. Feminist standpoint epistemologies cannot be reconciled with these assumptions, which include as yet unreconstructed infections of the same virulent strain that Virginia Woolf pointed to in the first place. The friendly gestures the philosophers et al. periodically make toward feminist approaches to science are almost invariably rooted in a fundamental misunderstanding of feminist approaches to science. They see gender as a social variable or as an exemplification that can be rather easily subsumed within their own respective analytic schema. They do not see it as the difference that makes the difference: the definitive difference that requires reconstruction of the scaffolding of critical social theories of science as well as science itself. In the end, they resist the radicalism of feminist standpoint epistemologies, and ignore Stuart Hall's warning that "all social practices and forms of domination—including the politics of the Left—are always inscribed in and to some extent secured by sexual identity and positioning."[31] They seek to resolve the contemporary crisis in knowledge by containing it. In contrast, feminist standpoint epistemologies see the current epistemological crisis of the modern West, which they have contributed to, as "a fruitful moment" to quote Harding, who recently speculated: "Is it too grandiose an evaluation to say that this crisis, and the changing social formations producing it, may well have effects as extensive as those that followed the Copernican, Darwinian, and Freudian revolutions, and that feminist epistemology is fully part of the moment? Perhaps not?"[32]

NOTES

1. Sue Curry Jansen, "Is Science a Man? New Feminist Epistemologies and Reconstructions of Knowledge," *Theory and Society* 19 (1990): 235–46.

2. Woolf, Virginia, *Three Guineas* (London: Hogarth Press, 1938), 253.

3. Sandra Harding, *The Science Question in Feminism* (Ithaca, N.Y.: Cornell University Press, 1986), 9.

4. Thomas S. Kuhn, *The Structure of Scientific Revolutions* (Chicago: University of Chicago Press, 1962).

5. David Bloor, *Knowledge and Social Imagery* (London: Routledge & Kegan Paul, 1977).

6. Carolyn Merchant, *The Death of Nature* (San Francisco: Harper & Row, 1980).

7. Mary Hesse, *Models and Analogies in Science* (Notre Dame, Ind.: University of Notre Dame Press, 1966).

8. Evelyn Fox Keller and Catherine Grontkowski, *The Mind's Eye, Discovering Reality*, ed. Sandra Harding and Merrill Hintinkka (Dordrecht, Netherlands: Reidel, 1983).

9. Evelyn Fox Keller, *Reflections on Gender and Science* (New Haven, Conn.: Yale University Press, 1985), viii.

10. Keller's response to questions about her use of these theories during a session of the National Endowment in the Humanities Summer Institute, Science as a Cultural Practice, at Wesleyan University, Middletown, Conn., 1991.

11. Ruth Bleier, ed., *Feminist Approaches to Science* (New York: Pergamon Press, 1986).

12. Donna Haraway, "Primatology Is Politics by Other Means," in *Feminist Approaches to Science*, ed. Ruth Bleier (New York: Pergamon Press, 1986): 77.

13. Hilary Rose, "Hand, Brain and Heart," *Signs* 9, no. 1 (1983): 73–90.

14. Ruth Bleier, *Feminist Approaches to Science*, 1.

15. Susan Bordo, *The Flight to Objectivity: Essays on Cartesianism and Culture* (Albany: State University of New York Press, 1987).

16. Harding, *The Science Question in Feminism*.

17. Catherine A. MacKinnon, "Feminism, Marxism, Method and the State: An Agenda for Theory," *Signs* 7, no. 3 (1982): 515–44.

18. Lewis Mumford, "Authoritarian and Democratic Technics," *Technology and Culture* 5, no. 1 (1964): 1–8.

19. Rose, "Beyond Masculinist Realities," in *Feminist Approaches to Science*, ed. Ruth Bleier (New York: Pergamon Press, 1986), 69.

20. Arthur Kroker and Marilouise Kroker, "The Age of Ultracapitalism," *Canadian Journal of Political and Social Theory* 9, no. 1–2 (1988): 5.

21. Hans Georg Gadamer, "Comment," *Theory, Culture and Society* 1 (1988): 25.

22. Thomas Frank, *Conquest of Cool: Business Culture, Counterculture and the Rise of Hip Consumerism* (Chicago: University of Chicago Press, 1998).

23. Sandra Harding, "Feminism, Science, and the Anti-Enlightenment," in *Critiques in Feminism/Postmodernism*, ed. Linda J. Nicholson (New York: Routledge, 1990), 83; see also Sandra Harding, "Conclusion," in *Epistemological Questions in Feminism and Methodology* ed. Sandra Harding (Bloomington: Indiana University Press, 1987), 181–90.

24. Sandra Harding, ed., *The Racial Economy of Science: Toward a Democratic Future* (Bloomington: Indiana University Press, 1993).

25. Sandra Harding, *Whose Science? Whose Knowledge? Thinking from Women's Lives* (Ithaca, N.Y.: Cornell University Press, 1991).

26. Merchant, *The Death of Nature*; Keller, *Reflections on Gender and Science*; Bordo, *The Flight to Objectivity*; Rose, *Hand, Brain and Heart*; Rose, *Beyond Masculinist Realities*; Brian Easlea, *Fathering the Unthinkable* (London: Pluto, 1983);

and Carol Cohn, "Sex and Death in the Rational World of Defense Intellectuals," *Signs* 12, no. 4 (1987): 687–718.

27. Donna Haraway, "Situated Knowledges," *Feminist Studies* 14, no. 3 (1988): 575–99.

28. Thus, for example, even Richard Dawkins, who is profoundly unsympathetic to feminist approaches to science, asserts, "Skill in wielding metaphors and symbols is one of the hallmarks of scientific genius." Richard Dawkins, *The Rainbow: Science, Delusion and the Appetite for Wonder* (Boston: Houghton Mifflin, 1998), 186.

29. Paul R. Gross and Norman Levitt, *Higher Superstition: The Academic Left and Its Quarrels with Science* (Baltimore: Johns Hopkins University Press, 1994).

30. Sue Curry Jansen, "My Dinner with Sandra," *A Different Voice* newsletter, Muhlenberg College (Fall 1990): 4–5.

31. Stuart Hall, "Brave New World," *Marxism Today* (October 1988): 29.

32. Sandra Harding, "Comments on Walby's 'Against Epistemological Chasms: The Science Question in Feminism Revisited': Can Democratic Values and Interests Ever Play a Rationally Justifiable Role in the Evaluation of Scientific Works?" *Signs* 26, no. 2 (2001): 523–24.

Chapter Six

What Was Artificial Intelligence?

We are all astronauts in this technological age, but the astronautic body of technological functioning there on the launch pad prepared and ready to depart the earth is a masculine figure. And the shadow of the abandoned body, the body left behind, exiled, imprisoned, and enchained, is the figure of the woman.

—Robert D. Romanyshyn,
Technology as Symptom and Dream (1989)

PROMETHEUS REBOUND: EVOLVING MODELS OF MIND

The strong research program for developing artificial intelligence was a Cold War ideological formation. Describing the artificial intelligence movement in the past tense is an ironic reversal since it always described itself in the future tense. It never fully existed in the present. It was always becoming: its success forever contingent on a next step, a discovery that was just across the frontier of knowledge.

The artificial intelligence movement (AIM) emerged as an identifiable, if not yet organized, approach in the early 1950s. The computer, a technology with a long prehistory, became a reality at the end of World War II. With the subsequent invention of the transistor in 1949, the stage was set for the computer to become the defining technology of the late twentieth century.

Germinal ideas for artificial intelligence (AI) can be traced to separate but related attempts by Pascal and Leibniz to build machines that could calculate and thereby simulate functions of the human mind. The modern conception of artificial intelligence entered into the discourse of computer science with the 1950 publication of Alan Turing's manifesto, "Computing Machinery and

Intelligence," which outlined a plan for creating computers that could think: a feat that Turing predicted would be achieved by the year 2000. A two-month long conference of leading computer scientists in 1956, the Dartmouth Summer Research Project on Artificial Intelligence, marked the formal emergence of artificial intelligence research as a "movement."[1]

Immediate inspiration for the project was drawn from the work of four generative thinkers of early computing. In addition to Turing, whose 1936 paper "On Computable Numbers" described the theory of, specifications for, and limitations of "logic machines," they included John von Neumann, who headed the research team that designed and developed the modern, memory-based, computer central processing unit (CPU), the computer architecture that is still used today; Norbert Wiener, who envisioned a new science of "cybernetics"; and Claude Shannon, who developed information theory and inspired early interest in the social scientific study of communication. The researchers who actually formed and led the movement to develop AI included, among others, Alan Newell and Herbert Simon, both jointly affiliated with the Rand Corporation and Carnegie Institute of Technology (now Carnegie-Mellon University); Marvin Minsky and Seymour Papert of Massachusetts Institute of Technology; and John McCarthy of Dartmouth and later Stanford. Most contemporary AI scientists have studied with one or more of these pioneers.

What brought these men together was a common commitment to move beyond the then-prevalent understanding of computers as mere tools, advanced adding machines, which could only do what they were told to do. The dominant view of the time was expressed in the familiar programmer's motto: "garbage in, garbage out." The goal of the AIM was to create computers that could "think" and learn. As Simon put it, the statement that "computers can do only what they are programmed to do—is intuitively obvious, indubitably true, and supports none of the implications that are commonly drawn from it."[2] AIM sought to create programs that would simulate the complexity of the human mind. These simulations would, however, amplify human reasoning powers, and would ultimately be more powerful than any single human mind: "It will be a program that analyzes, by some means, its own performance, diagnoses its failures, and makes changes that enhance its future effectiveness."[3]

AIM is now a half-century old. Some former enthusiasts speak of it in the past tense: as a self-correcting intellectual movement that has transcended itself by serving as a launchpad to other endeavors.[4] Others conceive of the movement as ongoing, but view its history as made up of two distinctive periods. Various pairing of adjectives have been used to define the shift in emphasis. The first period, in which the "strong," "top-down," or "traditional" approach envisioned by Simon and Newell held sway, extended from the inception of the field to the mid-1980s. The second period of "weak," "bottoms-up," "emergent," or "new wave" approaches emerged in the mid-1980s. The bottoms-up approach does continue some of the research program launched by the older, top-down tradition, for example, developing expert systems, robotics, and other commercial applications of AI. What marks the new wave as distinctive, however, is the reconfiguration of the metaphoric definitions of the field of inquiry. Logico-mathematical models give way to or merge with biological metaphors as the research goal is reconceived as the creation of artificial life ("A-life") rather than artificial intelligence.[5]

The top-down approach focuses on patterns and rules operating at the high-level, symbol-processing structures of the brain, while ignoring its lower-level physical processes. The bottoms-up approach was a reaction against the failure of the top-down approach to produce significant results after more than thirty years of research. Whereas the top-down approach ignored biology, the bottoms-up approach took the position that the physical structure of the brain may account for its cognitive capacities. The bottoms-up approach seeks to design computing devices that mimic the structure of the brain's neural networks: that is, devices, modeled on child development, which can observe and learn.[6] This approach is also known as "connectionism" and is encompassed under the broad umbrella of the "new sciences of complexity."[7] Some chroniclers of the history of AI see the publication of Minsky's *The Society of Mind* (1987) as the benchmark; some date it to a conference on A-Life in 1987.[8] Most regard it as a more gradual shift away from the original vision: an evolutionary shift rather than a revolutionary displacement of paradigms.

While the top-down versus bottoms-up distinction is useful for explaining the internal history of AI, it is already in some ways an arcane and, in the current fast-paced environment of technological change, archaic distinction. The end of the Cold War triggered a restructuring of big science that was far more rapid, pervasive, and, by its own measures, much more successful than even the movers and shakers of this transformation anticipated in their most optimistic projections. The new research and development model streamlined and mainstreamed the old defense model for research and development by creating new, comprehensive partnerships of government, university, and corporate research and development initiatives: a model the Japanese had pioneered, to the dismay of the U.S. government, in the 1970s and 1980s. Computer science and technologies, genetics, and bioengineering have been the leading edges of this new technological initiative; and commercialization of these fields fueled the unparalleled growth of U.S. stock markets during the 1990s. The infusion of corporate capital has produced rapid advances in computer networking, robotics, and nanotechnologies that have transcended AI without leaving it behind. Some of the leading AI scientists and all of the sites that housed leading AI laboratories continue to be key players in the creation of the scientific and technological infrastructure of the information economy. It is not too much of a stretch to say that many of the technovisions that were incubated in AI laboratories have been mainstreamed into our brave new info-world. Just a decade ago, the utopian and dystopic projections of AI manifestos seemed unbelievable, woolly headed sci-fi fantasies. Now, we are building the global infrastructure that support them.

The rise and fall of the "strong" artificial intelligence program roughly parallels the duration of the academic careers of the founding generation, although Minsky, who was a graduate student when he participated in the formative Dartmouth summer project, serves as a bridging figure. Its rise and decline also appears to coincide with the influence of the unity of science movement, of which it was part. The funding and fate of top-down AI were closely tied to the duration of the Cold War, with the bottoms-up transitional period coinciding with the U.S. government's expansion of its defense funding priorities to include economic "competitiveness." The competitiveness thrust created the preconditions for jump-starting the information economy by underwriting the so-called greening of artificial intelligence: the period when entrepreneurial AI scientists began aggressively promoting the commercial applications of their work, sometimes to the dismay of more idealistic AI founders like John McCarthy.[9]

PURE SCIENCE AND THE COLD WAR

Like virtually all university-based computer science research during the Cold War, AI research was funded by the Department of Defense's Advanced Research Projects Agency (ARPA). Therefore, it was a player in the arms race with the Soviet Union and later the "competitiveness" race with Japan. Taken at face value, it was not a very effective player. In fact, it might have been viewed as an academic boondoggle: a metaphoric equivalent of a $7,000 Pentagon hammer. But taking AIM at face value grossly underestimates its accomplishments. Scientists associated with the movement made definitive contributions to the development of robotics and expert systems, which have had significant military and commercial applications. Top-down AI was also a very successful learning experience that taught scientists a great deal about the complexity of the brain and thereby provided the impetus for the development of what would become a new branch of psychology, cognitive science.

Artificial intelligence was part cover story as well as an important part of the real story of the early development of computer science. It leveraged the spectacular successes of the generation of Turing, von Neumann, Wiener, and Shannon, whose work had been supported by unlimited wartime resources, into an equally ambitious ongoing program for basic research in computer science. "Basic" and "pure" were crucial adjectives for naming and claiming significant degrees of intellectual autonomy for government-funded research during the Cold War. The terms referred to research that did not have immediately apparent instrumental applications: for example, developing a computerized chess game that was smart enough to defeat the world's top chess champions and thereby pass the Turing test for intelligence. This relative non-instrumentality was, of course, very instrumental to the research programs and careers of computer scientists.

"Basic" still retains some of this patina in scientific grantsmanship. "Pure" was, however, a crucial descriptor in the ideological and institutional struggles of the early Cold War period. Scientists, who chased defense dollars, professed their purity to try to fend off charges of scientific prostitution in the days when the government's growing presence in the funding of private universities was unsettling to many in the academy. The unsettled ranged from traditionalists, who wanted to preserve the relative insularity (cum purity) of the ivory tower, to liberals and leftists, critical of the Cold War policy and of threats to intellectual freedom posed by what President Eisenhower called "the military-industrial complex."[10]

When I use the term "pure" here, I am not suggesting a pristine practice free of social and political influences and interests. To the contrary, I treat it as a strategic, ideological stance that artificial intelligence and other scientists used during the Cold War to justify their dual careers as defense researchers and academics. The ideology of pure science also sometimes served as a temporary safe harbor during a politically complex and compromising era: the dark period of U.S. government interrogations and purges of academics, intellectuals, writers, and other culture workers by the House Un-American Activities Committee and by Senator Joseph McCarthy.

Scientists doing defense work were, by definition, always under intense scrutiny as potential national security risks. Much of their work was classified and only accessible to those with government security clearances. In those days, the purer the science, the safer the scientist. I am not, however, suggesting that the scientists who embraced the sanctity of pure science were cynics, liars, propagandists, or scientific prostitutes, although some individual scientists may have been. Rather, I am saying that pure science was an ideal, an aspiration that had pragmatic as well as intellectual resonance. Like all potent ideological formations, it was a complex and fluid construct; part truth, part self-serving shield; it was a tool of power that could sometimes be used to hold the powerful accountable.

The technovisions that now support the growth of the domestic U.S. economy and its globalizing thrust are inspired to a significant degree by the

achievements of the pure and impure sciences of AIM.[11] Although some influential figures associated with AIM are now uncharacteristically modest
about their achievements, and, it would seem, almost eager to acknowledge
their "failures," the distance from the AI laboratories to the information economy is small. In fact, in some instances, it is just across the threshold: that
much-vaunted next step. Both figuratively and literally, it is a step, sometimes
direct, sometime faltering, from publicly funded military research to publicly
and privately supported applications of digital technologies, including the Internet. "Convergence," the hot techno buzzword of the 1990s, is being actu-
alized in this century as a reengineering of society as well as technology.[12]

The significance of this reengineering is profoundly transformative. An
Wang, founder of Wang computers, maintained, "The digitalization of information in all of its forms will probably be known as the most fascinating development of the twentieth century."[13] Ivan Illich underscored the revolutionary structural changes that digitization is bringing about. Conceiving of
computers as agents of a new enclosure movement, he warns that computers
"are doing to communications what fences did to pastures and cars did to
streets."[14] In short, the digital revolution marks a deep structural shift in how
we think, what we think about, how we communicate, how we relate to the
material world and to one another, how we organize our work, and how we
construct communities.

CONTEXT AND LIMITS OF THIS CHAPTER

The purpose of this chapter is not to assess the successes or failures of AI science as science. That is beyond my expertise. My goal is much more modest:
to explore the rhetoric and mythopoetics of the parascientific discourse of artificial intelligence scientists. By parascientific discourse, I mean the programmatic descriptions, manifestos, and interviews that artificial intelligence
scientists have used to explain what they think they are doing when they do
AI science.

This paradiscourse might be conceived as functioning in academic science
in the way that mission statements function in the corporate world. Both articulate the values, means, goals, and hopes of their enterprises. Like corporate mission statements, parascientific statements are, in a special sense, also
public relations efforts. That is, they are purposively constructed to cultivate
and promote positive perceptions; in the case of the parascientific discourse
of AI, the intended audience appears to be other scientists, potential government and private sponsors, science buffs, and the general public. During the
heyday of top-down AI, the forefathers and the founders of AI functioned as

the practical philosophers of computer science; their influence was not limited to AI practitioners.

The rhetoric of the parascientific discourses of the artificial intelligence movement is remarkable on a number of counts. It does not use the flat, carefully measured language that experts on scientific writing recommend. To the contrary, it is frequently provocative and hyperbolic. Aphorisms, puns, and slogans are common, as are learned allusions to philosophy, literature, art, and music. Intrinsically interesting numerical and visual puzzles and paradoxes are often used to illustrate points, and, I suspect, to engage and entertain readers who cannot fully follow or who might be bored by the accompanying technical explanations. Self-depreciating modesty and humor are sometimes deployed, but they are usually accompanied by dissembling winks. Expressions of self-doubt are, however, hard to find. Normally authorial voices that aggressively flaunt their superiority, even hubris, disturb and alienate readers; however, in the parascientific discourse of AI, this mode of address functions as a seductive hook. It uses inclusive pronouns and generous displays of encompassing "of course" constructions to flatter readers. It models readers as peers, colleagues, knowing and supportive companions; if readers take the hook, this mode of address seems to say that they too will be admitted to Mount Olympus where they will also see like gods and be like gods (or astronauts). Some AI spokesmen have spent most of their careers modeling natural language; they are acutely aware of how languages work, and how irony, poetry, and Aesopean indirection resist, mislead, and charm AI modeling attempts. And some of these men are very adept at using these tropes to engage readers. For example, Minsky's discussion of metaphor is cutting-edge poststructuralism, but it has been cleanly shaven into clear, concise, and easily accessible prose.[15] When these writers use synecdoche, they mean it: for Minsky, mind is a "society." Top-downers are prone to what bottom-upper, Douglas Hofstader, refers to as "'Buck Rogers' fantasies."[16] Some of these fantasies are presented in whimsically, engaging prose, prefaced by almost child-like "what ifs." Most of the writing is artful. A few authors need to be taken seriously as writers as well as thinkers: Hofstader won a Pulitzer Prize for his remarkable book *Godel, Escher, Bach* (1979). Clever, arrogant, self-serving, engaging, propagandistic, literate, playful, often facile, occasionally profound, sometimes outrageous, and usually interesting, the parascientific discourse of AIM inspires believers and incenses critics.

While parascientific texts are clearly intended as a form of scientific outreach, frequently even proselytization, nonscientists are not encouraged to critically interrogate them. The late Isaac Asimov, who is regarded as the patron saint of "robotic ethics" by the AI community, celebrated this resistance to external criticism of science in "Every Real Problem Can and Will Be Solved":

> I'm a great one for iconoclasm. Given half a chance, I love to say something shattering about some revered institution, and wax sarcastically cynical about Mother's Day or apple pie or baseball. Naturally, though, I draw the line at having people say nasty things about institutions, I personally revere. Like Science and Scientist, for instance (Capital S, you'll notice).[17]

Parascientific discourse is frequently treated with the same reverence as science. Where in traditional (preconstructivist) philosophies of science, the scientist is seen as a kind of miner who goes off and discovers precious ore, the parascientific writer, even the nonscientists among them, seem to see themselves as sharing the charisma of scientific discovery.[18] They go off and mine the texts and the talk of scientists, translate what they find into reader-friendly language, and then offer to share that precious metal with readers. Sociological analysis and rhetorical criticism seems to be all but proscribed.[19]

Turing himself imputed theological and philosophical significance to AI modeling; as a result, philosophers, unlike sociologists, have been part of AI paradiscourse almost since its inception. They have extensively criticized the ontological, logical, and linguistic assumptions of the models of mind proposed by top-down AI scientists; see, for example, Dreyfus, Searle, Boden, Collins, and Penrose.[20] Elsewhere (chapter 4), I explored some of the ways that the logical structures of top-down AI models incorporate gendered assumptions.[21] See, for example, the comparisons and conflations of Maruyama's concept of "classificatory information" and Gilligan's typification of masculine modes of decision-making, or "morality of rules."

My purpose here is not to reiterate the philosophical critiques, but rather to use some of their scaffolding as support for investigating some of the underexamined social constituents of the AI project. These constituents include the gendering of the language and assumptions of AI paradiscourse, and, to a lesser extent, the historically specific Cold War social formations of that gendered language, for example doomsday thinking.[22]

AIM is an especially rich and unusually accessible site for excavating the poetry in the paradigms of scientific thought. The nature of the AI project itself, simulating or modeling minds, forced artificial intelligence scientists to consciously reflect upon the god-like roles they were playing in daring to try to create artificial life. It also required them to carefully weigh the qualities of the human mind they wanted to incorporate in their models and the qualities they wanted to leave behind.

AI science is unusual—an extreme case—in the history of Western science's long struggle with dualism. As a mind modeling mind, the artificial intelligence scientist is both subject and object: the observer and the observed.[23] He cannot deny his agency. Unlike other forms of scientific discourse, which attempt to erase all social fingerprints from scientific reason, artificial intelligence scientists recognize that their fingerprints are indelible. Some even seem to celebrate their presence: to engage in conscious myth-making about the significance of their work. For these reasons, the extreme case is also an ideal case for exploring the mythopoetics of scientific vision.

AI scientists have spoken very freely and often quite extravagantly about their roles as modelers and about the qualities of their models. During World War II, women played substantial roles in wartime computing; however, nearly all artificial intelligence scientists during the Cold War era were men. They formed the so-called nerd or, until it became a pejorative term, hacker masculine subcultures of elite science and engineering schools; it is therefore not surprising that the AI manifesto writers are all male.

Indeed the subworld of pre-PC academic and scientific computing was perhaps the purest post–World War II articulation of the monastic culture of science so painstakingly documented by David Noble in his underappreciated but groundbreaking contribution to both the history of science and the feminist critique of science, *A World Without Women: The Christian Clerical Culture of Western Science* (1992).[24] The nature of early computer technology and the rigid gender socialization of the Cold War era combined to make the subworlds of serious academic and scientific computing an exclusively male preserve. Use of mainframe computers was based on time-sharing. Typically, by day the mainframe did the routine business of the university, its instructional and administrative tasks, and perhaps some of the work of senior researchers. By night, computer centers belonged to engineering and computer science graduate students who basically lined up to run, then debug, then rerun the complex programs that demanded a lot of the computer's time and memory. These graduate students, who attended and taught classes by day, did their real work in and near the computer labs by night. Within the computer subculture, the mainframe was referred to as God, who determined the life (a successful run) or death (a glitch that needed debugging) of programs.

The lumbering technology of the machines themselves demanded a kind of de facto near-equivalent of a vow of celibacy from their supplicants. They were expected to demonstrate their seriousness by periodically eating, sleeping, and socializing in the building that housed the computer. The overachievers, the nerds and hackers, virtually lived in and for the nighttime worlds of the labs. Like most all-male subcultures, this one had a dark underside in which male bonding was frequently mediated by shared misogynist and repressed homoerotic fantasies, jokes, and storytelling. Technology itself is sometimes eroticized within the subcultures of elite science, creating a kind of technoporn "that rouses prurient interest, demeans the powerless, eroticizes domination," and sets up boundaries that signal they are off-limits to women and other outsiders.[25]

My analysis opens a rather narrow window onto that masculine subculture by exploring the mythopoetics of the technovisions of AI. It also examines the anxious image of masculinity that accompanies the generative metaphors that animate these visions.

DREAMS OF REASON: WHEN DREAMERS DREAM THEY ARE DREAMING, ARE THEY AWAKE?

Working largely independently of each other, constructivist and feminist analyses of science have exposed the fiction of "pure" science.[26] They have established that science, like other noble and ignoble human enterprises, is the work of mortal men and women, not of gods. Science is a social and cultural practice, which supports some of humankind's highest aspirations to and achievements of excellence.

Until the twentieth century and then only in atypical cases, for example Heisenberg's physics, Godel's Theorem, and AI modeling, science has been a practice that has been secured in denial of its own nature.[27] This denial has been deftly concealed and papered over for centuries by official histories and laundered origin stories. Anchored in the Western mind-body dualism, this denial makes doing science an "out-of-body experience." The scientist seeks domination over nature by denying, implicitly or explicitly, that he is part of nature. His pretense to objectivity is maintained by detaching his mind from his body and the world, and by denying his mortality. This stance allows the scientist to believe that he is spying on the world from afar: viewing it dispassionately through God's eyes or through the eyes of an astronaut. The gendering of the pronouns in this paragraph is conscious and purposeful, for in Western culture this kind of disembodied Promethean objectivity has been a masculinist preserve and privilege. Within its assumptions, woman has been conceived as part of nature, as "the sex," and always embodied. In his *Sixth Meditation*, René Descartes provides the definitive articulation of this (masculine) stance when he asserts, "I am truly distinct from my body, and . . . I can exist without it."[28]

AI's positioning vis-à-vis the mind-body problem is shot through with contradiction. On the one hand, the Cartesian flight from embodiment and materialism reaches one of its clearest and most thorough articulations in the visionary statements of AIM because the computer is "the embodiment of the world as the logician would like it to be," not as it is.[29] The goal of the AI scientist is to release mind from body: to download its contents into programs.

On the other hand, however, AI and the new sciences of complexity are futuristic visions: "dreams of reason." They are exercises of scientific imagination rather than faithful codings of empirical reality. The dreamers know they are dreaming: they are not in denial about that.

They simultaneously share and surrender the Cartesian dream of pure reason, of a "Promethean flight from embodiment," to borrow Susan Bordo's words.[30] Their top-down struggle to release mind from body has, in the course of the history of AI research, paradoxically pulled AI researchers back to biology. It is the body, the human biological system, with its brain, nervous system, nerve endings, and mercurial emotional apparatus, that weighs so heavily against AI and keeps its flight grounded. The more successful AI scientists are in advancing the Promethean dream, the more the model comes to resemble what they want to escape. From a bottoms-up perspective, Hofstader describes the paradox that locks the AI scientist in a recursive loop: "[A]ll intelligences are just variations on a single theme: to create true intelligence, AI workers will just have to keep pushing to ever lower levels, closer and closer to brain mechanisms, if they wish their machines to attain the capacities which we have."[31] The better the bottoms-up machines get, the slower they will get. The microworlds of the bottoms-up dream are the complete antithesis of the Buck Rogerian top-down supercomputer.

The resulting discourse is understandably profoundly ambivalent about embodiment. The body is the enemy as well as the portal to knowledge that can transcend the body. In the Buck Rogers versions of the dream, the program becomes the spaceship that allows the AI scientist-astronaut to escape from the enemy (e.g., the body, woman, mortality, or nuclear annihilation). The scientist moves into another dimension, no longer human or embodied. The best of what he has to offer survives in this new dimension. In Hofstader's scenario, however, the scientist assumes a Zenlike stance and learns to live with, even savor, the intellectual and aesthetic pleasures of contradiction. He faces the paradox of the recursive loop head-on and demonstrates the intellectual and aesthetic pleasures of life lived on its rim.[32]

Whether Hofstader's version marks the end of AIM, the point where it transcends itself and mutates into the new sciences of complexity, or whether it marks AI's rebirth as a mature research program may still be an open question. He describes the top-down approach as over—"Retrospects"—and the bottoms-up perspective in the future tense—"Prospects." These prospects are based on wholism rather than on reductionism, in computerese, parallel processing units and neural nets: "[M]any trains moving simultaneously down many parallel and crisscrossing tracks, their cars being pushed and pulled, attached and detached, switched from track to track by a myriad neural shunting-engines."[33]

THE POETRY IN THE PARADIGMS

Like Descartes and Boyle, AI researchers embrace mechanical metaphors of mind. They conceive of mind as machine: a computer, a grid of electrical relay switches, "many trains moving simultaneously," and so on. While some, like Turing, acknowledge the limitations of this conception within AI parascientific discourse and top-down AI modeling, the "program" is a metonymic surrogate for intelligence. AI constructs computer models of operations of mind by reducing its cognitive and biological processes to machine recognizable inputs. AI modelers assume that all interesting manifestations of intelligence can be "captured" and "contained within" programs.[34] According to one journalistic chronicler of AI, some AI modelers even believe it is possible to precisely quantify and program the "odd little chemicalelectrical cloud of activity that is our personality."[35]

Metaphors are usually thought of as tools of humanists not scientists. The eighteenth-century English poet William Wordsworth was apparently the first thinker to argue that poets and scientists share similar relationships to nature, even though their languages differ. The scientist uses Royal Academy prose and the poet uses meter to interpret nature.[36] Both approach the unknown through the portals of the known, and scientist, no less than poet, uses analogies to construct bridges between the two. Although scientists from Francis Bacon to the present wish it were not so, the bridges the scientist builds between the familiar and the mysterious, like the poet's spans, are constructed of bricks baked in the cultural and linguistic kilns of historical time.

Scientific vision, like poetic vision, is expressed most palpably through metaphors. The metaphors used by scientists are not, however, incidental to the scientific enterprise. To the contrary, they empower scientific vision; they provide the scaffolding for arguments, color the language of assertion, and guide inquiry. Indeed, Richard Dawkins claims, "Skill in wielding metaphors and symbols is one of the hallmarks of scientific genius."[37] In short, they are the magic carpets that make science possible.[38]

Metaphors are not, however, all that make science possible. Mathematics formalizes and refines scientific vision; instrumentation amplifies and standardizes it; and systematic, repetitive, and controlled observation tests its reliability. Yes, metaphors lurk within and enable these practices too—like Godel's Theorem, reminding us of the limits of all human knowledge. But lost at sea, who amongst us would not rather have a compass than a sonnet? Science has demonstrated its potency in practice. Studies in the history, philosophy, and sociology of science have nonetheless firmly established that metaphors are a necessary, though far from sufficient, component of scientific thought. Bacon was right! They are also mischief-makers that smuggle "the idols of the tribe" into science.[39] This mischief does not negate or invalidate scientific claims, but it does humanize them.

Social constructivist unpackings of the poetry in the paradigms have knit many scientific brows into exasperated consternation. But mythology! What are scientists to make of it? Hofstader would probably advise art, music, or some more science; and he would be right. Mythology is a testament to human aspirations, not just a graveyard of human fallacies and foolishness. We are all, in some sense, poets, although there are very few Wordsworths, Shakespeares, Byrons, Bacons, Turings, or von Neumanns among us.[40] All of our poetry, including the poetry of science is, however, a record of what humans value, aspire to, and fear.

The Enlightenment cast scientists in the role of supermen. In its cosmology, nature displaced God as first principle; the scientist replaced the priest as authoritative interpreter of the reality. Scientists were expected to see with the eyes of gods and to be nature's ventriloquists. The voice of scientific reason was conceived—impossibly—as the unmediated and therefore objective voice of nature. Scientific instrumentation and calculations created and preserved this construction of objectivity, which did, in fact, prove to be an extraordinarily productive way of interpreting and imputing patterns to nature. In short, the Kantian trick usually worked.[41]

In making their daring claims at the height of the Inquisition, the members of the Royal Society not only risked the wrath of the God (if they were wrong) but the swords of inquisitors (if they were right). To weather the fury of the storm, fear was repressed in the tough-minded, even macho, Baconian vision of the masculine future of science. It was a brave vision that took modern science far. Like most brave visions, however, its monological and monovocal structure and resonance left their imprimatur on both the vision and the visionaries.

Fear is, of course, a proscribed emotion for men in the West (perhaps for men everywhere); if they have it, they are supposed to repress it. Repressed sentiments and ideas do, however, have a habit of returning; mythology is a primary staging ground for this return. Male fear seems almost to be the axis upon which modern science has turned; and the momentum generated by this axis has been simultaneously constructive and destructive to the species and the planet. For example, scientists did not seek to understand natural disasters just because they posed interesting scientific problems. Well-warranted fear, as much or more than cool-headed rationality, provided the momentum for the quest for scientific predictability and control. Earthquakes, hurricanes, volcanic eruptions, fires, floods, deadly diseases, nuclear explosions, and, yes, women have variously terrified many scientists as well as fascinated them. Not surprisingly, both terror and fascination are encoded in the mythopoetics of scientific thought.

METAPHORS AND MINDS

Metaphors based upon images of sexual relations and reproduction are both common and deeply embedded in the discourses of Western science and culture.[42] Bacon himself incorporated them in the foundation documents of modern science, including his fragmentary *The Masculine Birth of Time* (1602 or 1603).[43] These metaphors place the scientist in a hierarchical relationship of domination and control of nature.[44] Within the mythopoetics of computer scientists, reproductive metaphors occupy a much more prominent position than copulative imagery, although the latter are invoked in predictable ways to represent inputs, circuitry, and connections.

Images of male birthing have been a common motif (even, for those so inclined, a Jungian archetype) of Western origin stories, for example Zeus giving birth to Athene from his head and God creating Eve from Adam's rib. Lionel Tiger claims rites of male bonding are "the male equivalent of child reproduction, which is related to work, defense, politics, and perhaps even the violent mastery and destruction of others."[45] Brian Easlea (1983) makes a similar point when he asserts:

> Men in prescientific societies, it may be generally argued, attempt to affirm masculine and, for them therefore, dominant status through secret exclusively male rituals. Quite often these rituals have a very direct "pregnant phallus" aspect to them, the male participants thereby demonstrating that through their special phallic powers they, like women, are able to give birth.[46]

Both Easlea and Evelyn Fox Keller demonstrate the continuing presence of the images of the "pregnant phallus" in the mythopoetics of contemporary science.[47]

Birth is the primary (perhaps even primal) source of most of the poetry in the paradigms of computer science. Computers are the sites of the generative process. They are, in the words of AI scientists, Roger Schank and Harold Abelson, "omnipotent"; Schank and Robert Abelson describe them as "god."[48] They are also incubators, (male) wombs that are conceived as mediums for generating new forms of life. According to David Gelernter, these incubators will soon produce "mirror worlds": you will be able to look into a "genie bottle on your desk" and see "reality." Computers will soon become "crystal balls, telescopes, stained glass windows—wine, poetry or whatever—things that make you see vividly." They will put "the universe in a shoebox." Why? Because, "A bottled institution cannot intimidate, confound or ignore its members; *they dominate it*" (emphasis in original).[49]

The virility and reproductive prowess of computers is expressed through three interconnected sets of birth images: images representing creativity, immortality, and progress.

IMAGES OF CREATIVITY

Much of the mythologizing of the computer science fraternity is conscious, intentional, and programmatic: it serves a community-building function in AIM. It makes the work and the sacrifices it requires—the deferred gratification of always becoming, never fully arriving—special, ordained, daring, and even god-like. In *God and Golem, Inc.* (1964), Norbert Wiener, widely referred to as the "father of cybernetics," maintains that machines that learn, reproduce themselves, and coexist with men pose profound theological questions. Wiener points out that if a contemporary of Francis Bacon had claimed to be able to make machines that could "learn to play games or that should propagate themselves," he would surely have been burned by the Inquisition "unless he could convince some great patron that he could transmute the base metals into gold, as Rabbi Low of Prague, who claimed that his incantations blew breath into the Golem of clay, had persuaded the Emperor Rudolf."[50]

According to the folklore of the computer science subculture, Wiener, John von Neumann, Gerald Sussman, Marvin Minsky, and Joel Moses all claimed to be actual descendants of Rabbi Low, perhaps the first mortal man to be credited with creating life without using woman as a vessel.[51] Moreover, Low's descendants believe they are carrying on the family tradition. By the mid-1980s, these latter-day alchemists maintained that they had already given birth to four generations of Golem. The labor pains they were then experiencing in their attempt to give birth to "the fifth generation" of computers were extraordinary because the "pregnant phallus" was more pregnant than usual.[52] It was struggling to bring forth very special progeny: a superchild who will be able to reproduce itself without the agency of either man or woman.[53]

Some enthusiasts herald "neural nets" as this special progeny. Indeed, to cross the border from one genre of scientific vision to another, an episode of *Star Trek* featured conscious, intentional, and ethical neural nets contemplating the injustices of their human sires. The crossover from science to science fiction is a common one: science feeds the imagination of science fiction writers, and many scientists feed off of science fiction. As Freeman Dyson puts it, "Science is my territory, but science fiction is the landscape of my dreams."[54] Scientist and science fiction writer share the same imaginative field and vocabularies of motive: they are both posed on the precipice of the possible and asking, "What if . . . ?" In Greek mythology, the lesser Greek god Prometheus incites the wrath of Zeus by giving fire to man. Contemporary Prometheans invert the flight trajectory: their leaps of imagination are intended to make them god-like. They seek to transcend embodiment, biology, and gravity, and give birth to a new, superior species of ideational forms.

IMAGES OF IMMORTALITY

According to the fathers-to-be, this much-anticipated superchild may cut through the genetic coding of the universe and produce "the next step in human evolution."[55] Some computer scientists believe this generation of computers will possess the power to transform their fathers into "supermen."[56] They claim this vaunted son of the computer god will allow them to download the contents of their own minds into programs and thereby achieve immortality.

One proud papa, Hans Moravec, director of the Mobile Robot Laboratory at Carnegie-Mellon University, maintains, "The things we are building are our children, the next generations. They're carrying on all our abilities, only they're doing it better."[57] In *Mind Children: The Future of Robot and Human Intelligence* (1988), Moravec acknowledges that today "our machines are still simple creations, requiring the parental care and hovering attention of any newborn, hardly worthy of the word 'intelligent.' Within the next century, however, he promises "they will mature into entities as complex as ourselves, and eventually into something transcending everything we know—in whom we can take pride when they refer to themselves as our descendants."[58]

The gender of these children is seldom in doubt. When references to AI or robotics are personified, male pronouns are typically used. Within the often too transparently Freudian imagery of the lore of infotech, however, software and software designs are sometimes personified as females, for example Eliza and Linda. This practice departs from common, humanistically inspired conventions of tech-talk because technology is usually personified as female.[59] Andreas Huyssen attributes this practice to fear of autonomous technology: "As soon as the machine came to be perceived as a demonic, inexplicable threat and as the harbinger of chaos and destruction . . . writers began to imagine the *Maschinenmensch* as woman."[60] This move also has mythological precedence, as, for example, Pandora's box.

For top-down AI, the signs are changed: the prospect of autonomous technology is exciting, a source of wonder and daring defiance of Judeo-Christian understandings of life and death and of conventional American values like God, motherhood, and apple pie. Sometimes this defiance gives practitioners pause, leads to self-interrogations of the ethical implications of AI. Yet, self-interrogations of the god-like powers of mind-makers are also, by definition, celebrations of those god-like powers, which separate the dilemmas of AI scientists from the problems of ordinary folks who are still stuck back in an earlier stage of evolution. An exception to top-downers embrace of autonomous technology is, however, made in the case of computer viruses, which carry the regressive stigma of biological life and usually infect only (female) software.

The telos of AI *is autonomous technology*. It is AI's ticket to immortality. Marvin Sussman, for example, conceives of the mind children, produced by AI, as delivering their fathers to the threshold of life everlasting: "[T]he machine can last forever," and "if it doesn't last forever, you can always dump it out onto tape and make backups."[61] As we shall see, bottoms-up AI is having difficulty sustaining this optimism. The return of biology not only refills Pandora's box; it also opens the door to Mary Shelley's humanist and feminist nightmare of the deformed progeny of phallic pregnancies: the Frankenstein monster.[62]

The Cartesian disconnection of AI researchers that permits them to conflate mind and machine also allows them to conceive of biological death as a minor episode in the life cycle of a superman: "If you make a machine that contains the contents of your mind, then that machine is you."[63] Indeed, within the mythos of AI modelers, biological man (as well as woman) becomes an obstacle to be conquered and rationalized.

The contents of the mind cannot be downloaded into immortality until the information channels are cleaned up. For this reason, AI simulation requires modelers to subject cognitive processes to the Law of the Hammer, albeit reluctantly and only for the time being until more complex forms of modeling become possible. The AI modeler must reduce complex cognitive and biological processes to a series of discrete and univocal binary commands. Modeling even a very simple movement like raising the arm of a man to press a lever may require identifying, mapping, and simulating hundreds, even thousands, of cognitive and neurological messages. Add to this the fact that within biological man, these messages are often confounded by the "noise" of indecision, procrastination, memory, reflection, love, lust, and other sentiments, values, and intentions that appear to be irrelevant to the immediate task at hand.

Cleaning up the information channels to create models that will program a robot to push a lever with the same cool efficiency, regardless of whether the lever releases bombs or coffee cups, is therefore a genuine achievement of Cartesian logic. Faulting the AI modeler for preferring clean channels to cluttered ones is like faulting the plumber for preferring clean drains to clogged ones. Both find their efforts blocked by the waste products of biological man. The AI modeler's dream of a clean machine is a dream of Cartesian transcendence, perhaps even redemption. But where Descartes wanted to control the noise of embodiment, AI researchers frequently express a desire to eliminate the body. The late Heinz Pagels, then-director of the New York Academy of Sciences, found serious humor in the Cartesian mind-body problem: the incompatibility of rationality and sexuality, in this instance male sexuality. He opens his survey of the sciences of complexity, *The Dreams of Reason: The*

Computer and the Rise of the Sciences of Complexity (1988), with a quotation from Robert Hutchins, "When the penis goes up, reason goes out the window."[64] Computers, it seems, can eliminate this distraction.

Rodney Brooks explains why he wants to eliminate "the wet stuff"— human bodies—from the equation: "We are sort of locked into our genetic structure. At the moment we might be able to tweak our genetic structure a little bit, but nothing severe."[65] Brooks sees "an advantage to building robots out of silicon and stuff like that, because we know how to control that fabrication process pretty well," whereas we have "trouble with" biology: "We can't add more brain cells to us, but we can add more processors, more silicon, to a robot."[66] In short, robots are easier to expand, repair, and control than their messy and unpredictable prototypes.

Because the legend of the pregnant phallus requires the scientist to make love to himself—to give birth to a "sacred image" of himself—it encourages narcissism.[67] Sherry Turkle reports the following conversation between AI scientists. Don Norman says, "I have a dream to create my own robot. To give it my intelligence. To make it mine, my mind, to see myself in it. Ever since I was a kid." Roger Schank responds, "So who doesn't? I have always wanted to make a mind. Create something like that. It is the most exciting thing you could do. The most important thing anyone could do." Gary Drescher tells Turkle, "We have the right to create life, but not the right to take our act lightly."[68] Drescher believes scientists have ethical obligations in a society where human and artificial intelligence live together.

Following the lead of science fiction writer, Isaac Asimov, Drescher entertains the idea that AI may make a new form of murder possible:

> People always talk about pulling the plug on computers as though when it comes to that they will be saving the world, performing the ultimate moral act. But that is science fiction. In real life, it will probably be the other way around. We are going to be creating consciousness, creating lives, and then people may simply want to pull the plug when one of these intelligences doesn't agree with them.[69]

IMAGES OF PROGRESS IN AI DISCOURSE

Some AI scientists acknowledge that the next step in evolution may render humans obsolete. Marvin Minsky thinks "people will get fed up with bodies after a while."[70] He predicts that like the dinosaurs we might disappear leaving behind a "society" of interacting and self-generating computer systems.[71]

Evolutionary analogies are common in AI discourse. They appear to represent a form of masculine display: a way of saying my science is bigger (more potent or pregnant) than yours. However, evolutionary images are also used to convey disdain for and distance from conventional conceptions of life, death, thought, and morality. That is, they are used to signal a radical departure from all previous ways of knowing and being in the world. Thus, Moravec asserts, "I have no loyalty to DNA," and Mike Blackwell claims, "Bodies have served their purpose."[72]

Moravec valorizes the departure, the irrevocable break with the past: "We are on a threshold of a change in the universe comparable to the transition from non-life to life."[73] On one level, AI scientists seem to be embracing a return to pre-Baconian animism in which matter, cum machine, is endowed with life and anthropomorphosized. There is, however, more to the equation. The transition is not to life. There is a change in signs, which negates the value of human life: machines evolve, humans download or die. Within AI's mechanistic reconstruction of evolutionary theory, the pregnant phallus finally achieves deliverance: mind is released from body and man is released from his biological dependence on woman. Moravec describes the brave new, "post-biological" world of AI:

> All our culture can be taken over by robots. It'll be boring to be human. . . . We can't beat the computers. So it opens another possibility. We can survive by moving over into their forms . . . because we exist in a competitive economy, because each increment in technology provides an advantage for the possessor. . . . Even if you can keep them (the machines) slaves for a long time, more and more decision-making will be passed over to them because of the competitiveness.
>
> We may still be left around, like the birds. It may be that we can arrange things so the machines leave us alone. But sooner or later they'll accidentally step on us. They'll need the material of the earth.[74]

REPRODUCTION AS DESTRUCTION IN AI DISCOURSE

In the transition from life to program, the clean machine supersedes its sweaty, plodding, loving, lusting, and aging progenitor. And, the pregnant phallus eliminates the "wet stuff" that permitted its prototype to penetrate Baconian "holes and corners."[75] The violence of the vision is neatly occluded by comic strip captions. Robots will accidentally step on "us," but that's okay because "we" won't really be there anyhow: "our" now immortal minds will be able to abandon mother earth entirely. Indeed, some AI scientists invoking the doomsday scenario believe it is imperative that "we" get some minds off of this nuclear and ecologically endangered planet and into space colonies before it is too late.

Inevitably the question must be raised: Which minds? Since the capacity of the most powerful parallel processing machines (connection machines) will be finite, not everyone will be able to get out of their bodies or off of the planet. Some of "us" will be stepped on, incinerated, or poisoned by toxic waste. So, who gets downloaded into the programs? The new evolutionary logic dictates the answer. The best minds, of course, the kinds of minds that are most readily available for modeling in the AI laboratories at MIT, Stanford, and Carnegie-Mellon University: minds of upper middle-class, white, American, predominantly male computer scientists. These are, not incidentally, some of the same minds and bodies that are most sought after by sperm bank entrepreneurs and their customers.

These are also some of the same minds that envision a future in which AI will render participatory democracy obsolete. Among them are minds that herald the coming of a time when machines, not people, will control the world's nuclear arsenals; when new forms of slavery will be introduced in which living machines (cyborgs) programmed to be "ethical" will serve as slaves; when robots will be programmed to meet all (in- and out-of body) erotic needs and thereby render human intercourse and biological reproduction redundant.[76] In short, these are minds that embrace what Neil Postman calls "technopoly," or totalitarian technocracy.[77]

The mythos and metaphors of AI talk and texts display a familiar design. AI discourse is a discourse of control; it builds hierarchy into the hard-wiring of its circuitry. The robotic fantasies of AI researchers presuppose the necessity of "the violent mastery and destruction of others."[78] Comic-book talk papers over the perversity of AI concepts of creativity, immortality, and progress, but MIT researcher and outspoken in-house critic of AI ideology and eschatology, Joseph Weizenbaum, cuts through the cartoon images and conceives the perversity within the same frame history has used to comprehend its previous incarnations: genocide.[79]

The faded mythology encoded in AI talk and texts demonstrates that AI is not the univocal discourse—not the pure Cartesian reason—that its architects thought they were encoding. Like the technostrategic discourse of the Cold War defense intellectuals analyzed by Carol Cohn, AI is also a discourse, which fails according to its own criteria: it is as far from a "paragon of cool-headed rationality" as was Francis Bacon's belief in the diabolical powers of witches.[80] Weizenbaum's characterization of AI scientists as big children who have not given up their "sandbox fantasies" or sublimated their dreams of omnipotence may be correct.[81] But lest we swell with the satisfaction of one-upping would-be gods, we should remember that we all harbor lost children within us, and that fear can usually be counted upon to release them from captivity. And fear was the generative core of Cold War cosmology.

Let us remind ourselves that the big children of AIM possess some of the best scientific and mathematical minds of the age. They are members of a powerful scientific elite: researchers, teachers, and gatekeepers of the most advanced and prestigious academic and commercial computer research centers in the world. The metaphors these men use to conceive nature, gender, and computer architectures are far more potent (and pregnant) than yours or mine. Donna Haraway contends biology has already undergone a cybernetic revolution, in which natural objects have been retheorized as "technological devices properly understood in terms of mechanisms of production and storage of information."[82] This metaphoric reconfiguration of the territory of science has fundamentally changed the character of scientific interventions in the biological and material worlds, and has thereby changed the nature of those worlds. The generative metaphors of information processing have transformed humans into cyborgs and astronauts—all of us: technophiles and technophobes, feminists and misogynists, acrobats and apple growers too.[83]

Unlike Bacon's patriarchal metaphors, which saw knowledge issuing from a chaste marriage between men's mind and nature, top-down cybernetic metaphors locate the genesis of knowledge in the marriage of men's minds and male machines. The mythos of male bonding encoded in AI discourse bears little resemblance to Plato's homoerotic vision. AI metaphors replace Eros with objects: fetishes made of circuits and chips. Where Baconian epistemology suppressed the female principle, AIM's technovisions negates the human principle, and as Weizenbaum points out, "There's nothing left after you've destroyed the human species."[84]

COITUS INTERRUPTUS

The strong top-down AI research program is both a tribute to and testimony against Western dualism and Enlightenment conceptions of reason. The self-correcting elements in the hyperrationality of the top-down AI program were powerful enough to discover AIM's own limits. This discovery, in turn, invalidated the essential tenet of AI's premise: that reason exists in a dimension apart from and beyond history, culture, and sentient beings. The failure of the top-down program was a triumph for biology: a regrounding of mind in body and of mental processes as human, learned, and socially situated. Promethean man was pulled back to earth, as he always is when he flies too high: too far from his origins. In the mythopoetics of Western dualism, the triumph of the body is a triumph of the feminine principle.

In AI parascientific discourse, the latent symbolic ascent of the feminine that accompanied the paradigmatic shift to the bottoms-up approach was never grasped, and appears in any case to have been ephemeral: a transitory return of the repressed feminine dimension. It was briefly ascendant at the point of impact and (yes, I will say it) intercourse of thesis (top-down) and antithesis (bottoms-up) and in the period of the reconceptualization and re-birthing of research programs for AI that immediately followed. That this moment of opening occurred at the same time that the larger social, cultural, and political formations of global power were also undergoing profound, even epochal, transformations is, as we have seen, not coincidental. The crises that the end of the Cold War posed for the defense industry and for research funded by the Defense Department were widely chronicled in the media in the late 1980s and early 1990s. The permanent war economy had been very costly, but it had insulated postwar America against the extremes of the boom and bust cycles of capitalism. What was at the time dubbed by the *New York Times* (March 12, 1989) as "risks of peace" included not only displacing the economic stabilization of defense spending but also displacing defense workers, which included a highly educated techno-scientific strata that could be very dangerous if it became alienated.[85]

The dramaturgical accompaniments of the Persian Gulf War launched what President George Bush called a "new world order," which, counterfactually, sought to keep the old power-knowledge of the military industrial complex intact. It did not work, except as television, and it was not, in any case, a strategy that held much long-term promise: it was too expensive and morally repellent, for example the U.S. military estimates that the brief war took somewhere between 100,000 and 200,000 Iraqi lives, most of them civilians. As a dazzling, well-edited, globally broadcast television display of the triumphs of American techno-culture, it did, however, foreshadow the future. The Clinton-Gore Administration defined that future in its technovision, the National Information Infrastructure, and in its policies, treaties, and legislative initiatives (NAFTA, GATT, and the omnibus U.S. Telecommunications Act of 1996), which supported the creation of an U.S.–dominated global information economy. Clinton-Gore went where no Republicans could have dared to go in accelerating the growth of corporate power and in defining corporate "competitiveness" as a defense initiative.[86]

The "smart" bombs profiled in the Persian Gulf War drama were prototypes for the smart technologies that would build the new information economy. By the early 1990s, the bombs were almost smart enough; and the research that produced them had already had some success in the consumer marketplace, for example the original computer game, Flight Simulator, and search-and-destroy video games. Virtual reality simulations showed commercial promise as techno-entertainments as well. AI research, like other forms of defense research, was encouraged to redefine itself, and generous government funding was dedicated to moving American science, scientists, and defense contractors through the transitional period. Research agendas were expanded to include educational, entertainment, biotechnologies, and other commercial applications. Visionary high-tech ideas were brought to bear on mundane tasks. Military and commercial agendas were often pursued in tandem. The development of robotic vision, for example, retains military applications, making those smart bombs even smarter in hitting targets, but its potential applications as prosthetics for the blind are also smart commercial (and humane) investments.

This commercialized technovision appears to support somewhat more humane agendas than the mature top-down AI approach insofar as it is less overtly tied to the monovocal agenda of Cold War demonology, for example eradicating the "evil empire." The level of fear and doomsday paranoia that accompanied the Cold War vision had largely disappeared from mass-mediated articulations of ideology and public policy until the 2001 terrorist attacks on the U.S. and the U.S.'s subsequent launching of its global War on Terrorism. This demonology continued to thrive in defense think tanks, and it prospers among fringe militia, survivalist, and white supremacist groups: groups made up primarily of white males who claim to be disenfranchised by the moderately more inclusive post–Cold War definitions of social reality.

Within computer science, doomsday scenarios have interestingly enough been transferred to the programs themselves. They revolve around fears of techno-terrorism, including hacker breaches of government and corporate security, scenarios of contamination of networked systems by massive self-replicating viruses, and dystopias involving techno-wars and extermination of the human race by a future species of intelligent robots.

WILL THE PREGNANT PHALLUS
DELIVER SELF-REPLICATING POWERS AND
A NEW GENERATION OF ANTI-HUMAN TERRORS?

What does the future hold? That is the perennial question that is posed to, and by, AI and robotics research and development scientists. The AI research community is no longer fully a male preserve: "a world without women." Women are a growing, though still small, presence within the ranks of AI and robotics research and development, although they have not yet issued any manifestos. Whether they will ultimately forge new metaphors and new ways of thinking about conceiving artificial life remains an open question.

At present the U.S. government, under President George W. Bush, is gearing up once more to strongly reassert its presence in computer science research and development by reviving development of the ill-fated (and, many scientists believe, ill-conceived) Cold War Star Wars missile defense system, originally proposed and funded under the Reagan–Bush I Administration.[87] It appears, at this point, that the War on Terrorism has given the Bush Administration the mandate it needs to override scientific reservations and congressional opposition to reviving the missile defense program. Moreover, the U.S. government has announced that it now needs aggressive as well as defensive weapons to conduct cyber-warfare. The huge reinfusion of defense funds will define the futures of AI and AL.

Will the mature research program of the bottoms-up approach of AI be more humane than the mature program of the top-down approach? There is no reason to assume it will; indeed, it could be more inhumane. The sandbox fantasies have not disappeared; in fact, they may have moved closer to becoming technological realities. Hans Moravec is still around, and still believes that "biological humans" will "be squeezed out of existence."[88] Danny Hillis, now known as the father of parallel processing, is still thinking about escaping the grim reaper: "I'm as fond of my body as anyone, but if I can be 200 with a body of silicon, I'll take it."[89] Ray Kurzweil is predicting we will become robots or fuse with robots.[90]

In "Why the Future Doesn't Need Us" (*Wired*, March 2000) Bill Joy, cofounder and chief scientist of Sun Microsystems and co-chair of a presidential commission on the future of information technology research, wonders how other techno-wizards can silently live with their fears. Joy reports that the kind of technology Moravec envisions will be feasible by 2030:

> What was different in the 20th century? Certainly, the technologies underlying the weapons of mass destruction (WMD)—nuclear, biological, and chemical (NBC)—were powerful, and the weapons an enormous threat. But building nuclear weapons required, at least for a time, access to both rare—indeed, effectively unavailable—raw materials and highly protected information; biological and chemical weapons programs also tended to require large-scale activities.
>
> The 21st-century technologies—genetics, nanotechnology, and robotics (GNR)—are so powerful that they can spawn whole new classes of accidents and abuses. Most dangerously, for the first time, these accidents and abuses are widely within the reach of individuals or small groups. They will not require large facilities or rare raw materials. Knowledge alone will enable the use of them.
>
> Thus we have the possibility not just of weapons of mass destruction but of knowledge-enabled mass destruction (KMD), this destructiveness hugely amplified by the power of self-replication.
>
> I think it is no exaggeration to say we are on the cusp of the further perfection of extreme evil, an evil whose possibility spreads well beyond that which weapons of mass destruction bequeathed to the nation-states, on to a surprisingly terrible empowerment of extreme individuals.[91]

Where the NBC technologies of the twentieth century were largely developed by the military in government-controlled laboratories, Joy points out, "We are aggressively pursuing the promises of these new technologies within the now-unchallenged system of global capitalism and its manifold financial incentives and competitive pressures."[92] He envisions scenarios where corporations may be forced into something like voluntary disarmament or the equivalent of biological weapons inspections if the species is to survive. Lest we blame the messenger, Joy is pushing the panic button precisely because he wants to initiate public dialogue about techno-futures, which, to date, have been shaped without it. He sees the astronautic fantasies of scientists, which call for evacuating the earth, as forms of denial that abdicate responsibility.

In the aftermath of the anthrax attacks on the U.S. Postal Service, Congress, the media, and the public that immediately followed the September 11, 2001, terrorist attacks in New York, Washington, and Pennsylvania, Joy's jeremiad resonates with even greater gravity. No one has taken responsibility for the anthrax attacks, which are at present assumed to be the work of a domestic terrorist, not the al-Qaida network. Government forces, from federal to local levels, remain on high alerts for further biological and chemical terrorist attacks. As a result, the scenario Joy describes takes on a new and chilling sense of reality.

Joy does not address the gendered components of these technovisions or the gender orders they will support, but he does try to see beyond the conventional horizons of Western science and culture. Siding with the biological life on planet Earth, he is a de facto ally in the struggle for a more human, and therefore a future friendlier to women, the species, and the planet. Moreover, by virtue of the authority his background gives to his argument, it is a valuable addition to the arsenal of ideas that can be mobilized in "the semiological warfare" that is required to interrupt the privatization of policy making that the new enclosure movement has empowered and normalized.[93] Joy's goal is to open up a broadly based dialogue about the deployment of technologies before they are deployed, not to provide lay readers with a definitive take on the science of the future. If his scenario is alarmist, then open, informed, critical, democratic dialogue can serve as a corrective. In any case, democratic dialogue about techno-futures is urgently needed if democracy is to retain (or recover) any meaning beyond the symbolic or spectral.[94]

NEW SCIENCE REQUIRES NEW
POETRY: RETURNING TO THE LAUNCH PAD

The process of interrupting and correcting the talk and texts of technoscience has just begun. Haraway describes such interventions as forms of practicing "politics by other means."[95] Yes, and poetry too! For the first step in scientific revolutions (as in political revolutions) is to change the names, because scientific revolutions are metaphoric redescriptions of nature, not (or not only) codings of revolutionary new insights into the intrinsic nature of phenomena.[96]

Most, though certainly not all, constructivist and Western feminist conceptions of nature and humankind break with the astronautic vision. Feminist perspectives support metaphors, models, and taxonomies for describing nature that are less hierarchical, more contextual and permeable, and perhaps more reflexive than their masculinist predecessors. The achievements (and perversions) of Western science have been possible because they have taken flight on transcendent metaphors, for example Prometheus, Icarus, Faust, Superman, cyborg, and astronaut.[97] These metaphors deny embodiment and mortality, whereas images of domesticity, embodiment, and material necessity—images drawn from women's experience—keep our feet on the ground. Fully human conceptions of nature and being must do both or both/and.[98] That is, they must allow us—all of us!—to dream dreams that make the impossible possible. But they must also recognize that it takes many dreamers—many diverse, self-reflexive, human agents—to dream life-affirming dreams: women and men in life sustaining communities, not insular enclaves of scientific geniuses or self-replicating forms of hardware and software.

This new way of thinking is, however, unlikely to emerge from truces, whether voluntary or mandated, in the so-called scientific wars. Adding women to science and stirring will not do the job. Indeed such a strategy, no matter how well intended, is likely to either kill the spirit of the women who are added to science or kill the spirit of science. Rather, species-friendly conceptions of nature are far more likely to find incubation within new generative metaphors that will, in turn, prove to be more illuminating, inspiring, and effective in meeting the life-sustaining challenges that lie ahead. Or, to put it pragmatically, expanding the landscape of the scientific imagination may prove to be more important to twenty-first-century earth science than it was to twentieth-century space science.

If scientists like Moravec, Kurzweil, Joy, and others are right about the future, survival of the planet now requires terminating the exterminating elements in the self-replicating technologies of genetics, nanotechnology, and robotics.[99] Our interventions need to attend to the problem from the launchpad rather than the space station. We need to cast our collective lot with earth, not the stars. We need to find our metaphors closer to home: to come back to earth, back to our aging, sweating, imperfect, mortal bodies. We need to face the responsibilities, tensions, ambiguities, and pleasures of a fully human life and death. In short, we need to dream a new cultural dream: a dream that requires nothing less than interruption and redirection of the out-of-body experiences of modern and postmodern science.

NOTES

1. The artificial intelligence movement has been widely chronicled. The brief overview of its history provided here draws primarily on the following sources: David Bolter, *Turing's Man: Western Culture in the Computer Age* (Chapel Hill: University of North Carolina Press, 1984); John L. Casti, *Paradigms Regained* (New York: HarperCollins, 2000); Douglas R. Hofstadter, *Godel, Escher, Bach: An Eternal Golden Braid* (New York: Random House, 1979); George Johnson, *Machinery of the Mind: Inside the New Science of Artificial Intelligence* (New York: Random House, 1986); and Sherry Turkle, *The Second Self: Computers and the Human Spirit* (New York: Simon & Schuster, 1984).

2. Johnson, *Machinery of the Mind*, 37.

3. Johnson, *Machinery of the Mind*, 37.

4. Sherry Turkle, who has extensively chronicled the computer culture at MIT, reports, "Mainstream computer researchers no longer aspire to program intelligence into computers but expect intelligence to emerge from the interactions of small subprograms." That is, scientists are no longer seeking to produce AI but rather AL (artificial life). The A-Life movement builds on the work of emergent AI research: a tradition that had been abandoned in the 1960s, but was rejuvenated by the shift to the bottoms-up tradition of AI. See Sherry Turkle, *Life on the Screen: Identity in the Age of the Internet* (New York: Simon & Schuster, 1995), 20.

5. I use Casti's shorthand terminology, top-down and bottoms-up, throughout rather than Turkle's AI and A-Life distinction, even though I am tempted by the greater drama of Turkle's terms. Casti's terms are cleaner and, in the case of bottoms-up, more encompassing. See Casti, *Paradigms Regained*. See also Hofstadter, *Godel, Escher, Bach: An Eternal Golden Braid*; and Johnson, *Machinery of the Mind*.

6. Casti, *Paradigms Regained*.

7. Heinz Pagels, *The Dreams of Reason: The Computer and the Rise of the Sciences of Complexity* (New York: Simon & Schuster, 1988).

8. Marvin Minsky, *Society of Mind* (New York: Simon & Schuster, 1987). See also Turkle, *Life on the Screen*.

9. Johnson, *Machinery of the Mind*.

10. For chronicle of how the Cold War climate impacted on university life in a variety of disciplines, as seen from left and liberal perspectives, see David Montgomery et al., *The Cold War and The University: Toward an Intellectual History of the Postwar Years* (New York: The New Press, 1997).

11. Many of the same cutting-edge AI scientists interviewed by Fjermedal and Turkle in the 1980s are the same cutting edge computer scientists that Bill Joy, a cutting-edge corporate scientist, interviewed for his current work on scientific futures. See Turkle, *The Second Self*; Grant Fjermedal, *The Tomorrow Makers* (New York: Macmillan, 1986); Bill Joy, "Why the Future Doesn't Need Us," *Wired* (April 2000): 1–15.

12. Robert W. McChesney makes notes the migration of this term in Corporate Media and the *Threat to Democracy* (New York: Seven Stories, 1997).

13. An Wang, quoted by Tom Forester, *High-Tech Society: The Story of the Information Technology Revolution* (Oxford: Basil Blackwell, 1987), 1.

14. Ivan Illich, "Silence is a Commons," *Development: Seeds of Change, Village Through Global Order* 1 (1985), 81. The analogy to the enclosure movement that Illich embraces has had currency in communications since the 1980s. More recently, and apparently independently, the trope has gained currency among legal scholars. For a summary of this work, see James Boyle, "Fencing off Ideas: Enclosure and the Disappearance of the Public Domain," *Daedalus* (Spring 2002): 13–25.

15. Minsky, *Society of Mind*.

16. Hofstadter, *Godel, Escher, Bach*, 601.

17. Isaac Asimov, "Every Real Problem Can and Will Be Solved," in *2,500 Years of Science Writing*, ed. Edmund Blarr Bolles (New York: W. H. Freeman, 1999), 5–6.

18. George Johnson points out, "In our society, we make a distinction between the history of science and the history of everything else." Within this proscription, only scientists are empowered to criticize science. Science writers, who assume the role of interpreters within the boundaries of this proscription, appear to share its protections. See Johnson, *Fire in the Mind: Science, Faith and the Search for Order* (New York: Random House, 1996), 5.

19. For an example of this proscription at work, see the hierarchical framing of references to (e.g., "down among the sociologists") and expressions of contempt for sociologists (Edinburgh constructivists) who presume to question science in Paul K. Gross and Norman Levitt, *Higher Superstition: The Academic Left and Its Quarrels with Science* (Baltimore: Johns Hopkins University Press, 1994).

20. Hubert L. Dreyfus, *What Computers Can't Do: A Critique of Artificial Reason* (New York: Harper & Row, 1979); Hubert L. Dreyfus, *What Computers Still Can't Do* (Cambridge, Mass.: MIT Press, 1992); John Searle, *Intentionality: An Essay in the Philosophy of Mind* (Cambridge: Cambridge University Press, 1983); Margaret A. Boden, *Computer Models of Mind* (Cambridge: Cambridge University Press, 1988); and Harry M. Collins, *Artificial Experts: Social Knowledge and Intelligent Machines* (Cambridge, Mass.: MIT Press, 1993).

21. See also Sue Curry Jansen, "The Ghost in the Machine: Artificial Intelligence and Gendered Thought Patterns," *Resources for Feminist Research/ documentation sur la recherche feministe* 17, no. 4 (1988): 4–7.

22. Cynthia Enloe, *The Morning After: Sexual Politics at the End of the Cold War* (Berkeley: University of California Press, 1993).

23. Hofstadter, Godel, Escher, Bach. From the beginning AI theorists were aware of this conundrum, but Hofstadter explores its implications with stunning virtuosity.

24. David F. Nobel, *A World Without Women: The Christian Clerical Culture of Western Science* (New York: Alfred A. Knopf, 1992).

25. Sally Hacker, "The Eye of the Beholder: An Essay on Technology and Eroticism," in *'Doing it the Hard Way' Investigations of Gender and Technology*, ed. (posthumously) Dorothy E. Smith and Susan M. Turner (Boston: Unwin Hyman, 1990), 214.

26. These perspectives were pioneered by sociologists associated with the Edinburgh School as well as by feminist scholars Dorothy Merchant, Donna Haraway, Ruth Hubbard, Evelyn Fox Keller, Sandra Harding, and many others. See David Bloor, *Knowledge and Social Imagery* (London: Routledge & Kegan Paul, 1977);

Donna Haraway, "A Manifesto for Cyborgs," *Socialist Review* 80 (1985): 65–107; Sandra Harding, *The Science Question in Feminism* (Ithaca, N.Y.: Cornell University Press, 1986); Evelyn Fox Keller, *Reflections on Gender and Science* (New Haven, Conn.: Yale University Press, 1985); Carolyn Merchant, *The Death of Nature: Women, Ecology and The Scientific Revolution* (New York: Harper & Row, 1985).

27. Hofstadter, *Godel, Escher, Bach.*

28. For a discussion and of the Cartesian principle in relation to the sciences of complexity, regarding the bottoms-up approach, see Pagels, *The Dreams of Reason.*

29. Bolter, *Turing's Man*, 73.

30. Susan Bordo, *The Flight to Objectivity: Essays on Cartesianism and Culture* (Albany: State University of New York Press, 1987).

31. Hofstadter, *Godel, Escher, Bach*, 579.

32. Hofstadter, *Godel, Escher, Bach.*

33. Hofstadter, *Godel, Escher, Bach*, 623.

34. Minsky, *Society of Mind.*

35. Fjermedal, *The Tomorrow Makers*, 7.

36. Hugh Kenner, *The Mechanic Muse* (New York: Oxford University Press, 1987).

37. Richard Dawkins, *Unweaving the Rainbow: Science, Delusion and the Appetite for Wonder* (Boston: Houghton Mifflin, 1998), 186.

38. Mary Hesse, *Models and Analogies in Science* (South Bend, Ind.: University of Notre Dame Press, 1966); Bloor, *Knowledge and Social Imagery*; and Richard Rorty, "The Contingency of Language," *London Review of Books* 17 (April 17, 1986): 3–6.

39. Bacon recognized that language contaminated the purity of science and longed for a purely scientific language, which would be culture-free. Most practicing scientists have, however, bracketed the problem of language and reported their results as if language were a neutral instrument.

40. George Lakoff has exhaustively explored the role metaphor plays in making ordinary language and thought possible. See George Lakoff and Mark Turner, *More than Cool Reason: A Field Guide to Poetic Metaphor* (Chicago: University of Chicago Press, 1989). See also George Lakoff and Mark Johnson, *Metaphors We Live By* (Chicago: University of Chicago Press, 1981); George Lakoff and Mark Johnson, *Philosophy in the Flesh: The Embodied Mind and Its Challenge to Western Thought* (New York: Basic Books, 1999); and George Lakoff, *Women, Fire, and Dangerous Things: What Categories Reveal abut the Mind* (Chicago: University of Chicago Press, 1981).

41. That is, at least at the level of empirical science, there appeared to be consonance in the patterns scientists discovered in or imputed to nature and the patterns perceived or constructed by the human mind.

42. Such understandings of generative metaphors are shared by nonfeminists as well as feminists. See, for example, Arthur Koestler, *The Act of Creation* (New York: Macmillan, 1967); Simone de Beauvoir, *The Second Sex* (New York: Vintage Books, 1974); Susan Stanford Friedman, "Creativity and the Childbirth Metaphor," *Feminist Studies* 13, no. 1 (1987): 49–78; and Evelyn Fox Keller, *Reflections on Gender and Science.*

43. Merchant, *The Death of Nature*; and Keller, *Reflections on Gender and Science*.

44. Merchant, *The Death of Nature*; Keller, *Reflections on Gender and Science*; Harding, *The Science Question in Feminism*; and Theodore Roszak, *The Gendered Atom: Reflections on the Sexual Psychology of Science* (Berkeley, Calif.: Conari Press, 1999).

45. Lionel Tiger, *Men in Groups* (New York: Random House, 1969).

46. Brian Easlea, *Fathering the Unthinkable* (London: Pluto, 1983), 17.

47. Easlea, *Fathering the Unthinkable*; and Keller, *Reflections on Gender and Science*.

48. Roger C. Schank and Robert P. Abelson, *Scripts, Plans, Goals and Understandings: An Inquiry into Human Knowledge Structures* (Mahwah, N.J.: Lawrence Erlbaum Associates, 1977).

49. David Gelernter, *Mirror Worlds or the Day Software Puts the Universe in a Shoebox . . . How it Will Happen and What it Will Mean* (New York: Oxford University Press, 1991), 1.

50. Norbert Wiener, *God and Golem, Inc.: A Comment on Certain Points Where Cybernetics Impinges on Religion* (Cambridge, Mass.: MIT Press, 1964): 49–50.

51. Turkle, *The Second Self*.

52. Easlea, *Fathering the Unthinkable*.

53. Edward A. Feigenbaum and Pamela McCorduck, *The Fifth Generation: Artificial Intelligence and Japan's Challenge to the World* (New York: New American Library, 1984).

54. Freeman Dyson, *Imagined Worlds* (Cambridge, Mass.: Harvard University Press, 1997), 9.

55. Hans Moravec, *Mind Children: The Future of Robot and Human Intelligence* (Cambridge, Mass.: Harvard University Press, 1988).

56. Michael Hirsch, "Computers Envisioned as Successors to Humans," *Buffalo News*, 14 June 1987, 16(E).

57. Hirsch, "Computers Envisioned as Successors," 16(E).

58. Moravec, *Mind Children*, 1.

59. Judy Wajcman, *Feminism Confronts Technology* (University Park: Pennsylvania State University Press, 1991); and Andreas Huyssen, "The Vamp and the Machine: Fritz Lang's Metropolis," in After the Great Divide: Modernism, Mass Culture, Postmodernism, ed. Andreas Huyssen (Bloomington: Indiana University Press, 1986).

60. Huyssen, "The Vamp and the Machine," 70; see also Judith Halberstam, "Automating Gender: Postmodern Feminism in the Age of the Intelligent Machine," *Feminist Studies* 17, no. 3 (Fall 1991): 439–61.

61. Sussman quoted by Fjermedal, *The Tomorrow Makers*, 8.

62. Mary Shelley, *Frankenstein* (New York: St. Martin's Press, 2000, original 1818).

63. Sussman quoted by Fjermedal, *The Tomorrow Makers*, 8.

64. Hutchins quoted by Pagels, *Dreams of Reason*, 19.

65. Brooks quoted by Fjermedal, *The Tomorrow Makers*, 33.

66. Brooks quoted by Fjermedal, *The Tomorrow Makers*, 33.

67. Donna Haraway, presentations and discussions at Science as Cultural Practice, a summer institute sponsored by The National Endowment in the Humanities, Wesleyan University, Middletown, Conn., July 1991.

68. Drescher quoted by Turkle, *The Second Self*, 261.

69. Drescher quoted by Turkle, *The Second Self*, 262.

70. Minsky in Fjermedal, *The Tomorrow Makers*, 7.

71. Minsky, *Society of Mind*.

72. Moravec and Blackwell quoted by Fjermedal, *The Tomorrow Makers*, 60.

73. Moravec quoted by Fjermedal, *The Tomorrow Makers*, 60.

74. Moravec quoted by Hirsch, "Computers Envisioned as Successors," 16.

75. Bacon quoted by Merchant in *The Death of Nature*, 168.

76. Fjermedal, *The Tomorrow Makers*.

77. Neil Postman, *Technopoly: The Surrender of Culture to Technology* (New York: Alfred A. Knopf, 1992).

78. Tiger, *Men in Groups*, 69.

79. Joseph Weizenbaum, *Computer Power and Human Reason* (San Francisco: W. H. Freeman, 1976).

80. Carol Cohn, "Sex and Death in the Rational World of Defense Intellectuals," *Signs* 12, no. 4 (1987): 717.

81. Joseph Weizenbaum, "Not Without Us," *Z Magazine* (January 1988): 94.

82. Donna Haraway, "The Biological Enterprise," *Radical History Review*, 20 (1979): 223.

83. Donna Haraway, "A Manifesto for Cyborgs," *Socialist Review* 80 (1985): 65–107; and Robert Romanyshyn, *Technology as Symptom and Dream* (London: Routledge, 1989).

84. Weizenbaum quoted in Fjermedal, *The Tomorrow Makers*, 140.

85. See chapter 7 for a fuller discussion of news-framing at the end of the Cold War.

86. Department of Defense website, <www.defenselink.mil> (accessed March 2000).

87. For a critical analysis and summary of the scientific and political debates about the Star Wars program, see Frances Fitzgerald, *Way Out There in the Blue: Reagan, Star Wars, and the End of the Cold War* (New York: Simon & Schuster, 2000).

88. Joy, "Why the Future Doesn't Need Us," 2.

89. Joy, "Why the Future Doesn't Need Us," 2. For a recent account, which demonstrates that AI's self-promoting hype continues despite claims a new humility within AI and AL, see Jim Krane, The Associated Press, "'Human' Robots March Forward—on Movie Screen and Off," *Allentown (Pa.) Morning Call*, 26 June 2001, 8(D).

90. Joy, "Why the Future Doesn't Need Us," 2.

91. Joy, "Why the Future Doesn't Need Us," 3

92. Joy, "Why the Future Doesn't Need Us," 7.

93. Umberto Eco, *Travels in Hyper-Reality* (New York: Harcourt Brace Jovanovich, 1986).

94. Guy Debord, *The Society of Spectacle* (New York: Zone Books, 1995).

95. Donna Haraway, "Primatology is Politics by Other Means;" in *Feminist Approaches to Science*, ed. Ruth Bleier (New York: Pergamon Press, 1986), 77–118.

96. Mary Hesse, *Revolutions and Reconstructions in the Philosophy of Science* (Bloomington: Indiana University Press, 1980); and Rorty, "The Contingency of Language."

97. See discussion in chapter 1 as well as Eve Tavor Bannet, "The Feminist Logic of Both/And," *Genders* 15 (1992).

98. Bordo, *The Flight to Objectivity; Clive Hart, Images of Flight* (Berkeley: University of California Press, 1988); and Romanyshyn, *Technology as Symptom and Dream*.

99. Joy, "Why the Future Doesn't Need Us."

Part III

POST-IDEOLOGICAL IDEOLOGIES

When people disagreed with him, he urged them to be objective.

—Joseph Heller, *Catch-22*

Chapter Seven

When the Center No Longer Holds: Rupture and Repair

During periods of historical rupture and repair, the normally invisible strata-gems that the powerful use to create, cultivate, and mobilize public consent become visible. Such periods are extraordinary living laboratories for stu-dents of political linguistics. The sudden collapse of the Soviet Union and the abrupt end of the Cold War left both sides of the long conflict with obsolete policies and political narratives. This chapter examines the efforts of Ameri-can policymakers, pundits, and the press to quickly repair and redeploy their respective semantic resources in the wake of the rupture; the completion of that repair work during the Clinton Administration; and some of the chal-lenges the September 2001 terrorist attacks on New York and Washington posed to America's image of itself.

Raymond Williams opens *Keywords: A Vocabulary of Culture and Soci-ety* (1976) with a brief account of his own experience with the conceptual and semantic shifts produced by the cataclysmic rupture of World War II. Returning to Cambridge, England, in 1945 after four and a half years of military service, Williams reports that he experienced a profound sense of estrangement. All of the familiar faces were gone and everything seemed different. After many disorienting days, he encountered an old acquain-tance who had also just returned from the army. They eagerly shared their impressions of the strange new world around them. Then, Williams writes, "We both said, in effect simultaneously: 'the fact is, they just don't speak the same language.'"[1]

Williams, of course, used scholarship to cope with his disorientation. He undertook an inventory, or to use a more fashionable term, a genealogy, of the formation of key terms and concepts in the English language. Originally in-tended to serve as an appendix to *Culture and Society*, Williams actually spent over a quarter of a century revising and refining his vocabulary of key-words before it was finally published in 1976.

According to Williams, each of the 155 keywords he examined "virtually forced itself" on his attention because the problems of its meanings appeared to be inseparable from the problems it was being used to discuss. According to Williams, the words are "key" in two connected senses: "they are signifi-cant, binding words in certain activities and their interpretation" and "they are significant, indicative words in certain forms of thought."[2]

Williams made modest claims for his compilation. Acknowledging that it was neither thorough nor neutral, he invited readers to become collaborators in the work. He even convinced the publisher of the original edition to include blank pages to encourage readers to make their own notes, as well as to sig-nal both that the inquiry remained open and that the author solicited correc-tions and amendments for future editions. Williams himself continued work on the project throughout his life. His final public lecture, "When was Mod-ernism?", which explicated postmodernism as an enemy ideological forma-tion, was in many ways a coda to this endeavor.

Raymond Williams died in January 1988. Since then, planet Earth has un-dergone epochal transformations that would appear to be rivaled in scale by the revolutionary political and cultural developments that precipitated the Western Enlightenment and the birth of modern political cultures in the eigh-teenth century.

These transformations have been accompanied by changes in the lan-guages, categories, and assumptions of contemporary politics and culture. Euro-American explanations of world politics underwent a profound inter-pretive crises in the late 1980s and early 1990s because the political ideolo-gies and rhetorics, secured by the mythologies of the Cold War, lost their res-onance. The old political mythos had collapsed, but the new discursive system (or systems) for making sense of world politics was still struggling to be born. The rhetoric of globalization and the technovisions of an emergent global information society, revolving on the axis of a commercialized Inter-net, had not yet even entered the contest for hegemonic dominance (although U.S. plans for an information or knowledge-based economy actually predate the *beginning* of the Cold War).[3]

The altered political landscape of the early 1990s was far more bewilder-ing than the milieu Williams encountered at the dawn of the Cold War. Pres-idents, premiers, policymakers, political pundits, and managers of global cor-porations—not just returning soldiers and old reds—experienced the disorientation and actively engaged in mass-mediated races to locate, secure, name, and claim key formations in this brave new world *dis*/order.

THE INTERPRETIVE CRISIS

This chapter examines some of the discursive practices and framing devices that Western policymakers, social theorists, and media organizations used to make sense of these changes. Most scholarship and speculation that emerged in the immediate wake of the fall of the Berlin Wall focused quite understandably on how these transformations were altering institutions and structures of knowledge in the former Soviet Union and Soviet Bloc nations, and how the emerging nations of Eastern Europe were being repositioned in relation to the West.

My analysis gives some attention to these questions, but its primary focus is on how these changes entered into discussions of and warrants for freedom of expression and the production of knowledge within liberal (or neoliberal) democracies, especially the United States. More specifically, I look at some of the domestic (U.S.) reverberations of the global shift in power relations that have attracted relatively little systematic commentary or analysis. My agenda is modest, painfully so. It opens a rather narrow window for analysis of post–Cold War keywords by revisiting the period between breakup of the Soviet Union and the triumphant (and triumphalist) U.S. embrace of globalization. It identifies some of the communicative constituents of the interpretive crises and explores some of their implications for social theory. That is, it attends to the sociocultural dimensions of the crises, to deployments of persuasion and propaganda, which accompanied—sometimes preceding, sometimes following—profound structural shifts in the foundations of the political economy of communication. These structural shifts, which are, in effect, the story behind my story—one might even say the "real" story—have been well documented by others.[4] This chapter looks at the ideological or the post-ideological cover that was used to disarm or mute opposition to government and corporate actions that would have been either unthinkable or illegal prior to the Reagan-Thatcher revolution (or counterrevolution).

In the U.S., the period immediately following the fall of the Berlin Wall was characterized by a contradictory mix of euphoria, apprehension, urgency, and sense of possibility. In retrospect, that period of hegemonic opening was remarkably brief in duration. In the United States, it can be more or less reliably dated from the fall of the Berlin Wall and the collapse of the former Soviet Union to near the end of the first year of the Clinton-Gore Administration (1993). I date the beginning of the end of the crises to the publication of the policy document, National Information Infrastructure (NII) Agenda for Action (September 15, 1993), which was followed by Al Gore's famous "information superhighway" address at the National Press Club on December

21, 1993. NII laid out the initial blueprint for globalizing an U.S.–led, technologically based, information economy.

Pluralization of the term "crises" requires emphasis because the end of the Cold War transformed configurations of power throughout the world and precipitated multiple and distinctive crises within all of those configurations. Yet, international news, especially international news circulated in the United States, focused almost exclusively on the crises in the nations that comprised the former Soviet Union and on the implications of those foreign crises for the U.S. Moreover, the solutions offered to these crises by U.S. government agenda setters, policy analysts, elite journalists, pundits, and think tankers tended to be conceptualized in univocal terms: one solution fits all, for example a New World Order or global information economy. This chapter explores some of the elements necessary for critical analyses of a fairly narrow and elite form of communication, international news, in light of the dissolution of its master narrative or defining trope, the Cold War.

I take international news to be (a) a site where government, corporate, and media elites communicate with one another, and compete for control over national and international agenda-setting processes; as well as (b) an arena where these elites rationalize, test, and seek to publicly legitimate political and corporate policies and practices.

Marketing studies sponsored by major media corporations seem to indicate that, except in periods of immediate crisis, most news consumers in the United States do not invest very heavily in consumption of international news; they do not regard it as having much relevance to their daily experience; and they do not conceive of themselves as participants in either the events or the discourses of international news.[5]

Because of high production costs, most international news is produced by elite media organizations and news agencies. Although the Internet has opened up new, albeit time-intensive, opportunities for accessing alternative media sources, including international news, most Americans still get most of their international news from mainstream media outlets. Media usage patterns during the weeks following the September 2001 terrorist attacks in the United States strongly reaffirmed this reliance on mainstream media, especially television.

Gaye Tuchman's claim, which is that most consumers of mainstream national media function largely as spectators or eavesdroppers on the conversations of political and journalistic elites, still largely holds; and it holds with even greater force when applied to international news.[6] The "conversations" of elites that make up the bulk of routine national and international news and commentary do, however, offer us one of the only opportunities we have for gaining access to the strategic thinking of elites on global issues, even though this access is through tightly secured ideological screens.

My eavesdroppings on these conversations are assembled into four interrelated textual moves. The first part of this chapter situates the inquiry within the assumptions and precedents of media-critical theory. The second part briefly considers the contributions that recent work in metaphor analysis can make to the study of keywords in contemporary political discourse. The third part considers some of the processes whereby terms become naturalized and amplified in mass-mediated forms of political discourse. The final part offers a brief case study of the meteoric rise and rapid but lingering decline of the keyword/phrase "New World Order." It also considers the traction, in both theory and practice, which its successor (and offspring) globalization has achieved. In addition, it briefly examines some of the semantic resources mobilized by the United States and its allies to fight the "War on Terrorism." The final section concludes with an assessment of some of the implications of "political linguistics" for liberal or neoliberal concepts of press freedom.[7]

MEDIA-CRITICAL THEORY AND POLITICAL DISCOURSE

The designation "media-critical theory" is used here to signal affiliation with approaches to critique that recognize both (a) the importance of sociological analysis of formations and structures of power and knowledge, including the power of media; media organizations, ownership patterns, and their positioning within market systems; and (b) the significance of cultural analysis of the complex hegemonic and sometimes counterhegemonic processes, whereby mediated messages acquire meaning and exercise influence in socially stratified, heterogeneous, industrial societies. The term is also intended to convey a continued appreciation of the critical spirit of the Frankfurt tradition of media analysis, especially its insistence that it is only "by the refusal to celebrate the present" that the possibility of a more humane future might be preserved.[8]

The hyphenated form, media-critical, is intended to convey an inclusive, eclectic, perhaps even somewhat preemptive positioning: one that attempts to foreground what Hanno Hardt characterizes as "a notion of critique that is inherent in the idea of democracy and can be defined as thinking about freedom and responsibility and the contribution that intellectual pursuits can make to the welfare of society."[9]

In characterizing "political linguistics" as the "armor of the establishment," Herbert Marcuse maintains that "one of the most effective rights of the Sovereign is the right to establish enforceable definitions of words."[10] Williams acknowledged that he found his interests in historical semantics "closely echoed" in some of the later works of the Frankfurt School, which combine "analysis of key words or key terms with key concepts."[11] Williams was presumably referring, at least in part, to Marcuse's analysis of political language.

Neither Marcuse nor Williams intended their decodings to serve only, or even primarily, as academic exercises. Both saw their critiques of political linguistics as acts of resistance and even as potential admission tickets to emancipatory praxis. Marcuse made this explicit by linking the idea of political linguistics to linguistic therapy. He acknowledged that the idea of linguistic therapy is a utopian vision, whereby art and politics—what he later called "the aesthetic dimension"—combine to rescue keywords from the control of hegemonic forces and recruit them to the service of emancipatory ends.[12] He offered no recipes for organizing these rescue missions, but he did provide some lucid illustrations, for example the refusal and inversion of the language of oppression by black civil rights leaders in the U.S. during the 1960s, a form of semantic intervention that, for a time, replaced resignation with a collective vision of transcendence.

Few scholars today share Marcuse's optimism about the redemptive powers of the aesthetic dimension. With the triumph of postmodern aesthetics in the 1970s and 1980s, the avant-garde and counterculture were largely subsumed by commerce and hip consumerism: "the conquest of cool."[13] Nevertheless the relentless intellectual passion Marcuse invested in what he called "the critical spirit" remains worthy of emulation.[14]

On the surface, Williams's project is more esoteric than Marcuse's: to chart historical changes in the range of meanings ascribed to key terms that are also associated with, or indicators of, shifting social formations. Yet, Williams's genealogies were also politically charged. He saw them as means of raising consciousness of the social conflicts present in and sometimes papered over by changes in language.[15]

Feminist approaches to historical semantics and linguistic therapy owe more to the linguistic insurrections of Mary Daly than to either Williams or Marcuse.[16] Nevertheless, feminist theorists have also used excavations of the language of the sovereigns, in this case, church fathers, the founders of modern sciences, the gatekeepers of literary, artistic, and philosophical canons, as well as lawmakers and statesmen, as ways of raising consciousness and mobilizing movements for social change. Their excavations have demonstrated that the keywords for which sovereigns usually assign enforceable definitions are metaphors, specifically controlling or generative metaphors, upon which many other related terms and subterms depend for their cultural coherence and resonance. In part II of this book, Impertinent Questions, these feminist contributions to metaphor analysis were extensively explored. In part III, I assume that many of the claims that feminist epistemologists have made about scientific objectivity apply with even greater force to the derivative and always far more shaky claims media organizations have made for journalistic objectivity.

THE WINNER NAMES THE AGE: GENERATIVE METAPHORS

In political and news discourses, as in scientific discourses, metaphors are used to map unknown territory. They make the unfamiliar familiar by taming and at least partially domesticating it. Metaphors do similar work in ordinary conversation. For example, for many generations of small children, a smiling man in the moon who is made of green cheese transforms the shift-shaping orbit that looms ominously in the night skies into a friendly, even reassuring, presence. Big children and their leaders and scribes, suddenly confronted with the implosion of prevailing political narratives, also crave the comforts of green cheese. In science, the cheese is packaged in the plain wrappers of formal language and tested against empirical reality, but metaphors are still the doors to discovery. In politics, the wrappers themselves are often what count.

Winners get to name the age: to coin the metaphors that others will live by. But they are often unprepared for this momentous responsibility. The sudden end of the Cold War is a dramatic case in point. It rendered the victors, if not speechless, without reliable scripts. President George Bush's attempt to make green cheese, "The New World Order" (State of the Union Speech, January 17, 1991), and President Clinton's subsequent "New World" (Inaugural Address, 1993) both drew upon hyperbolic, even counterfactual, metaphors since the former Soviet Bloc was, in fact, left in a dangerous state of disorder.

A decade later, President George W. Bush was literally speechless and without any script during the surprise attacks on New York and Washington, which he learned about in the same way as the rest of the world did—from the live television coverage. The script that was quickly produced in the aftermath, "The War of Terrorism," is still unfolding as this book goes to press. It is, however, clear that its keywords, war and terror, have taken on new meanings.

Hyperbole appears to be a constituent of all forms of power-knowledge. As James Baldwin put it in an address to the National Press Club (Washington, D.C., December 10, 1986), "Every society has a model of itself, and every one of those models is false." Socrates, Plato, Aristotle, Machiavelli, Marx, Burke, Bentham, Gramsci, Habermas, Foucault, and hundreds of other students of political and social theory have examined the meanings and implications of the disparity between theory (model-making) and practices.

The ability to effectively recruit and strategically position what Nietzsche called "mobile armies of metaphors" to fill and police the resulting voids is, of course, the hallmark of effective statecraft.[17] (And, conversely, the commitments of democratic covenants to closing the gaps that separate theory and practice provide the historic justification for protections of free speech and freedom of the press in democratic societies. Thus, for example, Thomas Jefferson's salutary description of the mission of the free press has become a sacred canon of the professional ideology of journalism: "The basis of our government being the opinion of the people, the first object should be to keep that right; and were it left to me to decide whether we should have a government without newspapers or newspapers without government, I should not hesitate to prefer the latter."

METAPHOR AND JOURNALISTIC OBJECTIVITY

The political press envisioned by Jefferson and James Madison is, of course, history. It was replaced in the U.S. and in most other parts of the world by the commercial press.[18] The commercial press has not entirely relinquished its claims to public service as the watchdog of democracy; however, profit, not politics, has become its primary master, so much so that A. J. Liebling's dictum, "Freedom of the press belongs to the man who owns one," is almost as well-known today as Jefferson's apology for an adversarial press.

The commercial press secured its claims to authority by embracing the rhetoric, though not the methodology, of scientific objectivity. The ideological constituents of this rhetoric have always been relatively transparent. Gaye Tuchman characterized journalistic objectivity as a "strategic ritual."[19] Dan Schiller characterized it as a "cultural form" and a "myth" in Barthes's sense.[20] Nevertheless, Herbert Gans contends that journalism is "the strongest remaining bastion of logical positivism in America."[21] In recent years, however, even this bastion has been eroding as critiques of scientific objectivity have been imported into critiques of journalistic objectivity.

Nevertheless, I think that the claim Sandra Harding makes for scientific objectivity—that, like democracy, it is one of the central cultural patterns of belief in the modern West—can also be extended to press freedom and journalistic objectivity. That is, it simultaneously contains progressive, liberating, and liberalizing elements as well as regressive, self-serving, ideological elements. Journalistic objectivity is, in Harding's term, one of the "indigenous" resources of the Western press. It is flawed, incomplete, and hyperbolic, but this configuration also harbors a tarnished fragment of democratic idealism that continues, at least in its best moments, to value the quest for something more than, and better than, simply reproducing elite definitions of social order.[22]

The tradition of muckrakers and crusading journalists was motivated by profit as much or more than by idealism. Yet, if idealism sold newspapers, it also drew upon and reinforced democratic values of social justice and accountability. It cultivated romantic identification with the underdog: the righteous, lone individual victimized by powerful individuals and institutions. This tradition not only helped clean up meat packing plants and oust corrupt politicians and police. It also made some journalists important allies in the labor, civil rights, anti–Vietnam War, and feminist movements, and it still makes journalists in many parts of the world today crucial points of contact in monitoring human rights abuses. Writing from the perspective of a seasoned practitioner, Pete Hamill offers a hard-nosed rationale for recuperating the romantic tradition in journalism. He maintains that the future economic viability of newspapers, other than the elite national newspapers, may actually depend on recovering the historic mission of the press:

> From the days when we were a colony and then right through the history of the Republic, newspapers have been essential to the American idea. As concrete examples of freedom, they were the essential instruments of American reform. They measured the promises of the Constitution against the sometimes evil and unjust realities of American life and forced the country to change. As we continue the long, heartbreaking process of becoming better versions of ourselves, newspapers will, I hope, continue to be the point of the spear. They should enable us, in the phrase of Albert Camus, to love our country, and justice, too.[23]

I am less sanguine than Hamill is about whether Americans in the twenty-first century, swelled with their sense of global empire and patriotic entitlement, have the will or moral character to seek to become better versions of themselves. In addition, I worry about the ways America's advertising-driven media are seeking to turn not only Americans but also everyone within the grip of their vast global reach into versions of the hedonistic consumers they valorize. Nevertheless, I also think the fragment of democratic idealism that is buried under and within the professional ideology of journalistic objectivity is worth excavating. Despite its conservative ownership and gatekeeping, journalism remains virtually the only consequential mass-mediated platform through which truth—even difficult and dangerous truths—can sometimes be spoken to and about the powerful. Not often, not reliably, and not without hazards to the health and careers of journalists; yet, even today some journalists do continue to take significant, calculated risks in the interests of what they see as the truth. See, for example, the cases documented in the award-winning documentary video, *Fear and Favor in the Newsroom* (1997) or the cases regularly documented in the *Index on Censorship*.[24]

In sum, I am suggesting that in addition to being an artifact of the commercial press, created in part to appease advertisers and counter the damage to credibility of yellow journalism, the strategic ritual of journalistic objectivity is also a democratic accomplishment, albeit a deeply flawed one. Further, I contend its functions and promises can best be plumbed by adopting both/and logics: logics that acknowledge the Janus-headed character of most powerful ideas.

NEWS AS A CULTURAL FORM

Since the early 1970s, a virtual cottage industry in news analysis and critique has developed both within communication research and in the alternative press. This work has examined the historical origins, ideological foundations, organizational routines, narrative structures, and (more recently) gendered constituents of journalistic objectivity.[25]

There are a number of reasons why news analysis became a growth industry during the last quarter of the twentieth century. The primary reason is, however, the increased presence, visibility, and social power of the mass media. As Stuart Hall points out:

> Quantitatively and qualitatively, in twentieth century advanced capitalism, the media have established a decisive and fundamental leadership in the cultural sphere. . . . They have progressively colonized the cultural and ideological sphere.[26]

Initially critiques of this colonization sought simply to document the ideological constituents of the framing conventions, narrative structures, and organizational practices used to accomplish the strategic rituals of objectivity.[27] That is, they demonstrated that news is made, not discovered, and that it is generally made in ways that are congruent with the dominant system of signification in the society that produces it. This was a crucial critical move because news is re-presented and marketed as a univocal and naturalistic rendering of events. Critical studies of news production demonstrated that news is, and must be, a historically and socially situated cultural form. In short, this early work not only exposed the presence of cultural values and ideological biases in the social construction of news; it also documented the historically dependent character of the concept of journalistic objectivity itself.

Building on these foundations, subsequent communication research conceptualized news (like science) as mediated by paradigms, and treated facts as rule-governed and paradigm-dependent.[28] This work also underscored the importance of analyzing the visual constituents of news narratives, including the functions visual metaphors perform in enhancing the intertextual, polysemic, and hegemonic dimensions of mass communications.[29]

Framing Conventions

By exploring the founding metaphors that secure political visions, communication scholars can begin to track the roles framing devices play in naturalizing and cultivating hegemonic constructions of social reality. The "paradigmatic crisis" produced by the collapse of communism has, for example, rendered visible long-established and largely unquestioned media practices for gathering, organizing, and constructing international news. For over forty years in U.S. news organizations, the master trope, The Cold War, provided the news net, the bifurcated categorical structures, and the framing devices for conceptualizing international news.[30]

During the period of open hegemonic rupture that extended from the fall of the Berlin Wall in 1988 until the start of the Persian Gulf War in January 1991, this paradigmatic crisis was evident as routine Manichaean strategies for encoding foreign news seemed to increasingly invite, even court, ironic decodings. The spirit of the times was captured in newspaper headers such as "The loss of an enemy is a frightful thing" (*Washington Post*, October 12, 1989) and "Three European views on the risks of peace" (*New York Times*, March 12, 1989). Similarly, the struggle to find new ways of organizing representations of events in Eastern Europe was transparently played out in the pages of *New York Times*, which first embraced metaphors of natural disasters in its running headers, for example, collapse, earthquake, and storm, then shifted for several months to evolutionary metaphors. In short, for a time "media frames" did not just mediate events; they acquired news value of their own. And, no appeals to the strategic rituals of journalistic objectivity could conceal their social, cultural, historical, rhetorical, and mythic character.

Derived from Wittgenstein's linguistic philosophy, the concept of "frame analysis" was introduced into sociology by Erving Goffman.[31] It gained currency in news analysis as a result of the contributions of Gaye Tuchman, Stuart Hall, and Todd Gitlin.[32] Gitlin defines media frames as "persistent patterns of cognition, interpretation, and presentation, of selection, emphasis, and exclusion, by which symbol-handlers routinely organize discourse, whether verbal or visual." According to Gitlin, these frames are normally "unspoken and unacknowledged" devices that organize the world for both journalists and, to a significant degree, for those who rely on their reports. Media frames are what "makes the world beyond direct experience look natural."[33] They endow messages with "an eerie substance in the real world, standing outside their ostensible makers and confronting them as alien forces."[34]

The term "frame," itself a metaphor, has been widely and promiscuously used by communication scholars in recent years—so much so that it has become almost synonymous with mediation per se.[35] In news analysis, the framing process is seen as a site of contention and a source of hegemonic power. For this reason, framing conventions have attracted a great deal of critical attention. Gitlin, for example, demonstrated how major media used frames derived from crime reporting to (mis)represent the antiwar movement. In short, frames have usually been analyzed as conduits of ideological distortion.

Criticism of the news, its biases, negativity, scandal-mongering, sensationalism, and other offenses against public sensibilities is as old as newspapers themselves. Even the great champion of the press, Thomas Jefferson, was highly critical of newspapers during his presidency. The so-called liberal bias of the press has been a perennial target of the right at least since the 1960s. Critical communication research in news analysis, like Raymond Williams's study *Keywords*, has generally been launched from counterhegemonic (left or left-liberal) positions. As a result, this research sometimes appears to be coming from less contaminated (because less immediately materially invested) epistemological locations. This perception, in turn, has continued to nourish the impossible dream of escaping from what Nietzsche called the "prison-house" of language. It has kept alive realism's dream of stripping away the frames and apprehending the real facts, the real reality. And, it has done this despite the phenomenological disclaimers of its more philosophically sophisticated practitioners.

Focusing on the role metaphors play in securing news paradigms and in advancing intextuality and polysemy bypasses this temptation. It serves as a constant reminder of the mediated character of *all* communication. It provides the critical resources necessary to identify and analyze "the armor of the establishment," as well as to envision alternative or counter-hegemonic frames for interpreting events. In short, it acknowledges that frames are sense-making devices—"semiotic technologies" or conceptual lenses—that expand human vision by narrowing it.[36]

This approach to critical media studies recognizes that real reality exists, but also that it can never be fully accessed or transcribed by mere mortals. We have to settle for less. What critical-media theory can do in the wake of this Promethean deflation is to recognize the radical historical contingency of knowledge, and set itself to the task of identifying the rhetorical and social constituents of media frames as well as tracking how they operate within fields of power-relations. Analysis of the roles metaphors play both in securing news paradigms and in acting as agents of ideological transfer would appear to be a very important part of this task in an era where mass media play central roles in cultivating hegemonic constructions of social reality.[37]

Metaphors do the border crossings that take messages of elites from think tanks to speeches, headlines, sound-bytes, sitcoms, and advertising slogans. Defining master or mythic tropes like "The Cold War" or its would-be successors, "The New World Order," 'the World Order," "globalization," "information society," and "War on Terrorism" are generative structures. These root metaphors shape, instantiate, strategically position, and ensure both the authority and mobility of keywords in ascendant forms of political discourse. They propel the conceptual leaps necessary to capture, contain, and communicate new realities, but do so by foreclosing alternative formulations. The mythos buried in these root metaphors readily call up and thereby privilege certain constellations of words and word associations that operate in political linguistics. Their operation in the ideological realm parallels the operations of what Lakoff and Johnson call "metaphors that we live by" in the conversations of everyday life.[38] This is how keywords do double duty as both/and terms: "significant, binding words in certain activities and their interpretation" and "significant, indicative words in certain forms of thought."[39]

KEYWORDS AND INFORMATION MARKETS

Williams's lament, "They just don't speak the same language," assumes new significance in the emerging global media marketplace. Political discourse is deliberately, carefully, cautiously, and collectively constructed in contemporary media cultures. Television, advertising, public relations, litigation, political action committees, and spinmeisters have largely eliminated spontaneity from the speech of U.S. politicians and policymakers. What little spontaneity that remains survives in the netherworld of revealing misstatements, malapropisms, slips, and errant off-the-record statements that are breached onto the record.

Writing from a neoconservative standpoint, Irving Louis Horowitz acknowledges, "Every epoch redefines what of the past remains relevant and what needs to be discarded." What distinguishes current forms of revisionism, according to Horowitz, is, however, "the hyper-consciousness with which this cultural redefinition is being constructed."[40] This hyperconsciousness extends to the ways policy positions are constructed, commodified, and marketed for media consumption; that is, the ways they are preframed and packaged as sound-bytes. Release and dissemination of policy positions are also carefully orchestrated for maximum impact using the most advanced advertising and marketing techniques. This typically involves simultaneous distribution through many different media windows to "bandwagon" public opinion. Successful media plans for the distribution of informational and policy positions now involve deliberate (and sometimes deliberately deceitful) exploitation of the ambiguity and polysemy that make commercial media, especially television, accessible to heterogeneous mass audiences.

Much has been written about the privatization of public resources, spaces, media, and information in liberal democracies.[41] This privatization movement has, of course, been accompanied by ideologies and policies that valorize the rationality and wisdom of the marketplace. Mainstream Western media organizations largely filtered their framings of the collapse of the former Soviet Union within the assumptions of these discursive screens. Market terms—in the case of the former Soviet bloc, development of market economies; in the case of the U.S., attending to national deficits, trade deficits, and interest rates—replaced political definitions of the relations of the old Cold War rivals in international news constructions. Reports from Central and Eastern Europe framed resurgence of ethnic rivalries as obstacles to development of market-based economies. In the U.S. discussions of the national deficit, taxes, entitlements, privatization of social security, the bullish or bearishness of the stock market, e-commerce, and the costs of healthcare—economic issues of unquestionable importance in the new economy—dominated, or more accurately, supplanted political discourse, except for Clinton scandals, throughout most of the 1990s. To be sure, swords were still rattled periodically, usually when defense budgets were being debated in Congress.

These structural transformations in global capitalism, long in the making in the West but significantly accelerated in the past two decades, have been theorized by neoconservatives as a transition to postindustrialism, by the left as a move to post-Fordism, and by many of all ideological gradations as the advent of an information or postmodern age. Writing from a neo-Marxian position, David Harvey describes this transformation in capitalist expansion as involving a new configuration, which he calls "flexible accumulation."[42] It is "characterized by more flexible labour processes and markets, of geographical mobility and rapid shifts in consumption practices." Within this configuration, access to and control over accurate and up-to-date information as well as capacities for instant data analysis become highly valued commodities. The value of scientific knowledge increases, and control over flows of information and "over the vehicles for propagation of popular taste and culture . . . become vital weapons in competitive struggle."[43]

The commodification of culture, including political discourse, makes explorations of political linguistics more difficult than they were when Williams began his work in 1945. Print-based references like the *OED* are largely irrelevant to the task at hand. Television and the Internet have turned up the heat and accelerated the pace of political discourse. These technologies and the advertising that generates their profits have cut the cord that, in the early years of the television, made visual images mere extensions or exemplifications of print narratives. Advanced media cultures privilege visual images and draw upon the distinctive conventions of their visuality to communicate and cultivate their messages.

The disjunctive narratives of the new media culture are not random, scattered, or meaningless as some print-biased postmodernist and postreferential theorists suggest. To the contrary, the MTV-ing of political discourse represents, in the cultural sphere, what the political economy models of communication, developed by the late Dallas Smythe, Herbert Schiller, and others, have long described within the structures of media markets.

In this discursive form, as in scientific discourse, metaphor acts as the agent of ideological transfer. Metaphor is the boundary-crosser, mediator, epoxy, and occasional translator that makes the new form of individualized and consumerist communications of the media culture possible. The new forms of sense-making that it cultivates are not forms that print-based thinkers and democrats like Williams or I comfortably recognize as wholly rational. Yet, in mediated discourse, as in scientific discourse, metaphor does facilitate "an adaptation of our language to our continually expanding world."[44] This adaptation may more closely approximate "rationalization" (in Max Weber's sense of that term) than it does the substantive kind of rationality valued by democratic philosophies, but it is nevertheless responsive to the changing material, social, and cultural arrangements of our time.[45]

Agenda-Setting Technologies

The new discursive forms of media cultures have been implicated in undermining the print-based binary logic that secured Cold War mythology. Some analysts see them as a contributing factors in the collapse of communism.[46] The friendly imperialism of the glamorous visual imagery, produced CNN-ed and MTV-ed throughout the world by Western media cultures, are seen as having cultivated desires for consumer products that state-controlled production systems could not and would not satisfy.

What was framed in the Western press as a clamor for democracy can perhaps be more plausibly reframed as a clamor for Western technologies and consumer goods, especially communication technologies, computers, cell phones, VCRs, faxes: what Ithiel de Sola Pool called "the technologies of freedom," and what I would call the technologies of consumerism.[47] Like all technologies, the designs of commercial technologies transmit more than just the material cultural markers imprinted in transistors and circuits. They also carry social values and designs for living. They are, as Dallas Smythe put it, agenda setters and teaching machines.[48] These technologies make it easier to say and do some things while making it difficult, although not impossible, to say and do other things.

Within media cultures, this agenda-setting process becomes a major site of cultural contest. Thus, for example, at one point during the 1992 U.S. presidential election campaign, Vice President Dan Quayle appeared to be running against Candice Bergen, the actress who played the lead role in a popular television series, rather than against Democratic contenders Bill Clinton and Al Gore. Charging that Bergen's character, Murphy Brown, was responsible for undermining family values, Quayle's position was a direct extension and reflection of the new post–Cold War agendas of conservative think tanks and policymakers. This agenda casts the entertainment industry and popular culture in the role of prime mover in America's cultural malaise and crisis of leadership—a populist move that resonates across political party lines. However, this strategic populism also deflects attention away from critical analysis of the high levels of hegemonic closure that now operate within elite news media in the U.S.

To be sure, this closure is not complete. The credibility and "strategic rituals" of the Western news media are dependent on circulation of some counterhegemonic messages. Proactive conservative lobbies, think tanks, and media, including the growing conservative presence in cable broadcasting (for example, the news programming and analysis on Pat Robertson's Christian Broadcasting Network, and the talking heads of CNBC and CNN) appear to be committed to finding ways to exercise greater control over the flow of left and liberal counterhegemonic messages.[49] Mainstream media organizations increasingly possess, but seldom overtly exercise, the power to undermine the authority and legitimacy of governments.[50] The Clinton impeachment can be seen both as evidence of this power and as evidence of its limits: during the impeachment proceedings, public opinion polls repeatedly indicated that the American public did not share the Republican Congress's or the media's framing of Clinton's scandalous philandering as a high crime against the nation. The culture power of the elite media is still largely contained by its dependence upon official sources and increasingly conservative think tanks for information.[51] The "End of History" debate (the thesis that the triumph of capitalism over communism completed history) and the press coverage of the Persian Gulf War are striking examples of the ways this dependence works.

THINK TANKS AND SOUND-BYTES

In identifying the keywords that are both "significant, binding words in certain activities and their interpretation" and "significant, indicative words in certain forms of thought" in the U.S., it is increasingly necessary to track their migration from think tank to sound-byte. Lawrence Soley has documented the growing reliance of elite journalists on think tanks, especially conservative think tanks, as news sources by comparing a sample of news reports from the late 1970s with a comparable sample for the late 1980s.[52] Washington-based think tanks, addressing national and international issues, are supplemented by regional institutes and foundations that supply the local press with information on domestic and regional economic and social issues. Soley has also examined the increasing presence of journalists as fellows-in-residence at these think tanks, which are generously funded by corporate contributions. Unlike academic knowledge producers, whose intellectual autonomy is protected, at least in theory, by academic freedom and tenure, the knowledge producers supported by think tanks must return to positions in commercial media after a year or two in residence. For this reason, Soley points out, they do not "want to be identified with unpopular political positions, such as supporting Nicaragua's Sandinista government."[53] (Within this context, the meanings of, and relationships among, knowledge, research, and the always problematic pursuit of objectivity are highly responsive to market conditions.

As a result of the growing dependence of news media on private, corporate-funded data and policy sources, many—perhaps even most—of the keywords that have acquired currency within U.S. political discourse since the early 1980s have been fabricated within such think tanks as the Heritage Foundation, the American Enterprise Institute, the Cato Institute, the Olin Foundation, Council for Social and Economic Studies, the Hudson Institute, the Foreign Policy Institute, and the National Institute for Public Policy. Moreover, such organizations have played crucial roles in supplying expertise, planning resources, and cognitive maps for restructuring and privatizing the state economies of the nations of Eastern Europe and the former Soviet Union. Indeed, some counterhegemonic readings of the process indicate that Western experts supplied Russian president Boris Yeltsin with media consultants and crafted a new "made for TV" persona for him, albeit one he often had trouble performing.

Keywords in a Global Village

The definitions of democracy and freedom exported by these think tanks to former communist nations conflate democracy and capitalism: terms that always coexisted in modern Western Liberal societies in uneasy and occasionally conflictual unions.[54] Within this new vocabulary, the keyword of liberalism, democracy, is increasingly drained of its critical, resistant resources and becomes fully synonymous with free enterprise and consumer sovereignty.

Here, a set of terms—freedom of expression and freedom of choice—that were borrowed from politics and used metaphorically by U.S. manufacturers and advertisers in the early part of this century to herald the promises of consumerism become literalized. The equation of free enterprise and freedom from government regulation with political freedom by conservative think tanks, consultants, and advisors reinforces one-dimensional interpretations of democracy.

When such interpretations become naturalized within the political discourse of leaders and citizens of Eastern Europe and the former Soviet Union—people who have little access to or presumably interest in the prehistory or metaphoric associations of the languages of Western democracy—the meaning of democracy changes. Freedom of choice becomes the freedom to choose between Sony, IBM, Zenith, or Toshiba. When this political discourse is reimported as "news" from Eastern Europe and represented in Western news media, virtually all residue of its site of origination—U.S. think tanks— is scrubbed away. To be sure, this import also bears the imprimatur of its reception and reinterpretation from the perspectives of the experiences and national identities of the former communist nations. Nonetheless, naturalizing market definitions of democracy within these reports also gives these definitions added traction when they are recirculated within the Western press.

The following examples illustrate the way this migratory process works. When, for example, representatives of the American Enterprise Institute appear on U.S. television news programs like *Nightline* or PBS's *News Hour*, their affiliations are noted and sometimes moderated by the presence of an expert representing an alternative position. This practice is a lingering residue of the FCC fairness doctrine. Always problematic in theory and practice, this mandate nevertheless reinforces strategic rituals of objectivity.

CONSTRUCTING OBJECTIVE ACCOUNTS: EXPORTING AND IMPORTING "FACTS"

When, in contrast, positions developed in U.S. think tanks are refracted back to the U.S. from Eastern Europe, the signatures of the expertise of the American Enterprise Institute or the Rand Corporation are no longer attached. For example, in the period immediately following the dismantling of the Berlin Wall, when Gorbachev's or Yeltsin's advisors issued policy positions after meetings with former U.S. Secretary of State James Baker's staff and their advisors, they were portrayed as articulating Soviet or Russian positions, not Rand positions. These articulations become "fact"; within the practices of U.S. journalistic objectivity, facts do not require the same kinds of qualifiers

as "opinions" do. By packaging their reportage within the established structures of news narratives and relying on routine news-gathering practices—in
short, by conducting business as usual—U.S. news organizations were
thereby affirming rather than monitoring U.S. foreign policy.

The U.S. news media are also implicitly contributing to a kind of collective social amnesia regarding the history and constituents of liberal democracy. That is, they are providing their readers/audiences with unreflexive representations of the views that U.S. foreign policy experts and corporate
developers are exporting to countries that do not have established institutional
structures for regulating, monitoring, taxing, or resisting privatizing initiatives. In doing so, they are also further eroding their own, already severely
compromised, ideological claims to autonomy: claims that provided the historical warrant for privileging press freedom in the First Amendment to the
U.S. Constitution.

Perhaps no term, phrase, or metaphor better displayed the hyperconscious
effort by those in power to redefine social reality and cultivate new keywords
within contemporary political discourse than the first Bush Administration's
counterfactual valorizations of the New World Order (NWO). Political slogans have, of course, been a characteristic of American politics since the
American Revolution: Manifest Destiny, the New Deal, the Square Deal, the
New Frontier, and of course the Cold War are all master tropes that mobilized
advanced visions of American futures. Moreover, the Cold War was a media-
made term, coined by journalist Walter Lippmann in response to Winston
Churchill's announcement on March 5, 1946, in a speech in Fulton, Missouri,
that an "iron curtain" had descended upon Europe.

The New World Order

The conception of the New World Order was, however, articulated within a
new communication environment: one in which hyperconscious myth-making
has immediate and global resonances. Moreover, the New World Order and
the occasion of its articulation represented extraordinarily innovative exercises in political linguistics for several reasons. First, its articulation in a televised speech by U.S. President George Bush on January 17, 1991, two days
into the Persian Gulf War, when television audiences throughout the world
were acutely attentive to U.S. news, ensured unprecedented levels of immediate global visibility.

Second, coupling the articulation of this vision with the announcement of
the massive bombing of Iraq elevates poststructuralist doubts about the ways
words may be said to refer to the world to the level of political praxis. So
much so, that the late Herbert Schiller suggested that the president's assertion

that mass bombing of urban centers constitutes "the rule of law, not the law of the jungle" raises a "psychiatric question."[55]

Third, the term represents a hyperconscious attempt to appropriate counterhegemonic languages and practices at a number of levels. Schiller examines the most immediate and obvious antecedents of the term in United Nations initiatives, the New International Economic Order and the New International Information Order. Responding to pressures from Third World nations, the NIEO and NIIO were designed to redistribute both economic and information resources in ways that redressed some of the enormous inequities between industrialized societies and the rest of the world. Supported by more than 125 nations, these initiatives were opposed by the U.S. government and largely ignored by U.S. media.[56] NWO also appropriated the language of another international effort that was less well-known but nonetheless prestigious. The World Order Models Project, founded in 1966, which publishes the journal *Alternatives*, is a transnational association of scholars and political figures engaged in research, education, dialogue, and publication of materials aimed at "promoting a just world peace." Its advisory board has included, among many others, left and liberal social reformers like Paulo Freire, Else Boulding, and Henryk Skolimowski. In addition NWO appropriates or piggybacks onto the language of U.S. government sponsored 1492–1992 commemorations of Columbus's "discovery" of the new world. The term, of course, also has other less salutary historical associations in the rhetorics of both Mussolini and Hitler, who used the term extensively.[57]

Fourth, these appropriations have amplified the resonance, ambiguity, and polysemy of NWO, but also of course its openness to ironic renderings.

Fifth, the first Bush Administration's articulations of the vision of the NWO was accompanied by sophisticated scripting of visual representations, especially during the Persian Gulf War, where sets, video technology, and mythic narrative patterns, developed for television coverage of sports, specifically football, were simulated in military "press briefings." These briefings were actually live U.S. government broadcasts directly to the people of the "global village" that were, presumably, intended to negate the power of journalistic mediation and to directly beat the drum of American global triumphalism. Photo opportunities were effectively used to convey the layers of hierarchy, the distributions of power, and the gender order of the NWO.[58]

The war naturalized the NWO metaphor. It became familiar furniture in editorial headers and talk-show conversation. It also quickly infiltrated the language of the television talk show circuit. After the war, the press transferred this framing to analysis of events—the destabilization and disorder—in the then-disintegrating Soviet Union. The resonance of the phrase appeared to owe as much to its openness to ironic inversions as to its bandwagoning effects. Moreover, the vastness and vagueness of its terms permit an unusually broad range of meanings to find refuge under its umbrella, so much so that the titular author of the concept has been plausibly charged with misunderstanding it. Thus Lester Thurow (C-SPAN, *Booknotes*, May 31, 1992) claimed that President Bush, "the Cold War President," understood less about the New World Order than most policy analysts since he conceived of it primarily as a military phenomena, when actually the most dramatic structural transformations were occurring in global market systems, not in military formations.[59] This example is doubly significant because it is one of hundreds that demonstrate the migration and naturalization of the metaphor, NWO, into the statements and publications of would-be oppositional mediated voices and publications. The NWO metaphor slowly faded into the background after Clinton defeated Bush in the 1992 presidential election. It is, however, periodically resuscitated, usually by critics of the original. For example, the cover story of *The Nation* (July 9, 2001) was "AIDS and the NEW WORLD ORDER" (capitals in the original).

This brief analysis of NWO only scratches the surface. It demonstrates that the term is not new, that the "world" it evokes is highly selective both economically and geographically, and that the "order" it celebrated had, at the time it was being widely bandwagoned, no material referents. In Williams's sense, NWO constitutes an exemplary case of a set of keywords that disorient because the problems of their meanings are inseparable from the problems they are being used to discuss.

"Everything Has Changed": September 11, 2001

The sense of American invincibility—America's image of itself as the sole architect of world order, which emerged with its lone superpower status at the end of the Cold War—was shattered on September 11, 2001. Almost immediately the phrase "Everything has changed" began circulating within the media and among the people. It became the dominant framing device for attempts to comprehend the gravity of the events themselves, as well as their policy implications. Exactly how things had changed would be the subject of semantic contests for weeks, and months, and perhaps will be for years to come.

The attack on New York was, of course, covered live on television. The very real terror experienced by the victims, near victims, witnesses, and survivors, combined with the psychological terror of the population at large about what would happen next, immediately made "terrorism" a key term in the vocabularies of all Americans. The anthrax attacks on the U.S. Postal Service that followed added biological and chemical terrorism to this vocabulary. Even the international news agency, Reuters, retreated from its policy of using the term "political violence" instead of terrorism: a policy that recognizes the heavy ideological load that use of the term carries.[60]

Ground Zero, a metaphor borrowed from the language of nuclear war and used to describe the devastated site of the World Trade Center—the symbolic and actual nerve center of global capitalism—also acquired immediate traction. The word surreal, used paradoxically to refer to the reality of the Hollywood-like images captured by television cameras of the attacks on the WTC and their aftermath, resonated widely even among adolescents: it seemed to mean that the reality of the attacks is more unreal, unbelievable, and disorienting than the fictional narratives of action films. "Homeland security" is another term that quickly entered the American vocabulary when former Pennsylvania governor Tom Ridge was appointed to a new cabinet position as director of homeland security.

Official response to the attacks from top government leadership was delayed several hours because the president and vice president were in the protective custody of the Secret Service in undisclosed locations. This clearly alarmed television commentators, who were left to fill the semantic void. When President George W. Bush did respond, he initially used crime metaphors to describe the crisis: the attackers were described as perpetrators to be brought to justice by law enforcement agencies, and the dead and injured were characterized as victims. In a colorful phrase that was widely quoted, and which he himself repeated, the president drew upon the language of the old American West to describe the perpetrators as "wanted dead or alive."

A few hours after the attack, Senator Joseph Biden compared the surprise nature of the attacks and the devastating loss of life that they produced to Pearl Harbor. War metaphors soon merged with and largely displaced crime metaphors as victims became casualties, attackers became enemies, rescue workers became heroes and patriots, and military action became the logical recourse. The name given to the proposed military action went through multiple drafts as the administration mobilized an international coalition to fight a War on Terrorism. The immediate target of this unorthodox war against a largely invisible enemy, Osama bin Laden's al-Qaida network, was the Taliban regime of Afghanistan, which had provided a refuge for al-Qaida. President Bush also subsequently declared war on "all terrorism," on "the evil ones," and on "evil doers"; he rattled sabers at what he called "the axis of evil," Iraq, Iran, and North Korea. The president made a point of distinguishing between good Moslems (most Moslems) and bad Moslems (an aberrant minority of fundamentalist fanatics). However, he also repeatedly invoked religious metaphors, which seemed to be designed to cultivate the impression that the West was embarking on a holy war against the self-styled holy warriors of the Jihad. This double move was presumably intended to appeal to the president's own Christian fundamentalist supporters as well as to send a message of determined ferocity to all Moslems.

The term "war" has also soaked up new shades of meaning, which cover both domestic and international covert activities by U.S. and foreign law enforcement and intelligence agencies, as well as more conventional forms of military activity.[61] The president initially compared the War on Terrorism to the War on Drugs, but then retreated from that comparison because the War on Drugs has been notoriously unsuccessful. The War on Drugs was subsequently reconfigured as part of the War on Terrorism. The president has settled into a pattern of referring to the War on Terrorism as a "new kind of war" in which all citizens are warriors.

What is certain is that President G. W. Bush's messages are now carefully scripted, despite his reputation for malapropisms. Despite the highly criticized early silence and some inarticulate misfires and nervous improvisations that followed it, the Bush Administration rapidly recovered control over deployment of political linguistics, and organized what the *New York Times* describes as a broad "campaign to create a 21st century version of the muscular propaganda war that the United States waged in the 1940's."[62] In addition to using persuasion and censorship to ensure the cooperation of a corporate media that was not showing any signs of not cooperating, White House Communication Director Karen Hughes set up a communications "War Room." Although Hughes has since resigned her White House post, the War Room provides a clearinghouse where top communication strategists, including high-profile veterans who have run presidential campaigns, talk regularly, monitor news reports, issue press statements countering negative news, and develop methods to continue to cultivate and capitalize on the national outpouring of patriotism that followed the attacks. The State Department, in turn, hired Charlotte Beers, a former advertising executive, to launch an international campaign to sell a positive image of America to the world. These efforts appear to be succeeding, at least domestically: the Bush Administration has achieved and so far (July 2002) maintained record levels of popularity in opinion polls. The popularity has continued even in the wake of the corporate scandals that dominated the news for several months in 2002. The superficiality and reliability of such polls are, of course, always open to question. Conversely, critics of the administration's news management, restriction on civil liberties; detention without charges of Middle Eastern men suspected of having connections with al-Qaida; and plans for massive deportations, without hearings, of resident aliens receive very little coverage in mainstream media, especially television news.

Democracy and the Critical Spirit

The difference between the keywords in contemporary political linguistics and the keywords that troubled Williams in 1945 is that the obfuscation that accompanies their articulation is more deliberate and hyperconscious. When Herbert Marcuse wrote *One-Dimensional Society* in 1964, the book's title and its argument were correctly criticized as hyperbolic. The thesis he put forth is still somewhat overdetermined, but present structural relationships for the production and distribution of knowledge and their representations in news media now come much nearer to approximating Marcuse's model. Ironically, conservative think tanks mastered Marcuse's lessons on political linguistics and are now very effectively practicing what he preached against. In a speech to the European Bank for Reconstruction and Development, Jacques Attali described the new global market formation in these terms: "The world is becoming an ideologically homogeneous market where life is being organized around common consumer desires, whether or not those desires can be fulfilled."[63] Within this new postindustrial or post-Fordian world order, political candidates, positions, and programs are brought to market like music videos, waffle irons, and dandruff shampoos. War and national images can now be added to Attali's list.

Whether the keyword of Euro-American political linguistics during the first half of the twentieth century, democracy, can retain its historic resonance within this new world is open to question. Citizens and scholars committed to its preservation would be well-advised to accept Hanno Hardt's challenge to recover the critical spirit "that is inherent in the idea of democracy and [that] can be defined as thinking about freedom and responsibility and the contribution that intellectual pursuits can make to the welfare of society."[64]

NOTES

1. Raymond Williams, *Keywords: A Vocabulary of Culture and Society* (New York: Oxford University Press, 1976).

2. Williams, *Keywords*, 13.

3. See, for example, the essays C. Wright Mills wrote during the final years of World War II, in which he discusses the coming transition from wartime to peacetime economy. Clearly these ideas were already very much in the intellectual air at the time. See C. Wright Mills, *Power, Politics and People: The Collected Essays of C. Wright Mills* (New York: Ballantine Books, 1962).

4. See, for example, Herbert I. Schiller, *Who Knows: Information in the Age of the Fortune 500* (Stamford, Conn.: Ablex Publishing, 1981); Herbert I. Schiller, *Information and the Crisis Economy* (Stamford, Conn.: Ablex Publishing, 1984); Vincent Mosco, *The Political Economy of Communication: Rethinking and Renewal* (Thou-

sand Oaks, Calif.: Sage, 1996); Robert W. McChesney, *Rich Media, Poor Democracy: Communication Politics in Dubious Times* (Champaign: University of Illinois Press, 1999); and Dan Schiller, *Digital Capitalism: Networking the Global Market Systems* (Cambridge, Mass.: MIT Press, 2000); and much of the work of Dallas Smythe.

5. Pete Hamill, *News Is a Verb* (New York: Ballantine, 1998). Academic communication researchers have generally accepted these findings, but some journalists question the validity of these claims, seeing them as functioning in part as convenient rationales for corporate cost-cutting since international reporting is a very expensive commodity to produce. The journalistic doubters usually cite the following points. First, the U.S. population is primarily an immigrant population, and even third- and fourth-generation American news consumers retain an interest in coverage of their ancestral homelands. Second, and more immediately, during the past quarter-century, the U.S. has experienced an enormous expansion in its immigrant population. There is a strong demand among these recent immigrants for news from home. Most of these people do not, however, occupy the upscale market segments that advertisers are eager to reach; as a result, servicing these readers/audiences is not a business priority. Third, globalization has greatly expanded the contacts of U.S. citizens abroad. More Americans are traveling abroad and more American students are studying abroad than ever before. This would suggest an increase, rather than a decrease, in interest in foreign cultures and developments. Fourth, the U.S. now has one of its largest, permanent, peacetime, international deployments of military troops in its history; this deployment has created a market among the families and friends of these military personnel for news from the countries in which these military personnel are stationed. Finally, the enthusiasm with which many Internet users report their international Web browsing and messaging as well as the strong reliance of Hispanic-Americans on the Internet as a news source, also suggests that many Americans are not nearly as isolationist as media moguls would like to believe. While the World Wide Web and Internet-based interactivity does open up vast new opportunities for proactive consumers of international news to access online versions of newspapers from abroad and ideologically diverse websites, this remains a time-intensive activity that only the most dedicated are likely to pursue on a regular basis. Cable television stations targeting specialized groups, for example Univision: the Spanish Television Network, the International Network, Black Entertainment Network, and print materials targeted to the new immigrant groups also provide other alternatives. I owe debts for parts of this analysis to John Pittman, former *Voice of America* correspondent in Africa, visiting classroom lecturer, Muhlenberg College, March 7, 2000.

6. Gaye Tuchman, *Making News* (New York: The Free Press, 1978).

7. Herbert Marcuse, *An Essay on Liberation* (Boston: Beacon Press, 1969), 73.

8. Martin Jay, *The Dialectical Imagination: A History of the Frankfurt School and the Institute of Social Research, 1923–1950* (Boston: Little, Brown, 1973), 299.

9. Hanno Hardt, *Critical Communication Studies: Communication, History and Theory in America* (London: Routledge, 1992), xi.

10. Herbert Marcuse, *An Essay on Liberation* (Boston: Beacon Press, 1969), 73.

11. Williams, *Keywords*, 22.

12. Herbert Marcuse, *The Aesthetic Dimension: Toward a Critique of Marxist Aesthetics* (Boston: Beacon, 1978).

13. Thomas Frank, *Conquest of Cool: Business, Culture, Counterculture, and the Rise of Hip Consumerism* (Chicago: University of Chicago Press, 1998). For a sardonic, journalistic analysis of the impact of hip consumerism on contemporary U.S. intellectual culture, see David Brooks, *Bobos in Paradise: The New Upper Class and How They Got There* (New York: Simon & Schuster, 2000).

14. Herbert Marcuse, *Negations* (New York: Columbia University Press, 1989).

15. Alan O'Connor, *Raymond Williams: Writing, Culture, Politics* (New York: Basil Blackwell, 1989).

16. Some of the essential feminist sources are Mary Daly, *Beyond God the Father: Toward a Philosophy of Women's Liberation* (Boston: Beacon, 1973); Mary Daly, *Gyn-Ecology: The Metaethics of Radical Feminism* (Boston: Beacon Press, 1979); Sandra Harding, *The Science Question in Feminism* (Ithaca, N.Y.: Cornell University Press, 1986); Sandra Harding, *Whose Science? Whose Knowledge? Thinking from Women's Lives* (Ithaca, N.Y.: Cornell University Press, 1991); Donna Haraway, "Situated Knowledge: The Science Question in Feminism and Privilege of Partial Perspective," *Feminist Studies* 14, no. 3 (1988): 575–99; Donna Haraway, *Primate Visions: Gender, Race, and Nature in the World of Modern Science* (New York: Routledge, 1989); Carolyn Merchant, *The Death of Nature: Women, Ecology and the Scientific Revolution* (New York: Harper & Row, 1980); and Evelyn Fox Keller, *Reflections on Gender and Science* (New Haven, Conn.: Yale University Press, 1985).

17. For a succinct explication of Nietzsche's approach to metaphor, see Richard Rorty, "The Contingency of Language," *London Review of Books* 17 (April 17, 1986): 3–6.

18. Dan Schiller, *Objectivity and the News: The Public and the Rise of Commercial Journalism* (Philadelphia: University of Pennsylvania Press, 1981); and Michael Schudson, *Discovering the News* (New York: Basic Books, 1978).

19. Gaye Tuchman, "Objectivity as Strategic Ritual: An Examination of Newsmen's Notions of Objectivity," *American Journal of Sociology* 77, no. 4 (1972): 660–79.

20. Schiller, *Objectivity and the New*. See also Roland Barthes, *Mythologies* (New York: Hill and Wang, 1972).

21. Herbert Gans, *Deciding What's News* (New York: Pantheon, 1979), 184.

22. Sandra Harding, presentation to the Women's Professional Group, Muhlenberg College, April 26, 1992.

23. Pete Hamill, *News Is a Verb* (New York: Ballantine, 1998), 95.

24. Beth Sanders and Randy Baker, *Fear and Favor in the Newsroom*, videotape (Seattle, Wash.: Northwest Passage Productions, 1987).

25. See for example Tuchman, "Objectivity as Strategic Ritual"; Schudson, *Discovering the News*; Gans, *Deciding What's News*; Schiller, *Objectivity and the News*; John Hartley, *Understanding News* (London: Methuen, 1982); Lana Rakow and K. Kranich, "Woman as Sign in TV News," *Journal of Communication* 41, no. 1 (1991): 8–23; Stuart Allan, *News Culture* (Buckingham, England: Open University Press, 1999); and Robert K. Manoff and Michael Schudson, eds., *Reading the News* (New York: Pantheon Books, 1986).

26. Stuart Hall, "Culture, the Media, and the Ideological Effect," in *Mass Communication and Society*, ed. James Curran, Michael Gurevitch, and Janet Woolacott (London: Arnold, 1977), 340–41.

27. See, for example, Gans, *Deciding What's News*; Todd Gitlin, *The Whole World is Watching: Mass Media in the Making and Unmaking of the New Left* (Berkeley: University of California Press, 1980); and Tuchman, "Objectivity as Strategic Ritual."

28. See, for example, Farrell Corcoran, "KAL 007 and the Evil Empire: Mediated Disaster and Forms of Rationalization," in *Rhetorical Dimensions in Media*, ed. Martin J. Medhurst and Thomas W. Benson (Dubuque, Iowa: Kendall/Hunt Publishing Company, 1991), 162–82; and R. A. Hackett, "Decline of a Paradigm? Bias and Objectivity in News Media Studies," *Critical Studies in Mass Communication* 1 (1984): 229–59.

29. Medhurst and Benson, eds., *Rhetorical Dimensions in Media*.

30. E. P. Thompson, "END and the Beginning: History Turns on a New Hinge," *The Nation* (January 29, 1990): 117–18, 120–22; Corcoran, "KAL 007 and the Evil Empire"; and Ed Herman, *The Myth of Liberal Media: An Edward Herman Reader* (New York: Peter Lang Publishing, 1999).

31. Erving Goffman, *Frame Analysis* (New York: Harper & Row, 1974).

32. Tuchman, *Making News*; Stuart Hall, "Encoding and Decoding in the Television Discourse" in *Culture, Media, Language*, ed. Stuart Hall, D. Hobson, A. Lowe, and Paul Willis (London: Hutchinson, 1980), 128–38; and Gitlin, *The Whole World Is Watching*.

33. Gitlin, *The Whole World Is Watching*, 6–7.

34. Gitlin, *The Whole World Is Watching*, 2.

35. For this reason, some scholars believe the concept of "frame" has largely become meaningless within communication theory. My own view is that, while the term is certainly overused and loosely used, it nevertheless retains some explanatory value in news analysis.

36. Haraway, "Situated Knowledge," 598–99.

37. See, for example, Mary Hesse, *Models and Analogies in Science* (South Bend, Ind.: Notre Dame Press, 1966); David Bloor, *Knowledge and Social Inquiry* (London: Routledge & Kegan Paul, 1977); Merchant, *The Death of Nature*; Keller, *Reflections on Gender and Science*; and Rorty, "The Contingency of Language."

38. George Lakoff and Mark Johnson, *Metaphors We Live By* (Chicago: University of Chicago Press, 1980).

39. Williams, *Keywords*, 13.

40. Irving Louis Horowitz, "The New Nihilism," *Transaction: Social Science and Modern Society* 29, no. 1 (November/December 1991): 27–32.

41. See, for example, Dallas W. Smythe, *Dependency Road: Communication, Capitalism, Consciousness, and Canada* (Norwood, N.J.: Ablex, 1981); and Phillip Elliott, "Intellectuals, the 'Information Society' and The Disappearance of the Public Sphere," in *Mass Communication Review Yearbook* 4, ed. Ellen Wartella, D. C. Whitney, and Swen Windahl (Beverly Hills, Calif.: Sage, 1982).

42. David Harvey, *The Condition of Postmodernity* (Oxford: Basil Blackwell, 1989), 123.

43. Harvey, *The Condition of Postmodernity*, 160.

44. Hesse, *Models and Analogies in Science*, 177.

45. Max Weber, *Theory of Social and Economic Organization* (Glencoe, Ill.: The Free Press, 1947).

46. E. P. Thompson, "END and the Beginning"; R. Wilson, "Techno-euphoria and the Discourse of the American Sublime," *Boundary* 2, no. 19 (1992): 204–29; and others.

47. I. S. Pool, *Technologies of Freedom* (Cambridge, Mass.: Harvard University Press, 1984).

48. Smythe, *Dependency Road*.

49. J. J. O'Connor, "For the Right, TV is Half the Battle," *The New York Times*, 14 June 1992, (2)1.

50. Robert M. Entman, *Democracy without Citizens: Media and the Decay of American Politics* (New York: Oxford University Press, 1989).

51. Lawrence Soley, *The News Shapers: The Sources Who Explain the News* (New York: Praeger, 1992).

52. Soley, *The News Shapers*.

53. Soley, *The News Shapers*, 64.

54. Samuel Bowles and Herbert Gintis, *Democracy and Capitalism, Property, Community, and the Contradictions of Modern Social Thought* (New York: Basic Books, 1986); and Sue Curry Jansen, *Censorship: The Knot that Binds Power and Knowledge* (New York: Oxford University Press, 1988).

55. Herbert Schiller, "Whose New World Order?" *Lies of Our Times* (February 1991): 12–13.

56. Schiller, *Whose New World Order?*

57. R. Rundle, "The New World Order," *Boundary* 2 (1992): 1.

58. Sue Curry Jansen and Don Sabo, "Sport/War: The Gender Order, the Persian Gulf War, and The New World Order," paper presented at the annual meeting of the International Communication Association, Miami, Florida, May 1992.

59. Lester Thurow, *Booknotes*, C-SPAN (May 31, 1992).

60. Jackie Loohaus, "New Terms Shred Old Definitions since Sept. 11 Terror Attacks," *Allentown (Pa.) Morning Call*, 2 November 2001, 2(D).

61. For a thorough trenchant analysis of the metaphors used by the administration and the media to make sense of this crisis, see George Lakoff, "Metaphors of Terror: The Power of Images," *In These Times.com* (October 29, 2001), <www.inthesetimes.com> (accessed November 4, 2001). See also Ellen Goodman, "The Language of Evil," *Buffalo News*, 28 October 2001, 3(H).

62. Elizabeth Becker, "In the War on Terrorism, A Battle to Shape Opinion," *New York Times*, 11 November 2001, 1(1).

63. Jacques Attali, *Vital Speeches* 57 (1992).

64. Hardt, *Critical Communication Studies*, xi.

Chapter Eight

Football Is More than a Game: Masculinity, Sport, and War

In American popular culture, some of the primary sites for cultivation of Promethean visions of male achievement are the playing field, sports reporting and biographies, superhero and science fictions, action adventures, and war stories. These are places where idealized images of masculinity are represented, tested, and introduced into children's play. For most boys, exposure to this kind of fantasy and play is a central part of the socialization process. These symbolic resources provide boys with opportunities to experiment with conceptions of themselves as independent agents, acquire masculine values and skills, begin to see themselves as heirs to a male tradition, experience male bonding, and learn to dream the cultural dream of male mastery. For many, perhaps even most, boys, these rites of passage are self-affirming experiences that promote ego development and gratification, and establish their dominant positioning within the sex and gender hierarchies of Western patriarchal cultures. For some boys, of course, these rites are marked by psychic pain and trauma. A boy who is perceived by his peers as running or throwing like a girl is a boy whose entire sense of self and positioning in the world is called into question.

Sports media and sports entertainments make it possible for their (mostly male) consumers to participate in and celebrate the Promethean rites of youth from cradle to grave. Within the storytelling routines of sports journalism, unlike other forms of reporting, mythic narratives are the standard storytelling conventions. The historical amnesia that is so endemic in contemporary culture, especially American culture, is suspended in sport media. Reports of peak athletic performances always reference history, as great contemporary performances are routinely compared with great performances of the past and record-breakers are lionized into legends. The facts (sports statistics) are launchpads to hyperbole, which is often used consciously by sports writers and announcers, sometimes wryly, sometimes with deadpan seriousness. Athletic heroes, like Prometheus, defy the normal limits of human embodiment: they run faster, hit harder, jump higher, and throw farther, faster, or with greater precision than ordinary mortals.

Playing fields have historically served as training grounds for battlefields, instilling such values as discipline, rule-orientation, aggression, competition, risk-taking, denial of pain, loyalty, and teamwork, which serve equally well on both fields. As a result, the language of the two realms have traditionally intersected in ways that have lent themselves to exploitation by old men seeking to enlist young men (and sometimes young women) to fight their wars for them.

This chapter presents a case study of the political linguistics that were mobilized by the United States government and corporate interests, including media, to propagandize the Persian Gulf War. It is an especially interesting case because the Persian Gulf War took place: (a) in the immediate wake of the end of the Cold War, when America was triumphantly redefining its position in the world; (b) when the U.S. military was organized on an all-volunteer basis, with most of the volunteers coming from the ranks of racial minorities and the poor; (c) in the period after the second wave of feminist struggles for equality had crested and women had entered the paid workforce, including the military, in unprecedented numbers; and (d) when entertainment, with sports representing an especially robust sector, had become one of the most rapidly growing segments of the U.S. economy, with cultural products claiming the lion's share of American foreign exports.

SPORT/WAR

A world that can be explained even with bad reasons is a familiar world.

—Albert Camus, *The Myth of Sisyphus*[1]

The mixing of metaphors of sport and war played a historically unique social, rhetorical, and ideological role during the Persian Gulf War. The traditional homologous relationship between sport and war provided the U.S. government, military, sport industry, and mass media with an easily mobilized and highly articulated semiotic system and set of values to advance and justify their respective plans, actions, and interests.

Sport/war tropes are crucial rhetorical resources for mobilizing the hierarchical values that construct, mediate, maintain, and, when necessary, reform or repair hegemonic forms of masculinity and femininity. The prominence of sport/war–based rhetorical devices in mass-mediated discourse during the

Persian Gulf War resonated with values and sentiments in the larger society that legitimate the practices of the military, sport, and media. In the process of doing this ideological work, these rhetorical practices also valorized and reaffirmed many of the structured inequalities that comprise the American gender order.

The analysis developed in this essay is situated in what McKay and Rowe called the "critical paradigm" of sport and media studies, in which strands of structuralism, political economy, and cultural studies find theoretical confluence in an effort to show how media "reproduce and legitimate relations of domination in patriarchal capitalist societies."[2] Feminist frameworks are used to emphasize gender relations as central to radical theories of sport.[3] Gender is viewed as a key linking concept that holds together a broad configuration of structural, ideological, institutional, semiotic, and psychological processes that formed the basis for the brief, but extraordinary, hegemonic unity that was present in government and media representations of allied actions during the Persian Gulf War. Our approach does not, however, in any way discount the very real role press restrictions and military censorship played in generating this unity; to the contrary, these measures are regarded as integral structural features of the configuration that created the unity.

Even before the Allied Forces initiated their attack, the prominent use of the sport/war metaphor in presidential rhetoric, Pentagon pronouncements, and reportage was evident. This chapter examines the positioning of the sport/war metaphor as a salient motif in military, government, and media interpretations and explanations of events in the Persian Gulf War and beyond it. How did such a commonplace, even clichéd, metaphor come to assume so much importance in the dramaturgy of staging and reporting the war? Where did it derive its symbolic power? What purposes were served by the sport/war discourse? Whose interests were involved and upheld?

We explore these questions in the following way. First, we examine the framing and cultivation of sport/war metaphors within mass media and related institutional contexts and formations during the war. Second, we develop the argument that the sport/war metaphor is embedded within a "deep structure" of patriarchal values, beliefs, and power relations that, in turn, reflect and advance the agendas of hegemonic masculinity.[4] Third, we briefly identify and explore some of the semiotic constructions and operations of hegemonic masculinity. Finally, we examine the processes through which sport/war metaphors reflected and reinforced the multiple systems of domination that not only enabled the Persian Gulf War to be rationalized and fought, but also extended and strengthened the "triumphalist" ideological hegemony of Euro-American male elites at the end of the Cold War.[5]

SPORTSPEAK AND INSTITUTIONAL FORMATIONS

Convergence and conflation of the vocabularies of sport and war in both official briefings and reportage of the Persian Gulf War attracted widespread commentary and some analysis during the war.[6] Football was the favorite sport of most of the participants in this language game. The language of football has always drawn heavily on military (and sexualized military) argot: *attack, blitz, bombs, ground and air assaults, offense, defense, penetrations, flanks, conflicts,* and *battles for territory* are standard terms in sportscasters' vocabularies. When the game/conflict is over, coaches/generals publicly glory in their *victories*, lament their *defeats*, and mourn their *casualties*. Thus, for example, after a particularly difficult game, one National Football League coach told an interviewer, "Our boys were out there fighting and dying today on the frontlines."[7] During the Persian Gulf War, sport, specifically football, functioned as a kind of synecdoche within U.S. domestic propagandizing for the war; it served as a mobile metaphor that traveled freely across multiple institutional and informational contexts including the government statements, military briefings, war news, analysis, punditry, and sport media.

SPORTSPEAK IN THE GOVERNMENT AND MILITARY

Conflation of the metaphors and specialized vocabularies of sport and war provided the U.S. government and its military wing, represented by the Pentagon and military briefers in the theater of operations, with a vehicle for mobilizing support for the war that possessed what Barthes has called an "imperative buttonholing character."[8] This vehicle was used to communicate the military rationales for the war as well as the objectives of the Western coalition to the American public and to the world community.

Sport/war metaphors have had currency in U.S. politics at least since the Civil War.[9] By the time the Watergate tapes were produced during the Nixon Administration, football imagery had become the root metaphor of American political discourse. Indeed, Richard Nixon mixed football and political metaphors to the point where the boundaries between the two realms blurred. He selected *Quarterback* for his code name as president and developed the habit of regularly telephoning the coach of the Washington Redskins to discuss strategy before big games.

One of the most compelling and widely quoted examples of sport/war imagery during the Persian Gulf War was provided by General Norman Schwartzkopf when he characterized the strategic plan of the ground war as "the Hail Mary play in football." By the time Schwartzkopf offered this simile, however, sport and gaming analogies had become the salient metaphors in both official government statements and media representations of the war, with expressions drawn from football achieving special prominence. The first pilots returning from bombing raids on Baghdad described the action to reporters as "like a big football game" and "like a football game where the defense never showed up." The general and his pilots, moreover, were echoing their Commander-in-Chief George Bush, who had accused Saddam Hussein of "stiff-arming" the prewar diplomatic negotiations.

Military training exercises and battle simulations are, of course, routinely called "war games." During the war, the Pentagon public relations officers seemed to consciously cultivate vocabularies and images of sport. The press briefing room in the field closely resembled the sets used by producers of television sport media for pre- and postgame analyses and interviews with coaches of professional football teams. Equipped with video instant replays and chalkboards for reviewing the game plans of the invasion, the sets as well as the choreography of briefings themselves possessed "high production values." Ironically, entertainment-based props and protocols of presentation not only enhanced the drama of the briefings, but also seemed to enhance their authenticity. The dramaturgical effect was further heightened by the persona of General "Stormin'" Norman Schwartzkopf, whose on-camera presence bore an uncanny resemblance to some of the mythic tough-talking coaches of football/entertainment legend: Buddy Ryan, Vince Lombardi, even Pat O'Brien playing the lead in the film version of the Knute Rockne story.

Gaming—sport and entertainment—metaphors were so deeply embedded in the cognitive maps for military public relations protocols that even when their extravagant use began to attract some criticism, they were not abandoned. Thus, for example, in rejecting characterizations of the war as a video game, General Schwartzkopf nevertheless contended such comparisons were not useful "at this stage of the game" (Cable Network News, January 26, 1991). In a briefing a few days earlier, a Defense Department spokesman prefaced a showing of videos of air attacks by cautioning, "This is not a video game," but also qualified his statement by saying, "This is a serious game" (National Public Radio, January 21, 1991). Some analysts believe the military origins of info-tech, which naturalize models of total control, not only conflate but also confuse simulation and reality.[10]

SPORTSPEAK IN WAR JOURNALISM

News producers and war correspondents reinforced and embellished the sport/war metaphors of the president and the men in the field. They used these metaphors as vehicles to mobilize and promote their own war efforts in the competition for audience shares. In the early hours of the war, for example, CNN anchor Patrick Emory touted his organization's achievements in these terms: "Last night was about as close to the Super Bowl as you can get. It was as though we had Montana, Marino and Hostetler in together." Steve Friedman, executive producer of NBC news, also described his news "team's" efforts in a rather fully articulated football metaphor: "Jack Chesnutt . . . he's our defensive coordinator. Cheryl Gould, our senior producer, talks to the correspondents in the field, in the Middle East. She's our offensive coordinator." Friedman described himself as the "head coach": "I send in the plays. Tom [Brokaw] is the quarterback. . . . He makes the ultimate decision on the field, and the field to us is the screen."[11]

The wedding of sportspeak and newspeak predated the war. Team imagery has had currency in promotional and advertising campaigns for broadcast news organizations, especially television, for some time. Thus, for example, one prepackaged format for local television news that was widely used at the time was known as "first team news." Moreover, television has been largely responsible for making football a national and increasingly international sport, as well as one of its most lucrative profit makers.

Warspeak in Sport Media

With the action on real battlefields packaged in sports imagery for domestic consumption, the language and framing conventions of sport media faced special challenges during the Persian Gulf War. In the early days of the war, sportspeak continued unabated. While covering the January 19, 1991, Hula Bowl (four days into the war), for example, Charley Jones described a flanker reverse as "weaving through a minefield." By the time of the Super Bowl on January 26, however, the language of war no longer seemed to have a place on the playing field. Yet, sport/war metaphors are so deeply entrenched in the narrative structures of sport media that sport commentators for the NFL playoff games and the Super Bowl were sometimes at a loss for words because they had been instructed to respect the sensitivities of audience members with loved ones who might actually be "fighting and dying" on the "front lines."

Self-censorship of warspeak by sport media was, however, very short-lived. Not long after the war, *Sports Illustrated* ran a story entitled, "Big D-Day: The Dallas Cowboys Went on the Attack in the NFL Draft and Took All the Right Prisoners."[12] Moreover, the 1991–1992 football season witnessed the full recuperation and restoration of the prewar cadences, resonances, and hyperbolic excesses of warspeak.

WARSPEAK IN THE SPORT INDUSTRY

During the war, sport organizations used sport/war metaphors to further their own cultural and corporate agendas. On the eve of Super Bowl 25, eleven days into the war, National Football League Commissioner Paul Tagliabue said, "We've become the winter version of the Fourth of July celebration."[13] In response to some public pressure to postpone the Super Bowl, Tagliabue announced he would make the "best business decision." The game between the Buffalo Bills and the New York Giants was ultimately staged as a war spectacle involving a barricaded stadium, X-ray security searches of 72,500 fans, antiterrorist squadrons in the stands, hand-waving sized American flags distributed to every seat, a rousing rendition of the national anthem by Whitney Houston, and a halftime speech by President Bush. The drama was heightened by the probability of interruptions of the game coverage for news bulletins about new Scud missile attacks on Israel or Saudi Arabia or other combat action.

The live domestic audience for the event was in excess of 100 million viewers with a worldwide audience of three-quarters of a billion including about one-third of the troops in the Persian Gulf.[14] Patriotism, helmet-thumping, and profit-taking combined to make the silver anniversary celebration of the Super Bowl an extravaganza of colossal scale. It attracted then-unprecedented television advertising revenues of $800,000 for a thirty-second spot.[15]

The links between sport media, profit-seeking, and displays of patriotism were also evident in intercollegiate athletics. Malec surveyed the sports information directors of 152 randomly selected colleges and universities in order to discover whether a patriotic symbol was worn on sports team uniforms during the Persian Gulf War period. Fifty-eight percent of teams wore patriotic patches of some kind. Most "of the schools that did wear a patch were the larger schools which belonged to NCAA Division I and which, therefore, were not only more generously funded but also more likely to appear on regional and national television."[16]

Globalization of the Sport Industry: Exporting Sportspeak

The institutional border crossing of sportspeak reflects and reinforces the increased structural integration of sports and mass media in North American cultural industries.[17] Sport has been used to promote newspaper sales, to sell advertising space, and to win lucrative contracts for television and radio airtime. In turn, sport media have helped to sell spectator sports and attendant sports-related consumer products to the public. The Super Bowl itself was wholly an invention of network television; and it now draws much of its revenues from the companies that make up the multibillion-dollar sport marketing industry.

In recent decades, the integration of sport and media industries has become more complex as well as more global. For example, Maguire's analysis of the development of American football in England and Europe since 1978 documents the growth of interdependence between sport organizations, media, and marketing organizations within the "media/sport production complex."[18] Maguire points out that sport organizations now depend on media exposure to gain followings that, in turn, allow them to attract corporate sponsorship. Reciprocally, athletic events provide television and news media with predictably large audiences at relatively low production costs. Sport, relying on action rather than on language and plot development, is also easy to export; once a market for it has been cultivated, it can serve as the advance guard in the globalization of the U.S. sport marketing industry.

In sum, the media-sport production complex is becoming a global formation, and sportspeak appears to be one of the export agents that package and naturalize the values of American contact sports for distribution in global markets.[19] The value and standards of performance within these sports not only are patriarchal, they also *embody* instrumentalism, aggression, and the zero-sum concepts of competition that dominate corporate capitalism.

The remainder of this essay examines the success of sport/war imagery in "buttonholing" U.S. citizenry, in rallying the troops, and in creating relatively univocal mythic and explanatory structures that cut across institutional contexts.

THE DEEP STRUCTURE OF THE SPORT/WAR METAPHOR

A number of plausible explanations for the widespread currency of sport/war tropes during the Persian Gulf War were offered in both popular and scholarly accounts at the time. With appropriate parodic aplomb, Tom Callahan of *U.S. News and World Report* speculated whether war had become the "moral equivalent of football" in the postmodern age.[20] Robert MacNeil, moderator of the *MacNeil-Lehrer News Hour* and author of several books on the English language, attributed the conflation of the languages of politics and football to a decline of formal literacy in contemporary culture that had led to a "flattened use of language": by world leaders.[21] A McLuhanesque extension of MacNeil's theory would identify electronic media as the catalyst for this transformation. Fred Mish, editor-in-chief of *Merriam-Webster Dictionary*, embraced this argument to explain why television has made sport a major source for the growth of new words in recent decades. As a result, he claimed, he was not surprised that President Bush "has taken football words to war."[22]

Edelson saw the president's rhetorical move as a propaganda technique.[23] She maintained that "sports-language and battle euphemisms not only are inaccurate, tiresome, and unoriginal, but they sanitize the atrocities of war as effectively as any government-imposed censor." Gridiron imagery was used to deflect the public's attention away from the real horrors of war by rallying support for the "home team." As a propaganda device, sport/war bandwagoning proved doubly productive: sports were used to promote the war and the war was used to promote sports, especially the Super Bowl.

Feminist scholars conceive of the conflation of the languages of real violence and ritualized violence as involving gender politics as well as *realpolitiks*.[24] Within the assumptions of recent feminist epistemological inquiries, sport and war metaphors would be perceived as masculinist (or androcentric) forms of discourse.[25] From this perspective, the apparent intensification of such usages and their widespread acceptance during the war are interpreted as indicators of a renewal of the language, values and practices of male dominance.

GENDER ORDER AND HEGEMONIC FORMATIONS

Each of the interpretations considered so far has some explanatory power. In order to comprehend the ways the border-crossing activities of the sport/war trope function to express and legitimate the increasing integration of corporate, military, and entertainment industries, however, a more comprehensive theory is needed. We can craft the building blocks for such a theory by combining some ideas derived from the new feminist epistemologies (examined in part II of this book), the so-called strong program in the sociology of knowledge, and rhetoric that is broadly conceived to include recent theories or metaphor and strategies for textual analysis, with the theory of hegemonic masculinity developed by Connell.[26] Connell's sociologically based approach integrates and synthesizes Gayle Rubin's feminist analysis of 'the sex/gender system" with a Gramscian approach to theorizing hegemony.[27]

Connell uses the term "gender order" to refer to a "historically constructed pattern of power relations between men and women and definitions of femininity and masculinity" that emerge and are transformed within varying institutional contexts.[28] The prevailing cultural definitions of masculinity or hegemonic masculinity are essentially ideological constructions that serve the material interests of dominant male groups. Hegemonic masculinity reflects, supports, and actively cultivates gender inequality (male domination), but it also allows elite males to extend their influence and control over lesser status males through an "inter-male dominance hierarchy."[29] This theoretical scheme is flexible enough to facilitate analyses of social structures in general rather than forcing the researcher to place a priority on class or gender relations.[30]

Within this framework, we were able to identify three propositions that help explain how sport/war tropes fit into current formations or the U.S. gender order: (a) the "language games" of sport and war share and are generated by the rules of a common categorical "deep structure"; (b) this deep structure is homologous with as well as an artifact of the sex/gender system of American society; and (c) this structure preserves and amplifies male dominance in several important theaters for public performance and myth-making in American society, including politics, sports, and the military.

The theory suggests that the extravagant mixing of metaphors surrounding the Persian Gulf War not only reasserted the presence of American political power on the world stage, but also celebrated and conspicuously displayed elite male power at home. Use of sport/war tropes allowed the allied nations and white Western males to flex their muscles and, to use President Bush's own sport/war metaphor, "kick some ass."[31] Ironically, while elite white males made ample use of images of hegemonic masculinity in rallying around the flag (i.e., athletic and combat images of physical strength, aggressiveness, violence, hardness, emotional stoicism, competitive zeal, Promethean transcendence, and denial of death), they actually waged war at a safe distance through the use of computers and so-called smart bombs and with military forces comprised primarily of lower-middle-class, lower-class, and minority males.

BORDER CROSSINGS:
METAPHORIC CONSTRUCTIONS OF MASCULINITY

Metaphors keep language alive. Davidson claims metaphors do "the dreamwork of language," while Stevens describes them as "the symbolic language of metamorphosis."[32] Metaphors build bridges between the familiar and the unknown. They empower new visions and act like relay switches for transferring meaning, myth, and ideology from one pocket of cultural understanding to another.[33] In short, they make cultural coherence, homology, and hegemony possible.

Although metaphors make sense by making new or novel connections, the kinds of things they use to advance understanding of other things do not represent promiscuous couplings.[34] They are not simply fortuitous slips of the tongue. To the contrary, they embody, exhibit, police, and preserve the mythologies that create social order and make communication possible. The "faded mythology" preserved within Indo-European languages and categorical structures is organized around what Harding called the "totemism of gender."[35] This totemic organizes words, thoughts, images, objects, people, and experiences into polarities that encourage binary perceptions and categorizations of difference such as male/female, human/nature, and subject/object. Moreover, this process of binary coupling is weighted by hierarchical assumptions that implicitly attach primacy to the first term in the system: the male, human, subject. The concept of hegemonic masculinity provides a tool for analyzing the ways this primitive totemic is articulated within contemporary gender relations. At the societal level, as distinct from the interpersonal level, the realm of lived experience (where a wider range of behavioral variation is tolerated), portrayals of masculinity and femininity become simplified, highly stylized, and impoverished. They are the prototypes and templates for what Goffman called "gender advertisements."[36] According to Connell, the social and semiological systems that link these advertisements are "centered on the single structural fact, the global dominance of men over women" at the level of mass social relations.[37] Connell maintained:

> This structural fact provides the main basis for relationships among men that define a hegemonic form of masculinity in the society as a whole. "Hegemonic masculinity" is always constructed in relation to various subordinated masculinities as well as in relation to women. The interplay between different forms of masculinity is an important part of how a patriarchal social order works.[38]

During the Persian Gulf War, constructions of hegemonic masculinity were frequently articulated within the sport/war tropes: analogies, metaphors, and narrative structures that were used to legitimate, report, and analyze the war.

THE WAR GAMES OF HEGEMONIC MASCULINITY

Sport/war tropes exaggerate and celebrate differences between men and women. They idealize and valorize men and masculinity, and reciprocally, they trivialize and devalue women and their activities and interests. These tropes also lionize strong and aggressive men as Promethean supermen, while simultaneously marginalizing and emasculating men who appear to be weak, passive, or pacifist.

Policing the Boundaries of the Gender Order

Some critical feminist scholars maintain that sport, especially contact sport, has functioned primarily as a homosocial institution through which hegemonic masculinity has been constituted, particularly in the recent historical periods when men's superiority has been challenged by organized feminist activity.[39] That is, they suggest that sport operates, in part, as an institutionalized mechanism for venting, galvanizing, and cultivating resistance to gender-based forms of social equality. Similar arguments have been made about warfare, where male hegemony is bolstered by the association of men with power and violence in a situation that not only has historically excluded women, but has also frequently portrayed them as victims [and victimized them] as well as politically marginalized them.[40]

The tropes of sport/war help to police the borders that secure the gender system within discrete binary categories that require hyperbolic and hierarchical renderings of difference. As Edwards pointed out, there is a "massive institutional and popular commitment to thinking of war as an essential test of manhood and [like football] a quintessentially masculine activity."[41] Hegemonic masculinity is, by definition, an idealization that comes into being and exists in opposition to other counterhegemonic constructions of masculinity.

Sport/War and Male Solidarity

During the Persian Gulf War, sport/war tropes and explanatory structures were also sites of and mechanisms for constructing and reconstructing intergroup relations. As Carrigan, Connell, and Lee pointed out: "The construction or hegemony is not a matter or pushing and pulling between ready-formed groupings, but is partly a matter of the formation of these groupings."[42]

Sport/war analogies express and contribute to male solidarity at several levels. First, the social organization of both war and sport follows a pattern of sex segregation. Military socialization and athletic socialization occur in mainly same-sex contexts, and attempts to initiate coeducational military education and coeducational athletics have met with much and very similar forms of resistance. Second, the elevation of male soldiers and athletes to the status of heroes reinforces the overall idea that "masculine" contributions to society are more important than "feminine" contributions. Thus, for example, sport/war tropes frame male instrumental actions like throwing a touchdown pass or dropping a bomb as much more important than giving birth to or nurturing a child. Third, the language of sport/war represents the values of hegemonic masculinity (i.e., aggression including denial and defiance of death, competition, dominance, territoriality, and instrumental violence) as desirable and essential to the social order while at the same time, either explicitly or implicitly, marginalizing other types of masculinities within the culture (i.e., protest masculinities, pacifist or profeminist masculinities, and weak, sensitive, or emotionally vulnerable masculinities). The resulting pressures toward conformity contribute to enhancing real and perceived forms of solidarity among male elites, self-styled "manly men."

It's All in the Game: Football and Male Dominance

Bryson identified two ways that sport rituals cultivate male dominance: (a) by linking maleness to highly valued and visible skills, and (b) by linking maleness with the positively sanctioned use of aggression, force, and violence.[43] Football, especially professional football, is one of the most highly stylized displays of the contrasts between manly men and vulnerable women in contemporary American culture (exceeded today only by the quasi-sport cum male soap opera of professional wrestling). Thus, for example, journalists and fans sometimes refer to the top college football players drafted by the National Football League as "prime beef." When this prime beef is herded onto the playing field, it is very carefully and deliberately packaged for presentation to the consumers of the media-sport production complex. In helmets, spiked shoes, and padded uniforms, men who are already exceptionally, perhaps even unnaturally, large appear larger than life and as menacing as comic-book superheroes and villains.[44] Similarly the teams are usually named after objects or beings that, from the perspective of the faded mythology of U.S. history and culture, are variously perceived as wild, savage, bestial, powerful, predatory, swift, and wily. Frequently racist and generally sexist, this mythology has given us Redskins, Giants, Jets, Chiefs, Rams, Raiders, Bengals, Cowboys, Eagles, Bears, Broncos, Chargers, Packers, and others. The primary appeals of the game itself are the physical daring and danger that it involves as well as its ritualized violence that plays at the edge of, and sometimes breaks into, real violence. While the spotlights, cameras, and the eyes of the fans are focused on the displays of brute force by manly men, the only women allowed anywhere near the field are scantily clad, leaner-than-lean cheerleaders. Wearing out-of-season short-shorts or miniskirts that expose as much flesh as possible even in freezing climates, these cheerleaders jump up and down waving delicate pom-poms in cheering routines that are choreographed to erase any telltale signs of the very real athleticism, rigid training, and diet regimens that the performances actually require.

Like women, small, weak, and physically unfit men, as well as all men past their prime, are also barred from the scene; the only exceptions are coaches and attendants who serve as coordinators and officiants for the ritual itself.[45] Only the burliest men "take the field" and engage in football's strategic battles for territory. All others—the families of players, the technicians and strategists, the coaches in their high-tech headphones on the sidelines, the fans in the stands, and the millions of television viewers—are denied access to the field. Yet, their eyes remain riveted to the field or screen as everyone closely follows and identifies with the actions and outcomes of the "game."

Media Representations of Manly Men and Womanly Women

The strategic "inferiorization" of females and femininity, implicit in the framing practices and storytelling routines of mainstream sport media, became explicit in the discourses of sport/war. Linkages between masculinity, technical expertise, and applications of aggression, force, and violence were pervasive during the Persian Gulf War. Under heavy military censorship, cameras and texts focused most media coverage on "our men in uniform." Thus, for example, a special commemorative issue of *Newsweek* (January 28, 1991) featured a subsection on the war.[46] The visuals included photographs of fifty-one males and just two females. The females represented were wives: first lady Barbara Bush and the wife of another government official, who were pictured praying. Similarly, Time-Life Books used the alliterative advertising hook, "The Men, The Machines, The Missions," for its mail-order book series on the Gulf War, "From Desert Alert to Desert Storm." Under "The Men," the copy reads, "First-person accounts give you the inside perspective of today's electronic warrior—top guns, supercommandos, sky soldiers and silent hunters of the deep—so you can find out just how it feels." In this marketing move, war, like football, is explicitly framed as a spectator sport.

There was some media coverage of female warriors, particularly casualties and the female prisoner of war. The dominant framing device used to represent female experience during the Gulf War was, however, to focus on women's roles as mothers, wives, daughters, and girlfriends: loved ones and survivors. The fact that women participated more fully in the military action in this war than in any previous American war could not be easily accommodated by the mythos that secures the discourses of sport/war. While generals and congressmen debated whether women belonged in combat or whether they were as skilled at warfare as their male counterparts, many women soldiers and fliers sought greater access to battlefield roles. Although women did in fact fight and die in battle, female pilots and soldiers were marginalized by the official rhetoric and media representations of the war. Some of the marginalization of women warriors was no doubt strategic: an attempt by the U.S. government to downplay the challenge that the partial gender integration of the U.S. military posed to the conservative gender regimes of its Middle Eastern allies. The struggles over women's rights and roles in the military have continued since the end of the Persian Gulf War. After the war, the ideological forces that support beliefs in essentialized gender differences were challenged on April 28, 1993, by Defense Secretary Les Aspin, who directed Pentagon officials and Congress to lift restrictions that have barred women from a variety of combat roles. The debate, however, continues to resurface.

Sport/war tropes not only marginalized women in the U.S. military, but also licensed homophobia. Gay and lesbian efforts to gain access to military careers were officially rebuffed. Legal prohibitions that bar homosexuals from the military were reaffirmed during the first Bush Administration, although they relaxed somewhat under the "Don't Ask, Don't Tell" policy of the Clinton Administration. The military ambitions of lesbians may have been perceived as an affront to male authority and traditions, but their activism posed no real threat to gender expectations for manly men. In contrast, the demands of gay men for equal access to positions within the intermale dominance hierarchy were a fundamental challenge to the canons of hegemonic masculinity. Homophobia and the official exclusion of gays and lesbians from the military, which even the Clinton policy supported, continue to be crucial for the maintenance of hegemonic masculinity.

During the Persian Gulf War, the armed services and the mythos of sport/war proved flexible enough to accommodate some heterosexual women who were, at least metaphorically, willing to *act like* manly men. Nevertheless, the core values of the institutions of sport and war, as well as the rhetorical practices that support them, remained steadfastly heterosexist. Open acceptance of gay soldiers could not be tolerated within the U.S. gender order because it would have destroyed the root structure of a system of relationships and homophobic sentiments that depend upon both equations of sport and war and binary pairings of masculinity and femininity. In contrast, cultivation and amplification of the mythos of sport/war allowed hegemonic masculinity to emerge from the Persian Gulf War slightly transformed but still culturally and politically ascendant.

Framing Out Resistance

The extensive media use of and the apparent public receptivity to sport/war tropes rendered articulation of resistance to the war extremely problematic. Criticism of the war effort seemed to cut both across and against the grains of sport, gender, and patriotism. Some war resisters actively invested in the rhetorical opportunities that the language game of sport/war made possible. For example, in his address to the Washington, D.C., peace rally on January 26, 1991, New York Congressman Charles Rangel accused the press of "cheerleading the military Super Bowl" (WKFW, Pacifica Radio). The pervasive use of sport/war imagery in the media and in unmediated discussions of the war made it extraordinarily difficult to express counterhegemonic interpretations of the war. As Sallach argued, the propagation of hegemony by dominant groups "involves not only the inculcation of its values," but also "the ability to define the parameters of legitimate discussion and debate over alternative beliefs, values, and world views."[47]

Scott observed that "in making long overdue room for the analysis of ideological domination *per se*, many of Gramsci's successors have . . . substituted a kind of ideological determinism for the material determinism they sought to avoid."[48] The ideological hegemony during the Persian Gulf War was never complete. There was an ongoing struggle to resist the war effort, to challenge what some claimed was misguided patriotism, and to reveal the underlying political and patriarchal roots of the war process. But this resistance was to a large extent muted, derailed, and marginalized in its relation to social forces that adopted and deployed the sport/war trope. Indeed, the use of the sport/war metaphor in the discourse of government, military, war journalism, sport media, and the sport industry helped to make ideological hegemony a reality by masking the ideological diversity in the American polity and curbing (and erasing visibility of) resistance to the war.

SPORT MEDIA AND THE MODERN WAR SYSTEM

Sports, especially team sports, are vehicles for cultivating and displaying community and national values and identities. This is demonstrated on local and regional levels by home-team loyalties, and in the nationalism that provides the edge of excitement in the Olympic Games and other international sporting competitions. Sport also plays a crucial role in contemporary forms of nation building by transcending social divisions and affirming political loyalties to the nation as a whole.[49]

The Persian Gulf War took place in the wake of the collapse of the Cold War ruling strategy that had served as the primary means of unifying U.S. and Western policy and ideological constructions since the end of World War II. The West had lost the enemy, "world communism," that had provided it with a common purpose and basis for solidarity. American defense intellectuals, policy think tanks, and State Department analysts were actively seeking new ways of making sense of—and thereby exercising some control over and within—the new worldwide realignments of power relations.

The reassertion and amplification of the values of hegemonic masculinity generated by the Persian Gulf War created a very timely opportunity to consolidate and reintegrate what Connell called "multiple systems of dominance": the hierarchical relations of social inequality that provide the auspices for hegemony in both national and international arenas of power.[50]

The New World Order, the ideological centerpiece of President Bush's January 1991 State of the Union speech, articulated the terms of the renewal of

U.S. and Western power. His speech drew heavily upon the mythos of sport/war in saluting the toughness, aggressiveness, sacrifices, patriotism, and bravery of the manly men who were defending the honor of the U.S. and the Western coalition in the Persian Gulf.

Official versions of the war—the versions that were presented by the proactive public relations strategies of the Defense Department and filtered through the tightest screen of military censorship the U.S. had experienced up to that point—articulated a new hierarchy in which white men remained clearly positioned at the pinnacle of the pyramid. They were, however, flanked by men of color: African-American military personnel including General Colin Powell and troops from Saudi Arabia, Syria, and Bangladesh. Moreover, women were not entirely excluded from the pyramid, although they were largely positioned at the margins.

Because the war involved wealthy Arab nations, the media spotlight on the Middle East deflected attention away from the dramatic structural inequalities that separate industrial nations and developing nations. The discussion of gender stereotyping, both within Arab nations and in the U.S. military, raised issues of social equality, but representations of the war itself reinforced hegemonic definitions of masculinity. The marginalization of gays and lesbians during and after the war eroded the potential for articulations of genuinely counterhegemonic definitions of gender within the emerging structures of power relations. Moreover, the unprecedented (until September 2001) waves of patriotism and nationalism, fueled by the mythos of sport/war, enabled predominantly white ruling groups to effectively confuse and diffuse opposition to the war among the African-American population in the U.S., the group that made the greatest sacrifices during the war. In both sport coverage and war coverage, the already muted colors of race were further obscured by the bright foreground of red, white, and blue.

The multiple systems of domination that are constituted by power relations in American society are increasingly part of the emerging global system of warfare. Within the framework of the changing world order, Reardon defined the "war system" as

a competitive social order which is based on authoritarian principles, assumes unequal value among and between human beings, and is held in place by coercive force. The institutions through which this force is currently controlled and applied are dominated by a small minority, elites who run the global economy and conduct the affairs of state. These elites are men from industrial countries, primarily Western, and for the most part educated to think in Western, analytic terms. Although their relationship is competitive within the elite structures, there is a common objective that holds the elites together: the maintenance of their control and dominance.[51]

The growing presence of sports programming in international communications media, including the increasing prominence of American professional team sports in European sport media, may indicate that sport/war tropes and scenarios, derived from the images and icons of U.S. history and popular culture, are becoming part of the semiological structure of the global "war system." Sport/war media framing devices, which were so widely used during the Persian Gulf War, have tapped into and revitalized the deep structure of patriarchal meanings and values that have pervaded hierarchies of domination in all Western societies for millennia.

The sport/war trope in the Persian Gulf War not only produced, at least briefly, extraordinary levels of patriotic solidarity within the U.S. and enabled the military to achieve its immediate objectives in the Middle East, but also demonstrated how effectively the government can control mass media during national and international emergencies. The U.S. government provided the press with very little news at a time when the public had an insatiable appetite for it. Under these circumstances, media, especially electronic media, were forced to draw more heavily on "soft" or mythic—associative rather than fact-based—storytelling routines and framing devices and conventions in producing their news programming. These mythic frames, in turn, appear to have worked to reassert the power of white, upper-class males within the changing gender order of the late twentieth century.

Some of the rules of the language games and practices of hegemonic masculinity were slightly modified by the experiences, representations, and responses to the Persian Gulf War; those slight modifications did nonetheless represent hard-won victories for African-American and female military personnel. Despite these victories, however, the first-string players continue to be recruited from the same elite Western colleges and universities that controlled the action on the fields of power before Third World nations gained their independence, before the second wave of feminism pressed its claims for equality, and before the Berlin Wall crumbled. The New World Order subsequently transmuted into globalization, and globalization, in turn, is currently developing what appears to be a permanent military wing, mobilized to fight the War on Terrorism. Within the emergent system, "manly men" still possess, assert, and largely control mediated constructions of agency, subjectivity, and power.

CODA: THE FUTURE OF SPORT/WARS

Throughout the 1990s, the market largely displaced the state as the generative site of post–Cold war political linguistics. The dollar, rather than the flag, represented the terms of U.S. global engagement. The competition to name the age presupposed U.S. hegemony. Retro–Cold War narratives still periodically reappeared in the news in stories about China, North Korea, and Cuba, for example, the 1999 saga of the six-year-old Cuban refugee Elian Gonzalez. Resistance to U.S. hegemony, which received sparse coverage in mainstream media, was more likely to be mobilized to target economic rather than political power, for example, the protests at WTO meetings and hackers' assaults on e-commerce.

With the September 2001 attacks on the U.S., the post–Cold War period came to an end; a new war, both metaphoric and real, hot and cold, began. According to President George W. Bush, the War on Terrorism will be a new kind of war. It will be covert and overt; domestic and international; involve law enforcement and intelligence agencies as well as conventional troops; and it will be conducted on many fronts, military, economic, political, and technological. It will entail unprecedented government surveillance powers and suspension of some civil liberties, especially the civil liberties of aliens and resident aliens. Congress quickly provided the president with these extraordinary powers in the "Patriot Act."

Many of the key players mobilizing this new war are the same players who led the Persian Gulf initiative. So far (circa late-2002) this new war is proving more popular with the American people than the Persian Gulf War. Moreover, at this point, it appears the G. W. Bush Administration has the resources (symbolic and material) necessary to avoid the quick ebb of popularity that followed the Persian Gulf War. The new war, like the Cold War but unlike the Persian Gulf War, involves a permanent war economy. That is, it is a conflict that is expected to last for the foreseeable future. Unlike the industrially based Cold War, however, the new war will have a kind of post-Fordian flexibility that allows anti-terrorist initiatives to move swiftly and invisibly, using private resources as well as public, and improvising strategies, including legal procedures, as it evolves. Yet, in terms of government mobilization of symbolic resources, there are remarkable parallels with the Persian Gulf War.

The sport/war packaging of the Persian Gulf War was, on one hand, stunningly successful. It effectively rallied the troops and the American public around the flag. It deflected American attention away from the massive scale of U.S.–inflicted human carnage in Iraq. It successfully delayed disclosure of tactical errors and failures of the U.S. military, and it decisively asserted U.S. global dominance at a defining moment in the early post–Cold War period. On the other hand, however, it was also problematic because the highly restrictive media censorship triggered widespread criticism, both during and after the war. Journalists expect some censorship during wars, for example to protect troops and military tactics, but the level of censorship imposed during the Persian Gulf War was unprecedented in modern U.S. history.

The military had learned the lessons of Vietnam, and seemed determined to leave nothing to chance in packaging the Persian Gulf War for dissemination to the news media. Indeed, the military framed its messages for direct broadcast to the U.S. public in an apparent attempt to bypass journalistic mediation as well as to mute the effects of postbroadcast media punditry. As a public relations cum propaganda strategy, it was a brilliant move, but its short-term success had long-term costs. The sound-byte, video enhanced, public relations coached delivery of the military's message was too slick, too orchestrated; the high production values of the military briefings did not "fool the foolers." What played well on live television, as television qua television, and as a collective mobilizer of the American public, could not pass the cynical crap detectors of experienced journalists, especially print journalists. To compete with the electronic media in the era when history is broadcast live, print journalists needed the story behind the story. In short, the military fed the broadcast media a banquet, but it starved print media. The war was very good for the television industry. It made CNN a lucrative profit center for Turner Broadcasting for the first time in the cable network's history.

Print media shared the war profits, but elite newspaper journalists as well as editors and writers for journals of opinion were stung by their displacement in the news hierarchy. Their role as mediators and interpreters of government leaks, as insiders and brokers of in-depth stories was largely negated. They fought back. A coalition of journalists and publications filed First Amendment lawsuits against the government. The blank news holes, created by government censorship, were filled with criticisms of government censorship. By the end of the short war, even print-based sports reporters were parodying the sport/war packaging.

The military learned the lessons of this war too—and very quickly! President George Bush's sequel to the Persian Gulf War, billed as "a humanitarian war," premiered to live cameras on location in Somalia only days before Bill Clinton took office after defeating Bush in the 1992 election. The military subsequently brought us a number of global "peace-keeping missions." These U.S.– or United Nations– mediated wars in the former Third World could not have been successfully billed as sport/wars. The adversaries are too poorly armed to qualify—or to be inflated into—real competition in war games of manly men. Rather, they were represented as "victims" to be rescued by American led coalitions.

The feminized rhetoric used to frame these wars was presumably designed not only to make them play well in the U.S. and Europe (where the global presence of the U.S. military is widely criticized) but also to convey the real differences in the "national interest" that the U.S. had in these wars as compared to the regional wars of the Cold War. That is, the U.S.'s strategic interest is in keeping markets and access to resources stable, not in keeping dominos from falling into communist hands.

Sport wars require a special brand of enemy: a technologically advanced adversary who is deemed capable of posing significant threats to U.S. national security or to the security of global markets. Nations, large or small, with nuclear weapons or the capability of producing nuclear weapons—what the Pentagon calls "weapons of mass destruction"—qualify as worthy enemies, as do terrorists and hackers (cyber-warriors) capable of sabotaging the electronic infrastructure of the government or the global economy.

Saddam Hussein himself continued to qualify as a manly man and as a legitimate target for sport/warriors, as George W. Bush's 2001 bombing raids demonstrated. However, the September 2001 attacks on America not only produced a new kind of war, they also introduced a new kind of enemy to Americans.

All wars have civilian casualties; sometimes the civilian casualty toll is horrific as, for example, in the U.S. atomic attacks on Japan that ended World War II. But the governments and military leaders conducting such wars invariably claim that civilian casualties are unavoidable and regrettable costs (so-called collateral damage) of achieving military objectives. Such claims, even when they are false, conform to the values and mythos of sport/war. Within the twisted logics of war talk, the airline passengers and the civilian employees of the Pentagon who died in Washington on September 11 might conceivably be considered collateral damage. That is, their deaths could be viewed as means to military or paramilitary ends. The other passengers and the victims of the World Trade Center attacks could not, however, be rationalized by this kind of military logic. These civilians were targets qua targets.

The attackers were a multinational force that represented no state; in a sense, they were guerrilla warriors against global capitalism as well as perpetrators of a terrible crime against humanity. The language and ethos of sport/war are artifacts of nationalism. In the case of the WTC, the violations of the conventions of sport/war are so grievous that the metaphors simply do not apply: they were not used and they do not work. Conversely, however, by attacking the Pentagon (surely considered one of the most inviolate military fortresses in the world) and by using improvised weapons, minimal personnel, high intelligence, rigorous discipline, and lethal dedication, the al-Qaida network proved itself to be a formidable enemy of manly men. That is, Osama bin Laden's forces did what no modern nation-state or its military forces had previously dared to do: they attacked the military headquarters of a nuclear superpower. In short, they defied the hierarchical logic of world power relations.

The term terrorism is and should remain a contested term with the vocabulary of critical theory; yet, it has now become virtually impossible to avoid its use, at least in the U.S. The terror produced by the New York, Washington, and Pennsylvania attacks and by the anthrax attacks on the U.S. Postal Service that immediately followed unleashed an orgy of patriotic fervor among Americans that made the Persian Gulf War excesses pale to insignificance.

Compared to the poignant daily vigils of the news media at the rescue site in lower Manhattan, the somber dramaturgy of the many televised memorial services, the endless streams of obituaries of victims in the *New York Times*, and the spectacles of the celebrity fund-raisers for the families of the victims, the pageantry of the Super Bowl 36 was almost subdued. Yet, as with Super Bowl 25, the iconography of sport and war converged. Red, white, and blue filled the screens, and players and referees wore flags on their uniforms. Former President George Bush presided over the opening coin toss. Pretaped footage showed individual players, with American flags in the background, sending greetings and messages of support to U.S. troops in Afghanistan; live coverage showed the troops in Kandahar watching the game. The halftime entertainment, featuring Irish pop group U2, involved incongruous staging in which they performed their wildly energetic music in front of a screen listing the names of the victims of the September 11 attacks. At the end of the performance, the screen collapsed (which may or may not have been intended to simulate the collapse of the WTC towers), and the lead Irish performer opened his jacket to reveal that it was lined with an American flag.

The commercials, in 2002 costing $2 million dollars for a thirty-second ad, used mixtures of grief, gratitude, nostalgia, and humor to make their sales pitches.[52] Few traded directly on the September 11 attacks, although muted symbolic representations were present as, for example, in a Budweiser ad where a beer wagon pulled by the company's trademark Clydesdale horses seemed to be crossing a bridge into Manhattan where the horses paused and bowed their heads near the World Trade Center site. Two ads directly referenced the attacks. The first featured former Mayor Giuliani expressing his appreciation to all America's for helping New York after the attacks. The other, a government-sponsored antidrug ad attempted to directly tap the well of patriotism by warning audience members that if they buy drugs, they finance terrorists. What was strikingly absent from these ads was the high-tech, special effects that had come to define Super Bowl ads in the 1990s.

Security was understandably even tighter at the 2002 game than it was in 1991. What was similar to 1991, but different from the usual hoopla of Super Bowl games, was the subdued language of the announcers. Network executives had once again banned the language of war from the lexicon of sports announcers.[53] In its place, the commentators used muted descriptive language to report what may have been the most suspense-filled Super Bowl game ever as the underdog Boston Patriots triumphed over the St. Louis Rams in the final seconds of the game.

The following week, the themes of grief and patriotism continued to be played out for a global sports audience, estimated at three billion viewers, in the opening ceremonies of the Winter Olympics in Salt Lake City, Utah. After a dispute and controversy, the International Olympic Committee reversed an earlier decision and allowed the tattered remains of a flag that flew over the WTC site to be paraded through the Olympic stadium by an American Honor Guard.

These displays, controversies, and proscriptions are, of course, testaments to the generative powers of the metaphors of sport/war. They are also affirmations of the continuing resiliency of gender regimes, secured in hegemonic masculinity, which, in times of crises, seem to be able to reach deeply into taproots of traditional, even primitive, values, that still remain largely untouched after decades of feminist critique and activism.

NOTES

1. Albert Camus, *The Myth of Sisyphus* (New York: Random House, 1955), 5.

2. Jim McKay and David Rowe, "Ideology, the Media, and Australian Sport," *Sociology of Sport Journal* 4 (1997): 258–73.

3. Susan Birrell and C. L. Cole, "Double Fault: Renee Richards and the Construction and Naturalization of Differences," *Sociology of Sport Journal* 7, no. 1 (1990): 1–21; C. Critcher, "Radical Theorists of Sport: The State Play," *Sociology of Sport Journal* 3 (1986): 333–43; and Michael A. Messner and Donald F. Sabo, ed., *Sport, Men, and the Gender Order: Critical Feminist Perspectives* (Champaign, Ill.: Human Kinetics, 1990).

4. The concept of "deep structure" is drawn from Chomsky's generative transformational linguistic perspective, and is used as an analogy to suggest that deeply rooted cultural mythos akin to a collective unconsciousness partially conditions use and reception of language. See Noam Chomsky, *The Logical Structure of Linguistic Theory* (New York: Plenum Press, 1975).

5. For a discussion of U.S. triumphalism at the end of the Cold War, see Patrick Smith, "Dark Victory," *Index on Censorship* 28, no. 5 (September/October 1999): 42–43.

6. Ira Berkow, "Once Again, it's the Star-Spangled Super Bowl," *New York Times*, 27 January 1991: 6(B); and Marilyn Booth, "Crossing the Demarcation Line," *The Women's Review of Books* 8, no. 18 (May 1991); M. Capuzzo, *Philadelphia Inquirer*, 19 January 1991, 2(D); and P. Edelson, "Sports During Wartime," *Z Magazine* (May 1991): 85–87.

7. Capuzzo, *Philadelphia Inquirer*, 2(D).

8. Roland Barthes, *Mythologies*, sel. and trans. Annette Lavers (New York: Hill & Wang, 1972), 114.

9. L. A. Taylor, "Nationalism, the State, War and Sport: The Problem of Using Women as Patriotic Symbols," paper presented at the annual meeting of the North American Society for the Study of Sport, Milwaukee, Wisc., November 17, 1991.

10. Deborah Heath, *Computers and Their Bodies: Sex, War and Cyberspace*, unpublished manuscript (1991), Department of Sociology and Anthropology, Lewis and Clark College, Portland, Oreg.; and Les Levidow and Kevin Robbins, eds., *Cyborg Worlds: The Military Information Society* (London: Free Association Books, 1989).

11. Capuzzo, *Philadelphia Inquirer*, 2(D).

12. P. King, "Big D Day," *Sports Illustrated* (April 29, 1991): 42–48.

13. Berkow, "Once Again," 6(B).

14. G. Eskenazi, "Jitters Abound in Telecast," *New York Times*, 27 January 1991, 3(B).

15. D. Elliot, *USA Today* (1 February 1991), 2(C).

16. M. Malec, "Patriotic Symbols in Intercollegiate Sports during the Gulf War: A Research Note," *Sociology of Sport Journal* 10 (1993): 98–106.

17. Donald F. Sabo and Ross Runfola, eds., *Jock: Sports and Male Identity* (Englewood Cliffs, N.J.: Prentice-Hall, 1990).

18. J. Maguire, "The Media-Sport Production Complex: The Case of American Football in Western European Societies," *European Journal of Communication* 6 (1991): 315–35; J. Maguire, "Globalization, Sport Development, and the Media Sport Production Complex," *Sport Science Review* 2, no. 1 (1993): 29–47; and Sut Jhally and Barry Truchil, "The Spectacle of Accumulation: Material and Cultural Factors in the Evolution of the Sports/Media Complex," *Insurgent Sociologist* 12, no. 3 (1984): 41–57.

19. Donald F. Sabo, "Sociology of Sport and New World Disorder," *Sport Science Review* 2, no. 1 (1993): 1–9.

20. Berkow, "Once Again," 6(B).

21. Capuzzo, *Philadelphia Inquirer*, 2(D).

22. Capuzzo, *Philadelphia Inquirer*, 2(D).

23. P. Edelson, "Sports During Wartime," *Z Magazine* (May 1991): 85–87.

24. Marilyn Booth, "Crossing the Demarcation Line," *Women's Review of Books* 8 (May 1991): 18; Carol Cohn, "Sex and Death in the Rational World of Defense Intellectuals," Signs 12, no. 4 (1987): 687–718; and Donna Haraway, presentations and discussions at NEH summer institute, "Science as Cultural Practice," Wesleyan University, 1991.

25. Donna Haraway, "Science as Cultural Practice"; Sandra Harding, *The Science Question in Feminism* (Ithaca, N.Y.: Cornell University Press, 1986); and Catherine A. MacKinnon, "Feminism, Marxism, Method and the State: An Agenda for Theory," Signs 7, no. 3 (1982): 515–44.

26. R. W. Connell, *Gender and Power* (Palo Alto, Calif.: Stanford University Press, 1987).

27. Gayle Rubin, "The Traffic in Women: Notes on the 'Political Economy' of Sex," in *Toward an Anthropology of Women*, ed. Reyna R. Reiter (New York: Monthly Review Press, 1975), 157–210; and Antonio Gramsci, *Prison Notebook* (New York: International Publishers, 1971).

28. Connell, *Gender and Power*, 98–99.

29. Donald F. Sabo, "Pigskin, Patriarchy, and Pain," *Changing Men: Issues in Gender, Sex and Politics* 16 (1986): 24–25.

30. R. W. Connell, "The State, Gender, and Sexual Politics," *Theory and Society* 19 (1990): 507–44.

31. In what might be reconceptualized as an even more direct display of hegemonic masculinity, then–Vice President George Bush was first quoted in the press using this expression to describe what he intended to do to Democratic vice presidential candidate Geraldine Ferraro during a televised debate between vice presidential candidates in the 1984 election campaign.

32. Donald Davidson, "What Metaphors Mean," in *On Metaphor*, ed. Sheldon Sacks (Chicago: University of Chicago Press, 1979), 290–91.

33. David Bloor, *Knowledge and Social Imagery* (London: Routledge & Kegan Paul, 1977).

34. Mary Hesse, *Models and Analogies in Science* (South Bend, Ind.: Notre Dame Press, 1966); George Lakoff and Mark Johnson, *Metaphors We Live By* (Chicago: University of Chicago Press, 1980); and George Lakoff and Mark Johnson, *Philosophy in the Flesh: The Embodied Mind and Its Challenges to Western Thought* (New York: Basic Books, 1999).

35. Harding, *The Science Question in Feminism*, 104.

36. Erving Goffman, *Gender Advertisements* (New York: Harper & Row, 1979).

37. Connell recognized that "the sheer complexity of relationships involving millions of people guarantees that ethnic differences and generational as well as class patterns come into play. But in key respects the organization of gender on the very large scale must be more skeletal and simplified than the human relationship in face-to-face milieux. The forms of femininity and masculinity constituted at this level are stylized and impoverished." And, therefore, we would add, deeply oppressive. See Connell, *Gender and Power*, 183.

38. Connell, *Gender and Power*, 182.

39. M. A. Hall, "The Discourse on Gender and Sport: From Femininity to Feminism," *Sociology of Sport Journal* 5 (1988): 330–40; Bruce Kidd, "Sports and Masculinity" in *Beyond Patriarchy: Essays by Men on Pleasure, Power, and Change*, ed. Michael Kaufman (Toronto and New York: Oxford University Press, 1987), 250–65; Michael A. Messner, "Sports and Male Domination: The Female Athlete as Contested Ideological Terrain," *Sociology of Sport Journal* 5 (1988): 197–211; and David Whitson, "Sport in the Social Construction of Masculinity" in *Sport, Men, and the Gender Order*, ed. Michael A. Messner and Donald F. Sabo, 19–29.

40. Robert W. Connell, "Masculinity, Violence, and War" in *Men's Lives*, ed. Michael Kimmel and Michael A. Messner (New York: Macmillan, 1989), 94–100; Barbara G. Walker, *The Crone: Woman of Age, Wisdom, and Power* (San Francisco: Harper & Row, 1985).

41. Paul Edwards, "The Army and the Micro World: Computers and the Politics of Gender Identity," *Signs* 16, no. 1 (1990): 118; and Heath, "Computers and Their Bodies."

42. T. Carrigan, R. Connell, and J. Lee, "Toward a New Sociology of Masculinity," *Theory and Society* 14, no. 5 (1985): 551–604.

43. L. Bryson, "Challenges to Male Hegemony in Sport" in *Sport, Men, and the Gender Order*, ed. Michael A. Messner and Donald F. Sabo, 173–84.

44. Unnatural, because muscle mass is frequently augmented by anabolic steroids.

45. Donald F. Sabo and J. Panepinto, "Football Ritual and the Social Reproduction of Masculinity" in *Sport, Men, and the Gender Order*, ed. Michael A. Messner and Donald F. Sabo, 115–26.

46. *Newsweek* (special commemorative war issue), 28 January 1991, 12–34.

47. G. Sallach, cited by George H. Sage, *Power and Ideology in American Sport: A Critical Perspective* (Champaign, Ill.: Human Kinetics, 1990), 118.

48. Joan C. Scott, *Weapons of the Weak* (New Haven, Conn.: Yale University Press, 1987), 317.

49. James Riordan, "State and Sport in Developing Societies," *International Review for the Sociology of Sport* 21, no. 4 (1986): 288; and L. A. Taylor, "Nationalism, the State, War and Sport."

50. Connell, *Gender and Power*.

51. Riordan, "State and Sport," 288.

52. Skip Wollenberg, "Mixed Messages," *Allentown (Pa.) Morning Call*, 5 February 2002, 1(D)–2(D).

53. Jackie Loohauis, "New Terms Shed Old Definitions since Sept. 11 Terror Attacks," *Allentown (Pa.) Morning Call*, 2 November 2001, 2(D).

Chapter Nine

International News: Masculinity, Paradox, and Possibilities

A growing body of feminist research suggests that news, especially international news, is a form of communication that can be fully and critically understood only when seen through the prism of gender.[1] This research indicates that the cultural forms of objective journalism are currently alienating a significant segment of the potential audience: women, especially young women. From a pragmatic perspective, journalism's apparent indifference to the female audience makes no sense. In the United States, where commercialization of news production is most pronounced, women control or influence 80 percent of consumer decision-making. When advertising-driven news organizations ignore women, they ignore market imperatives.[2]

What accounts for this apparent resistance to the logic of capitalism? In this chapter, I argue that journalism's indifference to female audiences is a socially significant extension of current structures of global power, not simply a provincial souvenir of traditionalism. I treat gender as an important, perhaps even decisive, category in articulations of all power relations, including relationships among heterosexual men. By continuing to ignore the salient role that gender plays in communications and international relations, critical communication scholarship limits the range and power of its analytic lens, and fails to realize its emancipatory promise.[3]

There are four parts to this argument. First, I develop the claim that news, especially international news, is gendered and that this gendering both reflects and contributes to current global crises. Second, I unpack some of the gendered constituents of the mythology of the Cold War. Third, I analyze some of the opportunities and obstacles that the end of the Cold War posed for the global feminist movement, for the practice and study of international relations, and for media organizations themselves. Fourth, I briefly identify four crises that become fully visible only when gender is treated as a significant category for analyzing and reporting global politics.

NEWS AS A GENDERED FORM

In the United States, men still write most of the front-page newspaper stories. They are the subjects of most of those stories—85 percent of the references and 66 percent of the photos in 1993. They also dominate electronic media, accounting for 86 percent of the correspondents and 75 percent of the sources for U.S. network television evening news programs.[4] According to Margaret Gallagher, "Prevalent news values define most women and most women's problems as unnewsworthy, admitting women to coverage primarily as wives, mothers or daughters of men in the news: in their own right, they make the headlines usually only as fashionable or entertaining figures."[5]

Newspaper readership research indicates that heavy reliance on conflict-based news narratives alienates women.[6] Yet, stories framed in terms of conflict, confrontation, extremism, and sensationalism are the staples of journalism. Men are typically assigned to "hard" news, news that has significant public implications. Women, in contrast, cover "soft" news stories and stories related to topics traditionally associated with female responsibilities. Figures for U.S. newspapers show that men dominate coverage of war and the military (81.8 percent), sports (81.2 percent), government and politics (78.1 percent), human interest (75.4 percent), economics (75.3 percent), and foreign relations (72.6 percent). Women most frequently cover education (66.7 percent), health and medicine (43.9 percent), accidents and disasters (45.5 percent), and social issues (42.4 percent).[7] Gender also makes a difference in reading the news. In the United States, women read more than men generally, but men read more newspapers than women: approximately 65 percent of men and 60 percent of women are daily consumers of newspapers.[8]

Kay Mills maintains that Western journalism still views women as "outsiders, suspect, 'the other' . . . the anomaly, exceptions to the male norm"; as a result, "coverage of issues affecting women is not institutionalized, not part of the normal media mind-set."[9]

In international news coverage, women not only are marginalized, they are largely absent. As Cynthia Enloe points out, only on those rare occasions when women such as Margaret Thatcher or Indira Gandhi are present in news photographs of world leaders do we become consciously aware that nearly all leaders are men:

> Women's experiences—of war, marriage, trade, travel, factory work—are relegated to the "human interest" column. Women's roles in creating and sustaining

international politics have been treated as if they were "natural" and thus not worthy of investigation. Consequently, how the conduct of international politics has depended on men's control of women has been left unexamined.[10]

The socially structured silences or erasures produced by the routine practices of international news production contribute to the maintenance and reproduction of an international gender order that is secured by what Bob Connell calls "hegemonic masculinity."[11] Connell is, of course, describing the way patriarchal societies impute meaning and values to, and often exaggerate, sexual differences; he is not, however, arguing that patriarchy is destiny. To the contrary, he identifies himself as a feminist committed to the struggle for a more just world.

According to Connell, at the level of mass social relations, highly stylized and impoverished definitions of masculinity form the basis for dominant males' relationships to subordinate males and for the relationships of all males to females. This hegemonic principle is replicated, in abstract form, in the global ordering of relationships of dominant and subordinate nations. This principle is, in turn, reproduced in journalistic framing of international news.

Research stimulated by the feminist, gay, and lesbian liberation movements has, however, made it increasingly difficult to ignore the salience of gender as an explanatory category in social research. As Stuart Hall has observed, nothing less than a "revolution in thinking" follows in the wake of the recognition that all social practices and forms of domination, including all political positions—whether centrist, left, or right—are always marked by and secured in relation to sexual identity and positioning.[12]

This revolution requires radical reconstruction of the theories, research protocols, and journalistic practices used to conceptualize international relations and international news. Connell criticizes the outmoded, but still operative, approach: "The habit of mind that treats class, or race, or North-South global relationships as if gender did not matter is obsolete and dangerous."[13] To ignore gender is to ignore a major generative principle of international conflicts. Such ignorance contributes to practices that allow incipient conflicts to remain invisible until they escalate into major international crises. As Connell points out, even when gender is ignored:

> The facts of gender do not go away. Aid programs to Third World countries, by ignoring gender in principle, in fact give resources to men rather than to women. Industrial and nationalist militancy that ignores questions of gender reinforces men's violence and the patterns of masculinity that lie behind it. The question of human survival, in the face of a global arms race and widespread environmental destruction requires us to understand a play of social forces in which gender is a major part.[14]

Under the present global gender order, policymakers and journalists find it more manly to deal with guns, missiles, espionage, treaties, trade wars, and violent conflicts than with matters like female infanticide in China and India, the increased trade of children in the sex markets of Manila and Bangkok in the wake of the AIDS epidemic, the impact of the intifada on Palestinian women, or the political activism of groups such as the Women in Black, Israeli women who have supported the intifada.

Exceptions to this rule occur when exploitation or persecution of women acquires instrumental value in international news. For example, when the United States was mobilizing coalition forces to attack the Taliban regime in the wake of the September 2001 terrorist attacks on America, there was widespread coverage of the Taliban's persecution of women. Feminists had, of course, tried to publicize the Taliban atrocities since the regime took control in Afghanistan, but these feminist efforts were generally ignored by mainstream media. When American policymakers and the press did take up the plight of women in Afghanistan, the mission of the Western coalition was framed as both military and humanitarian: to hunt down the al-Qaida Network and to overthrow the Taliban as well as to bring food to the Afghan people and to *rescue* female victims of the Taliban rule.

THE GENDER ORDER AND COLD WAR MYTHOLOGY

In claiming that the Cold War hung "the hinge of history" on a narrow frame and thereby impoverished the political imagination of the period by reducing it to polarized terms, E. P. Thompson does not attend to the gendered constituents of this impoverishment.[15] They are, however, fairly transparent. The ideological framing on the Cold War cultivated and inflamed "reciprocal paranoias" by embedding analysis within the logic of worst-case scenarios, and by demonizing the people on the other side of the global divide as "an Enemy Other."[16] This polarizing code also nourished and fed cultural imagery of a heterosexist gender order, where good European and American women stayed in the kitchen and the bedroom and supported manly men in their valiant attempts to contain an "evil empire" (to use former President Ronald Reagan's description of the Soviet Union). Within this binary semantic code, homosexuals were conceived as "security risks": enemies within, to be coerced, brutalized, and confined to closets.

Brian Easlea, Helen Caldicott, Carol Cohn, and others have excavated the gendered constituents of "the dangerous-world syndrome" that fueled the mythology of the Cold War.[17] In a world pervaded by threats and violence—in which two superpowers were locked into a deadly game of brinkmanship—

risk-taking was justified in the name of avoiding a bigger risk.[18] Thus, for example, U.S. defense policy justified wars in Korea and Vietnam as necessary to stop Chinese and Soviet expansionism and thereby avoid a nuclear holocaust. The rationale for these bloodlettings, "the domino theory" put forth by John Foster Dulles, secretary of state in the Eisenhower Administration, is an exemplary case of a Cold War policy that "nourished and reproduced reciprocal paranoias."[19]

The Cold War may be over, but the dangerous worldviews of men in power show few signs of pacification or imaginative reconstructions. The Persian Gulf War was, among other things, a boy thing. Throughout the 1988 presidential campaign, Republican candidate George Bush was dogged by the charge, attributed to Evan Thomas of *Newsweek*, that he was a "wimp." Although Bush was a bona fide World War II hero and had served as head of the Central Intelligence Agency prior to becoming Ronald Reagan's vice president, his genteel social class background and sometimes effeminate speech patterns and mannerisms gave the charge some traction. President George Bush, however, demonstrated that he could, indeed, walk the walk of a macho man during the Persian Gulf War, proving—live and in technicolor— that his missiles were bigger, better, and much more potent than Saddam Hussein's.[20]

Bill Clinton also dramatically invoked the dangerous-world syndrome to justify renewal of bombings of Baghdad and to initiate nuclear saber-rattling with the last fully intractable Cold War enemy, North Korea.[21] Like Bush, who showed the U.S. media and the world that he was no wimp, Clinton's moves also closely followed the Cold War's prescriptions for manly men at the brink. Even though the Cold War is now a distant memory, this kind of symbolic brinkmanship continues unabated today, with George W. Bush picking up where his father left off. From the moment of his entry on the national stage, George W. Bush was portrayed by the U.S. media as a man's man, an anti-intellectual fraternity boy who sewed his wild oats with the best of them. One of the first international actions of the younger Bush's administration was to resume the bombing of Iraq to show that he too means business. The War on Terrorism has, however, cast G. W. Bush in the role of avenger of Western values: as the metaphoric stern "father" protecting his nation against the demonic forces of "evil."[22]

When elite males define the world as a dangerous place, "masculine men and feminine women are expected to react in opposite but complementary ways."[23] In such a world, manly men are supposed to suppress their own fears and assume the role of protector of women and children. Women, in turn, are expected to look to their fathers, husbands, brothers, or their symbolic surrogates for protection against the dangerous men on the other side. In exchange for this protection, women are expected to be self-sacrificing: to put the interests of their husbands, children, and nation before their own. According to Easlea, Cohn, and, by extension, Keller, the erotics of power knowledge of this masculinist order are, paradoxically, homoerotic, misogynist, and necrophilic—involving male bonding secured by exclusion of women and sealed by the daring defiance of death.[24]

Under the form of hegemonic masculinity that defined global politics since the end of World War II,

> [i]deas of masculinity have to be perpetuated to justify foreign-policy risk-taking. To accept the Cold War interpretation of living in a dangerous world also confirms the segregation of politics into national and international. The national political arena is dominated by men but allows women some select access; the international political arena is only for those rare women who can successfully play at being men, or at least not shake masculine presumptions.[25]

Madeleine Albright, Clinton's secretary of state, was an interesting and ultimately affirming test case of this proposition. Her tough talk was at least as tough as that of any of her predecessors as was her presentation of self. Yet, alternative presentational possibilities for women in international leadership roles may be emerging. Mary Robinson, Ireland's first woman president and the United Nations' commissioner of human rights, is pioneering a more independent and nuanced model of female (and feminist) leadership, which combines a strong sense of agency with sensitivity to the human consequences of international law and policy initiatives. Even Condoleezza Rice, G. W. Bush's national security advisor, who holds a less visible position than Albright did, projects a softer version of the "new" woman, presumably designed to make her (and her boss) palatable to U.S. conservatives. Her media image is that of a glamorous, approachable, even affable woman who is very smart but committed to advancing traditional values, not challenging them.

A dangerous world is, however, an unambiguous world. For this reason, it is, paradoxically, a comfortable world for some males in the defense establishment and the press. As Larry Eichel noted in a September 11, 1989, article in the *Philadelphia Inquirer* entitled, "Wall Kept Things Simple," some experts on international politics had already begun to miss the Cold War: "They say the day may come when the world looks back on the 40 years after World War II as the good old days—when life was simple, people knew which side they were on and a standoff between superpowers kept the peace."[26] In a 1990 interview, Jeremy Azrael, a Rand Corporation Soviet analyst, acknowledged that "the Cold War world has been very good" to the military, the defense industry, and its apologists. With the prescience of a seasoned warrior, he worried: "There is a terrible danger that defense intellectuals will have to go whoring. Folks in the services will go looking for threats out there."[27]

OPPORTUNITIES AND OBSTACLES TO EXPANDING THE POLITICAL IMAGINATION

In 1990, when E. P. Thompson announced that history is now turning on a "new hinge," he was optimistic about the possibilities for expanding the breadth, depth, and quality of the political imagination.[28] Nevertheless, the semantic void left by the spies, speechwriters, and policy wonks who came in from the cold remained unfilled throughout the 1990s to the considerable frustration of editors of publications like *Foreign Policy* who wanted to dispense with post–Cold War analysis and invent themselves anew to attract a new generation of readers.[29] Neither subsequent historical events nor mass-mediated accounts of these events provide much to support Thompson's optimism. Instead, it seems, new threats to the existing order, domestic or foreign terrorists, hackers, cyber-warriors, and rogue nations are almost seamlessly retrofitted in the trappings of Cold War scenarios of evil. In effect, these retrofittings are rehanging the old hinge of history. Ronald Reagan's "evil empire" appears to have been born again as G. W. Bush's "axis of evil." The enemy has changed, but the binary rhetorical frames live on.

While he was president of the new, now former Czechoslovakia, Vaclav Havel offered a very different and far more pessimistic take on the events of the late twentieth century than Thompson had constructed. Havel maintained that the collapse of communism not only profoundly challenged the assumptions of Eurocentric political and social theories but also undermined the very foundations of rational inquiry itself:

> The end of Communism has brought a major era in human history to an end. It has brought an end not just to the 19th and 20th centuries but to the modern age as a whole. . . . The large paradox at the moment is that man—a great collector of information—is well aware of all of this, yet is absolutely incapable of dealing with the danger.[30]

According to Havel's postmodern dangerous-world scenario, the modern West's uncritical faith in scientific and technological progress—its instrumentalism—has delivered us to the eleventh hour: "We are looking for new scientific recipes, new ideologies, new control systems, new institutions, new instruments to eliminate the dreadful consequences of our previous recipes, ideologies, control systems, institutions and instruments."[31]

If Havel's analysis and the cultural practices he describes are reexamined through the lens of gender, very different readings are not only possible but are, in fact, already well advanced in the work of many feminist and postmodernist theorists. James Hillman unpacked this legacy eloquently and succinctly:

The specific consciousness we call scientific, Western and modern is the long sharpened tool of the masculine mind that has discarded parts of its own substance, called it *Eve, female and inferior.* What is required to recover and heal *political man* is not simply to add woman and stir. Rather masculinity and femininity must be reinvented, new political and social theories must be written, and new forms of politics and eroticism must be created.[32]

Cynthia Enloe suggests a new feminist (and, I believe, planet- and species-friendly) recipe that may contribute to this political and personal renaissance.[33] She reflects on the rhetorical power that C. Wright Mills's claim that the "the personal is political" had in mobilizing the activism of the late 1960s, including the second wave of U.S. and global feminism. Mills considered the phrase to be a palindrome; that is, as Enloe explains, it can be read backward as well as forward:

Read as "the political is personal," it suggests that politics are not shaped merely by what happens in legislative debates, voting booths or war rooms. While men, who dominate public life, have told women to stay in the kitchen, they have used their public power to construct private relationships in ways that bolstered their masculinized political control.[34]

According to Enloe's recipe, to understand a nation's political order, its gender order must be analyzed. The "political is personal" concept not only renders visible the roles women play in the global assembly line—as laborers, servants, guest workers, diplomatic wives, immigrants, refugees, tourists, sex workers, bank clerks, and peace activists—but it also exposes men as men, as policymakers, husbands, fathers, humanitarians, pimps, and so on. As Enloe points out, governments qua elite males devote considerable resources to controlling women, and women, it should be noted, devote considerable resources for developing multiple overt and subterranean strategies for resisting and subverting these controls.[35]

A crucial point that is too often ignored or underemphasized in feminist analyses is that elite males' efforts to control women usually have much more to do with optimizing control over other men than over women per se: men as migrant workers, soldiers, diplomats, intelligence operatives, potential defectors, overseas plantation and factory managers, and even bankers and stock portfolio managers. This control includes control over what Herbert

Marcuse called political linguistics: "the right to establish enforceable definitions of words."[36] Legitimacy is secured within and arises under the terms of the current international gender order: "ideas about *adventure*, *civilization*, *progress*, *risk*, *trust*, and *security* are all legitimized by certain kinds of masculinist values and behavior, which makes them so potent in relations between governments."[37]

Within the economy of signs produced by prevailing patterns of political linguistics, icons of popular culture such as Rambo, the Terminator, and search-and-destroy scenario video games are not simply entertainments. The extreme exaggerations and sexualization of differences between men and women that are present in the imagery currently produced by the U.S. culture industry for global consumption suggests that the retro-gender order of the Cold War is now playing its trump card—the threat of brute force—in an attempt to repel feminist threats to hegemonic masculinity. In this deadly contest, airbrushed images of violent, steroid-pumped, manly men with suprahuman bulging muscles are presented as counterpoint to starving, pencil-thin but surgically enhanced, fashion-modeled forms of femininity: physical types that are so different that, if they were found in other parts of the animal kingdom, scientists might mistake them for members of different subspecies. Within this reconstruction of the gender order, however, corporations—advertising, fashion, sports, film, video, and related consumer industries—rather than governments define and police the new internalized landscapes of the dangerous-world syndrome. Indeed, these consumerist definitions are often at odds with governments and the United Nations policies intended to advance the equality of women.

The gender-based news blackout does not involve malevolent plots or conspiracies by retro-male editors. Women editors and journalists also create and enforce policies and practices that perpetuate it. This blackout reflects the survival of ancient mythic narratives in news as well as the continuing influence of both Cold War and commercial news values that privilege dangerous-world scenarios: sensational stories about violent conflicts and disruptions of order. There are, to be sure, very real dangers in the world today, which constitute legitimate and important news; most of these dangers are still primarily under the control of male agents, government and corporate leaders and perpetrators of political violence, for example, nuclear threats, disposal of nuclear weapons, global warming, and chemical and bio-terrorism.

Within the terms of current formulas for international news production, however, the occasional stories about women that do make the news typically represent them as sexualized objects or victims of male violence, whether in Bosnia, Kuwait, Afghanistan, or in the mean streets of urban centers throughout the world. Such stories are news: hard political news, not just human interest or crime stories. Nevertheless, this kind of news represents a very narrow range of women's experiences: the actual and narrative terrain where hegemonic masculinity overtly and often brutally surveys and disciplines females into political subordination as "comfort women," sexual slaves, abused wives, and so on.

There are many significant stories about women that seldom make the news: stories about women's collective efforts to become agents rather than victims of history. Some dramatic and dramatically underreported efforts, which fit within the agonistic frames of conventional news, are, for example, women's organized efforts on behalf of "the disappeared" in Argentina, Chile, and Guatemala; the political mobilization of women's rights organizations in the wake of the slaughter of female engineering students in Montreal; mass demonstrations of Moroccan women to protest police violence against women after a police commissioner was convicted of raping more than 500 girls; the takeover of highways in northern Buenos Aires by 300 women on foot and bicycles to protest privatization of Argentine highways; and the role that Vox Femina and other Serbian women's groups played in mobilizing the vote against Slobodan Milosevic.[38]

The news blackout is nearly total when women organize to address issues that involve structural exercises of elite male power. Examples can be found worldwide: women meeting in Japan to examine and redress the status of migrant workers and proxy brides, women in New York tracking the global prostitution industry, women in the Netherlands and Finland monitoring gender-related impacts of global trade and arms agreements, women in Mexico City organizing to address labor issues, women meeting in Brussels to examine the implications of the unification of the European Community, and women worldwide organizing to protest George W. Bush's policy curtailing U.S. support for family planning in poor nations.[39]

How many readers of this book know that women have established a feminist radio station, *Radio Tierra*, in Chile? How many know that they are producing and distributing feminist videos throughout the Americas?[40] How many know that women in Sri Lanka have formed underground media collectives to produce videos documenting human rights violations?[41] How many are aware that women in Uruguay have used the legal division in that country between commercial and noncommercial speech to win concessions from advertisers that have resulted in less sexist images of women in the media of that country?[42] How many know that the Manushi Collective in India has published a successful magazine that confronts the oppression of women in that society?[43] Conversely, how many media scholars are aware that similar efforts in Kenya by the editorial staff of *Viva* magazine were halted by transnational advertising agencies? These agencies threatened to withdraw advertisements if the advertising-dependent magazine continued to address issues like prostitution, birth control, female circumcision, polygamy, and sex education. How many know that the Asian-Pacific Institute for Broadcasting Development in Kuala Lumpur is distributing internationally a resource kit on changing media images of Asian women?[44]

Such stories have low or no news value within the framing conventions of mainstream objective media. To locate such stories, readers must seek them out at the margins of journalism in feminist and left magazines, in human rights and religious periodicals and electronic postings, and in low- or no-budget newsletters. History will not be hung on a new hinge until the gender-related constituents of commercial news practices and the forms of knowledge they represent are critically analyzed and reconstructed.

WHAT GENDER ANALYSIS MAKES VISIBLE

In this section, I briefly identify and discuss four crises that either become visible or look quite different when they are examined through the lens of the global politics of the gender order: global overpopulation, the international child sex trade, female genocide, and Islamic fundamentalism.

Global Overpopulation

In a book that received extensive praise in U.S. media, *Preparing for the Twenty-First Century* (1993), Paul Kennedy examined demographic projections indicating that the world's population had more than doubled in the past forty years to 5.5 billion. Current projections indicate that it will reach between 7.6 and 9.4 billion by 2025, with most of the growth occurring among people currently living in developing nations. In Kennedy's dangerous-world scenario, imbalances between "richer and poorer societies form the backdrop to all other important forces for change that are taking place."[45] The developing nations will face famine, ecological devastation, and massive emigration, but Kennedy points out that the effects of the population explosion are also going to be very "painful for the richest one-sixth of the earth's population that now enjoys a disproportionate five-sixths of its wealth."[46]

Until the appearance of reviews of Kennedy's book, population issues had received little coverage in the U.S. press since the early 1980s. Coverage had been so meager that some media coverage treated Kennedy's thesis as if it were "news," even though it drew on data that are readily available in undergraduate sociology textbooks. After a few months of intense coverage in journals of opinion, the population crisis once again disappeared from public fora. Why?

The repeated eclipse or erasure of the population crisis from news and public agendas can be explained, at least in part, as an intrusion of the domestic gender politics of the U.S. into world affairs as a result of the combined leverage of U.S. superpower dominance and of U.S. global media dominance. For the past thirty years, the abortion debate has been a political hot potato in the U.S. for both of the major political parties. The so-called gender gap in U.S. politics is, at least to some extent, an artifact of the ways the two parties have responded to this debate. While there have been strategic splits within the ranks of Democrats on this issue, the national party platform has been consistently pro-choice. This stance has, however, eroded the Democrats' historic claim to the Catholic and blue-collar voting blocs; so, the abortion issue is a problematic issue for Democrats as well as Republicans. The Reagan Administration and both Bush Administrations (father and son) have, however, been anti-choice and anti-feminist. Both Bushes banned U.S. aid to international population planning agencies that condone abortion in any way. In the developing nations, it should be noted, family planning, which requires regular access to contraceptives, medical care, and calendar-based calculations, is often not an option. In these nations, ending access to abortion or sterilization ends birth control.

In effect, neither of the major U.S. political parties nor U.S. advertising-driven commercial media have anything to gain by foregrounding the population crisis: an issue that is inextricably tied to the right of women to control their reproductive capacities. To the contrary, placing the population crisis on the agenda for public discussion invites boycotts by powerful lobbies, loss of advertising revenues, and loss of votes.

To view the population issue as a national issue is, of course, absurd. Overpopulation in the developing world produces famine, wars, depletion of the rain forests, exacerbation of global warming, as well as migration of displaced refugees to the developed world. To view it as a gender-neutral problem is even more absurd. Women have babies.

Kennedy says nothing about global feminism in any of his well-informed 428 pages but devotes four pages to "The Role of Education and the Position of Women." He notes that for the developing world, "the evidence linking the depressed status of women to population explosion, acute poverty, and economic retardation seems clear."[47] In Kennedy's view (and in the view of women's rights groups), education of women in the developing world is the essential key to solving the population explosion.

Who is "depressing" women? Who is denying them access to education? Kennedy does not take the next, and obvious, analytic step. He does not examine the gendered constituents of the structures of power that are producing the ecological nightmare. As a result, Kennedy does not see what can only be described, from an ecological perspective, as a strong ray of hope on that is clearly visible on the horizon: the global feminist movement, a movement committed to expanding women's literacy rates and reproductive choices. Research that focuses on human reproduction without examining the gender order does not have the power to analyze effectively the related constituents of international trade policies, employment practices of transnational corporations, the global communications and financial revolutions, the growing homogenization and commodification of culture, or international law.

Child Sex Trade in Poor Nations

The AIDS pandemic has received enormous global media coverage since the mid-1990s. Much of the coverage has, of course, been shown to reflect strong heterosexual and heterosexist biases.[48] Coverage of the AIDS crisis in Africa has also been widely criticized by both Africans and international media critics.[49]

The AIDS crisis is highly visible. Factors that remain relatively invisible are its impact on child slavery and prostitution in poor nations and the role that men from prosperous nations are playing in dramatically increasing the sexual traffic in children.

Stories about sex and prostitution are not usually framed as political news, let alone as international news. The only significant exception seems to be sex scandals involving princes, presidents, and prime ministers. Routine practices in the sex trades are generally unreported or underreported. The roles global structural inequalities play in trafficking in children typically make the news only when special commissions of the United Nations or human rights watch groups produce press releases. Such reports indicate that "child catchers" in poor countries like Thailand, Haiti, Bangladesh, the Philippines, Indonesia, and war-torn parts of Africa frequently purchase or kidnap children for employment that, in many cases, amounts to enslavement in mines, plantations, and sex trades.[50]

An unintended side effect of AIDS education, according to a 1993 UNESCO-sponsored conference, has been an increased demand for very young girls or boys, who are marketed by pimps as being clean or virgins. In Manila, Bangkok, Rio de Janeiro, and Frankfurt, such children draw premium prices on the international sex market. In Viet Nam, the influx of businessmen from Japan, Hong Kong, and Taiwan is generating a boom market in children. Statistics are both rare and of questionable reliability, but one UNESCO study estimated that 2 million Thai women work in the sex trades and that as many as 800,000 of them may be adolescents or children. The report indicated that the demand for young girls comes mainly from Asians, and the demand for young boys comes primarily from Westerners.[51] Another UNESCO study estimated that more than

10,000 boys between the ages of six and fourteen work as prostitutes in Sri Lanka, where most of their clientele consists of foreign men.[52] The forty-nation organization End Child Prostitution and Trafficking (EPAT) estimates that more than 2 million children worldwide are employed in the sex trades, and that 25 percent of their abusers are Americans, the largest percentage of any national group.[53] A recent national survey of U.S. judges indicates that child prostitution is also a very serious but largely unreported or underreported problem within the U.S., especially in rural areas, where judges report a dramatic increase in the last five years. Rural judges, who perceived an increase, reported a 73 percent rise in child prostitution cases on their dockets since 1995. Significantly men and women judges perceive and define child prostitution differently, with female judges seeing more cases of child prostitution in their courts than men (85 percent and 68 percent respectively).[54] The Internet has proven to be a particularly useful tool for expanding, advertising, and managing international sexual tourism, especially in rural areas. It has also, of course, become the hub for the global distribution and sale of child pornography.

The relative silence regarding child sex workers represents the routine workings of news organizations under a gender order secured by hegemonic masculinity. The repellent practices of the international sex trades do not appear to pose any immediate threats to manly men, their wives, or their children. (However, versions of this story have periodically found their way through the news net when the U.S. government has issued travel advisories warning U.S. travelers that the pre-adolescent prostitutes of the developing world, no matter how young, are not clean and not free of the HIV virus or other sexually transmitted diseases.)[55] The wall of silence shielding the sexual abuse of poor children and the long-term global health crisis their abuse precipitates do, however, become immediately visible when viewed through the lens of gender-order theory. When these children are seen as subjects, as full human beings rather than as commodities in impersonal exchanges, the gravity of the crimes against them cannot be denied. Few men or women anywhere in the world would publicly (or privately) defend these crimes against children. But silence about these abuses renders them invisible and reduces them to dirty little secrets that public officials and journalists can ignore with impunity.

Female Genocide in Bosnia

In response to activism by international women's organizations protesting "gynocide" in Bosnia, rape was finally defined as a war crime in 1993.[56] Although sexual forms of torture, including systematic military use of rape, were documented in the post–World War II Nuremberg and Toyko trials, perpetrators were not prosecuted.[57] During the past decade, as a result of activism by Japanese and Korean feminists, the Japanese government has acknowledged that Korean women were systematically used as "comfort women" for Japanese troops during the war; and reparations have been made to the remaining survivors.[58] A 2001 United Nations tribunal established "sexual enslavement" as a crime against humanity. The judge ruled that "the evidence shows" that "rapes were used by Bosnian Serb armed forces as an instrument of terror—an instrument they were given free rein to apply whenever and against whomever they wished."[59] Rape was reportedly used as a weapon by all sides in the Bosnian war: a European Union report estimates that 20,000 women were assaulted in 1992 alone as a result of the Bosnian "systematic rape policy."[60] The U.N. tribunal went beyond just punishing three Bosnian Serb defendants for systematically raping and torturing women and girls in "rape camps" during the war to establishing legal precedent for prosecutions in future wars. The ruling recognizes that women and girls are often viewed as the spoils of war. That same week in early March 2001, Amnesty International released a report that the torture of women and girls is a widespread global phenomena that goes beyond rape and torture during armed conflicts to include abuse of women by partners, in police custody, in forced labor, in sexual trafficking, and by family members in so-called honor crimes.[61] These developments, which received relatively modest coverage in the U.S., have contributed to international momentum for establishing a permanent international war crimes tribunal, under U.N. auspices, which would serve as a court of last resort if nations refuse to discipline their own troops. The U.S. once supported the creation of such a tribunal, but now opposes it along with an unlikely group of allies: Libya, Iraq, Iran, and China. It is, however, under heavy international pressure to reverse this stance.

Female gynocide in Bosnia represents an extreme case. Naming it as a gender behavior marks a turning point in the history of war. Women have become historical agents by organizing, publicizing, and seeking international political condemnation of these acts as war crimes. In doing so, they are making visible a form of military aggression that has historically violated men as well as women. Because women have been regarded as the property of men under patriarchy, rape not only brutalized and dehumanized enemy women, but it also robbed, emasculated, and demoralized enemy men. In short, it is a military strategy that, under regimes of hegemonic masculinity, powerful males in many countries have used, covertly and sometimes overtly, to motivate their own troops and to dominate enemy males and all females.

Islamic Fundamentalism

Since the 2001 attack on America by Osama bin Laden's al-Qaida network, the patriarchal, even (from a Western perspective) misogynist, gender politics of radical Islamic fundamentalism have received considerable attention in Western news media. The extreme case, the Taliban regime, has frequently been treated as the paradigmatic case in the superficial analyses of Western media. In an extraordinary move in the period immediately following the attack, CNN repeatedly broadcast Saira Shah's documentary film *Behind the Veil*, which graphically recorded Taliban abuses of women and girls. In doing so, CNN broke with normal television practices in both form (repeat broadcast in short time intervals of a grainy, low-budget, independently produced documentary) and content (radical feminism). Because CNN framed its coverage of the aftermath of the attacks under the logo "America's New War," Shah's documentary provided the cable network with a "scoop" of sorts. It made an invisible enemy visible, although the visible Taliban actually functioned as stand-ins for the elusive al-Qaida fighters who remained hidden in caves in the Afghan mountains. This contributed to conflating the differences between the two groups in the minds of Western audience members, who generally know little about the Middle East because, except for the Israeli-Palestinian conflict, there has been little international coverage of the region since the Persian Gulf War.[62] The fact that bin Laden and most of the September 11 attackers were actually natives of Saudi Arabia, America's long-time strategic ally, received less attention in the media, although it was not ignored.

Despite CNN's scoop, there is nothing new about the role of women as the flashpoint where domestic Islamic responses to Westernization are played out. In the late nineteenth and twentieth century, when Middle Eastern women from elite families began to travel in the West and even, in some instances, to be educated in the West, the conflict between modernity and traditionalism became, in part, a conflict within the gender order. This conflict also, of course, has deep economic roots as well as generational dimensions, although the generational dynamic has been ignored by the ahistorical news media.

Under colonialism, the relative personal freedom of a small number of Middle Eastern women from the elite families who made up the indigenous administrative cadres posed no threat to the stability of the region. In the pre–World War II era, some of these women even embraced Western feminism; for that generation, dress—to wear Western garb or traditional garb, especially the veil—was an important political decision for women. The end of colonialism and the founding of the Nation of Israel after World War II were, however, accompanied by a rejection of Western values and a resurgence of traditional religious practices in Islamic nations.[63]

To be sure most elites, including some elite women, continued to enjoy their freedoms behind closed doors and during their travels to the West. However, part of the rejection of Western values included rejection of Western dress;

many women, even educated women, saw the return to the veil and to modest dress as expressions of both religious virtue and of solidarity with Third World liberation movements. During the 1970s and 1980s, when young women in the West were rebelling against the constraints of patriarchy, a countermovement was taking place in Islamic countries as daughters rejected the Western values of their mothers and grandmothers. These women consciously, and from their perspectives, rationally, rejected Western gender roles; their return to the veil was, for some, part of that generational rebellion, especially during and after the Islamic revolution in Iran. That is, these women exercised significant agency in crafting the gender regimes that, from Western and human rights perspectives, now oppress them. They were not the docile sexual slaves that some caricatures of them in Western media suggest.[64] In sum, it is a complex story, and not one that fits within the usual narratives of international news (or that can be adequately told in a short synopsis like this). Such stories are not sexy: they are not the typical fodder of a profit-driven media.

If the prism of gender had been used to craft Middle Eastern policy and to report news from the Middle East, the events of September 2001 probably could not have been predicted or averted. However, they might have been better understood and possibly even, to some extent, anticipated. Since the attacks, critical academic experts, normally ignored by mainstream American media, have enjoyed their fifteen minutes of fame. They have told us that the presence of U.S. forces in Saudi Arabia since the Persian Gulf War, particularly the presence of women military personnel, is a prime factor in explaining bin Laden's hatred of the U.S. They have also cited globalization of U.S. popular culture, particularly its highly sexualized representations of strong women, as central factors in Islamic fundamentalism's hatred of the West. The close alliance between the U.S. and Israel has fanned the flames of anti-Americanism in the Middle East. The vast economic inequalities separating elites and masses in the oil-rich nations of the Middle East, which U.S. policy supports in the interests of "stability" in oil markets, are also primary sources of hostility. However, the gender regimes of these nations are deeply implicated in reproducing these social inequalities.[65]

War may be hell, as Ernest Hemingway claimed, but it is a form of hell that has some beneficiaries: the commanders, commissars, and capitalists on the winning side. Efforts of human rights, peace, and feminist organizations to make the gender order of war and other forms of political violence visible may ultimately contribute to making it more difficult to stoke the fires of future hells. It may also make it more difficult to maintain the media blackout that marginalizes or erases women's politics qua politics.

A new, still largely underground or alternative journalism dedicated to breaking this code of silence is emerging in the wake of global feminism. The major media conglomerates generally ignore it; or, in some places, actively work to repress it, by censoring it directly or indirectly by withdrawing advertising. More often, however, major media respond to the changing roles of women worldwide by seeking to influence the directions of that change: by channeling it into new forms of consumerism that increase profits while minimizing challenges to the status quo. That is, they cultivate images of the good life for the new, liberated woman that selectively draw upon feminist rhetoric in ways that colonize it so that individual women can change their personal destinies (or appear to) without changing the world. One current version of the new postfeminist woman, ratified by the corporate produced popular culture, is a type Benjamin DeMott calls "the killer woman": a ruthless corporate operative, with plenty of money to spend, who is also a supercharged sexual bombshell.[66] Feminist political and social agendas play no part in, indeed are antithetical to, the killer women's life world despite the fact that the media represents her as a product of feminism.

In the U.S., there is some evidence that the killer woman is currently winning the war for young women's minds, or more accurately, their consumer dollars.[67] It is, however, unlikely that she will triumph globally, despite the power of the U.S. media industry. The killer woman image is too imbued with violent, masculinized, individualized American values of potence to achieve traction in either developing nations where women are still struggling for basic human rights, not looking for new forms of recreational shopping. Similarly, the rest of the world—as Americans discovered to their surprise after September 2001— is becoming increasingly disdainful of American corporate triumphalism and the popular culture it has produced (as, for example, international coverage of President George W. Bush's June 2001 trip to Europe made clear).

The events of September 2001 and their aftermath have not posed any serious threats to hegemonic masculinity, beyond eliminating the extreme form practiced by the Taliban regime. Indeed, in many ways they have affirmed its resonance.[68] They did, however, at least for a time, force gender onto the agendas of global politics and international news.

NOTES

1. This chapter owes an enormous debt to Cynthia Enloe's groundbreaking feminist scholarship in international studies, especially her *Bananas, Beaches, and Bases: Making Feminist Sense of International Studies* (Berkeley: University of California Press, 1989) and *The Morning After: Gender Politics at the End of the Cold War* (Berkeley: University of California Press, 1993). While Enloe's focus is not on news per se, her provocative analyses are full of implications for the study of mediating processes and agents.

2. Susan Miller, "Opportunity Squandered: Newspapers and Women's News," *Media Studies Journal* (Winter/Spring 1993): 167–82. Pete Hamill also examines this puzzling conundrum of the news business in *News Is a Verb: Journalism at the End of the Twentieth Century* (New York: Ballantine, 1998). Indeed, he ties the survival of the daily newspaper to recovering and expanding the female readership. Industry reports indicate that circulation of newspapers continue to decline, and that publishers are responding by raising prices, which, industry analysts predict, will further contract their readership base. See Set Sutel, Associated Press, "Newspapers issuing earnings warnings," *The Buffalo News*, 7 March, 2001, 4(E).

3. Gaye Tuchman did pioneering work in the study of gender and media. See Gaye Tuchman, "The Symbolic Annihilation of Women by the Mass Media," in *Hearth and Home: Images of Women in Mass Media*, ed. Gaye Tuchman, Arlene Kaplan Daniels, and James Benet (New York: Oxford University Press, 1978); Gaye Tuchman, *Making News: A Study in the Construction of Reality* (New York: Free Press, 1978); and Gaye Tuchman, "Objectivity as a Strategic Ritual: An Examination of Newsmen's Notions of Objectivity," *American Journal of Sociology* 77, no. 4 (1978): 660–79. This work laid the foundations for current social constructivist feminist critiques of journalistic objectivity. Yet it left intact a self-privileging form of scientific objectivity that most contemporary feminist epistemologies no longer support.

4. Freedom Forum, "Who's Covering What in the Year of the Women?" *Media Studies Journal* (Winter/Spring 1993): 135.

5. Margaret Gallagher, *Unequal Opportunities: The Case of Woman and the Media* (Paris: UNESCO, 1981), 71. See also H. Leslie Steeves, "Gender and Mass Communication Context," in *Women in Mass Communication Challenging Gender Values*, ed. Pamela I. Creedon (Newbury Park, Calif.: Sage Publications, 1989), 91.

6. Miller, "Opportunity Squandered," 172.

7. Freedom Forum, "Who's Covering What," 138.

8. Miller, "Opportunity Squandered," 169.

9. Kay Mills, "The Media and the Year of the Woman," *Media Studies Journal* (Winter/Spring 1993): 20.

10. Enloe, *Beaches, Bananas, and Bases*, 3–4.

11. R. W. Connell, *Gender and Power* (Stanford, Calif.: Stanford University Press, 1987). Gayle Rubin, in a classic article, "The Traffic in Women: Notes on the Political Economy of Sex," in *Toward an Anthropology of Women*, ed. Rayna Reiter (New York: Monthly Review Press, 1975), identifies and theorizes this dynamic long before Connell; however, Connell's formulation is nevertheless more extensively developed. It is particularly useful since it recognizes that the global pattern of subordination of women in industrial societies is nevertheless negotiated and accommodated in culturally specific ways. Women are not passive objects in this sex trade. In *Gender and Power*, 183–84, Connell noted, "One form is defined around compliance with this subordination and is oriented to accommodating the interests and desires of men. I will call this *emphasized femininity*. Others are defined centrally by strategies of resistance or forms of non-compliance. Others again are defined by complex strategic combinations of compliance, resistance and co-operation. The interplay among them is a major part of the dynamics of the gender order as a whole."

12. Stuart Hall, "Brave New World," *Marxism Today* (October 1988): 29.

13. Connell, *Gender and Power*, 17–18.

14. Connell, *Gender and Power*, 18.

15. E. P. Thompson, "End and the Beginning: History Turns Hinge," *The Nation* (January 28, 1990): 120.

16. Thompson, "End and the Beginning," 120.

17. Brian Easlea, *Fathering the Unthinkable: Masculinity, Scientists, and the Nuclear Arms Race* (London: Pluto Press, 1983); Helen Caldicott, *Missile Envy: The Arms Race and Nuclear War* (New York: Morrow, 1984); Carol Cohn, "Sex and Death in the Rational World of Defense Intellectuals," *Signs* 12, no. 4 (1987): 687–718. The phrase "dangerous world syndrome" is borrowed from George Gerbner, who uses it to analyze the pervasive presence of violence and terror in U.S. prime-time television programming, a phenomena that I believe, may, at least in part, bear the imprimatur of the Cold War. See George Gerbner and Michael Morgan, *Television and its Viewers: Cultivation Theory and Research* (New York: Cambridge University Press, 1999).

18. Enloe, *Bananas, Beaches, and Bases*.

19. Thompson, "End and the Beginning," 120.

20. Abouali Farmanfarmaian, "Sexuality in the Gulf War: Did You Measure Up?" *Genders* 13 (Spring 1992): 1–29.

21. Even Fidel Castro sent some mixed signals in speeches and interviews in the 1990s.

22. George Lakoff, "Metaphors of Terror: The Power of Images," *In These Times.com* (October 29, 2001): 1–10, <www.inthese.times.com> (accessed November 14, 2001).

23. Enloe, *Bananas, Beaches, and Bases*, 12.

24. Easlea, *Fathering the Unthinkable*; Cohn, "Sex and Death"; and Evelyn Fox Keller, *Reflections on Gender and Science* (New Haven, Conn.: Yale University Press, 1985). Conversely, the presence of this homoerotic element in the mythos of the Cold War gender order may, in turn, explain the centrality of its taboo on practicing homosexuality. Perhaps the idea could be entertained without threatening the dominance of manly men only if homosexual acts were strictly proscribed.

25. Enloe, *Bananas, Beaches, and Bases*, 12–13.

26. Larry Eichel, "Wall Kept Things Simple," *Philadelphia Inquirer*, 11 September 1989, 4(E).

27. E. J. Dionne Jr., "'Defense Intellectuals' in a New World Order: Rand Analysts Rethink the Study of Conflict," *Washington Post*, 29 May 1990, 7(D).

28. Thompson, "End and the Beginning," 117.

29. Martin Walker, "The New 'Foreign Policy'; Spiced Up, but Still Leavened with Insight," *Chronicle of Higher Education* (12 January 2001): 12–13(B).

30. Vaclav Havel, "The End of the Modern Era," *The New York Times*, 1 March 1992, 15 (E).

31. Havel, "The End of the Modern Era," 15(E).

32. James Hillman, *The Myth of Analysis* (New York: Harper & Row, 1972), 250.

33. Enloe, *Bananas, Beaches, and Bases*.

34. Enloe, *Bananas, Beaches, and Bases*, 195. See also C. Wright Mills, *The Sociological Imagination* (New York: Oxford University Press, 1959).

35. Enloe, *Bananas, Beaches, and Bases*, 195.

36. Herbert Marcuse, *An Essay on Liberation* (Boston: Beacon Press, 1969), 73.

37. Enloe, *Bananas, Beaches, and Bases*, 200.

38. Catherine MacKinnon, "Turning Rape into Pornography: Postmodern Genocide," *Ms.* (July/August 1993): 24–30. See also Swanee Hunt, "Learn from the Women Behind the Fall of Milosevic," *International Herald Tribune*, July 10, 2001, 8.

39. Enloe, *Bananas, Beaches, and Bases*, 189; and Angharad Valdivia, "International Communications and Feminist Studies," *Feminist Scholarship Interest Group Newsletter*, International Communication Association (Spring 1993): 4.

40. Valdivia, "International Communications and Feminist Studies."

41. "Women Breaking the Silence," *Index on Censorship* 19, no. 9 (October 1990): 2, 7–36.

42. Valdivia, "International Communications and Feminist Studies."

43. Steeves, "Gender and Mass Communication."

44. Gallagher, *Unequal Opportunities*; and Steeves, "Gender and Mass Communication."

45. Paul Kennedy, *Preparing for the Twenty-first Century* (New York: Random House, 1993), 46.

46. Kennedy, *Preparing for the Twenty-first Century*, 46.

47. Kennedy, *Preparing for the Twenty-first Century*, 341.

48. Randy Shilts, *And the Band Played On: Politics, People, and the AIDS Epidemic* (New York: St. Martin's Press, 1987).

49. Belinda Cowdy and David Royle, *Assignment Africa*, videocassette (New York: New Atlantic Productions, 1986).

50. Marlise Simons, "The Sex Market: Scourge on the World's Children," *New York Times*, 9 April 1993, 3(A).

51. Simons, "The Sex Market," 3(A).

52. Simons, "The Sex Market," 3(A).

53. Gerry Volgenau, KRT News Service, "Travel Industry is Shamefully Silent about Child-Sex Tourism," *Allentown (Pa.) Morning Call*, 14 November 1999, 4(F).

54. Jane O. Hansen, Cox News Service, "Judges: Society Is Ignoring Increasing Child Prostitution," *Allentown, (Pa.) Morning Call* (14 January 2001), 5(F).

55. Volgenau, "Travel Industry Is Shamefully Silent," 4(F).

56. Anna Quindlen, "Gynocide," *New York Times*, 9 April 1993, 15(A). See also Alexandra Stigmayer, ed., *Mass Rape: The War Against Women in Bosnia-Herzegovina* (Lincoln: University of Nebraska Press, 1994).

57. MacKinnon, "Turning Rape into Pornography"; see also Jerome Socolovsky, Associated Press, "U.N. Tribunal Rules in 'Sexual Enslavement' Case," *Allentown (Pa.) Morning Call*, 23 February 2001, 3(A).

58. Margaret D. Stetz and Bonnie B. C. Oh, *Legacies of the Comfort Women of World War II* (New York: M. E. Sharpe, 2001). See also Katha Pollitt, "Cold Comfort," *The Nation* (June 11, 2001): 10.

59. Socolovsky, "U.N. Tribunal Rules," 3(A).

60. Unsigned editorial, "War Crimes: A Measure of Justice," *Buffalo News*, 11 March 2001, 2(H).

61. Associated Press (London), "Torture of Women and Girls Common Worldwide, Report Finds," *Buffalo News*, 7 March 2001, 2(A). Amnesty International, "Broken Bodies, Shattered Minds," report released March 6, 2001.

62. Molly Ivins, "The Media Must Share the Blame," *The Buffalo News*, 27 October 2001, 5(B).

63. Marilyn Gaunt, dir., and Elizabeth Fernea, prod., *A Veiled Revolution*, videocassette (New York: Icarus Films, 1982).

64. Lena Jayyusi, "Women of the Intafada," paper presented at the annual meeting of the International Communication Association, Dublin, Ireland, July 12, 1992.

65. Benjamin R. Barber's 1995 book is now on the best-seller list. See Benjamin Barber, *Jihad vs. McWorld* (New York Random House, 1995). Bernard Lewis's new book immediately became a best-seller on release. See Bernard Lewis, *What Went Wrong? Western Impact and Middle East Response* (New York: Oxford University Press, 2002). Lewis's work has, of course, been a long-standing target of critique by Edward Said. For a recent contribution of that critique, see Edward Said, "Impossible Histories: Why the Many Islams Cannot Be Simplified," *Harper's*, July 2002, 71–77.

66. Benjamin DeMott, *Killer Woman Blues: Why Americans Can't Think Straight about Gender and Power* (New York: Houghton Mifflin, 2000). As an analysis of feminism, DeMott's book leaves much to be desired, but as a compendium of representations of women in recent American popular culture, it is suggestive of the ways "corporate feminism" is framing images of women as agents. See also Martha Irvine, Associated Press, "New Breed of Female Icons Are Hardly Wilting Flowers," *Allentown (Pa.) Morning Call*, 9 May 2001, 13(A). Suffice to say, I am not advocating a return to wilting flowers; the title of this article is a good example of the way the binary frames of American journalism frame issues in polarized terms that reduce the range of human behavior to caricatures. In this case, the choice is between "too tough" and "wilting flower."

67. Irvine, "New Breed of Female Icons," 13(A). Cassie Ederer, vice president of youth strategies for Convergent Mediagroup, a San Francisco firm that advises companies on how to cultivate markets for their products among young people, told Irvine that the aggressive image is the wave of the future.

68. The ways in which hegemonic masculinity played itself out in the United States' response to September 11, 2001 has received less attention. See Sue Curry Jansen, "Media in Crisis," *Feminist Media Studies* 2 (Summer 2002): 139–141.

Coda

NOBLE DISCONTENT

The choice is between teaching and acting according to our most deeply felt values, whether or not it meets approval from those with power over us—or being dishonest with ourselves, censoring ourselves, in order to be safe.

—Howard Zinn

Several [scholars blacklisted or interrogated by the House Un-American Activities Committee] are bold enough to ask what, exactly, university faculty in the post-repressive era have done with the freedom of expression that others went to jail to secure.

—Felicia Kornbluh

Chapter Ten

A Fly on the Neck:
"Noble Discontent" as
the Duty of Critical Intellectuals

We end where we began: with the proposition that creative scholarship starts where satisfactory explanations end: in failed conversations, broken logical chains, paradoxes, silences, and erasures. In this sense, all creative scholarship is also critical scholarship.

Yet, the term "scholarship," both etymologically and practically, denotes a societal good. That is, it refers to a practice that operates within institutional settings for the production, social reproduction, and preservation of knowledge: schools, colleges, universities, libraries, museums, monasteries, and so on. In that sense, its mission is both constructive and conservative.

There is, however, always a political tension built into the scholarly trust. Because critique begins in ignorance—in gaps in existing knowledge—its outcomes cannot be fully anticipated. Consequently critical reason always poses risks to its hosts.[1] Hosts, in turn, learn to insulate themselves against these risks. Established institutions and systems of knowledge develop mechanisms for containing, deflecting, or channeling internal criticism in system-enhancing directions. These strategies are not, of course, always successful.

Scholars themselves are often proactive participants in these policing efforts. Philosophers, self-proclaimed "lovers of wisdom," are among the highest stakeholders in the critical enterprise. Yet, they have historically set themselves up as gatekeepers of knowledge who not only promote critical thought but also aggressively patrol its epistemological boundaries: boundaries that are, of course, socially constructed, fluid, and shaped by human interests. Because serious scholarship frequently involves an existential quest as well as a form of intellectual labor, scholars usually have deep emotional as well as practical investments in defending what they think is right, rational, true, factual, valid, and just.[2] Indeed, that is why they establish "disciplines," create hierarchical standards of excellence, and press for paradigmatic coherence.

235

Even within knowledge systems themselves, then, there are strong conservative pressures toward closure despite the fact that advancement of knowledge requires openness to critique. Alvin Gouldner evokes this dynamic tension in dramatic terms when he asserts, "Every theoretical system has another system inside it struggling to get out. And every system has a nightmare: that the caged system will break out."[3]

In our own time, powerful forces within the academy and the larger society exert formidable controls to keep unruly ideas in check. The idealistic "marketplace of ideas" that Justice Holmes envisioned in the early part of the twentieth century—a metaphoric open space where all ideas were free to enter and receive a fair hearing—has given way to a literal marketplace. To enter the marketplace and receive a public hearing, ideas must now demonstrate that they are marketable commodities. Market values now exercise a kind of systemic censorship within the cultural sphere; with the end of the Cold War, the practice of conflating democracy and laissez-faire capitalism, which has a long, complex, and contested prehistory, became the dominant and largely uncontested practice. The political linguistics of what Patrick Smith calls the American "victory culture" named, claimed, and cultivated this view as the only reasonable view:

> In the name of our triumph, Americans have closed down public discourse, or—better perhaps—prevented it from opening up at a moment when it is urgent that it should. This is producing an alarming corrosion of American political life. Urgent questions go undebated. A widespread complacency—both in and out of government—threatens the institutions of democracy by encouraging Americans to assume that their common inheritance is eternal, requires no vigilance, and can withstand any abuse.
>
> In turn, this has produced a dedication to globalism that borders on religious belief. We may define globalism as the spread of neoliberal economic principles around the world: deregulation, the wholesale privatization of public institutions, and an unshakable faith in the primacy of unfettered markets. But let us understand the term as it is actually meant. As even its most convinced advocates acknowledge, globalisation amounts to Americanization. . . . We have attached a certain finality to this proposition: history has ended; the Hegelian process has run its course, and its end result is the U.S. model. . . . Americans today suffer a kind of narcissism, a failure of vision. As we did after WW II, we have chosen not to see others as they are, or to see ourselves as we are—or finally to see ourselves among others. This is the true meaning of US triumphalism: Wherever we look, we see only reflections of ourselves.[4]

The sense of American invincibility was shattered by the al-Qaida attacks on America in September 2001. Ordinary Americans, long insulated against world opinion by a commercial news culture that had grown comfortable harvesting the easy profits of scandal, celebrity, and infotainment, appeared genuinely shocked to discover that America has enemies. "Why do they hate us?" people asked in plaintive tones that seemed to express sincere bewilderment during the period of national mourning that followed the attacks.

Those who dared to answer—especially those who spoke up immediately—found their loyalty, humanity, integrity, judgment, and intelligence challenged. There have been some openings to critical analysis as the immediate pathos of the national trauma has ebbed; however, if public opinion polls are any indicator of the national psyche, it would appear that most Americans still do not want to probe very deeply into why "they" hate us. Moreover, the swift vengeance that the America-led coalition took against the al-Qaida network and their Taliban allies in Afghanistan, and America's subsequent unilateral warnings to Iraq, Iran, and North Korea—what President George W. Bush has labeled "the axis of evil"—has left little doubt in the rest of the world that America has the might and resolve to defend and reaffirm its superpower status.

The victory culture has emerged from this challenge to its hegemony with more resources in its arsenal than its most ardent true believers could have imagined possible prior to the assault. The defense budget has grown robust once more, the CIA and the FBI have been given new and broader powers, new public-private and national-international law enforcement powers have been enfranchised, and the U.S. government now has unprecedented surveillance powers, both domestically and internationally. In short, globalization, cum Americanization, now has a global and domestic police force, which can function routinely and systemically; it no longer has to rely on the kind of ad hoc, crisis-by-crisis, initiatives that had sustained it up to this point.

The War on Terrorism has imposed a new bifurcated template on the world, dividing it into those who accept, or at least do not actively resist, neoliberal economics and those who do not. Within this configuration, those who resist find themselves contained within the ring of terror: terrorists, rogue nations, and the axis of evil. The lessons of the Cold War era have taught us that such templates have very little tolerance for ambiguity. It is too early to tell where the lines will be drawn. We do know, for example, that the civil rights of resident aliens from suspect nations, which include some such as Saudi Arabia that are at least formally U.S. allies, can be readily suspended under the new rules of engagement. How much intellectual dissidence will be permitted remains an open question. Some, although not all, of the institutional attempts to gag dissident academics that occurred in the immediate wake of the attacks have now been reversed. Yet, there is no doubt that these administrative censures have had chilling effects.

These are therefore very uncertain times for those who conceive of their intellectual mission as speaking truth to power. This mission is already under fire, ridiculed and dismissed by the same think tankers and talking heads who launched earlier and successful attacks on feminism, multiculturalism, affirmative action, political correctness, and other flavors of the day that were perceived to be left or liberal.[5] Critical theory is one of several venerable traditions of scholarship, by no means always left or liberal, which views speaking truth to or about power as an intellectual trust and a civic virtue.

GADFLIES AS HISTORICAL AGENTS

Critical theory is work for gadflies and troublemakers. It is for those who refuse to accept the conclusions of the victory culture that history is now frozen and that all of the resources of democratic or postdemocratic societies must be dedicated to keep it from thawing. It is for those who refuse to believe that the democratic experiment is over or that it has failed or proven impractical. It is for those who reject the pessimism of so many contemporary intellectuals who, as Günter Grass' puts it, "today swallow everything, and it gives them nothing but ulcers."[6]

To accept what is or what has been as the best that can be is to resign oneself to a future in which man's inhumanity to man is a given. It renders struggles for social justice futile and abandons the remaining vestiges of what the great religious and philosophical traditions have defined as our moral responsibilities to one another and to the generations to come. It also denies the evidence of history, which tells us that every tyrant who has ever existed has claimed that his rule is the best that conditions permit and certainly better than any of the available alternatives, despite the fact that some people still must suffer.[7] Yes, some efforts to build a better world have failed tragically, as the horrors of the twentieth century amply attest, and all have produced imperfect results. If perfection is the standard, however, all human endeavors are failures. Moreover, if history tells tales, it tells us that when forces of domination press too hard for closure, their empires usually implode. And gadflies often ignite the fires that "jump start history."[8]

In the aptly titled *Disturbing the Peace* (1990), Vaclav Havel describes the calling of the gadfly: "The intellectual should constantly disturb, should bear witness to the misery of the world, should be provocative by being independent, should rebel against all hidden and open pressure and manipulations, should be the chief doubter of systems, of power and its incantations, should be witness to their mendacity."[9]

The tradition of the intellectual as gadfly, even as public nuisance, who insists on asking inconvenient questions and on telling the truth to those in power, goes back at least as far as Socrates. Drawing his inspiration directly from Plato's Socratic dialogues, Nietzsche said the thinker ought to be a fly on the neck of humankind.[10] Max Weber translated this Nietzschean premise into a pedagogical principle when he asserted that "the primary task of a useful teacher is to teach students to recognize 'inconvenient' facts." By this Weber meant "facts that are inconvenient for their party opinions."[11]

Contemporary American students are rarely strongly attached to political parties. Deployment of the Weberian pedagogical principle today would appear to require gadfly teachers to confront their students with the inconvenient facts of America's global positioning and its victory culture, the party that all Americans belong to now. The corporatized climate of American higher education is not a hospitable place to undertake such a trust; and many who do will surely be penalized for living their convictions.

Yet, this kind of risk-taking has a venerable history. Positioning itself as a fly on the neck of theocracy, the underground "Republic of Letters" provided the ideological warrants for the scientific revolution of the sixteenth and seventeenth centuries and for the democratic revolutions that followed.[12] It was also a touchstone of the Enlightenment: that flawed, bourgeois, and now much disparaged partial democratic vision that secured covenants based on liberty, fraternity, and equality for some. Blind to their own blindspots, all of these democratic movements to advance political and intellectual autonomy were, at best, partial victories for gadflies. With rare exceptions, these movements limited franchises for expression of heterodox ideas to educated, literate, well-spoken members of a dominant racial group (usually European and Euro-American): that is, people very much like those who led the movements. Women with big mouths were silenced as shrews or hysterics, and, in the late Middle Ages and early modern period, burned as witches. People of the "lower" classes with big mouths were dismissed as ignorant rabble. People of color with big mouths were coded as dangerous brutes and, in the United States, lynched on a relatively frequent basis well into the twentieth century. The catalogue of peoples who were exoticized, brutalized, and dehumanized, sometimes under the misguided authority of science, by "enlightened" nations is long: Africans, Asians, indigenous peoples of colonized lands, Jews, Moslems, Catholics, sexual minorities, and many more.

Yet, within our own time, we have seen massive social movements successfully mobilized by gadflies to right these wrongs and to complete the work of human liberation begun by the democratic revolutions of the Enlightenment. Big mouths throughout the world have engaged the critical spirit and used the vocabulary of democracy to prevail in David versus Goliath struggles against tyrannies that at first seemed invincible. Among those who have spoken truth to power with revolutionary results are Martin Luther King Jr., Lech Walesa, Nelson Mandela, Vaclav Havel, Simone de Beauvoir, and vast legions of feminists who launched the first grassroots, organized, global, social movement for equality, as well as gay and lesbian rights activists who refused to stay conveniently locked in closets. Even ordinary people like environmental activist Lois Gibbs, who had a common sense theory and the courage to act upon it, have demonstrated that, when conditions are right, small groups of people can change the world.[13] Most of these gadflies still walk among us. Indeed, some of us walked with them, whether literally or metaphorically, and in doing so also played essential roles in the mass movements that have changed the world. Why then should we, of all people, be persuaded that we cannot be historical agents? Clearly, the proposition is demonstrably false and patently absurd!

It is precisely because critical intellectuals have demonstrated just how powerful they are that the forces of reaction have responded by attempting to silence independent voices by narrowing access to fora of public discourse, eviscerating or displacing public controls over cultural institutions, and mobilizing monopoly controls over commercial media. The tragedy is that this strategy seems to be working, at least for the moment. In making these rather audacious claims, I do not assume that there is an organized conspiracy among the forces of reaction to repress democratic discourse; although, to be sure, lesser-scale conspiracies to corner a market, steal an election, or derail legislation have periodically been exposed.[14] Rather, I assume the obvious: that businesses are not democratic organizations, and that the strategies that work within business organizations to ensure efficient hierarchical control also "work" when business values and systems of authority colonize spaces vacated by civic values. The old metaphor of "the authorless theater" still applies to these large-scale, industry-wide patterns of market censorship, despite the fact that within specific media organizations more overt and authored interventions in representational practices are now much more common than in the past.[15]

POSTMODERN PAUSE OR FAILURE OF NERVE?

Why have critical intellectuals and academics allowed themselves to be gagged? Indeed, why do we gag ourselves? Why have we traded courage for ulcers?

Several explanations have been offered. First, some analysts attribute the failure to act or even to engage with political and social theory to postmodern paralysis. Cultural relativism has become a lived reality in a globally wired world. As a result, the Enlightenment's claims to universalism have been discredited; and the epistemological foundations of Western rationalism have lost their moorings. Speaking truth to power becomes a highly problematic enterprise when truth itself is an embattled epistemological construct. For some postmoderns, this antifoundationalism is a cause for despair; others see it as a warrant for returning to faith-based cosmologies. Still others view it as a liberating move, which releases intellectuals from the burdens of responsibility that Western rationalism imposed upon them. For the latter group, postmodernism provides, if only by default, a rationale for life devoted to the pleasure principle, for example physical, aesthetic, even consumerist.[16]

Second, the failure of social and political theorists on both the left and right to anticipate the sudden collapse of communism, as well as the effective demise of Marxism as a viable public platform for critique, have contributed to the failure of nerve among intellectuals, especially on the left. Capitalism and socialism were dialectical partners of Enlightenment thought. The critical tension between them kept them accountable to one another.[17] This tension also opened up a dialogical space that allowed for expression of a fairly wide array of voices ranging from left to right. The end of the Cold War undermined the intellectual grounds that supported this tension. It did not, however, solve the structural problems, the systemic social inequalities of capitalism, which had called the socialist critique into being in the first place. The end of the Cold War not only effectively muted the Marxist critique; it narrowed the entire spectrum of public political debate so that it now radiates around the central pole of neoliberalism. It thereby constricted the vocabulary of critical discourse. At a loss for words or out of the fear of being wrong again, many critical intellectuals remain silent.[18] Whether this silence is merely a critical pause—a time for renewal, for observing rather than changing the world (to reverse Marx's charge to intellectuals)—or whether it is a symptom of a deeper political resignation and fatigue remains to be seen. My own contrarian perception is that there is now much more creative left-critical, intellectual ferment bubbling up within the culture than those who rely on mainstream media for their reportage suspect. For example, despite mainstream U.S. media's framing of antiglobalization protests as the mischief of fringe groups, many of the issues raised by this broadly based movement have international resonance. Nonetheless, neoliberal perspectives are dominating the cultivation of the public memory of the Cold War, engineering globalization, mobilizing unprecedented powers to insure its stability, and exerting hegemony over mass-mediated visions of the future.

Third, given the consolidations of power and resources that now lie behind neoliberal visions of the future, pessimism is a rational response for critical intellectuals. Neoliberal governments have demonstrated an extreme reluctance to use their regulatory powers to constrain oligopolistic trends except in instances where the larger corporate good (e.g., stifling market growth) rather than the public good, is perceived to be at stake, such as the Microsoft intervention.[19]

Regulators have always been closely aligned with business interests. They have, however, been charged with serving the public interest, at least formally, and this quasi-fiction has periodically provided openings for democratic interventions. The Global Crossings, Enron, World.com, Tyco, and other corporate financial debacles, as well as the accounting scandals perpetrated by the once-illustrious Arthur Andersen accounting firm, may create such an opportunity. At this point (September 2002), there is no definitive evidence that it is producing a wellspring of popular sentiment for radical reform of the U.S. capitalist system, even though many middle-class Americans are angry and dismayed by the steep reductions in their retirement funds and other investments that such corporate manipulations have produced.

Critical intellectuals often do feel impotent as they contemplate the real world consequences of the consumerist future that the victory culture is exporting via globalization. Planet Earth cannot sustain global reproduction of U.S. consumer habits. Some responsible estimates indicate it would take eight planets of Earth's size and material resources to sustain that level of consumerism among the world's current population.[20] Resource limitations will necessarily set material limits on which countries and which social strata within those countries can actually participate in globalization and which ones cannot. These material limits will not merely preclude efforts to redress current global structural inequalities between "haves" and "have nots," they will further exacerbate them. In the long term, it is highly unlikely that neoliberalism will be able to sustain such global economic inequalities without resorting to more overt forms of repression. The War on Terrorism, like the Cold War, mobilized in response to real threats to U.S. national security, may well become a medium for systemic repression as it becomes institutionalized and bureaucratized, and as careers come to depend upon a steady supply of enemies as they did during the Cold War.

Fourth, for the present at least, the above developments have combined with the continued, if recession chastened, affluence of the victory culture, as well as a new vigilance regarding a dangerous and unpredictable world, to place an effective lid on utopian thinking. Proclaiming itself anti-ideological, neoliberalism continuously recycles "end of ideology" theses, which in effect mean the end of alternative ideologies.[21] Throughout history critical tensions between what is, what is missing, and what might be possible have been sources of intellectual creativity and critical political ferment in societies where "the power of persuasion has not been extinguished by force."[22] Alfred North Whitehead established this point decisively in his now neglected but still inspiring *Adventures of Ideas* (1933). Whitehead identified what he called "noble discontent . . . founded upon appreciation of beauty, and of intellectual distinction, and of duty" as the fundamental dynamic of the sociology of knowledge in Western cultures.[23] Noble discontent is what has kept these cultures and the ideas they have created vibrant and self-renewing. The decline of utopian thought, outside of the realm of technology, in our time has been widely documented and lamented.[24] The apparent disappearance of democratic alternatives to neoliberalism has generated a disabling pessimism among many left intellectuals. Without the utopian impulse, Russell Jaccoby maintains, "A light has gone out. The world stripped of anticipation turns cold and grey."[25] Without the utopian impulse, Thomas Jefferson could not have written the Declaration of Independence, and Martin Luther King Jr. could not have composed his "I have a dream" speech. And without the utopian impulse, noble discontent loses its nobility and degenerates into cynicism. Cynicism, wearing the mask of postmodern cool, has not only become a pervasive quality of intellectual discourse today, it permeates popular culture, journalism, advertising, and even adolescent subcultures.[26] This is why Pierre Bourdieu issued the following charge to critical intellectuals today: "[W]e must 'open our big mouths' and try to restore our utopia; because one of the defining qualities of these neoliberal governments is that they do away with utopias."[27]

Fifth, in the last half of the twentieth century, the structural positioning of critical intellectuals changed significantly, especially in America. It has become nearly impossible to live by the word, by publishing books and critical essays. Therefore, most intellectuals are now academics. With these institutional moorings, intellectuals have acquired relative financial security and the temptations that accompany security, including caution, conservatism, and consumerism. Through college- and university-sponsored retirement programs, most American professors are now significantly invested in the stock market, and the stock market growth of the last quarter-century, especially the dot.com bubble of the 1990s, made millionaires of a small but significant number of senior professors. The top segment of the professoriate, prominent researchers at elite research institutions, can no longer be adequately described as "servants of power"; they are also part of the "power elite" of the information economy.[28] In that sense, many of these academic elites are also implicated in what Christopher Lasch called "the revolt of elites": the abdication of a sense of responsibility to community, to historical continuity, and to democratic values.[29]

Sixth, the institutionalization of critique and its increasing dependence on profit-dependent forms of mediation have further contributed to the detachment of intellectuals from community and continuity by undermining the bohemian cultures that intellectuals have historically shared in large urban centers at least since the nineteenth century. By scattering intellectuals to remote and often isolating outposts in Iowa, Wisconsin, Oregon, and so on, academic employment has produced a much more fragmented, individualized, and specialized form of intellectual discourse about public issues in America than, for example, was the case in the first half of the twentieth century, when New York intellectuals set the agendas for and dominated journals of opinion. This development has opened up and enriched the conversation in many ways by moving it beyond East Coast domination, but it has also Balkanized it into disciplinary-specific enclaves, and tamed it by separating it from shared experiences of community. The new intellectuals may retain bohemian values and tastes. But without a community base and shared politics, bohemianism becomes a lifestyle choice that frequently manifests itself in upscale "hip" consumerism.[30]

Seventh, the structural shift described in the previous point has contributed to undermining the traditional gadfly concept of intellectual work by making it, in some significant senses, an avocation for academics. That is, the demands for professionalism and careerism in the academic's "day job" are often different from and in direct conflict with "the duty of noble discontent."[31] A distinction drawn from the older tradition, when intellectuals on both the left and right still felt the moral authority of this duty, remains instructive.[32] The early twentieth-century French conservative Julian Benda, responding in part to the Dreyfus Case, indicted what he saw as "the betrayal of intellectuals."[33] Benda distinguished between, "clerics," intellectuals who are bound by this moral authority, and "laity," who live in the world and pursue material advantage. Benda saw intellectual work as a sacred trust, a "vocation," that carries both moral authority and moral responsibilities. Benda cites Jesus's stricture, "My kingdom is not of this world," to define the parallel secular moral obligation that, he believed, the intellectual must embrace. In his view, the intellectual has to stand apart and to speak the truth to power with as much courage and eloquence as possible.[34] For Benda, this duty requires sacrifice: even, in some situations, the ultimate sacrifice.

In *Representations of the Intellectual*, Edward Said contemporizes Benda's distinction and applies it to an analysis of the current structural positions of American academics. He distinguishes between professionals and intellectuals and underscores the tensions between the two roles.[35] From the point of view of established institutions, including colleges and universities, those who embrace the moral/vocational approach are far more problematic than their nine-to-five professional peers. Although those who view intellectual work as a vocation may invest more of themselves in their efforts, they are, nevertheless, by definition, less predictable and potentially less loyal to the local agendas of their institutional employer than are the professionals. The gadfly vocation requires intellectuals to "deliberately not belong," to hold no allegiances to the media, governments, corporations, religions, parties, etcetera, in order to be free to "dissent against the status quo at a time when the struggle on behalf of underrepresented and disadvantaged groups seems so unfairly weighted against them."[36] Dissent, as we know, often begins at home, in internal criticism of the operations of the institutions in which intellectuals work: today, more often than not, that means—*or should mean*—criticism of the corporatization of higher education. Such criticism usually extracts high costs: costs that many academics today, like Benda's failed clerics, are unwilling to pay. Career-oriented academics prefer to do their day jobs, and retreat to the safety and comforts of the laity in the evening: to, in fact, enjoy the creature comforts of what David Brooks calls "bobos [bourgeois-bohemians] in paradise."[37]

The cumulative weight of these developments is discouraging. In cataloguing them, however, my intention is to encourage, not discourage. In virtually all of the trends explored here, critical intellectuals retain some agency. They can choose to remain silent, puzzled, conflicted, unsure, and unproductive, or they can choose to act: to do their work, to open their big mouths, to risk being wrong. Within the present climate, we are not asked to put our lives on the line, only our ideas. Unlike the brave souls who faced imprisonment to advance and defend academic freedom in American higher education during the early part of the twentieth century and again during the McCarthy era, we face, at most, loss of our jobs. To be sure, this is no small price to pay in a job structure where new opportunities are artificially repressed. As the ultimate price, it is, however, modest compared to what the great freedom fighters of the past paid. In reality, in the current litigious legal climate in the United States, very few will actually face this extreme sanction, especially if other big mouths rally to their support. More routinely, however, we do risk access to the perquisites of academic careers: desirable teaching schedules and course assignments, research subsidies, sabbatical leaves, promotions, collegiality, and so on.

Writing in 1996 on the occasion of the occasion of the twenty-fifth anniversary of *Theory and Society*, the journal founded by Alvin Gouldner, Janet Gouldner says of her deceased husband:

> Gouldner would have been saddened by the turn recent theoretical debate has taken among intellectuals. Not saddened at the challenge to objectivity and representation claims—he had long since challenged them himself. Not at the institutional constraints to intellectual life—he assumed that challenging those was part of the job. But saddened at the pessimism among contemporary intellectuals that theory is possible at all. He wanted intellectuals to be brave, profoundly passionate, daring to reach for the big picture, and bold enough to be wrong. Keep going, he would have said, do your work; people need it.[38]

Sound advice for us all! To it I would add that it is just possible that people need critical intellectual work now more than ever. Our pessimism may be rationally grounded, but our paralysis is an abdication of responsibility. Even in a post-Marxist world, Gramsci's dictum of "pessimism of intellect" but "optimism of spirit" remains a reliable motto for critical intellectuals.[39]

"NOBLE DISCONTENT"

Imputing moral authority and moral obligations to the role of the intellectual is, of course, a vestige of the origins of modern Western scholarship within the monastic tradition. The concept of vocation is also directly derivative. Max Weber presented one of the most comprehensive and emotionally tortured explorations of the secularized conception of intellectual vocations in his two prescient essays, "Science as a Vocation" and "Politics as a Vocation." Both of these works merit careful rereadings today.[40] Most publicly visible intellectual opposition to established institutions in the West in the last 100 years has been associated with left or left-liberal positions. There is, however, no necessary relationship between "noble discontent" and left political locations, as the history of dissent in the former Soviet Union amply demonstrated.[41] Since the 1960s, for example, conservative intellectuals in the U.S., despite the generous external funding that has been mobilized to support and publicize their views, have nevertheless seen themselves as an embattled intellectual minority within the academy. This may, in fact, be an accurate assessment at least in some institutional contexts some of the time, especially when conservatives take on such issues as speech codes, affirmative action, and multiculturalism.

Many, perhaps even most, academics, regardless of their political sympathies, probably feel some sense of existential, as opposed to purely careerist, commitment to their work; probably most academics, at least in the social sciences and humanities, privately aspire to be intellectuals. Many may commute between the poles of professionalism and intellectualism, in Said's sense of those terms. The distinction between career and vocational commitments is usually one of degree rather than kind, and where one is positioned along this continuum may vary in different seasons of one's personal and work life. Young faculty members with the double binds of the time-intensive responsibilities of young families and ticking tenure clocks, for example, normally have less time and leverage within the current institutionalization of intellect than do senior faculty members. So, noble discontent need not be a zero-sum game. For those who embrace the role, it imposes different, but usually incremental, responsibilities in the typical academic career cycle.

Historically, noble discontent has been a male prerogative: certainly Weber, Whitehead, Benda, and most other sociologists of knowledge conceived of it that way. The personal costs of dissent for women are still higher than the costs for men, although no longer out of reach.[42] For all historically marginal groups, women, racial and ethnic minorities, and others who still have not been fully integrated into academic cultures, the decision to stand apart requires greater courage and carries more risks than for those who fully enjoy the entitlements of membership in the academy. Said sees Virginia Woolf and Simone de Beauvoir as exemplars of female gadflies. I might add the names of Sojourner Truth, Emma Goldman, Margaret Sanger, Mother Jones, Alice Paul, Dorothy Day, Hannah Arendt, Bernadette Devlin, and Lani Guinier, among many others. The feminist movement (or, more accurately, movements) of the last quarter–century have decisively demonstrated that women can speak truth to power and with global consequences. Indeed, despite mainstream U.S. media's repeated requiems for feminism, the global feminist movement has weathered the end of the Cold War better than other Enlightenment based social movements. In fact, the end of the Cold War has significantly advanced the prominence of women's equality on the agendas of international human rights organizations.

Despite Said's gestures of inclusiveness and his own lived experience of marginality, I do not think he fully appreciates the personal and professional complexity that accompany embrace of the gadfly role by women, minorities, and academics and other intellectual workers at non-elite institutions. Not only must they, like Said, take on the world and their own institutions, but they must also confront the gadfly tradition itself, which is historically implicated in silencing and marginalizing the voices of women, minorities, lesbians, gays, and others. That is, these recently and still only partially enfranchised gadflies must critique the ongoing practices of their would-be (and should-be) ideological allies: gadflies like Said et al.

The record of the last forty years of internal, often disabling, strife within and among movements for social justice attests to the hazards of these internal confrontations. More often than not, they have splintered, factionalized, and inflamed; often they have done the enemy's work of dividing and conquering better than any enemy could. Yet, without these confrontations, the disenfranchised remain disenfranchised. Internal "semiological guerrilla" engagements among critical intellectual camps must continue. For these engagements to succeed, both old and new gadflies will need to rethink their goals and discursive strategies. "Old" gadflies will have to come to terms with the fact that "new" gadflies really are proposing a radical transformation of the tradition, not simply seeking accommodation or assimilation: a transformation that will require the old as well as the new to change. New gadflies, in turn, will, for the foreseeable future, have to continue to bear the exhausting burden of critiquing from within as well as from the trenches.

To reverse the polarization of the so-called culture wars and political correctness debates, stoked by conservatives, gadflies need to reclaim their own once-ironic language and restore community and solidarity building by building self-reflexivity and even humor into their internal self-criticisms. Internal criticism is, after all, a means, not the end of critical theory: it should start conversations, not finish them. An example from the art world, which joins serious critique, campy humor, and self-parody, may be instructive. The Guerrilla Girl Movement has captured the attention of art critics, garnered extensive press coverage, and mobilized women artists in several countries by using poster and performance art to critique discrimination, based on gender and color, in museums, among art critics, and in art markets.[43] The tools of the scholar's craft are, of course, different from the artist's or the actor's. I am not recommending importing performance art into our toolkits, although it may have a role to play in some disciplines, especially in the humanities.[44] I am, however, recommending that we take seriously the "new humility" that contemporary epistemologies mandate: that we use that humility to infuse our scholarly conversations with a new openness to discovery, and that we allow ourselves to enjoy, rather than fear, the unexpected turns that those conversations will take as they are enriched by a broader range of interlocutors. We might, for example, revisit the kinds of dialogic experimentation and intellectual playfulness that animated some of the more creative explorations of postpositive inquiries in and at the margins of the social sciences in the late 1960s and early 1970s before the sclerosis of angry factionalism shut down so many promising conversations.

In the previous chapters, I have discussed some of the ways in which discursive practices, paradigms, and models of critical reason have been implicated in enforcing socially structured silences. I have also stressed the necessity of radically rethinking, reinventing, and richly expanding the concept of rationality in light of what we now know about the limits of the Enlightenment model of rationality. Yet, like Said, Harding, Keller, Bordo, Haraway, Bourdieu, Grass, Habermas, Mannheim, Weber, and many others, I retain a belief in the constructive powers of critical scholarship. I believe in the possibility of crafting more adequate forms of substantive rationality, which can encompass models of complexity, incorporate ongoing epistemological work, retain sensitivity to context and community and to the communicative constituents of sense-making and knowledge construction, and give voice to the full panoply of human experience. In sum, I think that "discontent" begins at home, but that it achieves "nobility," in Whitehead's sense, through responsible engagement in the world.

Nobel discontent can be occasionally expressed, with significant results, within systems of power, although it is always difficult to stand apart in institutional contexts where pressures to close ranks are strong.[45] Nevertheless, some exceptionally talented insiders have successfully negotiated this perilous line. Most dissenters are, however, destined to exile, to living their lives on the margins of organizations, because their primary commitment is to criticism, not to governments, corporations, religions, or even to political or social movements with which they may identify. Said describes what he characterizes as the "romance" of this commitment:

> This is not always a matter of being a critic of government policy, but rather of thinking of the intellectual vocation as maintaining a state of constant alertness, of a perpetual willingness not to let half-truths or received ideas steer one along. That this involves a steady realism, an almost athletic rational energy, and a complicated struggle to balance the problems of one's own selfhood against the demands of publishing and speaking in the public sphere is what makes it an everlasting effort, constitutively unfinished and necessarily imperfect.[46]

In embracing Said's notion of "almost athletic rational energy," I am not aligning myself with the Promethean claims of what Georg Lukacs called "phantom objectivity," nor am I reviving the imperialistic God's eye of Western rationalism.[47] Rather, I am endorsing the fully human and humane stance of critical realism that recognizes the powers and pleasures as well as the limits of the human capacity to know. Nor, it should be clear, am I suggesting that the intellectual cannot be a political activist or a partisan, but rather that the intellectual's first commitment, her or his moral imperative, is to be responsive to the demands of reason. To remain silent in the face of abuses of power—to invoke the false gods of objectivity and neutrality—is, as Benda argued, a betrayal of the duty of the intellectual, not just a personal failure of courage. There are, however, always tensions built into alliances of reason and organized action. That is why reasonable people can disagree profoundly, and that is why intellectuals are often contentious allies.

Yet, there are historical circumstances and causes that are so desperate that the responsible exercise of intellect may compel some intellectuals to commit their whole beings to action because there are no viable alternatives. In *Between Hell and Reason: Essays from the Resistant Newspaper Combat, 1944–1947*, Albert Camus describes such a context when he writes that "the men who joined the Resistance found themselves in the solitary position of choosing shame or action."[48] Assuming the dual roles of intellectual and partisan does, however, carry special intellectual and moral responsibilities. Reflexive self-criticism, the obligation of all intellectuals, is a special obligation of partisan intellectuals; although, unfortunately, the hard realities of contemporary political struggles almost always preclude public displays of reflexivity, doubt, or regret. Yet, doubt is a precondition for critical reason, and self-doubt is a hallmark of wisdom.

The demands that intellectual vocations place on those who accept them are not always, or even usually, as dramatic as the roles that have been played in the public sphere by the intellectuals I have cited in this essay: Weber, Benda, Woolf, Brecht, de Beauvoir, Bourdieu, Grass, Said, et al. For many, noble discontent may mean consistently and perhaps even inconspicuously practicing and enjoying what C. Wright Mills called "intellectual craftsmanship" in teaching, research, and writing.[49] Nevertheless, intellectual vocations are not for everyone. Here is one more place where I part company with Benda. Not everyone has the interests, convictions, spleen, stamina, or a big enough mouth to take on the gadfly role. In most scholarly fields in the U.S. today, the choice is not, as it was in Camus's time, between shame and action. The time may come when that is the choice; it may come sooner, and with greater intensity, in some areas of scholarly specialization than in others. At present, however, it is still possible for scholars in most fields to live lives of moral responsibility and personal satisfaction as a members of the laity.[50]

For those who believe "something is missing," however, discontent can only be ennobled by opening their big mouths and speaking truth to power. Yes, the postmodern anxiety over truth that is made, not discovered, is warranted. Stripped of the authority of Promethean theories of knowledge, we must now stake more modest claims.[51] We must recognize that our methods for converting the evidence of our senses, the testaments of our reason, and fruits of our conversations into knowledge are always fallible, incomplete, and prone to error. But we must also recognize that they always have been, and that, in the past, we were ignorant of, deluded by, or willfully denying these contingencies. The wings of Prometheus have taken the Western mind far. The adventures of this lesser god have given us great art, literature, philosophy, and the wonders of modern science, but Promethean illusions have also been responsible for many tragic misadventures.

The loss of a false sense of certainty is, however, also a gain: perhaps even a step forward in the history of human consciousness. Viewing knowledge as a wholly human construct recognizes the awesome powers of our species as well as our mortal limits. If gods have not walked among us or stolen fire from the heavens for us, some very powerful human intellects have nevertheless illuminated our world for us. And some of them, sensing that something was missing, have used their noble discontent to launch some amazing "adventures of ideas."[52]

Now that we humans are forced to face our problems alone, with "steady realism" rather than with Promethean delusions, we are, in fact, far better positioned than ever before to avoid misadventures in ideas and in society. When imagining something better, we are now forced to do so without invoking superhuman powers or principles—divine rights, laws of historical immanence, racist perversions of evolutionary theory, concepts of compulsory heterosexuality, and so on—which have too often tragically twisted our utopian human impulse to do better into a totalitarian impulse, which has invariably done worse. The new humility requires us to recognize that all of our efforts to build better theories and better worlds must always remain works in progress, that all of our solutions to intellectual and social problems are necessarily tentative, and that every extension of the franchise of democracy is easily reversed.

Those who imagine that their victories are permanent—that they have powers to end ideology or freeze history—entertain dangerous Promethean fantasies. Immanuel Kant warned,

> Out of the crooked timber of humanity, no straight thing was ever made. And for that reason no perfect solution is, not merely in practice, but in principle, possible in human affairs, and any determined attempt to produce it is likely to lead to suffering, disillusionment, and failure.[53]

Better to reclaim the steadying stick of critical realism, to recognize our human limits as well as our opportunities, and to do our work. The world still needs it.

NOTES

1. This note is intended primarily for readers who may be reading this book out of chronological sequence. When I refer to reason, I am, of course, referring to it in light of the postmodern critique, but not from within the radical postmodern surrender to relativism. Throughout this book I argue for a new, more modest construction of rationality, which leaves behind Promethean illusions and Western ethnocentrism. This form of reason recognizes that rationality is a human construct, which is always tentative, incomplete and subject to correction, but it also recognizes the value of the Sisyphean struggle to seek better, more reliable, ways of knowing as well as more humane ways of living. That is, it argues for a critical realism that leaves the doors open. Elsewhere I have referred to it, in the words and spirit of Llewellyn Z. Gross, as "good rationality." See Sue Curry Jansen, *Censorship: The Knot that Binds Power and Knowledge* (New York: Oxford University Press, 1988), 250, n. 6.

2. Michael Polanyi, *Personal Knowledge* (Chicago: University of Chicago Press, 1958).

3. Alvin Gouldner, *The Two Marxisms* (New York: Seabury, 1980), 380. Writing twenty years after Gouldner, I would pluralize his formulation of repressed or caged systems.

4. Patrick Smith. "Dark Victory," *Index on Censorship* 28, no. 5 (September/October 1999): 42–43.

5. For a highly publicized recent conservative contribution to this critique, see Richard A. Posner, *Public Intellectuals: A Study of Decline* (Cambridge, Mass.: Harvard University Press, 2001).

6. Günter Grass in Günter Grass and Pierre Bourdieu, "A Literature from Below," *The Nation* (July 2, 2000): 28.

7. Gouldner, *Dialectic of Ideology and Technology* (New York: Seabury Press, 1976).

8. Francis Fukuyama, "The End of History?" *The National Interest* (Summer 1989): 3–18.

9. Vaclav Havel, *Disturbing the Peace: Conversation with Karel Hvizdala* (New York: Vintage Books, 1990), 167.

10. Friedrich Nietzsche, *Richard Wagner in Bayreuth*, cited from the German language edition in Walter Kaufman, *Nietzsche* (Cleveland, Ohio: World Publishing, 1956), 124.

11. Max Weber, *From Max Weber: Essays in Sociology* (New York: Oxford University Press, 1946), 147.

12. Pierre Bayle, *Nouvelles de la republique des lettres* (Geneva: Slatkine Reprints, 1966, original 1687).

13. Lois Gibbs was the determined young mother who organized and led the neighborhood association that forced the Love Canal crisis on the public agenda. For years people in Niagara Falls, New York, were aware, through direct observation, of the devastating despoilation of the environment by the chemical industry despite blanket denials by corporate spokesmen. Gibbs was, however, especially persistent in questioning the incidences of childhood illness and mortality in the La Salle neighborhood. The corporate stonewall might have been sustained if incumbent Democratic Governor Hugh Carey had not been facing a difficult reelection campaign in 1978 with a well-funded opponent. He could not compete in the media blitz, but, as governor, he could command media coverage if big news could be generated from Albany. Enter the Love Canal crisis: Carey declared a state of emergency, presented himself to the media as a champion of the underdog (the traditional working-class constituency of the Democractic voters), generated national press coverage, and won the election.

14. In a climate where concentration of ownership is accelerating, and government regulation is lax, as it is under the laissez-faire climate of neoliberalism, one can assume such organized efforts are becoming increasingly common, and perhaps even the norm in some facets of contemporary life.

15. Louis Althusser, *Lenin and Philosophy and Other Essays* (New York: Monthly Review Press, 1971).

16. For a survey of the range of postmodernisms, see Walter Truett Anderson, ed., *The Truth about the Truth: De-confusing and Re-constructing the Postmodern World* (New York: Putnam, 1995).

17. Grass in Grass and Bourdieu, "A Literature from Below," 26.

18. In the former Soviet Bloc nations, the reinvention of the academy in the wake of the collapse of communism has been ongoing. For example, it ended many careers and

opened up academic opportunities for former dissidents. In the West, the rupture has been less wrenching, although some scholars have seen interest in their specialties wane (e.g., Russian Studies), research funding and publishing opportunities dry up, and new job opportunities or job mobility decline or disappear. The sting of the conservative orchestrated "political correctness" debates should not be underestimated either, despite the fact that many of the arguments are lightweight or inaccurate. University administrators, who are increasingly drawn from business rather than academic backgrounds, have brought with them corporate, top-down authority models. In some institutions, they now have significant voice in academic affairs, including curriculum directions and hiring. For a trenchant account of the malaise that has infected the communication field, see Robert W. McChesney, "The Political Economy of Communication and the Future of the Field," *Media, Culture, and Society* 22, no. 1 (January 2000): 109–116.

19. This example demonstrates the effects of the conflation of the public good with the corporate good, in this case, defined as the good of corporations disadvantaged by Microsoft's exercise of its monopolistic muscle.

20. The present course would therefore appear to be leading almost inescapably to unprecedented global environmental crises. Without sustained, cooperative, international planning and interventions, this course will not only produce further destruction of the rain forests and exacerbation of global warming. It will also accelerate rates of extinction of species and the exhaustion of nonrenewable resources, which not only include the fossil fuels that keep the engines of the developed world running, but also fresh water supplies upon which life itself depends. In the poorest countries in the world, it will also contribute to increasing population pressures that result in genocidal regional wars, disease, starvation, and the creation of large refugee populations.

21. Russell Jaccoby traces the academic lineage of the "end of ideology" thesis in social science and historical writing. Those who have arrived, including academics, it seems must convince themselves that their good fortune is permanent and invincible. See Russell Jaccoby, *The End of Utopia: Politics and Culture in an Age of Apathy* (New York: Basic Books, 1999).

22. Alfred North Whitehead, *Adventures of Ideas* (New York: The Free Press, 1967, original 1933), 20. Bertolt Brecht's famous line from *Mahagonny*, "Something is missing," is cited by Jaccoby, through the intermediary of Ernst Bloch, as the key to the utopian impulse. Jaccoby, *The End of Utopia*, 181.

23. Whitehead, *Adventures of Ideas*; Karl Mannheim, *Ideology and Utopia* (New York: Harvest Books, 1936); and Karl Mannheim, *Essays on the Sociology of Knowledge* (London: Kegan Paul, 1952).

24. Jaccoby, *The End of Utopia*; Ishaiah Berlin, "The Decline of Utopian Ideas in the West," in *The Crooked Timber of Humanity*, ed. Ishaiah Berlin (Princeton, N.J.: Princeton University Press, 1990). This Western atrophy of optimism is exported to the rest of the world through media; yet, it may be the ideology of victors, which, as you read this, may be calling forth utopian reactions—in Mannheim's sense—in other parts of the world. See Mannheim, *Ideology and Utopia*.

25. Jaccoby, *The End of Utopia*, 181.

26. I recently witnessed a generational difference in idealism versus cynicism in audiences responses to a talk on political campaign reform. Paul Taylor, founder of

the Alliance for Better Campaigns, evoked a nostalgic spark of idealism among faculty, while students responded with cynicism by claiming Taylor must have an angle, must be a front for some interests, or must be profiting personally from his efforts. Paul Taylor, "Campaign Reform," lecture, Muhlenberg College, Allentown, Pa., October 17, 2000.

27. Bourdieu in Grass and Bourdieu, "A Literature from Below," 26.

28. One could argue that elite scientists and intellectuals in corporate and university research centers and think tanks now comprise a new presence in what C. Wright Mills called "the power elite." Alvin Gouldner forecast the value of intellectual capital in the world that was evolving in the last quarter of the twentieth century. His forecast was, however, far more optimistic than the reality that actually has, to date, taken form. That is, he saw intellectuals forming a "new class" and advancing a culture of "critical discourse" that would displace the "old class" of both capitalist and socialist domination. His faith in the relative intellectual autonomy of the intellectuals has not yet proven warranted. Yet, one can cite some examples of noble discontent among the new class of information intellectuals. See, for example, Bill Joy's "Why the Future Doesn't Need Us," *Wired* (April 2000): 1–30, which is discussed more fully in chapter 6 of this book. See also C. Wright Mills, *The Power Elite* (New York: Oxford University Press, 1956). Gouldner attributes the term "servants of power" to Loren Baritz. See Alvin Gouldner, *The Future of Intellectuals and the Rise of the New Class* (New York: Seabury Press, 1979), 40.

29. Christopher Lasch, *The Revolt of the Elites and the Betrayal of Democracy* (New York: W. W. Norton, 1995).

30. David Brooks, *Bobos in Paradise: The New Upper Class and How They Got There* (New York: Simon & Schuster, 2000).

31. The "day job" reference is from a talk given by Andrew Ross, who was contrasting his job as a professor in New York with his job as a writer who wanted to spend a year gathering material on Disney's planned community, Celebration, in Orlando, Andrew Ross, "Celebration," lecture, Muhlenberg College, October 18, 2000. Since then, I have also noticed this flippant dichotomy used in the *Chronicle of Higher Education* in reference to other academic celebrities, who within the *Chronicle*'s take, are often English professors, for example Scott Heller, "Harold Bloom Plays His Biggest Role," *Chronicle of Higher Education* (10 November 2000): 8(A). Disciplinary differences may be at play here; it is hard for me to imagine social scientists, who still carry the burden of the direct and indirect influences of Max Weber's ascetic approach to scholarship, finding this kind of verbal play "cool."

32. Julian Benda, *The Treason of the Intellectuals* (New York: Norton, 1969, original 1928). Edward W. Said makes extensive use of Benda's work in his *Representations of the Intellectual* (New York: Vintage, 1994). I, in turn, draw heavily on both Said and Benda's works.

33. Benda, *The Treason of the Intellectuals*.

34. Benda, *The Treason of the Intellectuals*.

35. Edward Said, *Representations of the Intellectual*.

36. Edward Said, *Representations of the Intellectual*, xxii.

37. Brooks, *Bobos in Paradise*.

38. Janet Gouldner, "Opening Remarks: Alvin Gouldner's Theory and Society," *Theory and Society* 25, no. 2 (April 1996): 165.
39. Antonio Gramsci, *The Antonio Gramsci Reader* (New York: New York University, 2000).
40. Both essays are in Weber, *From Max Weber*.
41. While the Western press used Western liberal/conservative labels to describe Soviet intellectuals during the period of Cold War détente, the Western press's and the Western left's responses to Aleksandr Solzhenitsyn's demonstrates the limits of these categories. American conservatives who embraced his denunciation of Soviet totalitarianism reframed him as eccentric when he criticized Western materialism.
42. Weber was sympathetic to the feminist arguments of his time, and supported women, including his wife, Marianne, in intellectual pursuits. The language and assumptions of his own writings on intellectuals are, however, classically masculinist. Said strives for greater gender inclusiveness in his discussion of intellectuals; however, he does not consider the by-now vast literature on the special challenges that most women academics and intellectuals still face in adopting a vocational approach to scholarship.
43. The Guerrilla Girls movement demonstrates that it is not enough for women to have access to clay, brushes, or art juries when the criteria the judges use preclude subjects, forms, and sensibilities drawn from women's experiences. Characterizing themselves as "the conscience of the art world," these feminist activists see themselves as the counterparts of the male tradition of anonymous do-gooders like Robin Hood, Batman, and the Lone Ranger. The Guerrilla Girls began in 1985 when the Museum of Modern Art (MOMA) in New York held an exhibit entitled, "An International Survey of Painting and Sculpture," which touted itself as a definitive inventory of the most significant contemporary art in the world. Of the 169 artists exhibited, only thirteen were women. All were white, either European or American. The curator advised any artist who was not included in the show to rethink "his" career. A protest by women artists in front of the museum was ignored. Following the example of the gay activist group, Act Up, the Guerrilla Girls decided to use their art to disturb, shock, outrage, and implode the masculine hegemony of the art world through posters, billboards, bus ads, magazine spreads, protest actions, letter writing campaigns, broadsheets in the bathrooms of major museums, interviews, and, most recently, books. Adopting the names of dead women artists, members of the group sought to both protect themselves from blacklisting by museums and from the emergence of a self-serving star system within their own ranks. A fairly typical example of their efforts is a 1997 poster protesting another MOMA exhibit, which reads, "3 white women, 1 woman of color and no men of color—out of 71 artists." The poster shows six gorillas in a hairy teacup on a hairy saucer. Detachable postcards congratulate the curator of the show on managing to "redefine the still life to exclude women and artists of color from the practice"; it advises MOMA to change the name of the exhibit from "Objects of Desire: the Modern Still Life" to "The Objects of MOMA's Desire are Still White Males." Supporters sent the museum thousands of the postcards; according to the Guerrilla Girls, all of the reviews of the exhibition commented on its discriminatory aesthetics. In art, a practice that bears the self-parodic legacy of Marcel Duchamp, the

Guerrilla Girls strategies are, insofar as the words are elastic enough to apply, both logical and rational. As a result, the group has attracted worldwide attention, and its tactics have been emulated by women artists in several countries. See *The Guerrilla Girls Bedside Companion to the History of Western Art* (New York: Penguin, 1998) and the movement's website <www.guerillagirls.com/interview/index.html> (accessed February 11, 2002).

44. Here I find myself ambivalent about Martin Jay's controversial essay, "The Academic Woman as Performance Artist." I share Jay's commitment to Gouldner's ideal of cultures of critical discourse: a form that I believe retains promise, if it still eludes us in practice, in the social sciences, history, philosophy, and public life. I even share, with some minor reservations, his conclusion that the women "performers" that he discusses do not meet that ideal, and probably do not aspire to. Yet, there is a scolding quality about Jay's essay that I reject. Performance, as opposed to rational-critical models, are on the ascent in many areas of the humanities and even in interdisciplinary studies; within their assumptions, shock, absurdity, street theater, parody, inversion, and other nonlinear discursive forms have achieved legitimacy. Perhaps Jay's own interdisciplinary fence-sitting, which has enriched so much of his work, is a liability here. See Martin Jay, *Cultural Semantics* (Amherst: University of Massachusetts Press, 1998).

45. For a recent chronicle of a critical intellectual's "insider" attempts to speak truth to power, see Benjamin Barber, *The Truth of Power: Intellectual Affairs in the Clinton White House* (New York: W. W. Norton, 2001).

46. Edward Said, *Representations of the Intellectual*, 23.

47. Georg Lukacs, *History and Class Consciousness* (Cambridge, Mass.: MIT Press, 1971, original 1922).

48. Albert Camus, *Between Hell and Reason: Essays from the Resistance Newspaper Combat, 1944–1947* (Hanover, N.H.: Press of New England for Wesleyan University Press, 1991).

49. Without taking on the full weight of a vocational commitment, one can strive for "intellectual craftsmanship" in C. Wright Mills's sense, or a similar construct, what Alasdair MacIntyre calls excellence in "practice." See C. Wright Mills, "On Intellectual Craftsmanship," in *The Sociological Imagination* (New York: Oxford University Press, 1959), appendix; and Alasdair MacIntyre, *After Virtue* (Notre Dame, Ind.: University of Notre Dame Press, 1981).

50. Here I not only part company with Benda, but with uncompromising traditions on both the left and right that assume that one size fits all. I do, however, conversely hold those who profess commitments to the vocational model to the standards of that tradition, which on some issues, find little room for compromise. In short, I expect more fidelity to noble discontent from clerics than laity.

51. Polanyi, *Personal Knowledge*.

52. Whitehead, *Adventures of Ideas*.

53. Immanuel Kant, quoted by Berlin, *The Crooked Timber of Humanity*, 48.

Selected Bibliography

Ackerman, Bruce A. *Social Justice in the Liberal State*. New Haven and London: Yale University Press, 1980.

Agger, Ben. "A Critical Theory of Dialogue." *Humanities in Society* 4, no. 1 (Winter 1981): 62–84.

———. "Work and Authority in Marcuse and Habermas." *Human Studies* 2 (1979): 191–208.

Allan, Stuart. *News Culture*. Buckingham: Open University Press, 1999.

Anderson, Walter Truett, ed. *The Truth about the Truth: De-confusing and Reconstructing the Postmodern World*. New York: Putnam, 1995.

Balsamo, Anne. *Technologies of the Gendered Body: Reading Cyborg Women*. Durham, N.C.: Duke University Press, 1996.

Bannet, Eve Tavor. "The Feminist Logic of Both/And." *Genders* 15 (Winter 1992): 1–19.

Barber, Benjamin R. *Jihad vs. McWorld*. New York Random House, 1995.

Barthes, Roland. *Mythologies*. Edited and translated by Annette Lavers. New York: Hill and Wang, 1972.

Barzun, Jacques. *From Dawn to Decadence: 500 Years of Western Cultural Life, 1500 to the Present*. New York: HarperCollins, 2000.

Beauvoir, Simone de. *The Second Sex*. New York: Vintage Books, 1974.

Benda, Julian. *The Treason of the Intellectuals*. New York: Norton, 1969; original 1928.

Beniger, James R. *The Control Revolution*. Cambridge, Mass.: Harvard University Press, 1986.

Bernstein, Basil. *Class Codes and Control*. London: Routledge and Kegan Paul, 1971.

Bleier, Ruth. *Science and Gender: A Critique of Biology and its Theories on Women*. New York: Pergamon, 1984.

Bloor, David. *Knowledge and Social Imagery*. London: Routledge and Kegan Paul, 1977.

Boden, Margaret A. *Computer Models of Mind*. Cambridge: Cambridge University Press, 1988.

Bolter, David. *Turing's Man: Western Culture in the Computer Age*. Chapel Hill: University of North Carolina Press, 1984.

Bookman, Ann, and Sandra Morgen, eds. *Women and the Politics of Empowerment*. Philadelphia: Temple University Press, 1988.

Bordo, Susan. *The Flight to Objectivity: Essays on Cartesianism and Culture*. Albany: State University of New York Press, 1987.

Bowles, Samuel, and Herbert Gintis. *Democracy and Capitalism, Property, Community, and the Contradictions of Modern Social Thought*. New York: Basic Books, 1986.

Braverman, Harry. *Labor and Monopoly Capital: The Degradation of Work in the Twentieth Century*. New York: Monthly Review Press, 1974.

Burke, Kenneth. *A Grammar of Motives and Rhetoric of Motives*. Cleveland: Meridian, 1962.

Caldicott, Helen. *Missile Envy: The Arms Race and Nuclear War*. New York: Morrow, 1984.

Camus, Albert. *Between Hell and Reason: Essays from the Resistance Newspaper Combat, 1944–1947*. Hanover, N.H.: Press of New England for Wesleyan University Press, 1991.

———. *The Myth of Sisyphus*. New York: Random House, 1955.

Carrigan, T., R. Connell, and J. Lee. "Toward a New Sociology of Masculinity." *Theory and Society* 14, no. 5 (1985): 551–604.

Cockburn, Cynthia. *Brothers: Male Dominance and Technological Change*. London: Pluto, 1983.

———. *Machinery of Dominance: Women, Men and Technical Know-How*. London: Pluto Press, 1985.

Cockburn, Cynthia, and Susan Ormrod. *Gender and Technology in the Making*. Thousand Oaks, Calif.: Sage, 1993.

Cohn, Carol. "Sex and Death in the Rational World of Defense Intellectuals." *Signs* 12, no. 4 (1987): 687–718.

Coles, Robert. *Doing Documentary Work*. New York: Oxford University Press, 1998.

Collins, Harry M. *Artificial Experts: Social Knowledge and Intelligent Machines*. Cambridge, Mass.: MIT Press, 1993.

Connell, R. W. *Gender and Power: Society, the Person, and Sexual Politics*. Palo Alto, Calif.: Stanford University Press, 1987.

———. "Masculinity, Violence, and War." In *Men's Lives*, edited by Michael Kimmel and Michael A. Messner, 94–100. New York: Macmillan, 1989.

———. "The State, Gender, and Sexual Politics." *Theory and Society* 19 (1990): 507–44.

Cowan, Ruth S. *More Work for Mother: The Ironies of Household Technology from the Open Hearth to the Microwave*. New York: Basic Books, 1983.

Creedon, Pamela I., ed. *Women in Mass Communication Challenging Gender Values*. Newbury Park, Calif.: Sage Publications, 1989.

Croteau, David. By *Invitation Only: How the Media Limit Political Debate*. Monroe, Maine: Common Courage Press, 1994.

Davidson, Donald. "What Metaphors Mean." In *On Metaphor*, edited by Sheldon Sacks, 290–91. Chicago: University of Chicago Press, 1979.

DeMott, Benjamin. *Killer Woman Blues: Why Americans Can't Think Straight about Gender and Power*. Boston: Houghton Mifflin Company, 2000.

Dervin, Brenda. "Users as Research Inventions: How Research Categories Perpetuate Inequities." *Journal of Communication* 39, no. 3 (Summer 1989): 216–32.

Dervin, Brenda, Larry Grossberg, Beverly J. O'Keefe, and Ellen Wartella, eds. *Rethinking Communication, Vol. 1: Paradigm Issues*. Newbury Park, Calif.: Sage, 1989.

Easlea, Brian. *Fathering the Unthinkable: Masculinity, Scientists, and the Nuclear Arms Race*. London: Pluto Press, 1983.

Edelman, Murray. *Political Language: Words that Succeed and Politics that Fail*. New York: Academic Press, 1977.

Edwards, Paul. "The Army and the Microworld: Computers and the Politics of Gender Identity." *Signs* 16 (1990): 102–27.

———. "Border Wars: The Science and Politics of Artificial Intelligence." *Radical America* 19, no. 6 (1985): 39–50.

Eisenstein, Zillah, ed. *Capitalist Patriarchy and the Case for Socialist Feminism*. New York: Monthly Review Press, 1979.

Enloe, Cynthia. *Bananas, Beaches, and Bases: Making Feminist Sense of International Studies*. Berkeley: University of California Press, 1989.

———. *The Morning After: Sexual Politics at the End of the Cold War*. Berkeley: University of California Press, 1993.

Ferguson, Kathy. *The Feminist Case against Bureaucracy*. Philadelphia: Temple University Press, 1984.

Finlay, Marike. *Powermatics: A Discursive Critique of New Communications Technology*. London: Routledge and Kegan Paul, 1987.

Fitzgerald, Frances. *Way Out There in the Blue: Reagan, Star Wars, and the End of the Cold War*. New York: Simon and Schuster, 2000.

Fraser, Nancy. *Unruly Practices: Power, Discourse and Gender in Contemporary Social Theory*. Minneapolis: University of Minnesota Press, 1989.

Friere, Paulo. *Pedagogy of the Oppressed*. New York: Seabury Press, 1970.

Frisson, Valerie, ed. *Gender, ITC's and Everyday Life: Mutual Shaping Processes*. Amsterdam: European Commission, 1997.

Gallagher, Margaret. *Unequal Opportunities: The Case of Woman and the Media*. Paris: UNESCO, 1981.

Gans, Herbert. *Deciding What's News*. New York: Pantheon, 1979.

Garnham, Nicholas. *Capitalism and Communication: Global Communication and the Economics of Information*. London: Sage, 1990.

Garson, Barbara. *The Electronic Sweatshop*. New York: Simon and Schuster, 1988.

Gerbner, George, Hamid Mowlana, and Herbert I. Schiller, eds. *Invisible Crisis*. Boulder: Westview Press, 1996.

Giddens, Anthony. *The Constitution of Society: Outline of the Theory of Structuralism*. Berkeley: University of California Press, 1974.

Gilligan, Carol. *In a Different Voice: Psychological Theory and Women's Development*. Cambridge, Mass.: Harvard University Press, 1982.

Gitlin, Todd. *The Whole World Is Watching: Mass Media in the Making and Unmaking of the New Left*. Berkeley: University of California Press, 1980.

Goffman, Erving. *Gender Advertisements*. New York: Harper and Row, 1979.

———. *Frame Analysis*. New York: Harper and Row, 1974.

Gouldner, Alvin, *The Dialectic of Ideology and Technology*. New York: The Seabury Press, 1976.

———. *The Future of Intellectuals and the Rise of the New Class*. New York: The Seabury Press, 1979, 40.

———. *The Two Marxisms*. New York: Seabury, 1980.

Gramsci, Antonio. *The Antonio Gramsci Reader*. New York: New York University Press, 2000.

———. *Prison Notebook*. New York: International Publishers, 1971.

Grass, Günter, and Pierre Bourdieu. "A Literature from Below." *The Nation* (July 3, 2000): 25–28.

Gray, Ann. *Video Playtime: The Gendering of a Leisure Technology*. London: Routledge, 1992.

Guerrilla Girls. *The Guerrilla Girls' Bedside Companion to the History of Western Art*. New York: Penguin, 1998.

Habermas, Jurgen. *Knowledge and Human Interests*. Boston: Beacon Press, 1971.

Hacker, Sally. *'Doing it the Hard Way': Investigations of Gender and Technology*. Edited by Dorothy E. Smith and Susan M. Turner. Boston: Unwin Hyman, 1990.

———. *Pleasure, Power, and Technology: Some Tales of Gender, Engineering, and the Cooperative Workplace*. Boston: Unwin and Hyman, 1989.

Hackett, R. A. "Decline of a Paradigm? Bias and Objectivity in News Media Studies." *Critical Studies in Mass Communication* 1 (1984): 229–59.

Hall, Stuart. "Brave New World." *Marxism Today* (October 1988): 24–29.

———. "Encoding and Decoding in the Television Discourse." In *Culture, Media, Language*, edited by Stuart Hall, D. Hobson, A. Lowe, and Paul Willis, 128–38. London: Hutchinson, 1980.

Hamill, Pete. *News Is a Verb*. New York: Ballantine, 1998.

Haraway, Donna. "A Manifesto for Cyborgs: Science, Technology, and Socialist Feminism in the 1980s." *Socialist Review* 80 (1985): 65–107.

———. *Primate Visions: Gender, Race, and Nature in the World of Modern Science*. New York: Routledge: 1989.

———. "Primatology Is Politics by Other Means." In *Feminist Approaches to Science*, edited by Ruth Bleier, 74–85. New York: Pergamon Press, 1986.

———. "Situated Knowledges: The Science Question in Feminism and the Privilege of Partial Perspective." *Feminist Studies* 14, no. 3 (1988): 575–99.

Harding, Sandra, ed. *The Racial Economy of Science: Toward a Democratic Future*. Bloomington: Indiana University Press, 1993.

———. *The Science Question in Feminism*. Ithaca: Cornell University Press, 1986.

———. *Whose Science? Whose Knowledge? Thinking from Women's Lives*. Ithaca, N.Y.: Cornell University Press, 1991.

Harding, Sandra, and Merrill B. Hintikka, eds. *Discovering Reality*. Dordrecht, Netherlands: D. Reidel, 1983.

Hardt, Hanno. *Critical Communication Studies: Communication, History and Theory in America*. London: Routledge, 1992.

Hartsock, Nancy. *Money, Sex, And Power: Toward a Feminist Historical Materialism*. New York: Longman, 1983.

Harvey, David. *The Condition of Postmodernity*. Oxford: Basil Blackwell, 1989.

Havel, Vaclav. *Disturbing the Peace: Conversation with Karel Hvizdala*. New York: Vintage Books, 1990.

Hawkesworth, Mary. "Knowers, Knowing, Known: Feminist Theory and Claims of Truth." *Signs* 14, no. 3 (Spring 1989): 557–73.

Herman, Ed. *The Myth of Liberal Media: An Edward Herman Reader*. New York: Peter Lang Publishing, 1999.

Hesse, Mary. *Models and Analogies in Science*. Notre Dame: University of Notre Dame Press, 1966.

———. *Revolutions and Reconstructions in the Philosophy of Science*. Bloomington: Indiana University Press, 1980.

Hillman, James. *The Myth of Analysis: Three Essays in Archetypal Psychology*. Evanston: Northwestern University Press, 1972.

Hofstadter, Douglas R. *Godel, Escher, Back: An Eternal Golden Braid*. New York: Random House, 1979.

Horkheimer, Max. *Critical Theory: Selected Essays*. New York: Seabury Press, 1972.

———. *Eclipse of Reason*. New York: Seabury Press, 1974.

Horkheimer, Max, and Theodore W. Adorno. *Dialectics of Enlightenment*. New York: Herder and Herder, 1972.

Hubbard, Ruth, M. S. Henefin, and B. Fried, eds. *Biological Woman, the Convenient Myth: A Collection of Feminist Essays and a Comprehensive Bibliography*. Cambridge, Mass.: Schenkman, 1982.

Hull, Gloria T., Patricia B. Scott, and Barbara Smith, eds. *All the Women Are White, All the Blacks Are Men, but Some of Us Are Brave: Black Women's Studies: A Black Feminist Statement*. New York: Feminist Press, 1982.

Jaccoby, Russell. *The End of Utopia: Politics and Culture in an Age of Apathy*. New York: Basic Books, 1999.

Jansen, Sue Curry. *Censorship: The Knot that Binds Power and Knowledge*. New York: Oxford University Press, 1988.

———. "Is Science a Man? New Feminist Epistemologies and Reconstructions of Knowledge." *Theory and Society* 19 (1990): 235–46.

Jhally, Sut, and Barry Truchil. "The Spectacle of Accumulation: Material and Cultural Factors in the Evolution of the Sports/Media Complex." *Insurgent Sociologist* 12, no. 3 (1984): 41–57.

Johnson, George. *Machinery of the Mind: Inside the New Science of Artificial Intelligence*. New York: Random House, 1986.

Joy, Bill. "Why the Future Doesn't Need Us." *Wired* (April 2000): 1–15. <www.wired.com> (accessed April 2000).

Kaufman, Michael, ed. *Beyond Patriarchy: Essays by Men on Pleasure, Power, and Change*. New York: Oxford University Press, 1987.

Keller, Evelyn Fox. *Reflections on Gender and Science*. New Haven, Conn.: Yale University Press, 1985.

Keller, Evelyn Fox, and Christine Grontowski. *The Century of the Gene*. Cambridge: Harvard University Press, 2000.

Kramarae, Cheris, ed. *Technology and Women's Voices: Keeping in Touch*. New York: Routledge and Kegan Paul, 1988.

Kuhn, Annette, and Ann Marie Wolpe, eds. *Feminism and Materialism: Women and Modes of Production*. London: Routledge and Kegan Paul, 1978.

Lakoff, George. "Metaphors of Terror: The Power of Images." *In These Times.com*, October 29, 2001.

———. *Women, Fire, and Dangerous Things: What Categories Reveal About the World*. Chicago: University of Chicago Press, 1987.

Lakoff, George, and Mark Johnson. *Metaphors We Live By*. Chicago: University of Chicago Press, 1981.

Lakoff, George, and Mark Johnson. *Philosophy in the Flesh: The Embodied Mind and Its Challenge to Western Thought*. New York: Basic Books, 1999.

Lakoff, George, and Mark Turner. *More than Cool Reason: A Field Guide to Poetic Metaphor*. Chicago: University of Chicago Press, 1989.

Lent, John A., ed. *A Different Road Taken: Profiles in Critical Communication*. Boulder: Westview Press, 1995.

Levidow, Lev, and Kevin Robbins, eds. *Cyborg Worlds: The Military Information Society*. London: Free Association Books, 1989.

Lewis, Bernard. *What Went Wrong? Western Impact and Middle East Response*. New York: Oxford University Press, 2002.

Lukacs, Georg. *History and Class Consciousness*. Cambridge, Mass.: MIT Press, 1971; original 1922.

MacCormack, Carol P., and Marilyn Strathern, eds. *Nature, Culture and Gender*. Cambridge: Cambridge University Press, 1980.

MacIntyre, Alasdair. *After Virtue*. Notre Dame, Ind.: University of Notre Dame Press, 1981.

MacKinnon, Catherine A. "Feminism, Marxism, Method and the State: An Agenda for Theory." *Signs* 7, no. 3 (1982): 515–44.

———. "Globalization, Sport Development, and the Media Sport Production Complex," *Sport Science Review* 2, no. 1 (1993): 29–47.

Maguire, J. "The Media-Sport Production Complex: The Case of American Football in Western European Societies." *European Journal of Communication* 6 (1991): 315–35.

Mander, Mary S. ed. *Communications in Transition: Issues and Debates in Current Research*. New York: Praeger, 1983.

Mannheim, Karl. *Essays on the Sociology of Knowledge*. London: Kegan Paul, 1952.

———. *Ideology and Utopia*. New York: Harcourt, Brace, 1936.

Manoff, Robert K. and Michael Schudson, eds. *Reading the News*. New York: Pantheon Books, 1986.

Marcuse, Herbert. *The Aesthetic Dimension: Toward a Critique of Marxist Aesthetics.* Boston: Beacon Press, 1978.

———. *Eros: A Philosophical Inquiry into Freud.* Boston: Beacon Press, 1955.

———. *An Essay on Liberation.* Boston: Beacon Press, 1969.

———. *Negations.* New York: Columbia University Press, 1989.

———. *One-Dimensional Man.* Boston: Beacon Press, 1964.

Martin, Randy. *Chalk Lines: The Politics of Work in the Managed University.* Durham, N.C.: Duke University Press, 1999.

Maruyama, Magoroh. "Information and Communication in Poly-Epistemological Systems." In *The Myths of Information*, edited by Kathleen Woodward, 28–40. Milwaukee: University of Wisconsin Press, 1980.

Marx, Karl, and Friedrich Engels. *The German Ideology.* New York: International Publishers, 1970; original 1846.

McChesney, Robert W. "The Political Economy of Communication and the Future of the Field." *Media, Culture, and Society* 22, no. 1 (January 2000): 109–116.

———. *Rich Media, Poor Democracy: Communication Politics in Dubious Times.* Champaign: University of Illinois Press, 1999.

McNeil, Maureen, ed. *Gender and Expertise.* London: Free Association Books, 1987.

Merchant, Carolyn. *The Death of Nature: Women, Ecology and the Scientific Revolution.* New York: Harper and Row, 1980.

Messner, Michael, and Donald F. Sabo, eds. *Sport, Men, and the Gender Order: Critical Feminist Perspectives.* Champaign, Ill.: Human Kinetics Books, 1990.

Mills, C. Wright. *The Sociological Imagination.* New York: Oxford University Press, 1959.

Minsky, Marvin. *Society of Mind.* New York: Simon and Schuster, 1987.

Montgomery, David, ed. *The Cold War and The University: Toward an Intellectual History of the Postwar Years.* New York: The New Press, 1997.

Morgall, Janine. *Technology Assessment: A Feminist Perspective.* Philadelphia: Temple University Press, 1993.

Mosco, Vincent. *The Political Economy of Communication.* London: Sage, 1996.

Mumford, Lewis. "Authoritarian and Democratic Technics." *Technology and Culture* 5, no. 1 (Winter 1964): 1–8.

Nash, Jane, and Maria Patricia Fernandez-Kelly. *Women, Men, and the International Division of Labor.* Albany: State University of New York Press, 1983.

Noble, David F. *A World Without Women: The Christian Culture of Western Science.* New York: Knopf, 1992.

Oakley, Ann. "Interviewing Women: A Contradiction in Terms." In *Doing Feminist Research*, edited by Helen Roberts, 30–61. London: Routledge and Kegan Paul, 1981.

O'Brien, Mary. *Reproducing the World: Essays in Feminist Theory.* Boulder: Westview: 1989.

O'Connor, Alan. *Raymond Williams: Writing, Culture, Politics.* New York: Basil Blackwell, 1989.

Peters, John Durham. "Information: Notes Toward a Critical History." *Journal of Communication Inquiry* 12, no. 2 (1988): 9–23.

——. *Speaking into the Air: A History of the Idea of Communication*. Chicago: University of Chicago Press, 1999.

Polanyi, Michael. *Personal Knowledge*. Chicago: University of Chicago Press, 1958.

——. *The Study of Man*. Chicago: University of Chicago Press, 1963.

Rakow, Lana, and K. Kranich. "Woman as Sign in TV News." *Journal of Communication* 41, no. 1 (1991): 8–23.

Romanyshyn, Robert. *Technology as Symptom and Dream*. New York: Routledge, 1989.

Rose, Hillary. "Hand, Brain and Heart: A Feminist Epistemology for the Natural Sciences." *Signs* 9 (1985): 73–90.

Roszak, Theodore. *The Gendered Atom: Reflections on the Sexual Psychology of Science*. Berkeley: Conari Press, 1999.

Rothschild, Jean. *Machina Ex Dea: Feminist Perspectives on Technology*. New York: Pergamon Press, 1983.

Rowbotham, Sheila. *Hidden From History: Rediscovering Women in History from the Seventeenth Century to the Present*. New York: Pantheon, 1974.

Rubin, Gayle. "The Traffic in Women: Notes on the 'Political Economy' of Sex." In *Toward an Anthropology of Women*, edited by Reyna R. Reiter, 157–210. New York: Monthly Review Press, 1975.

Sabo, Donald F., and Ross Runfola, eds. *Jock: Sports and Male Identity*. Englewood Cliffs, N.J.: Prentice-Hall, 1990.

Said, Edward. *Representations of the Intellectual*. New York: Random House, 1996.

Sanders, Beth, and Randy Baker. *Fear and Favor in the Newsroom*. VHS videotape. Seattle, Wash.: Northwest Passage Productions, 1987.

Schiller, Dan. *Digital Capitalism: Networking the Global Market Systems*. Cambridge, Mass.: MIT Press, 2000.

——. *Objectivity and the News: The Public and the Rise of Commercial Journalism*. Philadelphia: University of Pennsylvania Press, 1981.

——. *Theorizing Communication*. New York: Oxford University Press, 1996.

Schiller, Herbert I. *Information and the Crisis Economy*. Stamford, Conn.: Ablex Publishing, 1984.

——. *Who Knows: Information in the Age of the Fortune 500*. Stamford, Conn.: Ablex Publishing, 1981.

Schudson, Michael. *Discovering the News*. New York: Basic Books, 1978.

Scott, Joan C. *Weapons of the Weak*. New Haven, Conn.: Yale University Press, 1987.

Shelley, Mary. *Frankenstein*. New York: St. Martin's Press, 2000; original, 1818.

Smith, Dorothy. *The Everyday World as Problematic: A Feminist Sociology*. Boston: Northeastern University Press, 1987.

Smith, Patrick. "Dark Victory." *Index on Censorship* 28, no. 5 (September/October 1999): 42–43.

Smythe, Dallas. *Dependency Road: Communications, Capitalism, Consciousness and Canada*. Norwood, N.J.: Ablex, 1981.

Soley, Lawrence. *The News Shapers: The Sources Who Explain the News*. New York: Praeger, 1992.

Spender, Dale. *Nattering on the Net: Women, Power and Cyberspace*. New South Wales, Australia: SpinFex Press, 1996.

Spivak, Gayatri Chakravorty. *In Other Worlds: Essays in Cultural Politics*. New York, Routledge, 1988.

Stetz, Margaret D., and Bonnie B. C. Oh. *Legacies of the Comfort Women of World War II*. New York: M. E. Sharpe, 2001.

Stigmayer, Alexandra, ed. *Mass Rape: The War against Women in Bosnia-Herzegovina*. Lincoln: University of Nebraska Press, 1994.

Suchman, Lucy. *Plans and Situated Actions: The Problem of Human-Machine Communication*. Cambridge: Cambridge University Press, 1987.

Sunstein, Cass. *Republic.com*. Princeton, N.J.: Princeton University Press, 2001.

Thompson, E. P. "END and the Beginning: History Turns on a New Hinge." *The Nation*, (January 29, 1990): 117–18, 120–22.

Tiger, Lionel. *Men in Groups*. New York: Random House, 1969.

Tuchman, Gaye. *Making News*. New York: The Free Press, 1978.

———. "Objectivity as Strategic Ritual: An Examination of Newsmen's Notions of Objectivity." *American Journal of Sociology* 77, no. 4 (1972): 660–79.

Turkle, Sherry. *Life on the Screen: Identity in the Age of the Internet*. New York: Simon and Schuster, 1995.

———. *The Second Self: Computers and the Human Spirit*. New York: Simon and Schuster, 1984.

Veblen, Thorstein. *The Higher Learning*. Piscataway, N.J.: Transition, 1992; original, 1918.

Wajcman, Judy. *Feminism Confronts Technology*. University Park: Pennsylvania State University Press, 1991.

Webster, Frank, and Kevin Robins. *Information Technology: A Luddite Analysis*. Norwood, N.J.: Ablex, 1986.

Weizenbaum, Joseph. *Computer Power and Human Reason*. San Francisco: W. H. Freeman, 1976.

Whitehead, Alfred North. *Adventures of Ideas*. New York: The Free Press, 1967; original, 1933.

Wiener, Norbert. *God and Golem, Inc. A Comment on Certain Points Where Cybernetics Impinges on Religion*. Cambridge, Mass.: MIT Press, 1964.

———. *Human Use of Human Beings: Cybernetics and Society*. New York: Morrow, 1986.

Williams, Raymond. *Keywords: A Vocabulary of Culture and Society*. New York: Oxford University Press, 1976.

———. *Problems in Materialism and Culture*. London: Verso, 1980.

Woodfield, Ruth. *Women, Work and Computing*. Cambridge University Press, 2000.

Woodward, Kathleen, ed. *The Myths of Information: Technology and Postindustrial Culture*. Sun Prairie, Wisc.: Baumgartner Publications and the University of Wisconsin, 1980.

Woolf, Virginia. *A Room of One's Own*. London: Hogarth, 1929.

———. *Three Guineas*. London: Hogarth Press, 1938.

Woolgar, Steve. *Science: The Very Idea*. London: Tavistock, 1988.

Zaretsky, Eli. *Capitalism, the Family, and Personal Life*. London: Pluto Press, 1976.

Zimmerman, Jan. *The Technological Woman: Interfacing with Tomorrow*. New York: Praeger, 1983.

Zoonen, Liesbet van. "Feminist Theory and Information Technology." *Media, Culture and Society* 14 (1992): 9–29.

Index